D1156717

Voices from Captivity

MODERN WAR STUDIES

Theodore A. Wilson
General Editor

Raymond A. Callahan
J. Garry Clifford
Jacob W. Kipp
Jay Luvaas
Allan R. Millett
Series Editors

Voices from Captivity

INTERPRETING THE
AMERICAN POW NARRATIVE

Robert C. Doyle

Base Library (FL473)
Bldg. 765, 60
McChord AFB, WA 98438-0000

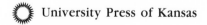 University Press of Kansas

Base Library FL4479
Bldg. 765, 6th St.
McChord AFB, WA 98438-5000

© 1994 by the University Press of Kansas
All rights reserved

Published by the University Press of Kansas (Lawrence, Kansas 66049), which was organized by the Kansas Board of Regents and is operated and funded by Emporia State University, Fort Hays State University, Kansas State University, Pittsburg State University, the University of Kansas, and Wichita State University

Library of Congress Cataloging-in-Publication Data

Doyle, Robert C.
    Voices from captivity : interpreting the American POW narratives / Robert C. Doyle.
        p.   cm. — (Modern war studies)
    Includes bibliographical references and index.
    ISBN 0-7006-0663-7 (hardcover : acid-free paper)
    1. Prisoners of war—United States. 2. Prisoners' writings, American. I. Title. II. Series.
    UB803.D69   1994
    813'.009358—dc20   93-41111

Printed in the United States of America
10 9 8 7 6 5 4 3 2 1

The paper used in this publication meets the minimum requirements of the American National Standard for Permanence of Paper for Printed Library Materials Z39.48-1984.

To the prisoners of war from the colonial period to Vietnam whose courage and fortitude in difficult circumstances radiate in their words; to those men and women who shared their experiences behind the wire. Theirs are the voices from captivity.

CONTENTS

Photographs follow page 88

FOREWORD

Captivity as a prisoner of war is the extreme circumstance in the human experience, for it entails great peril, physical and emotional torment, and the complete loss of the most basic freedom: control of one's destiny. The loss of freedom in any context is universally loathsome; to Americans, who assume general freedom is a given, such loss is anathema. To be thrust by circumstances into the hands of a hostile and often brutal enemy is the ultimate test of one's physical and emotional stamina. The situation forces the captive to carefully reassess the merit of personal values, especially as they do or do not equip one to deal with the grinding tedium and too-frequent terror of life as a POW.

As a POW for nearly five years in North Vietnam, my personal values were put to the test. In most cases, they were adequate, although sometimes my philosophical tools needed sharpening. However, on rarer occasions, I had to altogether abandon dearly held values to forge and temper new visions, ideas, and ideals. In these latter circumstances I, and those who served with and before me, experienced real growth as human beings.

Suffering similar ordeals over the past three-and-one-half centuries, many Americans have recorded for posterity their experiences in captivity. Viewed singly, any of these narratives might be dismissed as a merely interesting, if somewhat woeful, recapitulation of personal suffering and survival. When they are considered as a body of literature, however, a generally common pattern begins to emerge, or, as Robert Doyle calls it, a narrative contour. It is in reflecting upon this narrative contour that the historical, social, and philosophical significance of this book becomes apparent.

Happily for us, the author has placed all the voices in elegantly crafted settings of time, place, and social circumstance. By giving us an appropriate lens, Doyle clarifies our vision. Page by page, and phrase by phrase, he leads us through the experiences of hundreds of Americans whose misfortune it was to be held captive during time of conflict or war. What finally emerges is a profound understanding of the POW experience.

I believe that this refined understanding will inspire in the reader a sense of pride, not pity, for the hundreds of thousands of American men and women who suffered this sort of ordeal and who finally regained their dignity, their freedom, and their place in the history of our nation. I am richer for having read this magnificent pioneering work, and I am profoundly grateful to my dear friend, Bob Doyle, for bringing to us all a clearer understanding of the spirit of the American men and women whom we know only through their voices from captivity.

Giles R. Norrington, USN (Retired)
Norfolk, Virginia
May 1992

PREFACE

Voices from Captivity talks about American prisoners of war in enemy hands. Its purpose is to offer a new lens through which a reader can view more clearly the ordeal of captivity. The book strongly emphasizes the phenomenon of war psychosis (the escalating hatred for the enemy); traditional rules of war and international law relative to prisoners of war; differing traditional concepts of captivity among warring nations; the effect of neocolonialism on an army's treatment of its prisoners; and how foreign imperialism affects prison landscapes and treatment of prisoners of war.

Neither the incarceration and internment of prisoners of conscience, criminals, or internal political prisoners nor the behavior of American forces as captors is discussed in this book. The voices of native Americans who have been victims of colonization are also absent, and I do not write about the large corpus of nineteenth-century African-American slave narratives that has piqued the interest of Lawrence Levine, Eugene Genovese, and other scholars. This book is a cultural study of European civilian settlers caught in guerrilla wars and of American soldiers who found themselves in enemy hands. The absence of other voices in no way denies or demeans the sufferings of other groups.

I do, however, consider narratives of shipwrecks and North African captivity—though they may seem peripheral—for the victims of capture on the high seas were prisoners of war and their experiences lie within the scope of this book. Indeed, the sale of officers and crews into institutionalized slavery and the development of the practice of ransom, first between European and North African Islamic powers from the Middle Ages to the nineteenth century and then from 1793 to 1815 between the Barbary powers and the United States, were long-standing military practices.

This book organizes the captivity experience into three broad topical categories: (1) the context of the captivity experience in American culture; (2) the structure of the captivity narrative as represented by repeated event-scenarios; and (3) the legacies of captivity as they have been portrayed in folk and popular culture. Each chapter links the broad issues of successive American wars with the personal experiences of the prisoners of those wars. Chapter One defines military captivity literature, and subsequent chapters contain examples of representative narratives.

Chapter Two traces the development of international law relative to prisoners of war, and Chapter Three contains examples of religious and secular antecedents derived from narratives of the forest wars. Chapter Four explains the meaning of the narrative contour and introduces seven consistently repeated event-scenarios. Chapters Five through Eleven examine those event-scenarios as they appear in representative narratives. Chapter Twelve examines the popular myth of the missing warrior: how the myth came into being, how it relates to popular beliefs in calculated government deceit, and how it seems to persist in American postwar culture of the twentieth century. The last chapter addresses concerns and values in the POW community and conflicts of truth and truthfulness; it also discusses the POW issue in light of a dangerous and unpredictable world.

Sources for the book range from biblical and folkloric forerunners of the captivity narrative to personal memoirs and international statutes and conventions from 1785 to the present. Other sources include unpublished accounts of military captivity, personal letters, unpublished poems, government and personal photographs, unpublished diaries, and other narrative documents, including oral and written histories given to me by former prisoners of war. Captivity literature includes autobiographical prose memoirs, biographies, oral histories, novels, poetry, folktales, folk verse and songs, television shows, paintings and prints, and Hollywood feature films. This material has three distinguishable though often tightly interwoven layers: (1) the memories and traditions carried by the victims into captivity—in other words, their cultural baggage; (2) the prisoners' own accounts of and interpretations of their captivity; and (3) accounts by second, third, and subsequent parties that use both tradition and narratives.

Some prisoners of war, from the Civil War to Vietnam, won the Medal of Honor for actions above and beyond the call of duty. Very few prisoners of war have attained the status of popular hero. In war, they continued their war behind the wire; in peace, they have been and will remain ordinary citizens who contribute to the quality of their own communities. To ignore them would mean ignoring what they did; when, where, and why they did it; and the enormity of the suffering they endured. From the forest wars to Vietnam and beyond, those American voices continue to define what it is to be human amid the horrors and sufferings of life behind barbed wire. They are the voices from captivity; they are ourselves.

No one researches and writes a book alone. I first wish to extend my warmest thanks and sincere appreciation to Stanley Weintraub, Evan Pugh Professor of Arts and Humanities at Penn State University, for his consistent advice and endless encouragement. Samuel P. Bayard, Professor Emeritus of English and Comparative Literature, assisted me at every step on the long way from idea to book, and Daniel Walden, Director of the American Studies Program at Penn State, gave me his full support and provided assistance in the form of research and travel grants from Penn State's American Studies Program and the Center for Cultural Heritage. Dr. Henry Albinski and Robert Brand of Penn State's Australia–New Zealand Studies Center facilitated my 1989 research trip to Australia; Dr. John Dalton, Department of Politics, Monash University, Melbourne, and Mr. Jeff Doyle, Department of English, the Australian Defence Force Academy, Canberra, gave me a great deal of assistance in understanding British, Australian, and Commonwealth perspectives. I am especially grateful to Giles R. Norrington, USN (Retired) and Colonel Norman A. McDaniel, USAF (Retired)—both POWs in North Vietnam, 1966–1973; Sergeant Carl Nash, USA (retired) of Harlem, Georgia—a Bataan defender and POW in the Philippines and Japan, 1942–1945; and Henry Burman of State College, Pennsylvania—a POW in Stalag Luft III, 1943–1945.

Lee Stout, Archivist at the Pattee Library of Penn State University, was of great assistance, Fred D. Crawford and J. D. Shuchter offered organizational and editorial criticism, and C. Sommers Miller of the University of South Carolina, Beaufort, provided both methodological criticism and hospitality during my site research at Andersonville, Georgia, Beaufort, and Columbia, South Carolina. I appreciate Lois Seitz's patience when transcribing POW audiotapes to typescript and owe a special loving thanks to my wife, Beate, for putting up with this book for so long. I am deeply grateful.

Introduction

Voices from Captivity examines what it is to be human in difficult and even dangerous circumstances, when captors forcibly remove the outer layers of culture from a captive. I have two general intentions: to clarify the important connections between narrative literature and society and to show that the civilian and military captivity narrative is an important literary form, one that has chronicled part of the American experience for three hundred years. Against a background of the prophet Jeremiah's Book of Lamentations and the secular oral traditions of Western folklore, I consider the nature of the captivity narrative and its place in the American experience of war. Captivity literature is a genre of perceptions and truths drawn directly from personal experience. In an age when heroes seem more fictional than factual, media images of dramatic bravado have often replaced the simple faith, rugged stoicism, and determined, self-less valor of men and women in captivity. I am interested in neither phony bravado nor false heroism but in analyzing the form, content, and context of the captivity experience as it was lived and, after repatriation, narrated by the prisoners themselves.

Throughout *Voices from Captivity,* the armed conflicts between European settlers and native American nations of the seventeenth and eighteenth centuries are characterized by the nineteenth-century term *forest wars.* The word "war" here reinforces the understanding that from the Pequot War in 1637 on, tribal nations formed alliances and fought deadly political wars against organized colonial militias and later against the government and army of the United States. Many prisoners in the forest wars were not soldiers but individuals actually living on the battlefield who became entangled in the settler-tribal conflicts of the time. As narrators they are vital to this study for several reasons: the forest wars were simultaneously wars of colonial armies and guerrilla wars that established a distinct mode of warfare between Euro-Americans and Indian nations up to 1890. Beginning with John Cotton's sermon in 1630, Puritans felt a spiritual, moral, and ethical imperative to destroy the Indian nations opposing them, and narratives from captives of the forest wars in part set the tone and establish purpose—narrative intent—for the captivity narratives written by American prisoners of war later.

Each war offered prisoners new battlefield landscapes: Indian villages during the forest wars; prison hulks during the Revolution and the War of 1812; slave bagnios in Algeria and Tripoli; hotels and haciendas during the Mexican War; large barren camps like Andersonville in rural Georgia, converted warehouses like Libby Prison in Richmond, islands like Johnson's Island in Ohio and Belle Isle in Richmond, and fairgrounds, insane asylums, and converted federal military facilities like Elmira during the Civil War. Our own century featured the stalags and oflags of the world wars in Europe; the Japanese death camps in East Asia; the frozen camps of North Korea; the jungle camps of South Vietnam and the Hoa Lo Prison in Hanoi, known as the "Hanoi Hilton." *Voices from Captivity* examines these myriad battlefields: what and where they were; why they existed as they did; how they functioned; and how prisoners responded to their captors, their prison communities, and their own consciences.

The way we understand our past is changing. Ernst Breisach, in *Historiography,*[1] suggests that we have to take the hard road; we must look beyond numbers and statistics to seek out individuals whose actions and moral choices were guided by values. The historical record of American wartime captivity fulfills this demand by generating firsthand knowledge from the experience of participants. The narratives provide a context for literature as well as questions about the values that govern everyday life. *Voices from Captivity,* then, establishes firm links between the values of a fleeting present and the distant past.

Incarceration, regardless of kind, strips prisoners of personal liberties and the general rights of citizenship. Nevertheless, for clarity's sake, some further definition is necessary. *Captives* are men and women who after being taken captive or hostage have no legal status and no protection under any laws other than individual utility or worth for ransom and who survive, or die, ultimately, at the whim of the captor. The term *hostage* implies that a free person is taken prisoner by a hostile power or political group and held in order to negotiate a political or financial ransom. An *internee* is a civilian prisoner in an international war in the twentieth century. Internees, such as nonmilitary medical people, wives and family members of business people, journalists, and diplomats, are often granted special status of protected personnel. An *evader* is an individual soldier, sailor, or airman whose unit is conquered or defeated in battle and captured by an enemy force but who is not captured himself and seeks to elude enemy forces. Often assisted by indigenous resisters, the successful evader returns alone to friendly lines or is rescued by friendly search-and-rescue units. The term *missing in action* or MIA applies to a member of a military force who is lost without trace during or after combat. After a reasonable amount of time, the status can change to *killed in action body not recovered* or *missing in action presumed dead* or to *prisoner of war* if the detaining power announces custody through the International

Red Cross or some other recognized means. A *prisoner of war* or POW is a member of a military service captured by an enemy force during or after engagement who becomes incarcerated in a prison camp or some other kind of penal facility and whose status is reported by the detaining power through the International Red Cross or another representative body or even by a credible witness.

These people left their stories to a world more accustomed to order by law than survival by luck, stealth, rules of war, international conventions, or the whim of the captor. Their dramas reflect the five major responses to captivity: resistance, survival, assimilation, evasion, and escape. Resisters bring the battlefield to the prison pen and oppose their captors by shunning cooperation or collaboration. This act places the resisting prisoner in extreme danger. Captors respond by applying varying degrees of torture and punishment, even to the point of death. Survivors, according to Terrence Des Pres in *The Survivor,*[2] can passively resist a captor's demands, but more often the survivor neutralizes or numbs the experience completely. Suffering daily personal humiliations by cooperating with the captors, even minimally, makes little or no difference; the survivor's objective is to live through captivity by avoiding the captor's attention. However, Des Pres argues that after liberation and repatriation, it becomes the survivor's duty to act as witness to the unbelievable. The survivor honors the dead by writing a narrative for the living. Assimilators partially collaborate with or fully assimilate to the captor's culture. If they opt to act on the captor's behalf, either in camp or actually on the battlefield, then assimilators become renegades. Escapers ignore danger to return to their own lines and have been represented as the luckiest, if not the most heroic, kind of prisoner. Evaders resemble escapers in their determination to be free; however, the evader is never a prisoner. Instead, the evader's drama focuses on the odyssey from enemy territory to the safety of friendly forces.

Captivity not only challenges individual prisoners to continue wartime conflicts with the captor but to face conflicts with themselves and with others in a community of prisoners. Grief challenges pain, the needs of the community strive with those of the individual, human nature confronts ideology and authority, competition undercuts cooperation, the wisdom of age competes with the desires of youth, boredom threatens the will to live, community loyalty attenuates personal friendship, and success becomes survival. Written narratives of this drama derive from a history of living traditions that ensure the salvation of human dignity, community identity, and a sense of order in a world of chaos. Successful prisoners reject guilt and shame in order to live. Human emotion, communication, and artistic creativity combine to enable individual prisoners to express the effects of those traditions, and thus have ideas generated actions. To survive captivity with dignity and honor, ordinary people must cling to the most basic ideas of life in their cages, where days turn into weeks, months, and, in many cases, years of limitless boredom.

When there is war, there are prisoners of war. Because human captivity challenges basic cultural assumptions about justice, the rules of war, tradition, humanity, and ethics, indeed about civilization itself, a critical examination of narratives and other literature of captivity necessarily questions the nature of humanity in the modern age. What does it mean to be human when most or all the other wrappings of civilization are removed? Arthur A. Durand reminds us in *Stalag Luft III* that we may gain much by scrutinizing the experiences of prisoners of war.[3] Although humanity seems slowly to be winning the peace, we have not yet come to terms with all the implications of war, especially the social and cultural implications of wartime captivity. There is no reason to despair, however, for hope lies in studying the experiences of prisoners of war. Such an enterprise is valuable even if it does no more than suggest that military prisoners in the modern world cannot yet count on receiving humane treatment or an early parole to prevent wasting valuable years of their lives.

From colonial times to the present day, hundreds, if not thousands, of captivity stories have been written and published in America, and most appeared within a few years of the writers' repatriations. The stories of Americans in captivity are walks through houses of horror where years of danger and boredom, acts of torture, and moments of terror are compressed into brief, gripping scenarios. Many of the narratives are accounts of military captivity; that is to say, the author was a POW. Even the Puritan narratives of seventeenth-century New England (Mary Rowlandson, Hannah Dustin, John Gyles, Mercy Short) and the Indian captivity narratives of Pennsylvania in the eighteenth century (Barbara Leininger, Regina Leininger, Mary Jemison, Peter Williamson, Marie LeRoy) were those of wartime captives. All the combatants, military and civilian alike, were members of communities under arms, especially during the frontier guerrilla wars of the seventeenth and eighteenth centuries. Students of American literature and culture often study the Puritan captivities of Mary Rowlandson, Hannah Dustin, John Gyles, and other prisoners of the forest wars who narrated their captivities for their own generations. We would all do well to realize that today's Rowlandsons and Dustins are our neighbors. Their voices are part of a national experience that extends well beyond the New England Puritans and the forest wars to POW narratives after the world wars, to the television images of returning prisoners of war from Korea in 1953, Vietnam in 1973, and Iraq in 1991, as well as of the hostages in Iran in 1980 and Lebanon in 1991 and 1992.

Although the eighteenth- and nineteenth-century prisoners are gone, their narratives, letters, and testimonies survive. Called to arms in their youth, the prisoners of the two world wars, Korea, Vietnam, and beyond have chronicled the lives of ordinary people who suffered the rigors of captivity. After repatriation, they told their readers that their captors peeled from them the outer rings of precaptivity culture—psychological security in familiar social and work-oriented surroundings; physical security in familiar food, clothing, and shelter; and the emotional security of contact with loved ones and friends—and that they had only ideas of home, family, religious faith, and community to preserve their lives or sanity. For some prisoners the acquisition and practice of religious faith took on a special role. In religion, some prisoners validated their experiences as a manifestation of the providence of God and their sufferings as acts of redemption. Others, more secular, sought, in an attitude that might be called "heroic stoicism," to validate the traditional martial value of duty under adverse conditions; they were supported by military codes that require prisoners of war to attempt escape when and where possible. Whereas the religious captive seeks spiritual redemption, the heroic captive seeks justice, including in extreme cases revenge. Both captivity themes are well represented in American tribal captivities and contemporary prison camp memoirs.

The American vision of success demands victory in war. Capture initially signals defeat and failure; captivity, however, does not. Finding a bridge between failure and success requires some analysis of what happened, for the experience itself takes place in sequential stages. First, the POW narrative searches for and explains the limits in negative terms that set the boundaries of the experience. Prisoners explain what went wrong; why they were forced to surrender, and how their world collapsed in front of their eyes. In the second stage, the narrative relates how the prisoner came to grips with captivity, how and why he resisted or collaborated with the captors, and how he defined the parameters of his existence. In the third stage, the prisoner laments the experience and shares his understanding of it. At the very least, one gains from POW narratives an appreciation for the realities of life-and-death conflicts, the struggles between personal and institutional concepts of duty, visions of individual heroism, and ultimately, the paradigmatic shift from defeat to victory in the captive's thinking about the nature of the experience itself.

Survivors of the POW experience from the forest wars to Vietnam had powerful desires to communicate their experiences, and their narratives appeared slowly but steadily after repatriation. For example, Elizabeth Head Vaughn wrote her narrative *Community under Stress*[4] first as a doctoral dissertation and then published it later. Many accounts were written by former prisoners, like Kenneth Simmons, who simply wanted to forget the experience and get on with their lives but found that the more they wrote, the more they remembered. In effect, they survived to become witnesses. Terrence Des Pres studied this natural human impulse in *The Survivor* (1976) and maintained that prisoners make special promises among themselves to narrate their experience to whomever will listen—to the world if possible. Whoever survives, talks and, if necessary, devises a new vocabulary to do so. For the narrator, the act of telling the story transcends the personal distress of the camp; for those who died, the narration becomes a testament to their sacrifice and renews the victims' faith in history. Not only do the narratives allow the survivors to bear witness, but they allow the dead to speak as well. Prisoners kept diaries and notes, wrote poems, and sketched scenes of prison life, some of which have found their way into print, sometimes long after repatriation.

Much has been written about the politics of the captivity stories. Some critics attack them as exaggerated and vindictive attacks against former captors; others criticize them as overly simple morality plays. Both these critical positions seem to neglect the important traditional aspects of American culture that inform this fascinating genre of American literature. Rooted in western folklore and strengthened by biblical precedents, the essential characteristic of the American captivity narrative is a common fund of ideas that characterize, qualify, and evaluate the right and wrong of personal and community conduct in captivity during armed conflict.

PART ONE

Backgrounds

CHAPTER ONE

Soldier Chronicles:
The Borders of Military Captivity

We . . . shall be remembered; we few, we happy few, we band of brothers;
for he today that sheds his blood with me shall be my brother.

William Shakespeare
Henry V

From the American colonial period to the Vietnam War, prisoner-of-war
narratives have followed a firmly established, widely disseminated oral
and literary tradition in Western culture. Before investigating the structural
and temporal links that distinguish these works from others, we need
a sense of the contextual continuity from Indian captivity narratives of
the colonial wars to the distinctly military POW narratives from the
Revolution onward. Thus this chapter furnishes a wide-angled, broad-
brushed vision of the issues and circumstances that prompted so many
former prisoners of war to bear witness to their captivities.

The narratives presented and discussed in this book represent only a
small number in a huge body of work. To the credit of the authors, in
general they present their captivity experiences in terms of the cultural
realities that resulted in individual and community survival rather than
dwelling on hegemony, lawlessness, or personal failure. By and large,
readers are asked to depart from romantic notions of heroism, xeno-
phobia, or imagined institutional success to focus on the hard facts of
individual courage, personal fortitude, and the determination of a
prisoner-of-war (POW) community to survive, if not defeat, the captor.
Surviving an experience that begins in the ignominy of failure and personal disgrace of captivity is hard enough; transcendence and reflection
are far more difficult. As ordinary people who found themselves in difficult circumstances, former POWs have explained how they coped with
the experience through active resistance, stoic heroism, escape, collaboration, or even assimilation.

Beginning in New England, the forest wars raged throughout the
colonies and kept the colonists and colonial soldiers in continuous combat
with the native American tribes and their allies from 1637 to 1814.[1] One
of the earliest and most detailed of the colonial POW narratives is John
Gyles's *Memoirs of Odd Adventures, Strange Deliverances, etc., in the*

Captivity of John Gyles, published in Boston in 1736.[2] In 1689, the French Canadians sent a force from Montreal to attack Albany, and Thomas Gyles, his wife, and his four children were captured by Indians at Fort Charles in what is now the state of Maine. Thomas's son, John, was about ten years old and spent six years with the Indians. After his repatriation, John Gyles became a commissioned officer in the British colonial forces, and because he had learned the French and Indian languages during his captivity, he acted as an interpreter. Gyles was a Puritan by faith, but rather than embroidering his narrative with biblical passages, he fills it with ethnographic data about his Indian and French captors. He discusses pow-wows, fables, common feasts, food customs, and survival details. As a keen cultural observer of rituals, Gyles takes note of Indians feasting before battle, mourning for their dead, and their marriage ceremonies.

From 1746 to 1747, Nehemiah How and several hundred other American colonials were prisoners in Quebec. How's diary, *The Narrative and Captivity of Nehemiah How, Who Was Taken by the Indians* (1748), is one of the earliest POW diaries to be published, and it ends with bitter condemnations of his captors. How was never released from captivity; he died in prison on May 25, 1747, of what was then called "prison fever."[3] Another representative narrative came from Thomas Brown, a young man who served with Roger's Rangers in 1756. Only sixteen years old when he enlisted, Brown was captured by the French and Indians, wounded several times, and taken to Montreal. He managed to escape for a brief period and journeyed to Crown Point, New York, before he was recaptured, returned to Montreal, and exchanged shortly thereafter. Still full of youthful fight, Brown enlisted again, fought again, was captured again, went to Montreal again, and was again exchanged after three years on the frontier and in captivity. *A Plain Narrative of the Uncommon Sufferings and Remarkable Deliverance of Thomas Brown* appeared in 1760.

By the time of the American Revolution (1775–1783), the British and their Indian allies had replaced the French as the public enemies of colonial America, and two major types of POW narratives stem from this period: the soldierly resistance narrative and sailor prison-ship narratives. A soldier's chronicle of captivity might contain a few military scenes interspersed among chapters of civilian life, but the bulk would consist of morbid descriptions of his imprisonment.[4] Focusing on harshness and political confrontation, the soldier's chronicle differed from earlier New England and mid-Atlantic Indian captivity narratives that focused on civil or religious providence, and it previewed the kind of POW narrative that was to appear in the nineteenth and twentieth centuries.

American privateers captured on the high seas were regularly incarcerated in English naval prisons. Benjamin Franklin became the first American

POW activist in the sense that from his home in Paris, Franklin spent a considerable amount of time trying to get Americans released or exchanged from British jails. Catherine M. Prelinger's "Benjamin Franklin and the American Prisoners of War in England during the American Revolution" (1975) tells the Franklin story, and William James Morgan's *Naval Documents of the Revolution* (1986) includes scores of diplomatic and personal letters to and from Franklin concerning requests for help and descriptions of the experiences of American privateers in English jails. One man whom Franklin knew well was Captain Gustavus Connyngham, who led thirty men out of Old Mill Prison in spring 1779. His adventures appear in Robert W. Nesser's *Letters and Papers Relating to the Cruises of Gustavus Connyngham* (1915).

Concerning American activities during the Revolution, disagreement has surfaced among historians. The American apologist Howard Appelgate lauded American resistance to British attempts at impressment in "American Privateersmen in the Mill Prison During 1777–1782" (1961). His position was challenged by John K. Alexander in "American Privateersmen in the Mill Prison, 1777–1782: An Evaluation" (1966). British interest in captivity during the Revolutionary War has been kept alive by the scholarly efforts of such historians as Olive Anderson, Francis Abell, Eunice H. Turner, and others. The most comprehensive source is Admiralty 98, held in the Public Records Office. It contains voluminous numbers of letters to the Secretary of the Admiralty, directives, and individual communications. The Public Records Office holds the old log books from the prison hulks in America as well. Representative scholarly works include John Howard's *The State of the Prisons in England and Wales* (1784); Francis Abell's *Prisoners of War in Britain, 1750–1815* (1914); Olive Anderson's "American Escapes from British Naval Prisons During the War of Independence" (1955); and Eunice H. Turner's "American Prisoners of War in Great Britain 1777–1783" (1959).

The New York City Historical Society Library contains Revolutionary War manuscripts like George Ralls's "Account of Captivity in England" and many others. Diaries of Americans in English prisons have appeared regularly in historical publications such as *Essex Institute Historical Collections, New England Historical and Geneological Register, William and Mary Quarterly, Mariners Mirror, English Historical Review,* and the *Pennsylvania Magazine of History and Biography*. Rich secondary sources include Charles H. Metzger's *The Prisoner in the American Revolution* (1971) and Larry G. Bowman's *Captive Americans: Prisoners during the American Revolution* (1976). George G. Carey published a collection of POW songs as *A Sailor's Songbag: An American Rebel in an English Prison, 1777–1779* (1976).

The first distinctly American POW book of the Revolutionary War to become a bestseller during and following the Revolution was Ethan Allen's *Narrative of Colonel Ethan Allen's Captivity Containing His Voyages and Travels,* covering the period of his captivity from May 1775 until his release in May 1778. It appeared first in 1779 as a serial in the *Pennsylvania Packet* and later in book form, reprinted in 1780, 1805, 1807, 1814, 1834, 1838, 1845, 1846, 1849, 1852, and 1854. It was last reprinted for the Fort Ticonderoga Museum in 1930. In 1775, prior to the Continental Congress's declaration of war against England, Allen and his Green Mountain Boys seized Fort Ticonderoga in New York "in the name of God and the Continental Congress." Later that year, Allen joined Benedict Arnold's invasion of Canada that ended in an American defeat at Quebec. Allen was taken prisoner near Montreal and was imprisoned by the English for three years. According to Allen, the men were treated with contempt by their captors. British policy was to kill the prisoners, said Allen, and he insisted that more than 11,000 Americans were killed in captivity during the war. In defying the cruelty, mockery, and derision of his captors, Allen believed that his patriotism was more severely tested than his religious faith. Like the authors of most POW narratives, Allen is vindictive and hateful toward his captors, and, in effect, for propaganda and nationalistic purposes, the British replaced the French and the Indians as the nation's enemies.

Thousands of American sailors, mostly privateers, became POWs during the Revolution, and those prisoners suffered the most extreme horrors of the war in the British prison ships anchored near the British-controlled coastal cities of America. Thomas Dring complained, like Allen, that his captors' objective was to kill the American prisoners; in his case, slowly, by malnutrition.[5] By and large, the only relief for the men in the British prison ships came from private cartels, as poet Philip Freneau discovered. Freneau was a passenger on the armed ship *Aurora* when he was captured in May 1780 and incarcerated in the prison ship *Scorpion* (see Appendix 2A).[6] Many prison-hulk accounts have been preserved. The narratives of Christopher Hawkins, Thomas Dring, William Burke, Andrew Sherburne, and Thomas Andros were standard fare.[7] Andrew Sherburne's memoir, written and published in 1782, chronicles his life aboard the *Jersey* and in the hospital ships, which he calls "death ships." Other narratives discuss British efforts to enlist captured Americans in the British navy. As in subsequent wars, especially in the Civil War, life in someone else's army or navy often seemed a reasonable alternative to death in captivity.

Seven months after the British surrendered to the Americans at Yorktown, an army of volunteer militia marched west from the Ohio River in a punitive expedition to destroy the hostile Indian villages at Sandusky (now Upper Sandusky, Ohio). "Punitive" expeditions in those days meant what modern tacticians would term "search and destroy," a military tactic that calls for aggressive operations against a guerrilla enemy. The Battle of Sandusky, June 4–5, 1782, resulted in the Americans' defeat by a combined force of Indians allied with the British and Butler's Rangers, one of many loyalist regiments fighting the American Continental army.[8] During the retreat, Colonel William Crawford, the American commander and a close friend of George Washington, was captured and executed by the Indians. The incident was narrated by John Knight, Surgeon, and John Slover, Crawford's guide. First published in the *Freeman's Journal* in 1783, both narratives were reprinted as part of Hugh Henry Brackenridge's *Indian Atrocities: Narratives of the Perils and Sufferings of Dr. John Knight and John Slover among the Indians during the Revolutionary War* (1867) and later reprinted in C. W. Butterfield, *An Historical Account of the Expedition against Sandusky under Colonel William Crawford in 1782* (1873). The Crawford execution appeared in many editions of nineteenth-century captivity anthologies, including E. G. Cattermole's *Famous Frontiersmen, Pioneers and Scouts* (1888) and Henry Davenport Northop's *Indian Horrors or Massacres by the Red Men* (1891), two of the most prescriptive anti-Indian works of the late nineteenth century. They recount the personal adventures of the narrators themselves, but Crawford's capture, stoic resistance, and torturous death is a central focus of both. Crawford was an unwilling but popular military leader of western Pennsylvania volunteers, and his death inspired cries for retributive justice. In effect, the call for action in these narrative accounts heralded the kind of punitive warfare that would characterize the conflicts between Indian tribes and the American government from 1800 to 1890.

Related to the military resistance and escape narratives of Dr. Knight and John Slover is the account of Colonel James Paul, the defeated soldier who was separated from the main body of his force and evaded capture. In Robert A. Sherrard's *Narrative of the Wonderful Escape and Dreadful Sufferings of Colonel James Paul* (1868), the author not only chronicles the ill-fated Crawford expedition in 1782 but also defends Colonel Paul, the sole survivor.[9]

The POW narratives of the American Revolution mark the beginning of the transition from civilians in Indian captivity to soldiers in military captivity. The narrators, especially officers like Ethan Allen, remind readers that they were combat soldiers (or sailors) performing their military duty until they were unable to carry on any further. In captivity, treated more as felons than soldiers, they complain bitterly about the contempt and retribution of the rear guard, both British soldiers and loyalist Tories, in whose care they were placed and at whose hands they suffered. The lesson these prisoners learned was that political, moral, ethical, and legal considerations dominate life off the battlefield. Similar concerns would plague every future soldier confined in a POW camp.

After the Revolution ended, American sailors found themselves in captivity more often from acts of piracy than from war. The British treated them as pirates or rebels, but many sailors found themselves in the hands of North African captors, who had a long tradition of hostage taking for ransom. There were two ways to become a prisoner in North Africa at the turn of the nineteenth century: capture at sea or shipwreck. More civilian than military, the resulting narratives were the memoirs of merchant seamen who were taken into captivity off the coast of North Africa during this volatile period, when few naval vessels were available to protect the merchant fleet. Shipwreck narratives include the *Narrative of Joshua Gee of Boston Mass., While He Was a Captive in Algeria of the Barbary Pirates 1680–1687;* the *Journal of the Captivity and Sufferings of John Foss* (1798); the *Narrative of Robert Adams, a Sailor Who Was Shipwrecked on the Western Coast of Africa in the Year 1810, Was Detained Three Years in Slavery by the Arabs of the Great Desert, and Resided Several Months in the City of Timbuctoo* (1816), one of the most bizarre narratives; James Riley's *Loss of the American Brig Commerce* (1817); Judah Paddock's *Narrative of the Shipwreck of the Ship Oswego* (1818); the *Authentic Narrative of the Shipwreck and Sufferings of Mrs. Eliza Bradeley* (1821); and *The Voyages and Five Years Captivity in Algiers of Doctor G.S.F. Pfeiffer* (1836). The adventures of military captives taken and held during this period appear in six volumes of *Naval Documents Related to the United States Wars with the Barbary Powers* (1942), and H. G. Barnby published a diplomatic history of the American-Algerian War of 1785–1797, *The Prisoners of Algiers* (1966).

Early in the War of 1812, the United States House of Representatives commissioned the *Report on the Spirit and Manner in Which the War Has Been Waged by the Enemy* (1813), which, based on letters and sworn affidavits from participants and witnesses of British and Indian atrocities, charged the British with several counts of unlawful treatment of prisoners. It stated the British detained American prisoners as British subjects, on the plea of nativity in the dominions of Britain or of naturalization; American commercial mariners had been detained as POWs if they were in England when the war was declared; naturalized American sailors were impressed as seamen on board British ships of war; British army officers violated flags of truce in the field; the United States was forced to ransom American prisoners held by Indians in the British service; British forces permitted Indian allies to massacre or execute by fire prisoners who surrendered; and British forces had committed outrages against unarmed civilians in Hampton, Virginia.[10]

On the northern battlefields, the War of 1812 might be remembered more accurately as a failed "War of Canadian Acquisition," since forces of the United States invaded Canada with hopes of evicting the British and bringing Canada into the American union. The Americans all but gave up their specious claims on Canada after the American army suffered two major defeats on the Canadian frontier, Hull's surrender at Detroit and the Battle of Queenston. Winfield Scott, then a very young Lieutenant Colonel in the American regulars, recalled his participation in the battle and his subsequent captivity as a "Queenston Prisoner" in his *Memoir* (1864) and in his biography *Winfield Scott: The Soldier and the Man* (1937), written by Charles W. Elliot.

The most dispassionate British history of American prisoners and POW life in England is Francis Abell's *Prisoners of War in Britain 1756 to 1815: A Record of Their Lives, Their Romance, and Their Sufferings* (1914). In America, Ira Dye's work deserves mention. Cooperating with the British Records Office, he developed two working papers for the HM Dartmoor staff, "The American Prisoners of War at Dartmoor" and "Deaths of American Prisoners of War at Dartmoor Prison During the War of 1812." His published works on the Dartmoor prisoners include his introduction to *Records Relating to American Prisoners of War 1812–1815* (1980); "America Maritime Prisoners of War 1812–1815" in Timothy J. Runyan's *Ships, Seafaring and Society; Essays in Maritime History* (1987); and "Physical and Social Profiles of American Seafarers, 1812–1815" in Colin Howell and Richard Twomey's *Jack Tar in History* (1991).

Without a doubt, the most anti-British POW narrative from the period is *The Prisoners' Memoirs, or Dartmoor Prison* (1815) by Charles Andrews. He describes Dartmoor in great detail and details American resistance against the prison warden, Captain Thomas George Shortland, RN, as well as their hatred and contempt for the American agent in London, Reuben Beasley. Andrews makes it very clear that the Americans in Dartmoor believed that, instead of looking after their interests, Beasley deliberately ignored numerous petitions for help, especially after a POW revolt precipitated by Shortland. Less anti-British is the work of Benjamin Waterhouse, M.D., who describes the life of American sailors imprisoned in England in *The Journal of a Young Man Captured by the British* (1815). Waterhouse chronicles the adventures of the young privateer surgeon who was captured at sea, kept first in the Halifax prison in Nova Scotia, and later sent to Dartmoor Prison in Devonshire, England. Waterhouse notes the presence of about 300 black POWs, most of whom the British captured as crewmen on American privateers. Robin F. A. Fabel's "Self-Help in Dartmoor: Black and White Prisoners in the War of 1812" in the *Journal of the Early Republic* (1989) offers an historic analysis of the same phenomenon. First among these black prisoners was a man who called himself "King Dick." The "King," whose real name was Richard Crafus, was a seaman on board the American privateer *Requin* when it was captured on March 6, 1814. He spent some time in the hulks at

Chatham before being sent to Dartmoor, where he spent 249 days. Not only did he dominate all the other black prisoners, he acted more like a monarch in Dartmoor than a POW. What is curious about Waterhouse's description of "King Dick" is its close resemblance to James Clavell's fictional American, Sam King, in *King Rat* (1962). Although the two prisoners, one real and one imaginary, were separated by 150 years and several wars, both men defied rank to rise above their peers. In addition to the journal of Waterhouse, other POW histories and narratives appeared in the popular press, such as Josiah Cobb's *A Greenhorn's First Cruise . . . Together with a Residence of Five Months in Dartmoor* (1841), James Fenimore Cooper's *Ned Myers; or, A Life Before the Mast* (1843), and Nathaniel Hawthorne's edited version of his neighbor's oral history of life in Dartmoor, *The Yarn of a Yankee Privateer* (1926).

On April 20, 1815, 263 Americans left Dartmoor; 5,193 prisoners followed a few days later. By December 1815, Dartmoor military prison was empty, and the naval component of the War of 1812 was over. In the end, the War of 1812 remained essentially a stalemate; the British had important and threatening problems on the European continent to worry about. Canada remained loyalist, and the United States would never again raise the issue of unification or Canadian conquest. Great Britain retreated from its fortifications in the United States and dropped the assumption that it could impress naturalized American citizens into naval or military service. The United States and Great Britain would not face each other again as enemies.

During the Mexican War (1846–1848), the American superiority over the Mexican army in successive battles created great numbers of POWs. Indeed, there were so many Mexican prisoners that about 10,000 were simply paroled home. Two incidents, however, relate to American POWs: the renegade Brigade of Saint Patrick and the captivity of the Louisville cavalry. Edward S. Wallace comments in "Deserters in the Mexican War" (1935) that the history of Brigade of Saint Patrick (San Patricio) dates to April 1846, when the Mexicans loosed a flood of anti-American propaganda on foreign-born Catholic soldiers. General Antonio Lopez de Santa Anna, of Alamo fame, based his proselytizing efforts on anti-immigrant, anti-Catholic sentiments rampant in the United States at the time. General Santa Anna was successful in recruiting two infantry units and one full artillery battery led by Sergeant John Riley, an immigrant Irishman who had been an amiable and well-respected artillery instructor at West Point. The Mexicans offered 320 acres of land and Mexican citizenship to all deserting privates, with higher offers for higher ranks.[11] An American occupation newspaper prepared and published in Mexico City from October 1847 to April 1848, the *American Star,* covered the story of the Saint Patrick Brigade. Written in English and Spanish, the articles include eyewitness accounts of imprisonment and news of the ceremonious hangings of the brigade members. Few Americans became POWs; however, members of the Louisville cavalry were not so fortunate. The anonymously written *Encarnacion Prisoners* (1848), privately published in Louisville, Kentucky, is a short monograph describing the Louisville cavalry's trip to Mexico and its capture, resistance, and heroic actions in captivity.

Captivity during the Civil War reflected rising military technology, uncertain political status, lack of international law on the subject of POWs, neglect, and an escalating war psychosis. About 211,400 Union POWs were taken, of whom 16,668 were paroled on the field. Each side killed the other side's prisoners in large numbers. About 30,200 Union prisoners died in Southern prisons. Of the 220,000 Confederates in Union prison camps, approximately 26,000 perished in the hands of the Union.[12] In the North, Southerners died from pneumonia generated by their inability to adjust to the cold, damp Northern winters. In the South, Union prisoners died from starvation, dysentery, and scurvy. In addition to unsanitary conditions and a dismal diet, both sides implemented "deadlines," a line of demarcation usually posted a few feet inside the walls of the compound over which no prisoner could step. Guards shot and killed on sight any prisoner crossing a deadline.

Official reports and testimonies of Civil War captivity are readily available in government publications, including eight volumes of *The Congressional Globe* (1861–1866), the United States War Department's *War of the Rebellion: A Compilation of the Official Records of the Union and Confederate Armies* (1880–1901), and the House of Representatives' *Report on the Treatment of Prisoners of War by the Rebel Authorities during the War of Rebellion* (1869). Full of the firsthand affidavits and testimonies of Union soldiers, these massive works are rich sources of otherwise unpublished sworn testimonies. Unpublished POW memoirs lie in regional and county historical societies, local libraries, and genealogical associations throughout the country. More important, specific regional Civil War collections are held by archives such as the Museum of the Confederacy in Richmond and the Southern History Collection in Wilson Library at the University of North Carolina. Manuscript collections at Emory University in Atlanta and in the South Carolina library at the University of South Carolina in Columbia are other rich sources in the South.

Fewer confederate narratives exist than those accounts written by repatriated Union soldiers. Representative examples include Joe Barbiere's *Scraps from the Prison Table at Camp Chase and Johnson's Island* (1868), John M. Copley's *Sketch of the Battle of Franklin, Tenn.; with Reminiscences of Camp Douglas* (1893); Samuel B. Davis's *Escape of a*

Confederate Officer from Prison, What He Saw at Andersonville, How He was Sentenced to Death and Saved by the Interposition of President Abraham Lincoln (1892); William H. Duff's *Terrors and Horrors of Prison Life, or Six Months a Prisoner at Camp Chase, Ohio* (1907); *Prison Life during the Rebellion; Being a Brief Narrative of the Miseries and Sufferings of Six Hundred Confederate Prisoners Sent from Fort Delaware to Morris Island to be Punished, Written by Fritz Fuzzlebug, One of their Number* (1869), by John J. Dunkle; Griffin Frost's *Camp and Prison Journal* (1867); Isaac W. K. Handy's *United States Bonds, or Duress by Federal Authority; A Journal of Current Events during and Imprisonment of Fifteen Months at Fort Delaware* (1874); Buehring H. Jones's *The Sunny Land* (1868); Anthony M. Keiley's *Prisoner of War, or Five Months among the Yankees* (1866); John H. King's *Three Hundred Days in a Yankee Prison: Reminiscences of War, Life, Captivity, Imprisonment at Camp Chase, Ohio* (1904); John R. King's *My Experience in the Confederate Army and in Northern Prisons* (1917); J. M. Minnich's *Inside of Rock Island Prison from December 1863 to June 1865* (1906); Henry E. Shepherd's *Narrative of Prison Life at Baltimore and Johnson's Island, Ohio* (1917), and the *Autobiography* of Henry Morton Stanley (1913).

Statements, testimonies, and correspondence challenging Northern accusations of a deliberate Southern policy to mistreat Union prisoners were collected and published as "The Treatment of Prisoners During the War Between the States" by the Southern Historical Society in March and April 1876, just before a nationwide centennial celebration. Included in this work are commentaries on the POW issue from the major Confederate actors: Jefferson Davis, Robert E. Lee, Alexander H. Stevens, Robert Ould, S. P. Moore (Confederate Surgeon General), numerous journalists, clergymen, and senior Confederate officers. Short captivity vignettes appear throughout the forty volumes of *Confederate Veteran,* the popular newsletter of the United Confederate Veterans. Personal diaries show that the defenders of the South returned home to tell their stories for a Southern rather than a national audience. Repeatedly, they insisted that the starvation and medical neglect suffered by Union POWs in the South was a direct result of the Union's sea blockade, Confederate military reverses in the field, and, most important, General Grant's decision to halt prisoner exchanges in 1864. Southern apologists have consistently disputed charges made by former union POWs that Confederate POW policy was retributive or intentionally murderous.

Narratives written by Union officers were far more genteel than those written by the enlisted men, for officers customarily received better treatment in captivity than the troops. Whether penned by officers or enlisted men, however, much Northern POW literature rails against the inhumanity of the Southern captors with descriptions of malnutrition, disease, and death paralleling the worst of the Indian captivity "penny dreadfuls" still in print and popular at the time. Meanwhile, according to the Confederate POWs, Yankee jailers were worse than the stereotyped Indians in the popular thrillers. Prisoners on both sides felt the intent was clear: to destroy the POW population and deny its future services to the enemy cause.

Several common threads run through all captivity narratives of the Civil War. Stories of deadlines, starvation, theft, mistreatment by guards, epidemic disease, punishment, heat, cold, and boredom fill the survivors' memoirs. With little or no hope of exchange, one Confederate officer, a POW on Johnson's Island, wrote of "the terrible ennui of prison life . . . an infallible sign of surrender when the men become listless and no longer cared for the things that had hitherto been either their work or their recreation."[13] Many narrators believed that as POWs they were pawns of the federal and Confederate governments. Very few narratives fail to show the prisoners' violent hatred for the other side, Union or Confederate, with the ultimate judgment that the captors wanted to murder their prisoners.[14]

As William Best Hesseltine points out in *Civil War Prisons* (1930), newspapers were the first print media to exploit POW narratives. Exaggerated and sometimes fictional accounts of POW life appeared in the prestigious *New York Times,* Philadelphia *Inquirer,* New York *Tribune,* Richmond *Dispatch* and *Inquirer,* Atlanta *Constitution, Harper's Weekly, National Intelligencer,* and innumerable smaller local newspapers. In print, Lieutenant Colonel James M. Sanderson, USA, complained that the Confederates at Libby Prison in Richmond fed mule meat to the Union prisoners. An editorial in the Richmond *Dispatch* replied to Colonel Sanderson's remarks. "Well, what of it? It was vastly too good for men who have essayed to bring starvation on a people who captured them, and they would have no right to complain if they were forced to that fate they designed for us. . . . Better men have eaten mule meat, and thought it very good. . . . The anatomist who detected the mule bones in the meat sent him was a charlatan, as Yankees generally are. He knows nothing of bones and makes no bones of lying."[15] As a result, jailers reduced rations, near riots began in the camps, and guard staff was increased throughout the Northern military prison system. While the war was fought on the battlefields, newspapers used the structure and often the descriptive style of the popular "penny dreadfuls" as models to describe massacres, torture, and foul treatment. Not to be confused with POW camp newspapers like the *Libby Chronicle* and others that were published and read by the prisoners themselves, popular newspapers raised the level of popular hatred and added new dimensions to an existing familiar body of popular thriller literature. The officers of the Southern prison system were described as brutes, and notions of their being indicted and later tried as war criminals were steadily planted in the minds of Northern readers.

Two prominent scholarly works examine Civil War captivity, William Best Hesseltine's *Civil War Prisons: A Study in Prison Psychology* (1930) and Ovid L. Futch's *History of Andersonville Prison* (1968). Hesseltine argues that treatment became increasingly worse on both sides as the war progressed, in what he calls a general "war psychosis"—the gradual elevation of hate for the enemy—exacerbated by newspapers and exaggerated POW narratives in the popular press. Futch defends the Southern position and never admits that Confederate prison policy might have been at least in some cases retributive or intentionally murderous, as many former Union prisoners charged. On the contrary, Futch argues that the vast number of Northern narratives were exaggerations at best, that they built on shaky memories, and in some cases were outright lies.

Book-length narratives began to appear as POWs escaped or were exchanged. One of the first Union narratives of Southern captivity was *The Journal of Alfred Ely* (1862). Ely, a civilian congressman who, like many Washingtonians, decided to watch the Battle of Bull Run from the sidelines, was captured in its chaotic aftermath and exchanged shortly thereafter. Ely traces the brutality in Southern prisons to mean-spirited prison administrators and guards, not to an order of the Confederate government. The *Captivity of General Corcoran* (1862) was the first full-length POW narrative published during the Civil War.[16] Corcoran, an Irishman with a reputation for bravado in the Sixty-Ninth United States Volunteers, or "Fighting Sixty-Ninth" from New York, called himself "the Hero of Bull Run" and wrote about the personal indignities he suffered as a prisoner.[17] More representative of prevailing sentiment, however, was James J. Geer's *Beyond the Lines, or, a Yankee Prisoner Loose in Dixie* (1864). A Methodist minister and staunch abolitionist, Geer's prose is full of accusations of barbarities. Even before Geer's narrative circulated among Northern abolitionists, cries were heard that POWs in the South were oppressed, and the inevitable response was that Confederate POWs in Northern prisons should be given similar treatment.[18]

By 1863, the treatment of POWs had begun to worsen on both sides, and Northern POW camps especially were deteriorating quickly with the arrival of increasing numbers of Confederates captured after successive Northern victories. General Benjamin Butler, United States Volunteers (USV)—"Beast" as he was known in the South—was apppointed Agent of Exchange, but the Confederates initially refused to deal with him because when he commanded victorious federal troops in New Orleans, Butler had issued orders against harassment of his officers by the New Orleans women. To be more specific, many of the ladies of the city threw full chamber pots on Union officers as they rode on horseback through the streets, which outraged Butler, and he gave orders that if the women acted like harlots, he'd treat them that way. Because women enjoyed an exaggerated, nearly cult status, in the antebellum South, Butler's action became epic throughout the Confederacy, and the Confederate government even declared him to be a war criminal on December 24, 1862. As the exchange agent in 1863, Butler suggested that the Confederate prisoners in the Union POW camp at Point Lookout (Maryland) should receive the same treatment federal prisoners received in Richmond.[19] His suggestion was ignored by Abraham Lincoln, but nonetheless conditions worsened.

Each side attempted to exonerate itself from charges of brutality. The well-known humanitarian Dorothea Dix testified to a congressional committee that federal prison hospitals were clean, that there was no robbery in the North, and that there was ample religious reading material (mostly Bibles) available to the Confederates. Published in 1864, the report of the United States Sanitary Commission, *Narrative of the Privations and Sufferings of United States Officers ad Soldiers while Prisoners of War in the Hands of the Rebel Authorities, Being the Report of a Commission of Inquiry Appointed by the United States Sanitary Commission, with an Appendix Containing the Testimony,* was lauded by the popular press as another truthful account of what was really going on in Dixie. Concurrently in the South, the Confederate government decided to look into the allegations made by the United States Sanitary Commission, Northern captivity narratives, and newspaper reports. It appointed a joint committee for this task, which concluded that the reportage represented nothing more than a successful propaganda effort on the part of the federal government. More significant, on March 3, 1865, in a "Report of the Joint Committee of the Confederate Congress Appointed to Investigate the Conditions and Treatment of Prisoners of War," the Confederate Congress declared that the North was totally responsible for the sufferings of the prisoners in the South, since General Grant had decided to refuse any more prisoner exchanges in 1864.[20] The Confederate government admitted nothing.

What remained were POWs on both sides of the conflict who would write their memoirs, many of which were based on prison camp memories, powerful and persistent camp hearsay, and personal diaries written while soldiers were incarcerated. Decimus et Ultimus Barziza published his captivity memoir, *The Adventures of a Prisoner of War and Life and Scenes in Federal Prisons: Johnson's Island, Fort Delaware, and Point Lookout by an Escaped Prisoner of Hood's Texas Brigade,* in Houston, Texas, in 1865 before the war ended.[21] More an escape narrative than an indictment of Northern brutality toward Confederate POWs, it had little effect on a defeated South. Colonel Buehring H. Jones, CSA, a POW at Johnson's Island, Ohio, published *The Sunny Land* (1868), a collection of romantic POW narratives, poetry, and prose. Like POW diaries of the revolutionary war, many Southern memoirs remain hidden in state, regional, and local archives.

From the popular and influential Northern perspective, enough captivity narratives were written after the war to leave little doubt that life in a Confederate military prison was difficult, if not deadly. Whether recalling Libby Prison in Richmond, Camp Sorghum in Columbia, South Carolina, Belle Isle in Virginia, or Cahaba Prison (Castle Morgan) in Alabama, the Union prisoners—officers or enlisted men—cared little about the politics of exchanges, letters from General U. S. Grant, or the good works of Dorothea Dix; they cared about food, clothing, and the treatment they received at the hands of the Confederates. Everything else was secondary, especially in Camp Sumter in rural Georgia, better known as Andersonville. Three significant books came out of the Andersonville experience: John McElroy's journalistic account, *Andersonville: A Story of Rebel Military Prisons, Fifteen Months a Guest of the So-Called Southern Confederacy: A Private Soldier's Experience* (1879), John Urban's *Battle Field and Prison Pen; or, Through the War and Thrice a Prisoner in Rebel Dungeons* (1882), and *John Ransom's Diary,* first published by the author in 1881 under the simple title *Andersonville.* McElroy and Ransom rail vindictively against their captors; Urban is less vicious.

In addition to the narratives, the issue of captivity was kept alive after the war by the formation of active veterans' organizations such as the Andersonville Survivors Association, the Grand Army of the Republic (GAR), and the United Confederate Veterans. In 1893, Libby Prison was removed from Richmond and erected in Chicago as an exhibit in the World's Fair. In 1905, the Georgia chapter of the United Daughters of the Confederacy started a fund and erected a monument to Henry Wirz at Andersonville. The Andersonville prison site was administered first by the Woman's Relief Corps and later by the federal government, which converted it into a historic site and national cemetery. North and South continue to disagree on who bears responsibility for the suffering and horrors that arose in the war itself, especially in the military prisons that housed, starved, and in thousands of cases killed Union and Confederate POWs.

The Spanish-American War (1898) lasted only three months, during which the United States took about 150,000 Spanish POWs, all of whom were repatriated after peace accords in August 1898. In the advance on Santiago, Cuba, a naval battle took place that made Lieutenant Richmond Pearson Hobson, USN, at once a naval hero, a Medal of Honor winner, and a POW. The Hobson-*Merrimac* episode made its way into major newspapers and the postwar "thrilling adventure" books nearly without exception. Marshall Everett's *Exciting Experiences in Our Wars with Spain and the Filipinos* (1900) records it in prose, poetry, and prints.

The American government had been deeply involved with the POW problem from the beginning of hostilities in Europe in World War I. From 1914 through 1917 the United States served as the protecting power for Allied POWs in Germany, a role that required representatives of the United States to visit the camps, interview prisoners, and report their findings to the International Red Cross. One visitor, the former senator Albert J. Beveridge, reported in 1915 that Germany held 586,000 POWs, of whom 310,000 were Russians, 220,000 French, 40,000 Belgian, and 16,000 British. At the time, Germany's missing numbered 154,000.[22] Beveridge was an observer for the International Red Cross, and after his 1915 visit he commented that feeding these prisoners meant providing enough food to supply the whole German nation for about three days out of a year. "Yet," wrote Beveridge, "it is firmly expected in Germany that the number of prisoners taken by the German forces will be very greatly increased during the present year, and Germany is preparing for that contingency.[23] Beveridge was not the only important American in Germany from 1914 through 1917; James W. Gerard, the former American ambassador to Imperial Germany, was distraught at the alleged atrocities committed by German soldiers against their prisoners and was one of the most "hawkish" Americans at the time.[24] His polemic, *Face to Face with Kaiserism* (1918), contains many reasons why he thought the United States should declare war on Imperial Germany in 1917.

After the fighting started in France in 1914, some Americans refused to accept the American government's official policy of neutrality, and adventurers departed the United States bound for service in foreign armies, air forces, and ambulance corps. The noted American poet e. e. cummings was one such man for whom the lure of adventure was just too overpowering to ignore. After arriving in France, however, with the exigencies and dangers of war surrounding him, cummings found that service in an ambulance corps was a dirty business. He preferred Parisian nightlife to filthy trench warfare. Complaining in letters about their boss, the French, and the war in general, cummings and a colleague were seized by the French military police for seditious behavior and jailed. Fortunately, cummings's father contacted President Wilson and begged him to intercede for his son. The president managed to persuade the French to release cummings. After his deportation back to the United States, cummings published *The Enormous Room* (1922), more a literary work rather than a simple, unadorned POW narrative. Nevertheless, it remains one of the most reflective and ingeniously descriptive examples of prison life in World War I.

The United States and Imperial Germany were actually at war for a relatively short time, from April 6, 1917, to November 11, 1918, but the fighting was intense. American forces lost more than 100,000 lives to disease and combat (see Appendix 3A).[25] Of the 4,120 American POWs during World War I, only 147 died in captivity, and 3,973 were repatriated following the cessation of hostilities. Following the war, escape narratives caught the public eye, especially stories about pilots who dared to plot their way home. Norman Archibald's book *Heaven High, Hell Deep 1917–1918* (1935) was widely read, as was an anthology of escape narratives by H. C. Armstrong, *Escape* (1935). Although Armstrong's book focused on British feats, it did include the daring escapade of Harold B. Willis, an American volunteer pilot who flew with the Franco-American volunteer squadron, the Lafayette Escadrille. Willis's escape partner in Germany was Lieutenant Edouard Isaacs, USN, who wrote his own narrative, *Prisoner of the U-90* (1919). James Norman Hall published an escape narrative as part of his personal memoir, *My Island Home: An Autobiography* (1952). Ralph D. Paine's *The First Yale Unit* (1925) chronicles the adventures of Lieutenant Artemus L. Gates, USNR, who after being shot down attempted to escape from a train while being moved to the permanent officers' POW camp. Less common after World War I were captivity narratives of common soldiers. Henry Berry's collection of oral histories includes only one POW narrative, Corporal Mike Shallin's "The Guest of the Kaiser," in *Make the Kaiser Dance* (1978).[26]

Both officer and enlisted POWs describe capture, internment, resistance, and repatriation. Many narratives raise the issue of chivalry among soldiers, especially among the fliers, and detail the derring-do of committed escapers like Isaacs, Gates, Hall, and Willis. Although POWs during World War I suffered extreme physical privation, narrative accounts indicate no intentional political or military policies to murder POWs or starve them to death. The evidence of the memoirs suggests that German captors made a significant effort to keep the provisions of the Hague Convention.

After World War II (1939–1945), places like Camp O'Donnell, Billibid, Davao Penal Colony, Palawan, Santo Tomas, and Cabantuan prison camps in the Philippines, Changi in Singapore, Mukden in Korea, and Karenko in Formosa found their way into the pages of American captivity narratives. Some POWs witnessed unspeakable acts committed against prisoners, acts that in 1945 and 1946 were finally defined legally as war crimes. In the European theater of operations, life in POW camps for *Kriegies*— short for *Kriegsgefangener* (POW in German)—was hard, but with food packages from the Red Cross, sports materials from the YMCA, other relief agencies, and home, life was at least bearable. German military compounds were known as *Stalags* (*Stammlager* for enlisted soldiers), *Oflags* (*Offizierlager* for officers), *Stalag Luft* (*Stalags* operated by the German Air Force for Allied airmen), *Straflager* (punishment camps), *Marlags* (Navy POW compounds), and *Lazarets* (field hospitals) and were very different from the SS-operated civilian death camps. In 1960, Morris Jano-witz observed that Americans developed a style of warfare that replaced what appeared as heroic chivalry in World War I with the legalities of land warfare and the correct treatment of prisoners of war.[27] To their credit, most of the officers and men of the German air force and the German army were soldiers who understood and obeyed the rules of the 1929 Geneva Convention. Returned Americans reported consistently that the guard dogs were more vicious than the guards. The International Red Cross inspected the camps and attempted to certify that food packages and even mail arrived from time to time. Although some former POWs say that they had more food than the German civilians in 1945, the vast majority of the 90,000 American Kriegies in Europe were always dan-gerously hungry. Life was boring and dreary. "Barbed-Wire Disease"—giving up hope and preferring death to further incarceration—was always a possibility.

In all the theaters of war during World War II, approximately 130,200 Americans were captured and interned as POWs. Of that number, 14,072 died in captivity, mostly in Asia, and 78,914 were repatriated at the end of the war. There remain 78,773 men still listed as missing in action (MIA) from World War II and like their predecessors in World War I, they are presumed dead. The problem faced by liberated and repatriated ex-pris-oners returning to the United States was that the United States was vic-torious in spite of them, not because of them. In their postwar narratives, the authors admit to a sense of loss and failure, but counterbalance those losses by a heavy emphasis on individual and collective selflessness and heroism. Thus the POW narrators from the European theater of opera-tions (ETO) stated their case: as individuals and prisoner-units they con-tinued to resist their captors every bit as much behind the wire as they had as armed soldiers before capture. Togetherness was a soldierly vir-tue; individualism was suspect. Collaboration was rare.[28]

The American POWs in World War II are distinguished from their prede-cessors in earlier wars most significantly by the horror of war crimes and crimes against humanity committed by the Japanese Army. The extent of ill treatment in captivity during World War II is reflected in the capture-death or morbidity rates. In Europe, for example, 235,473 British and American POWs were taken by the Germans and Italians. Of this num-ber, 9,348, or 4 percent of the total, died. In the Pacific, the Allied death rate was 27 percent.[29] Beginning with the Bataan Death March and con-tinuing throughout the war, prisoners were stupefied by the cold ferocity of their Japanese captors.

Before captivity, Americans had little notion of the Japanese concept of Bushido, the soldier code that forbade surrender to the enemy on the battlefield, and were aghast at the extreme punishments and frequent

executions of fellow POWs for the most trifling transgressions of the captors' harsh rules. Defying international law, the worst of these rules was
the death sentence for anyone who tried to escape. On March 9, 1943,
the Japanese prisoner of war regulations were amended to permit escaping
prisoners to be punished in the same way as deserters from the Japanese
army. "The leader of a group of persons who have acted together in effecting an escape shall be subject to either death, or imprisonment for a minimum of ten years. The other persons involved shall be subject to either
the death penalty or a minimum imprisonment of one year."[30] In effect,
the worst fears emanating from the "Yellow Peril" stereotype began to
come true in the eyes of the Allied POWs.[31] To them, it was clear that the
buck-toothed, popular newspaper character, Hashimura Togo, created by
Irwin Wallace before the war, was the captor who intended to kill them,
not quickly but slowly, not soldierly but disgracefully, not honorably or
lawfully but ignominiously. Japanese soldiers, in turn, believed that the
surrendered westerners had disgraced themselves and as soldiers they got
what they deserved. When these two titanic belief systems clashed, catastrophe occurred.

Published before the war ended, *The Dyess Story* (1944) described Japanese atrocities and William Dyess's escape from captivity in the Davao
Penal Colony in the Philippines. Dyess had suffered greatly in the death
march, and was one of the first American escapers to tell his tale to a
disbelieving and outraged American public. Two Marine Corps officer narratives, James P. S. Devereux's *The Story of Wake Island* (1947) and
Colonel Gregory "Pappy" Boyington's *Baa Baa Black Sheep* (1958) also
created lasting impressions. Devereux's narrative was a detailed explanation of how well his marines, naval personnel, and civilians defended
Wake Island against an overwhelming foe. The book served as an apology
for the surrender of the island. "Pappy" Boyington's captivity took up
the last third of his memoir. Boyington was a flamboyant and irritating
figure who by his own admission was a committed alcoholic. After his
shootdown and capture, like so many other American fliers and submariners, Boyington was carried as MIA because the Japanese refused to
report his capture to the International Red Cross. Everyone thought that
Boyington was dead. His repatriation surprised the nation so much that
his photo appeared in national newspapers and the Movietone newsreels.
What Gregory Boyington did not know at the time was that, as "Pappy"
Boyington, he became a new American popular hero. He received the
Medal of Honor, and his memoir was the basis for the popular although
thoroughly fictional television series "Baa Baa Black Sheep," starring
Robert Conrad. Boyington served as "technical adviser" to the series.

Perhaps one of the most notable army POWs, also a recipient of the
Medal of Honor, was the popular General Jonathan M. Wainwright, USA.

Wainwright commanded the forces that surrendered on Corregidor in 1942, survived captivity, and was so universally honored that Douglas MacArthur invited him to the USS *Missouri* for the Japanese surrender. Amid the euphoria of victory, popular journalist Robert Considine assisted Wainwright in creating *General Wainwright's Story* (1945) shortly after the war ended. Resembling Wainwright's narrative was Edward W. Beattie, Jr.'s *Diary of a Kriegie* (1946). Assigned to Europe before the war, Beattie learned German and befriended journalists and some German luminaries. As a uniformed newsman in the American army, he found himself quite capable of communicating with his captors when necessary, or, in some cases, being able to listen in on his guards' conversations. His capture in France in 1944, his remove by train to the prison camp, and his stay behind the wire became one of the most complete, observant, and comprehensively reflective statements about military captivity in Germany. John A. Victor narrated his resistance and survival in *Time Out: American Airmen at Stalag Luft I* (1951). With much less bravado, Kenneth W. Simmons relates his resistance and survival experiences in *Kriegie* (1960). At the end of his book, Simmons recalls that the POW experience refused to go away, despite time or his own will to forget it. Finally, he realized that he had to face the past. Simmons then took time off from work, rented a small cabin, and wrote his narrative—simply to expunge memories of the Kriegie experience from his system. Simmons's work and that of many others found national publishers; other POWs published their personal captivity narratives themselves. A few examples of self-published Kriegie narratives are Willis and Roberta Carpenter's *I Was the Enemy* (1990) and Delmar Spivey's *POW Odyssey* (1984); Samuel B. Moody, a survivor of the Bataan Death March and captivity in the Philippines and Japan, published *Reprieve from Hell* (1961).

Beginning in the 1980s a new narrative form began to appear in print, the oral history collection of first-person interviews, in which an author pieces together the history of a captivity environment from the memories of several participants, usually members of the same or similar POW communities. Although the oral history narrative is not new in itself, its application to the topic of American POWs is relatively recent. Donald Knox published an oral history collection of POW experiences in his *Death March: The Survivors of Bataan* (1981) after conducting scores of interviews with former POWs and visiting several conventions of the American Defenders of Bataan and Corregidor. Whether the topic is capture, torture, executions, the death march, escapes, hell ships, slave labor, or liberation, Knox lets his informants narrate their experiences in a natural way and leaves the reader exhausted from sharing the experiences not only of one POW but of many who made up part of an entire POW community.

Treatments critical of American behavior in captivity have often waited many years for publication. The matter-of-fact captivity diary of General W. E. Brougher, USA, Wainwright's fellow POW, *South to Bataan, North to Mukden: The Prison Diary of Brigadier General W. E. Brougher,* waited until 1971 for publication. In his terse notes, Brougher expresses many private and critical evaluations of his peers. Likewise unsettling are the reflections written by Commander Thomas Hayes, USN, while he was imprisoned in Manila's Bilibid prison. Hayes was a navy surgeon captured in the Philippines who commented on the lack of leadership exercised by senior officers, morale-breaking interservice rivalries even in prison camps, food stealing, and breakdowns of discipline due primarily to the ennui of prison life. Hayes's notebooks were found, edited, and published by A. B. Feuer as *Bilibid Diary: The Secret Notebooks of Commander Thomas Hayes, POW, the Philippines, 1942–1945* (1987). Robert E. Haney's personal account of the North China Marines captured at Corregidor in 1942 combined his diary and narrative and appeared as *Caged Dragons: An American P.O.W. in WWII Japan* (1991). Like Brougher and Hayes, Haney became very angry in captivity, not so much at the Japanese as at General Douglas MacArthur, whom he blamed for abandoning the American force in the Philippines in the first place. Joseph S. Frelinghuysen's *Passages to Freedom: A Story of Capture and Escape* (1990) recounts not only the shock of his capture by a unit of the German Afrika Korps in 1943 but focuses significant attention on the shockingly poor state of training in the American army in North Africa. His Italian captors were not nearly as terrible as his fellow prisoners, who acted as disgruntled individuals and waived the opportunity to become a resistance-oriented POW community. To make matters worse, the British senior ranking officer resembled Pierre Boulle's character Colonel Nicholson in *Bridge over the River Kwai,* more interested in his own authority, the prisoners' morale, organization, comfort, and camp hierarchy than in escape or individual resistance.

The Korean War (1950–1953) was not the first example of an icy cold war turned hot. The civil war in Greece in 1946 was a bloody affair; so too were the on-again, off-again confrontations between the communist Yugoslavians and units of the American army stationed near Trieste. The French were battling the Viet Minh in Indochina (Laos, Cambodia, and Vietnam) as early as 1946, and although the West was tired of war after defeating Nazi Germany and Imperial Japan, wars of liberation were beginning to ignite all over Europe and Asia. Euphemisms such as "police action" or "conflict" were invented to replace the word "war," which has legal, social, and moral connotations. Yet as we learned in Vietnam in the following decades, acts of public war consist of actions more than words or legal concepts. For the participants, Korea was a war, and the soldiers who fought it believed they possessed an individual and collective right to expect the basic rules, customs, and international laws concerning warfare, including treatment of POWs, to be obeyed by all the parties involved.[32]

In a little more than three years of warfare spanning nearly the entire length and breadth of the Korean peninsula, 7,140 American servicemen were captured and interned, of whom 2,701 were known to have died in captivity.[33] By the armistice in 1953, 4,418 POWs were returned to American military control. Choosing to remain with their captors, 21 Americans and 1 British Royal Marine refused repatriation. Of that group, only 2 remain in China today; 8,177 remain MIA.[34] Before hostilities ended, "Operation Little Switch" brought home 149 American sick and wounded among 684 UN POWs from April 20 to May 3, 1953. After the war was brought to a halt and the armistice signed in 1953, "Operation Big Switch" completed the POW exchange between the adversaries.

The vast majority of American POWs were shocked when their captors discarded the 1949 Geneva Convention as if it had never existed. In the BBC documentary "The Unknown War" (1990) North Korean officer veterans admitted candidly that they often executed American prisoners, especially if they resisted in any way or refused to beg for their lives. They forced the Americans to walk in subzero weather north to permanent camps in North Korea, and the relatively few captivity narratives indicate that about 70 percent of the early POWs died on that horrifying winter march.

After the Chinese People's Volunteers entered the conflict, military captivity took a different turn in Korea. Instead of being simply POWs, the Americans and other Allied prisoners became "students." An ideological war behind the wire caught unsuspecting, free-thinking Americans by surprise. The Americans and the other United Nations POWs discovered that the Chinese were skillful interrogators bent on completing their mission of reeducating their charges. New words crept into the popular consciousness: the term *brainwashing* was invented by the popular press to describe what the captors called reeducation; reactionaries were those prisoners who adhered to their soldier's oath and to the precepts of the Geneva Convention; progressives were those POWs who began the process of assimilation into the captor's culture.

At no other time in the history of American arms have military captors executed so many American POWs immediately after capture or, later, attempted radical political indoctrination of American prisoners—reeducation—at the rate and intensity exercised by the North Korean Army and the Chinese People's Volunteers. Writers in the popular media searched for a word to describe that process of indoctrination, and even though they decided on "brainwashing," no one's brain was ever "washed" at all. Rather, individual American prisoners were forced to confess to outrageously false charges of war crimes or die trying to resist doing so. Only five years separated World War II and Korea, but after hostilities ceased and the POWs were repatriated, the popular media made it look as if American fighting men in Korea were weak, amoral losers who had betrayed the fundamental values of the American dream. In the popular view, there seemed to be something very wrong with the American POWs in Korea, something that distinguished them psychologically from the defenders of Bataan and Corregidor and the Kriegies of the German Stalags.

Virginia Pasley's *21 Stayed: The Story of American GI's Who Chose Communist China—Who They Were and Why They Stayed* (1955) details the lives of each of the expatriate Americans who remained with their captors. Journalist Edward Hunter responded with *Brainwashing: The Story of the Men Who Defied It* (1956), a collection of interviews that suggests the communist Chinese used Pavlovian principles in an attempt to reeducate captured Americans in much the same manner as they had reeducated resisting members of their own population following the communist seizure of power in China. Hunter argues that the Chinese communists failed, but Eugene Kinkead counters in *In Every War But One* (1959) that the American soldier in the Korean War had abandoned the traditional soldierly values that had supported and distinguished the American prisoner in World War II. In Kinkead's view, the idealistic and long-suffering captive communities of European and Asian captivity gave way in North Korea to a synthesis of American creature-comfort materialism, what's-in-it-for-me pragmatism, and to-hell-with-everyone-else-but-me individualism. Kinkead was aghast that twenty-one Americans and one Englishman would decide to remain in communist hands after the cessation of hostilities. Looking for a scapegoat, Kinkead blamed not only the prisoners but also the social, economic, and educational system that had nurtured them.

Had Americans "gone soft" in captivity? So it looked when the foreign presses of the Chinese People's Committee for World Peace published two assimilation narratives written by or at least edited by some of those men who had decided to stay with their captors. *Shall Brothers Be* (1952) was loaded with claims made by numerous "progressive" prisoners of favorable treatment. Later, in 1955, nearly two years after the Korean armistice and "Operation Big Switch," assimilated POWs edited *Thinking Soldiers* as a propaganda "peace" text on behalf of the Chinese communists. The United States Department of Defense and Senate countered these expatriate, assimilation captivity narratives with *POW: The Fight Continues After the Battle: The Report of the Secretary of Defense's Advisory Committee on Prisoners of War* (1955) and *Communist Interrogation, Indoctrination, and Exploitation of Prisoners of War* (1956).

Outside the world of narrative, two prominent apologists, William Lindsay White and Albert D. Biderman, began to make their presence felt. Both authors attempt to refute Kinkead's assertion that Americans had "gone soft" in captivity. White published *The Captives of Korea* in 1957 and compares "their treatment of ours and our treatment of theirs." White concludes that, although imperfect from time to time, United Nations forces treated communist prisoners well, with POW policies corresponding to all the provisions of the 1949 Geneva Convention. White then documented communist practices that flouted the convention. Albert D. Biderman followed White's lead with *March To Calumny: The Story of American POWs in the Korean War* (1963). Especially valuable in Biderman's book is the definition of the four types of American and United Nations prisoners in North Korea: the relatively few diehard resisters, or reactionaries as the Chinese called them; the collaborators or progressives who cooperated temporarily with their captors; the handful of renegades who decided to cast their lot with the captors, and the vast majority of prisoners who decided to stay out of the captors' way and "play it cool" to maximize their individual chances for long-term survival. By using narrative records, official documents, and cross-references to affidavits from POWs, Biderman and White attempt to refute Kinkead's hypothesis that communist reeducation or brainwashing was more than minimally successful among American prisoners in North Korea. Hunter, Biderman, and White corroborate the individual accounts in memoirs written by the prisoners themselves and show conclusively that the Americans resisted their captors with an intensity at least equal to what they had displayed in previous wars.

Several important POW accounts of resistance became popular in the Korean postwar period. General William F. Dean, USA, the highest-ranking American POW in Korea, first narrated his experience in the *Saturday Evening Post* and then published it as *General Dean's Story* (1954). He told his audience how he was separated from his forces and evaded enemy forces for nearly a month. After he was captured, General Dean became a prize and received special attention from his captors until his release. The popular General Dean, like General Jonathan M. Wainwright in World War II, received the Medal of Honor.

Philip Deane, the pen name of Gerassimos Svoronos-Gigantes, was a British civilian journalist who covered the war with an American infantry unit and was captured when the unit was overrun by North Korean assault troops. Deane managed to return to the West by way of Manchuria and Moscow and later published an interesting civilian narrative and travelogue called *I Was a Captive in Korea* (1953). Ward Millar's escape narrative, *Valley of the Shadow,* and Clay Blair's journalistic biography of escapers and evaders, *Beyond Courage,* were both published in 1955 and reinforced the notion that Americans did not simply give in but actively resisted their captors. Sergeant Lloyd W. Pate describes the hard-boiled resistance he displayed to his communist Chinese captors in *Reactionary* (1956). Wallace L. Brown's *The Endless Hours: My Two and a Half Years as a Prisoner of War of the Chinese Communists* (1961) recounts the POW experience of an air force pilot who was shot down and captured near the war's end in 1953. Jailed in China, Brown was not released until 1955, when he and some other American fliers were taken to Hong Kong. Walker M. Mahurin's *Honest John* (1962) addresses the issue of germ warfare in Korea. He was one of the pilots who was forced to sign a phony confession, and he uses his narrative to set the record straight. John W. Thornton, a navy flier, was shot down and held for three years. His *Believed To Be Alive* (1981) is one of the most complete resistance narratives of the Korean War written from an officer's point of view, in spite of the fact that it appeared nearly thirty years after his repatriation.

The postwar battle of words, however, was not conducted only in published, book-length POW narratives; literary and legal trench warfare was conducted in some of America's prestigious military, legal, and popular journals. In the *Saturday Evening Post, Look, Life, Newsweek, Command Digest, Army Information Digest, Collier's, US News and World Report, Military Engineering, Military Review,* and many others, one could find numbers of articles concerning the Korean War POW issue. Josop L. Kunz's "The Chaotic Status of the Laws of War and the Urgent Necessity for their Revision" appeared in the *American Journal of International Law* in 1951 and called for reforms in international law relative to POWs. Pitman B. Potter's "Repatriation of Korean Prisoners of War" (1953) in the *American Journal of International Law* and George S. Prough's "Prisoners at War: The POW Battleground" (1956) in the *Dickinson Law Review* reminded legal scholars how and why the POW's battle continues in the POW camp. In the end, however, the 1959 Kinkead position seems to dominate the memories of Americans when they consider captivity in the Korean War, perhaps thanks to Richard Condon's popular novel *The Manchurian Candidate* (1959), which John Frankenheimer made into a popular film in 1962.

Concurrent with the Vietnam War was the capture of the USS *Pueblo,* a small freighter of World War II vintage designed and used for passive electronic intelligence-gathering. Although the captain of the *Pueblo,* Commander Lloyd M. Bucher, USN, claimed that he was outside the twelve-mile limit in international waters off the North Korean coast, the North Koreans claimed that the *Pueblo* had intentionally sailed into its territorial waters. As a result, the North Koreans attacked the *Pueblo* on January 23, 1968, and captured the crew, the ship, and all the intelligence equipment. One sailor, Duane Hodges, died in captivity; all the rest, eighty-two men, were released on December 23, 1968. No one escaped, and no one collaborated beyond the usual forced confessions. Yet for the navy, the capture of the *Pueblo* and its crew was an institutional embarrassment. This was the first time such an incident had taken place at sea between the United States and a hostile captor in peacetime since Captain William Bainbridge surrendered the *Philadelphia* to the Tripoli pirates in 1803 without a fight. For the American intelligence community, the *Pueblo* incident was a catastrophe; for the officers and crew, it was a nightmare. Following the navy's formal board of inquiry and an inquiry by a special subcommittee of the House of Representatives in 1969, Admiral Daniel V. Gallery's accusatory polemic, *The Pueblo Incident* (1970), presented the traditional navy's antiquated, hard-line point of view. Gallery condemns Bucher's surrender, his actions in captivity, and the terms of the release. The participants responded to Gallery's accusations. Bucher describes his captivity as the *Pueblo*'s commanding officer in *Bucher: My Story* (1970), and Stephen Harris, the ship's intelligence officer, supports Bucher's defense in *My Anchor Held* (1970).

In Vietnam, as in Korea, American POWs were treated as political criminals rather than as soldiers with rights. Several motifs of Vietnam POW narratives link them with narratives from the past: stoic heroism, torture, resistance, defiance, and cooperation with the captors. Survivors raise questions about the viability of military discipline in captivity, the validity (if not the legality) of the Code of Conduct, and the uselessness of the Geneva Convention when one side disregards its provisions. With ethnographic precision, the narratives examine the functions of the POW community and prison culture in ways very much like those of their predecessors. Vietnam POWs damned their captors, but, more important, they also attempted to understand them.

The first POW narratives of the Vietnam War were published before the war ended. James N. Rowe's *Five Years to Freedom* (1971) is a classic military resistance and escape narrative. After he graduated from West Point, Rowe joined the Army's Special Forces and found himself advising South Vietnamese forces in the Mekong Delta. After an ambush and a futile firefight he was captured in 1963, survived, and escaped his captors on December 31, 1968. In counterpoint to Rowe's book, George Smith's *POW: Two Years with the Vietcong* (1971) is an antiwar polemic and a partial-assimilation narrative. After his release by the National Liberation Front for political reasons, Smith joined the antiwar movement in the United States, testified at the Winter Soldier hearings, and dedicated his captivity narrative to his captors. As a result, Smith was detained by the army and threatened with a court-martial. In the end the United States Army gave Smith a general discharge for collaboration.[35]

Beginning in 1973, many of the early postwar Vietnam POW narratives, written by military officers for the most part, featured themes of religious resistance. Examples of this type include Larry Chesley's *Seven Years in*

Hanoi (1973), Ralph Gaither's *With God in a POW Camp* (1973), *From the Shadows of Death* by J. N. Helsop and D. H. Van Orden (1973), Jay Roger Jensen's *Six Years in Hell* (1974), Eugene B. McDaniel's *Before Honor* (1975), Charles Plumb's *I'm No Hero* (1973), and Norman A. McDaniel's *Yet Another Voice* (1975). Jeremiah Denton's *When Hell Was in Session* (1976) synthesizes the religious and the resistance narrative so well that it formed the basis of a made-for-TV movie (same title) starring Hal Holbrook as Denton and Mako as his North Vietnamese Army interrogator. Only one narrative was written as an apology for religious pacifism, James A. Daley's *A Hero's Welcome: The Conscience of Sergeant James Daley Versus the United States Army* (1975). Daley became a Jehovah's Witness in captivity and joined the Peace Committee inside the Hanoi Hilton. Most POW accounts of Vietnam contain testimony akin to the Puritan and French Jesuit narratives of the seventeenth century,[36] and the majority address resistance and survival in the style of the stoic captive hero. Zalin Grant, a former intelligence officer in Vietnam, took an oral-history approach in his POW study of nine noncareerist POWs in *Survivors* (1975), one of the first books to report on renegadism and the antiwar movement in captivity.

By 1978, former Vietnam prisoners were beginning to reflect on their experiences in terms of philosophy and ethics. Not only were some of these officers telling their audiences what happened to them in captivity, but they were also beginning to question how captivity challenged and possibly changed their individual and collective sense of being. Scott Blakeley's *Prisoner at War: The Survival of Commander Richard A. Stratton* (1978) tells the fascinating story of Commander Richard Stratton, USN, who broke in torture and wrote bogus war crimes confessions. Stratton's famous bow and his monotone confession pleased his captors at first, but embarrassed them later when they understood finally how much he disgraced them in public. Stratton knew that bowing was foreign to American culture; when he bowed not once but several times, he fully intended caricature. The Western press noticed immediately that his behavior was distinctly foreign to American culture in general and asked again if the POWs in Hanoi were being "brainwashed." The North Vietnamese were then forced to respond to international scrutiny of their treatment of the Americans they held. As a result of Stratton's bow at an international press conference in Hanoi, what looked like a propaganda victory to the North Vietnamese ended as an international resistance event and a vital turning point for the politics that would affect the Vietnam War in general and the American POWs in Hanoi until 1973. In Blakeley's contemporary reflection on the philosophy of military captivity, Stratton contended that the individual could withstand only so much torture before being made to confess anything. Resisting a torturer to the best of one's ability was the objective, not resisting to the point of total self-sacrifice. Stratton suggested that the Cold War prisoner should attempt to save his mind and body in order to continue the fight over the long haul rather than giving in to one's primal instincts to resist at all costs. Most importantly, Stratton, along with many of his prisoner colleagues, maintained that the greatest good for the greatest number of prisoners in a POW community begins with tolerance of failure, endures through forgiveness of others' weaknesses, limits resistance to what is absolutely necessary, and maintains strong links with the captive community at large. James A. Mulligan's struggle to resist in *The Hanoi Commitment* (1981), agrees, at least in spirit, with Blakeley's study of Stratton's captivity philosophy; so too does James and Sybil Stockdale's *In Love and War* (1984), Everett Alvarez's *Chained Eagle* (1989), Gerald Coffee's *Beyond Survival* (1989), and Larry Guarino's *A P.O.W.'s Story: 2801 Days in Hanoi* (1990).

In every war there are committed escapers, POWs who refuse to accept the inevitability of captivity. Dieter Dengler's *Escape from Laos* (1979) describes his escape as an act planned in concert with all the other POWs (Thai and American) in the camp. James N. Rowe was also a committed escaper. After several failed planned attempts, luck and opportunity presented themselves and he escaped. John Dramesi wrote *Code of Honor* (1975) as a pure resistance narrative from a committed escaper's point of view. Perhaps foolishly, perhaps heroically, Dramesi and Edwin L. Atterberry planned their escape meticulously, broke jail, and traveled several miles down the Red River before being discovered. His narrative criticized the existing policy advocating stoic resistance and seemingly in good faith accused his comrades in the Hanoi POW community of compromise in the face of the enemy. To escape or not remains one of the most disputed alternatives of military captivity; it is difficult to tell committed escapers not to go over, under, or through any barrier to their freedom.

As the context of the American captivity experience shifted from civilians in Indian hands to soldiers in enemy hands, the nature and intent of captivity narratives changed as well. Although in individual captures one soldier still surrendered to another, as the number of soldiers increased, so too did the number of soldiers who surrendered en masse to the enemy. As the technology of flight evolved into the science of aviation, mounted cavalry soldiers became pilots, and enemy gunners shot them down. The landscape of the Indian village shifted first to the prison hulks in Wallabout Bay and the prisons in England, to the bagnios of Tripoli and Algiers, to haciendas in Mexico, to the camps and penal colonies in the Philippines, Stalags in Germany, numbered camps in Japan and Korea and eventually to the prison system in Vietnam. Gauntlets disappeared, replaced by constant daily head counts. Ritual torture gave place to vindictive punishments in the Civil War and the world wars, then back to torture again in Korea and Vietnam. Despite all the contextual changes, six major narrative categories remain (religious redemption, military resistance, escape, evader, assimilation, and romance) and the natural flow of the basic event-scenarios continues, from precapture statements of status to liberation and lament.

CHAPTER TWO

The Evolution of POW Status:
Establishing Order in Captivity

Men who take up arms against one another in public war do not cease on
this account to be moral beings, responsible to one another and to God.
                                                        Francis Lieber (1863)

Public war obligates soldiers to kill for reasons of state only, not to fulfill
a personal vendetta, nor to gratify a perverse personal impulse, nor to
get rid of obnoxious people, nor simply to inflict suffering for its own
sake.[1] When the fighting stops at the moment of capture, the killing stops,
and some system of law has to regulate the actions of reasonable men
caught in temporarily unreasonable circumstances. Military captivity—
being a prisoner of war—carries no assumption of personal criminality,
nor does it imply in any way that a soldier was acting illegally while carrying out his combat duties in public war. Traditionally, military captivity
is the physical state of incarceration endured by a soldier after a personal
capture or group surrender. As a result, the prisoner is considered a public
enemy by the detaining power and, if physically fit for duty, may be held
for the duration of the war or until a suitable exchange can be made. The
customs of war and the statutes of international law require captors to
treat military captives humanely. Yet modern times have seen significant
shifts in the behavior of captors toward captives, shifts that have significantly affected the lives of nearly every POW.

Captivity denies civil rights to the captive and underscores the failure of
an assigned mission. For the soldier, captivity remains a most dangerous
experience. Hostile and punitive captivity, especially the kind that took
place in the Philippines, Japan, and indeed throughout the Pacific theater
during World War II, and later in North Korea and Vietnam, not only
threatens a soldier's mental well-being in the field during a national conflict
but can also cause continuing trauma to former prisoners who survive.

History shows the evolution of prisoner-taking in war. According to
Richard Garrett, to fight in publicly declared war or in private vendetta
made an unpleasant adventure something glorious, but being captured
in these circumstances left the fate of the captive to the whim of the
captor, to whom the captive was merely a combatant on the losing side
who did not run away fast enough. His loot added to the spoils of the

captor, his ransom recovered the cost of the war, and his person became a slave.[2] As early as the time of St. Patrick in Ireland (c. A.D. 461) the practice of slave-making through capture was denounced by prominent churchmen, especially by St. Patrick himself, who was captured as a boy and sold into slavery in Ireland. In his epistle to the soldiers of the British ruler Coroticus, St. Patrick condemned the practice in general along with the killing of noncombatants.

> These soldiers live in death, the associates of Scots and Picts who have fallen away from the Faith, the slayers of innocent Christians. . . . It is the custom of the Christians in Roman Gaul to send chosen men of piety with money to the Franks and other heathens, to ransom baptized captives. Thou slayest all, or sellest them to a foreign nation that knows not God. I do not know what to say about the dead of the children of God upon whom the sword has fallen beyond measure. The Church deplores and bewails her sons and daughters whom the sword as yet hath not slain but who are carried far away and transported into distant lands, reduced to slavery, especially to slavery under the degraded and unworthy apostate Picts.[3]

In medieval Europe, being a POW implied that the defeated soldier was wealthy or well connected, and the loser's ransom could enrich the captor's coffers considerably. Death awaited captured troops who had nothing but their lives to give. The medieval captivity paradigm excused mass murders of prisoners, with the general exception of royalty, but from time to time even they were caught in the slaughter.[4] This is not to say that war had no rules; the morality and political legitimacy of war have been the study of theologians, jurists, and diplomats from ancient times to the present. Historians often observe that early Christian pacifism from 100 to 300 A.D. contributed to the defeat of Rome's western empire, but as military historian Telford Taylor suggests, in the East, Constantine's conversion nullified the passivity of the West and fundamentally changed Christian attitudes toward war.[5]

War as a political act of nations was Christianized but not tamed by men such as St. Augustine of Hippo (354–430), St. Thomas Aquinas (1225–1274), Father Francisco de Vitoria (1548–1617), Jesuit theologian Francisco Suarez (1548–1617), and Hugo Grotius, the Dutch Protestant jurist of the seventeenth century. St. Augustine of Hippo, who saw some value in the rule by a democratic Christian community, lived in a fragile and dangerous political atmosphere. He discussed the nature of just and unjust war, saying that just wars were fought either to "avenge injuries or to restore what has been unjustly taken." "Indeed," wrote Augustine, "the aim of the just war is peace."[6] Saint Thomas Aquinas, a political monarchist who feared wrongful oppression by democracy and oligarchy, asked in *Summa Theologica* (1272) if warfare was always sinful. In his answer, he concluded that three fundamental conditions must exist for a war to be just in the eyes of God and man: (1) the authority of the prince (the state) has to be the basis for armed conflict, not vengeance, not greed, nor any other individual whim; (2) a war has to have a just cause, that is, the enemy must in fact deserve the war; and (3) the war has to have a good intention, that is, it must be an effort to secure peace.[7] The Dominican Francisco de Vitoria followed St. Thomas's concept of the "higher intention" when he defended Spanish conquests in the New World. Vitoria believed the acquisition of souls for God by armed force was morally valid and did not constitute an illegal act of war, although certain rules needed to be exercised because a wrong war could "bring great evil and ruin to multitudes."[8] The Jesuit theologian Francisco Suarez maintained that Christian rulers had the right to make war, but that these Christian (Catholic) rulers "must conduct their wars with at least some relation to natural law."[9] To Suarez, war was an act of political defense, and to him a defensive war was always legal when it was conducted in defense of life, property, or a friend who was unjustly attacked by an enemy.

Beginning with Thomas More, jurists began to take over the issues of POWs from the theologians. More's position in *Utopia* (1519) reflects the values of his age but also foreshadows the international law of later centuries. To More and his Utopians, war by its nature is manifestly brutal, yet it was "practiced by man more constantly than by any other beast."[10] According to More, when the Utopians win a battle, "they are more ready to take prisoners than to make great slaughter."[11] In More's *Utopia,* POWs become bondsmen (slaves), but they are well treated, and their offspring are free citizens. When the war is over, the conquered side pays the bill through taxes (war reparations) imposed by the winners.

One century later, Hugo Grotius (1583–1645), a Dutch Protestant lawyer, the "Father of International Law," and himself a former political prisoner (and escaper), wrote *De Jure Belli ac Pacis* (1625). The title was taken from Cicero's *Oratio pro Balbo,* in which Cicero summarizes all the subjects of the law of nations, "universum denique belli jus ac pacis."[12] By international law Grotius meant the Roman concept *jus gentium,* a system of laws that was applied to alien elements that infiltrated Roman society. Not Roman law at all, *jus gentium*—the assumption that a common law existed in and among all nations—was forced upon unwilling Roman jurists by the necessity of maintaining legal and political order in an empire that consisted of many peoples. What complicated the matter among the Romans was the superimposition of the Greek theory of the law of nature, or *jus naturale,* which assumed that there was a patterned superscript, a "natural law" for the physical world. Grotius synthesizes these two major legal assumptions of *jus gentium* and *jus naturale*.[13] *On the Law of War and Peace* is divided into three books: the first addresses the nature of *jus belli* as a conventional concept among nations and treats the different kinds of wars; the second addresses the causes of war, or the violation of public or private rights that justifies the taking up of arms; the third book examines the course of war and considers permissible behavior in war and the conventions or treaties which end it.[14] Grotius was the first statesman to advocate an end to chemical warfare, which, at the time, took the form of venom on arrows and poisoned wells. He pleaded, for the sake of nations, armies, and soldiers, for a recognized common law of war.

The Thirty Years War (1618–1648), fought in Europe during Grotius's lifetime, seemed to obscure both divine and human law behind open catastrophic frenzy—hellish war—which looses men to commit all sorts of unspeakable acts in the name of duty, or religion, or orders given by superiors. Grotius attempted to find a compromise position somewhere between the extremes of the military commander who wants to use only the force of arms to settle a dispute and the lawyer who rejects the force of arms completely. Simply stated, Hugo Grotius attempted to devise a set of rules that combatant nations could follow to their mutual advantage to wage war and establish peace. He suggested that nations should establish sets of international laws and an international forum to put them in place. Neither solution was wholly adopted, but Grotius did achieve a limited success. He publicized the problem and was responsible for the provisions in the Treaty of Westphalia (1648) that negated the idea that POWs should be treated as criminals. Grotius wrote, "It is the bitterest lot to be a captive by the laws of war."[15] No longer would prisoners of war forfeit all civil and personal rights upon capture, nor would captors be legally able to sell them into slavery. But beyond these provisions Christian Europe turned a deaf ear. The military commander had to ask whether restraint could operate when it came to seizing military objectives in the name of the state, and the lawyer was helpless when the force of arms replaced the jurisprudence of the courtroom. Thus, in Europe, despite Grotius's pleas, no rules existed beyond the rules of tradition and the specific treaties that concluded wars.

History has shown that warlust surfaces occasionally in world affairs. It is difficult to control and nearly impossible to eradicate. If no law exists to regulate the force of arms before and after battle, expediency alone will guide the actions of blooded soldiers. During the Middle Ages, combatants preferred to fight to the death than to be captured, for captivity meant butchery or enslavement. Gallantry was rewarded by the sparing of life after the battle, but the code of chivalry among Christian knights gave rise to fanatical ideologies, especially against the soldiers of Islam.[16]

European servitude to the Moslems began when Moslems from North Africa launched their campaign to conquer the Iberian peninsula in 711.[17] During the Middle Ages the ransom trade was often supported by religious orders, such as the Order of the Most Holy Trinity for the Ransom of Captives that traded people for cash in 1198 and the Order of Our Lady of Mercy that did much the same in 1218. After the expulsion of Arabs from the Iberian peninsula in the fifteenth century, Moslems frequently raided the coasts of Spain, Portugal, Italy, Greece, France, Ireland, Iceland, Sicily, Corsica, and Cyprus. They kidnapped Spaniards, Portuguese, and Italians and sold them into slavery as infidels.[18]

By 1748, the spirit of Grotius could be found in the French Enlightenment philosophers Montesquieu and Rousseau. Montesquieu claimed that the only right the captor held over the captive was prevention from harm. Jean-Jacques Rousseau urged captors to remove captives from the battlefield immediately following surrender.[19] By the nineteenth century, the concept of just and unjust wars was discarded because, as Donald Wells suggests, the twin doctrines of national sovereignty and military necessity erased all potential laws or rules of war.[20] Carl von Clausewitz's textbook, *On War* (1832), makes the case that "war is nothing but a duel on an extensive scale . . . an act of violence intended to compel our opponent to fulfill our will. Violence arms itself with the inventions of Art and Science in order to contend against violence. Self-imposed restrictions, almost imperceptible and hardly worth mentioning, termed usages of International Law, accompany it without essentially impairing its power."[21]

Captivity was not always a one-way trip to death or lifelong slavery. There were some pathways to freedom. Ransom was a system designed to free aristocratic prisoners who had wealthy families. As a favorite method for victorious captors to make losing captives pay for a war, it had been in place since antiquity. With the exception of Turkish kingdoms of Algiers, Morocco, Tunisia, and Tripoli in North Africa who ransomed prisoners until the nineteenth century, the European practice of ransom ended in the seventeenth century along with the general enslavement of military prisoners. The troops among the lower ranks of soldiers knew there was no ransom for them; as prisoners they could be kept forever, or sold as slaves, or killed at the whim of the captor. However, by the eighteenth century a system of pro rata cartels developed that sent prisoners home from both sides of the battlefield. Keeping the enemy's prisoners was expensive, and it was cheaper for one side to exchange its prisoners with an adversary during hostilities. This approach worked well for the troops, especially when there were large numbers of equal-ranking prisoners on both sides. Lastly, captors began to parole their prisoners who would promise not to escape and to wait for an exchange, ransom, or cartel to gain freedom. A paroled prisoner contracted with the captor for freedom from close confinement and relative freedom from jail within the confines of a defined area of control. In like manner, a prisoner could contract with the captors to parole him home. This arrangement was based on the captive's solemn promise not to bear arms against the detaining power after that freedom was granted. In either case, the basic requirement for parole was trustworthiness based on a person's word of honor and good name.

With the end of ransom and the introduction of cartels and parole, nations began to recognize that the prisoner was not a private practitioner of war but a servant of his government who could not be held responsible for the actions of his political masters.[22] Large cartels and individual paroles lasted into the twentieth century and were commonplace during the Civil War for prisoners on both sides. Today, parole is clearly understood by POWs, as evidenced by the provision against its use in the American guide for POWs, the Code of Conduct (1954, 1988). War thus came to be recognized as a public, political act of a nation, not a private action perpetrated by individual soldiers. This recognition led nations to international agreements concerning not only the nature of captivity but the very nature of warfare itself.

The United States attempted to regulate the treatment of POWs from its earliest experiences as a nation. The American Revolution (1775–1783) had no written rules of war between the American colonies and the British government. The political problem was sovereignty; the captive's problem was status. A POW at least enjoyed mutually understood customs and traditions among soldiers in the field of battle; if nothing else, soldiers commanded respect from one another. But the rebel had no status as a POW and could look forward only to a long prison stay as a criminal or the hangman's noose. By invoking the statutes of the North Act of 1777, the British government intended to reserve and exercise all its sovereign judicial powers of punishment. It would punish the American colonials for treason if they were captured on land, and for piracy at sea at the pleasure of the crown.[23] In effect, at the hands of the British the Americans were criminals, not POWs, and a mutual, reasonable understanding eluded both the principal combatant nations during the American Revolution. As a result, thousands of Americans suffered a punitive, criminal captivity, rather than receiving treatment commonly accorded officially recognized POWs.

In 1783, Benjamin Franklin, Thomas Jefferson, and John Adams formed an American delegation to devise a Treaty of Amity between the United States and King Frederick the Great of Prussia. Feeling rather stung by the prison-hulk experiences and the needless loss of citizen-soldiers and sailors during the Revolution, the new American government sought to eliminate even the slightest possibility of such things happening again. Ratified in 1785, two years before the Constitution was adopted in the

United States, the Treaty of Amity was the first time the United States and another nation addressed the treatment of POWs. Article 24 reads:

> And to prevent the destruction of prisoners of war by sending them into distant & inclement countries, or by crowding them into close & noxious places, the two contracting parties solemnly pledge themselves to each other & to the world that they will not adopt any such practice; that neither will send the prisoners whom they may take from the other into the East Indies or any other parts of Asia or Africa, but that they shall be placed in some part of their dominions in Europe or America, in wholesome situations, that they shall not be confined in dungeons, prison ships, nor prisons, nor be put into irons, nor bound, nor otherwise restrained in the use of their limbs, that the officers shall be enlarged on their paroles within convenient districts & have comfortable quarters, & the common men be disposed in cantonments open & extensive enough for air & exercise, and lodged in barracks as roomly & good as are provided by the party in whose power they are for their own troops, that the officers shall also be daily furnished by the party in whose power they are with as many rations & of the same articles & quality as are allowed by them, either in kind or by commutation, to officers of equal rank in their own army, and all others shall be daily furnished by them with such ration as they allow to a common soldier in their own service; the value whereof shall be paid by the other party on a mutual adjustment of accounts for the subsistence of prisoners at the close of the war. And the said accounts shall not be mingled with, or set off against any others, nor the balances due on them be withheld as a satisfaction or reprisal for any other cause real or pretended whatever: that each party will be allowed to keep a commissary of prisoners in possession of the other, which commissary shall be allowed to see the prisoners as often as he pleases, shall be allowed to receive and distribute whatever comforts may be sent to them by their friends, and shall be free to make his reports in open letters to those who employ him: but if any officer shall break his parole, or any other prisoner shall escape from the limits of his cantonment, after they shall have been designated to him, such individual officer or other prisoner shall forfeit so much of the benefit of this article as provides for his enlargement on parole or cantonment. And it is declared that neither the pretense that war dissolves all treaties, nor any other whatever shall be considered as annulling or suspending this.[24]

George Washington commented to the Comte de Rochambeau in a letter dated July 31, 1786, that "the Treaty of Amity which has lately taken place between the King of Prussia and the United States marks a new era in negotiation. It is perfectly original in many of its articles. It is the most liberal Treaty which has ever been entered into between independent powers; and should its principles be considered hereafter as the basis of connection between nations, it will operate more fully to produce a general pacification than any measure hitherto attempted amongst mankind."[25] A contributor to the *Monthly Review* of London commented at the same time. "This Treaty is a phenomenon in the history of nations—a Treaty replete with benevolence. Military powers uniting to alleviate the miseries of war, to lessen the horrors of bloodshed, and relieve the distresses of their enemies, is the best lesson of humanity which a philosophical king [Frederick II] acting in consort with a philosophical patriot [Franklin] could possibly give to the princes and states of the earth."[26]

After the signing and ratification of the Treaty of Amity in 1785, no state of war came to pass between the United States and Prussia until 1917, when Prussia evolved into Imperial Germany. Nonetheless, the Treaty of Amity theoretically remained in force regardless of the chaotic state of international politics. The real benefit was that POWs of both nations had something solid, an old and enduring treaty as well as the new Hague Convention of 1899/1907, to lean on and no longer had to depend solely on the whim of the captor or the customs and traditions of war.

The United States concluded a treaty with the sultan of Morocco in 1786, ending American tribute and Moroccan piracy. In 1793, the United States paid Algeria $40,000 for the relief of its prisoners and nearly $1,000,000 for a treaty in 1796. In 1798, the United States paid Tunis $107,000 in cash, jewels, small arms, and other presents for the ruling official of Algiers. From 1787 on, Tripoli wanted $100,000 yearly, but that sum was never paid. In all, the United States paid the Barbary powers more than $2,000,000 in ransom and tribute. The United States signed an agreement with Tripoli on June 4, 1805, stipulating that if war broke out between the United States and Tripoli, the POWs captured by either party should not be made slaves but should be exchanged rank for rank. It further stipulated that any deficiency on either side should be made up by the payment of five hundred Spanish dollars for each seaman. Most important, this treaty put a limit of twelve months on the period of incarceration.[27] President Thomas Jefferson, a pacifist at heart, realized that the country was going broke paying blackmail to the leaders of three of the four Barbary states and finally decided that it would be cheaper to build a new navy and Marine Corps. Because a naval force replaced tribute, the Barbary wars concluded finally in 1815 with treaties.

After assisting the United States in its fight against England, aristocratic France had become a republic. By 1797, French cruisers challenged the American navy in an undeclared trading war in the Caribbean. In February

1800, the new American warship *Constellation* intercepted the French ship *La Vengeance,* commanded by Captain Citizen Pitot. *La Vengeance* carried fifty-four guns, a crew of 320, eighty military passengers, and thirty-six American prisoners previously taken at sea. *La Vengeance* also carried a cargo of gold specie for the West Indies, and Captain Pitot had no desire to be taken by gold-hungry Americans. Captain Thomas "Terrible Tom" Truxtun fought *La Vengeance* for nine hours, sometimes in hand-to-hand fighting. Finally, Truxtun fired grapeshot across the enemy's hull and decks. After taking 168 rounds in the hull, *La Vengeance* swung around into the wind, her mizzen-topmast pitching overboard. In the last hour of the battle *La Vengeance* attempted to strike her colors, but Truxtun failed to see this. Finally, *La Vengeance* broke off the engagement in the middle of the night and beached at the mouth of the port of Curacao. The *Constellation,* also hurt badly, limped into Jamaica for repairs.[28] The Americans on board *La Vengeance* remained in captivity. On November 20, 1798, Captain William Bainbridge surrendered his warship *Retaliation* to the French without a fight. The officers of the *Retaliation* were held prisoner on board the French frigates, but the crew was confined in a loathsome prison at Brasseterre on St. Kitts.[29] This undeclared war with France had its rewards. During more than two years of fighting at sea, the American navy captured 111 French privateers and sank four. Additionally, the Americans recaptured seventy merchant ships that had previously been taken by the French.[30]

The second war between Great Britain and the United States was formally declared in a proclamation issued by President James Madison and confirmed by the Congress on June 18, 1812. By this act both nations opened hostilities with each other and soon began to capture each other's vessels on the high seas. Neither sovereignty nor status of prisoners was a problem for either side. The former colonies were no longer subject to the internal laws of Britain; they were the United States of America, a sovereign nation. As nations at public war, their military captives were legal POWs. No longer would Americans in British hands be considered either rebels or political criminals. The captives were collected from different ports and confined in different prisons. Some were sent to the prison ship at Chatham, some to Hamoze, and others to Forton prison in Portsmouth where British authorities took a strict census. Many of the officers were paroled to English villages such as Ashburton in Devonshire or Reading in Berkshire. The British government allowed them one shilling and six-pence per day which translated into the buying power of about thirty-four cents, not very much to purchase food, clothing, and shelter even in 1812. After giving their parole—a promise not to escape—the officers were permitted walks and enjoyed relative freedom but were still required to appear for daily roll call at appointed hours.[31]

Prison hulks were still in use in England during the War of 1812 and were supervised by the British Transport Board. With fresh memories of the *Jersey, Scorpion, Stromboli, Falmouth, Hunter,* and the other prison hulks the British used in America during the Revolution, Americans were terrified of prolonged confinement aboard these ships. The greatest number of prisoners were sent to the *Hector* and *La Brave,* moored by chain about two miles from Plymouth. Aboard the hulks, the Americans were counted, interrogated, and given a hammock, some coarse bedding, a thin blanket, and some chopped rags that were to last a year and a half before new provisions could be drawn. Sick prisoners received some medical attention on a hospital hulk, but few recovered from their illnesses. The prisoners were counted twice each day, once in the morning and once in the evening before being locked down for the night. Between counts, the prisoners were on their own for the most part except for assigned cleaning duties and the preparation of food. All correspondence was censored by the Board of Transport. No boats were permitted alongside the hulks without the captain's permission. Liquor, newspapers, and candles were contraband among the prisoners. The Board of Transport permitted the American prisoners to make items to sell to the general civilian community, but prohibited the manufacture of the very items the sailor-prisoners knew how to make. Netting, woolen products, straw hats, and bonnets were well within the sailor's arts, but their manufacture was forbidden. By the autumn of 1813, the English prison ships were full, and many restless Americans began to attempt escapes. Responding to the possibility of having to hunt down and recapture loose Americans, the Board of Transport decided to move many of them to more secure locations, one of which was the large, secure, and gloomy prison facility at Dartmoor. There they would stay until release and repatriation in April, 1815.[32]

There were two wars with Mexico in the nineteenth century: the first between the Mexicans and the Texans, the second between Mexico and the United States. In the war of Texan independence, the garrison at the Alamo in San Antonio offered General Santa Anna a stubborn defense, but they were defeated with no quarter by a superior Mexican force. Six defenders surrendered, including Davy Crockett, and begged for their lives. Santa Anna refused clemency, and the six were executed. Crockett was stabbed many times; Jim Bowie also died this way. After this slaughter, Texans could be provoked to action by the mere mention of the Alamo. In spite of the Mexican declaration of no quarter—all prisoners would be executed—against Texans fighting with the United States Army, prisoners were taken by both sides in the American national war with Mexico and in 1848 the peace treaty called for their exchange.

By the time of the American Civil War (1861–1865), there were still no written international statutes governing the conduct of war and the humane treatment of prisoners signed by possible belligerents except for the Treaty of Amity between the United States and Prussia and the agreements between the United States and the Barbary powers. At best, nations agreed to a kind of common law-by-tradition to regulate the conduct of international warfare, but nothing existed at all for internecine warfare.

In the international arena a system of common law-by-tradition worked when everyone abided by the same rules, but as President Abraham Lincoln discovered when hostilities began between the federal government and the forces of the Confederacy, without proper guidelines for his field commanders the war became a chaotic mess. The opposing sides even disagreed about what they would call it: the War of the Great Rebellion in the North, the War Between the States, or the War of Northern Aggression in the South. Acts of reprisal (hangings) were taken against prisoners who participated in raids and other acts of guerrilla warfare, and both sides provided utterly inadequate facilities for prisoners taken on the battlefield. Something had to be done quickly lest what had evolved from a rebellion between states to a full-blown civil war should evolve into a catastrophe of uncontrolled, retributive bloodletting. Through his adjutant general, Henry W. Halleck, Lincoln asked Francis Lieber, a professor of international law at Columbia College in New York City who had sons fighting on both sides, to use his training and experience to devise a practical set of rules to which both sides, Union and Confederate, could agree and adhere.

Francis Lieber understood war and soldiering. He was a Prussian German immigrant who had soldiered under Prussian rules and European military traditions with von Blücher at Liegnitz, Waterloo, and Namur. Earlier in his career, he had translated Hugo Grotius's *On the Law of War and Peace* into English. In this instance, he produced the first comprehensive codification of the rules of war used internally by any government anywhere and the first recognized published legal code pertaining to issues concerning the treatment of POWs. He delivered *Instructions for the Government of Armies of the United States* to General Halleck and President Lincoln. Lincoln called it *General Order 207: Instructions for the Government of Armies of the United States* and issued it on July 3, 1863, through the war department of the United States. Lincoln ordered the document delivered to every field commander in the Union and Confederate armies. At first some of the Confederates thought it all a trick. Many Confederate field commanders (General Lee not included) believed that the *Instructions* was merely propaganda from a hostile, advantage-seeking federal government.

With Lieber's document and Lincoln's vision came a new era in the protection of American POWs. The most important precepts in the *Instructions for the Government of Armies of the United States*—General Order 207,

3 July 1863, United States War Department, later known as General Order 100, *The Rules of Land Warfare*—concerning POWs include the following:

1. No belligerent has the right to declare he will treat every captured man at arms . . . as a brigand or a bandit.
2. A prisoner of war is subject to no punishment for being a public enemy, nor is any revenge wreaked upon him by the intentional infliction of any suffering, or disgrace, by cruel imprisonment, want of food, by malnutrition, death or by any other barbarity.
3. A prisoner of war . . . is the prisoner of the government and not of the captor.
4. Prisoners of war are subject to confinement or imprisonment such as may be deemed necessary on account of safety, but they are to be subjected to no other intentional suffering or indignity.
5. A prisoner of war who escapes may be shot, or otherwise killed in flight; but neither death nor any other punishment shall be inflicted on him for his attempt to escape, which the law of order does not consider a crime. Stricter means of security shall be used after an unsuccessful attempt at escape.
6. Every captured wounded man shall be medically treated according to the ability of the medical staff.
8. Prisoners of war will receive the same rations as the captors.
9. Honorable men, when captured, will abstain from giving to the enemy information concerning their own army, and the modern law of war permits no longer the use of any violence against prisoners, in order to extort the desired information, or to punish them for having given false information.[33]

Lieber acknowledged that there might be instances when a force, especially a small force tasked with a specific mission much as elite units are today, could not afford to take prisoners. These circumstances, although rare in large-unit military operations, are common in small-unit operations. There is an obvious moral problem in these circumstances, a dilemma that requires the field commander to make a life-or-death judgment concerning the fate of his prisoners. The rule of priority is this: first, the mission, second, one's own troops, and third, the lives of the prisoners. Although imperfect for all circumstances, this rule at least sets some guidelines for the responsibility and action of the combat unit commander in the field.

Fundamental to Lieber's thinking was the moral precept formulated by Hugo Grotius that recognizes an enemy as a fellow human being with lawful rights. If these rights were violated, the offender could be brought to trial. Thus, after hostilities ceased, Captain Henry Wirz, CSA, the Interior

Commandant of the Andersonville Prison (Camp Sumter) in Georgia, was arrested and charged with murdering Union prisoners in Andersonville. Exempted from the general amnesty for Confederate soldiers in 1865, Wirz was brought to Washington for trial. After a sham military trial with questionable procedures, Wirz was found guilty of murder and executed in the courtyard of the Old Capitol Prison in Washington. Captain Henry Wirz, CSA, would be the first person tried, convicted, and executed in America for mistreatment and murder of POWs.

Following the American lead, Europeans began thinking seriously about international rules of war and the protection of warriors in captivity. Henri Dunant's important book, *Un Souvenir de Solferino* (1862), describes the inhumane fate of victims of battle in Europe. Its popularity contributed to the formation of the International Red Cross in 1864. Meetings were called in Geneva in 1864, 1868, and 1906 to address relief for wounded combatants, regardless of flag. The Brussels meeting, called by the Imperial Russian government in 1874, was the first European conference to consider POWs as a humanitarian as well as a military issue. The representatives at Brussels incorporated many of Lieber's suggestions from *Instructions for the Government of Armies of the United States* (1863) into the parameters of modern European warfare and developed something very new in European culture, the Brussels Code, for the treatment of POWs.

The Hague Conference of 1899 was called by the Russian czar Nicholas II to address disarmament, war at sea, and the establishment of a world court to adjudicate international disputes in lieu of war. The POW provisions reflected the basic Brussels Code, and these were amended and reaffirmed in 1907 and ratified by the United States on December 3, 1909. The most significant POW provisions include Section 1, "On Belligerents," Chapter 2, articles 4 through 20:

Article 4   Prisoners of war are in the power of the hostile Government, but not of the individuals or corps who capture them. They must be humanely treated. All their personal belongings, except arms, horses, and military papers, remain their property.

Article 5   Prisoners of war may be interned in a town, fortress, camp, or other place, and bound not to go beyond certain fixed limits; but they can not be confined except as an indispensable measure of safety and only while the circumstances which necessitate the measure continue to exist.

Article 6   Prisoners may be authorized to work for the public service, for private persons, or on their own account. Work done for the State is paid for at the rates in force for work of a similar kind done by soldiers of the national army, or, if there are none in force, at a rate according to the work executed. When the work is for other branches of the public service or for private persons the conditions are settled in agreement with the military authorities. The wages of the prisoners shall go towards improving their position, and the balance shall be paid them on their release, after deducting the cost of their maintenance.

Article 7 The Government into whose hands prisoners of war have fallen is charged with their maintenance. In the absence of a special agreement between the belligerents, prisoners of war shall be treated as regards board, lodging and clothing on the same footing as the troops of the Government who captured them.

Article 8 Prisoners of war shall be subject to the laws, regulations and orders in force in the army of the State in whose power they are. Any act of insubordination justifies the adoption towards them of such measures of severity as may be considered necessary. Escaped prisoners who are retaken before rejoining their own army or before leaving the territory occupied by the army which captured them are liable to disciplinary punishment.

Article 9 Every prisoner of war is bound to give, if he is questioned on the subject, his true name and rank, and if he infringes this rule, he is liable to have the advantages given to prisoners of his class curtailed.

Article 10 Prisoners of war may be set at liberty on parole if the laws of their country allow, and, in such cases, they are bound, on their personal honor, scrupulously to fulfill, both towards their own Government and the Government by whom they were made prisoners, the engagements they contracted. In such cases their own Government is bound neither to require of nor accept from them any service incompatible with the parole given.

Article 11 A prisoner of war can not be compelled to accept his liberty on parole; similarly the hostile Government is not obliged to accede to the request of the prisoner to be set at liberty on parole.

Article 12 Prisoners of war liberated on parole and recaptured bearing arms against the Government to whom they had pledged their honor, or against the allies of that Government, forfeit their right to be treated as prisoners of war, and can be brought before the courts.

Article 13 Individuals who follow an army directly belonging to it, such as newspaper correspondents and reporters, sutlers and contractors, who fall into the enemy's hands and whom the latter thinks expedient to detain, are entitled to be treated as prisoners of war, provided they are in possession of a certificate from the military authorities of the army which they were accompanying.

Article 14   An inquiry office for prisoners of war is instituted on the commencement of hostilities in each of the belligerent States, and, when necessary, in neutral countries which have received belligerents in their territory. It is the function of this office to reply to all inquiries about the prisoners. It receives from the various services concerned full information respecting internments and transfers, releases on parole, exchanges, escapes, admissions into hospital, deaths, as well as other information necessary to enable it to make out and keep up to date an individual return for each prisoner of war. The office must state in this return the regimental number, name, and surname, age, place of origin, rank, unit, wounds, date and place of capture, internment, wounding, and death, as well as any observations of a special character. The individual return shall be sent to the Government of the other belligerent after the conclusion of peace. It is likewise the function of the inquiry office to receive and collect all objects of personal use, valuables, letters, etc., found on the field of battle or left by prisoners who have been released on parole, or exchanged, or who have escaped or died in hospital or ambulances, and to forward them to those concerned.

Article 15   Relief societies for prisoners of war, which are properly constituted in accordance with the laws of their country and with the object of serving as a channel for charitable effort shall receive from the belligerents, for themselves and their duly accredited agents every facility for the efficient performance of their humane task within the bounds imposed by military necessities and administrative regulations. Agents of these societies may be admitted to the places of internment for the purpose of distributing relief, as also to the halting places of repatriated prisoners, if furnished with a personal permit by the military authorities, and on giving an undertaking in writing to comply with all measures of order and police which the latter may issue.

Article 16   Inquiry offices enjoy the privilege of free postage. Letters, money orders, and valuables, as well as parcels by post, intended for prisoners of war, or dispatched by them, shall be exempt from all postal duties in the countries of origin and destination, as well as in the countries they pass through. Presents and relief in kind for prisoners of war shall be admitted free of all import or other duties, as well as of payments for cartage by the State railways.

Article 17 Officers taken prisoner shall receive the same rate of pay as officers of corresponding rank in the country where they are detained, the amount to be ultimately refunded by their own Government.

Article 18 Prisoners of war shall enjoy complete liberty in the exercise of their religion, including attendance at the services of whatever church they may belong to, on the sole condition that they comply with the measures of order and police issued by the military authorities.

Article 19 The wills of prisoners of war are received or drawn up in the same way as for soldiers of the national army. The same rules shall be observed regarding death certificates as well as for the burial of prisoners of war, due regard being paid to their grade and rank.

Article 20 After the conclusion of peace, the repatriation of prisoners of war shall be carried out as quickly as possible.[34]

Another conference was called in 1914, but the Great War interfered. The United States took the position that it was not party to the Hague Convention because there was a provision that stated that all belligerents needed to be signatories for it to be in force. Serbia and Montenegro were belligerents but not signatories; therefore, the force of the Hague Convention was immediately weakened. Nonetheless, the United States decided to comply with its provisions and hoped that the other nations would do the same. To ensure international compliance, the United States, France, and England concluded separate treaties concerning the treatment of POWs with the Germans in 1917 and 1918. Germany and the United States convened their conference on September 23, 1918, and signed their POW treaty on November 9, 1918, only two days before the armistice.

In 1929, after the horror of World War I, the Geneva Conference convened with the purpose of laying down humanitarian rules to mitigate the barbarism of war. In spite of the Brussels Code, the activities of the International Red Cross, the traditional international rules of war, the Hague Conferences of 1899/1907, and the separate treaties concluded by the belligerents in 1918, the abuse of POWs had continued occasionally on all sides during World War I, especially between the Germans and Russians. The gathering of nations in Geneva in 1929 attempted to establish rights and responsibilities for captives and captors alike and attempted to establish provisions to make sure that the statutes of the convention were observed. This convention dictated the basic rule for POWs during World War II: a new POW must tell captors his name, rank, and serial/service number but need say nothing more. It set minimum standards for medical care and life maintenance and prohibited physical labor for officer prisoners.[35] In other words, a prisoner had rights; still, there were loopholes in the convention. It did not include a clear definition of the status of partisans and commandos, a problem that led to Adolf Hitler's *Kommandobefehl,* the order to the Gestapo and the German Army's field units to execute all captured partisans and commandos as capital war criminals.

In spite of the difficulties and imperfections of the agreement, in 1929 the United States, (Weimar Republic) Germany, Italy, France, and Britain were all signatories. Japan had signed at Geneva, but because discipline inside the Japanese armed forces was stricter than that which could be imposed upon POWs in accordance with the 1929 Geneva Convention, Japan refused to ratify it at home. In the Japanese view, ratifying the document meant undermining the Bushido concept of unlimited discipline, the very basis of Japan's internal military structure.[36] The Soviet Union insisted that the Hague Convention already covered the POW issue and did not sign. Finally, although the attending nations felt bound by the convention's codes, other nations did not.[37] Therefore, throughout World War II, there were two camps among the belligerents: those nations who had signed and ratified the 1929 Geneva Convention and those who did not. Among the Allies, Britain, France, the United States, and the British Commonwealth nations were signatories; the Soviet Union was not. Nazi Germany upheld the Weimar Republic's commitment to the convention; Japan refused to consider it. No international statutes regulated how nations would or could treat their own people, implying that persecuted minorities were strictly internal problems. There was no such concept as a "crime against humanity" in 1939; such a term had to wait until December 11, 1946, when the *Nuremberg Principles* were published. According to the *Principles:*

1. Any person who commits an act which constitutes a crime against international law is responsible therefore and liable to punishment.
2. The fact that internal law does not impose a penalty for an act which constitutes a crime under international law does not relieve the person who committed [such] an act from responsibility under international law.
3. The fact that a person who committed an act which constitutes a crime under international law acted as Head of State or responsible government official does not relieve him from responsibility under international law.
4. The fact that a person acted pursuant to order of his government or of

a superior does not relieve him from responsibility under international law, provided a moral choice was in fact possible to him.

5. Any person charged with a crime under international law has the right to a fair trial on the facts and law.

6. The crimes hereinafter set out are punishable as crimes under international law:

   A. Crimes Against the Peace:

      (1) Planning, preparation, initiation or waging of a war of aggression or a war in violation of international treaties, agreements, or assurances;

      (2) Participation in a common plan or conspiracy for the accomplishment of any of the acts mentioned under (1).

   B. War Crimes: Violations of the laws or customs of war which include, but are not limited to murder, ill-treatment or deportation to slave-labor for any other purpose of civilian population in occupied territory, murder or ill-treatment of prisoners of war, or persons on the seas, killing of hostages, plunder of public or private property, wanton destruction of cities, towns or villages, or devastation not justified by military necessity.

   C. Crimes Against Humanity: Murder, extermination, enslavement, deportation and other inhuman acts done against any civilian population, or persecution on political, racial, or religious grounds, when such acts are done or such persecution are carried on in execution of or in connection with any crime against peace or any war crime.

7. Complicity in the commission of a crime against peace, a war crime, or a crime against humanity as set forth in Principle 6 is a crime under international law.

General Douglas MacArthur's comments confirming General Tomayuki Yamashita's execution order in 1946 for war crimes against Allied prisoners in the Philippine Islands synthesized Nuremberg's Grotius-based understanding of legality with St. Augustine's morality and St. Thomas's vision of justice and the good intention. "The soldier, be he friend or foe, is charged with the protection of the weak and unarmed. It is the very essence and reason for his being. When he violates this sacred trust, he not only profanes his entire cult but threatens the very fabric of international society. The traditions of fighting men are long and honorable. They are based upon the noblest of traits—sacrifice."[38] General Yamashita's execution order traveled to the United States Supreme Court for review. It was confirmed by the court on the American interpretation of the principle of martial law supported by *Ex Parte Milligan* (1866).

The world had tired of the outrageous violence of concentration and prison camps where torture, summary executions, death marches, starvation, and savage war crimes were perpetrated against Allied POWs, internees, political captives, and persecuted minorities in Europe and Asia. Enough was too much, but the Cold War would introduce new POW dilemmas. The 1949 Geneva Convention attempted to set new and lasting standards for the treatment of POWs; it also set the stage for later United Nations declarations against the crimes which caused millions of unnecessary noncombat deaths in World War II. The Soviet Union's political interest at the time turned toward support for wars of liberation in emerging Third World nations, many of which were former colonies of the prewar powers. The communist world view of 1947 divided the world into two Cold War camps: the imperialist Western states and the liberating communist ones. As stated by Andrei Zhdanov and Liu Shao Chi of the COMINFORM at the Trade Union Conference of Asian Countries, the duty of the communist states were to foment, encourage, and aid national liberation movements whenever possible in the developing nations.[39] Also in 1947, the issue of status for partisans and guerrillas was finally settled in the Third Geneva Convention. Article 4 of the 1949 *Geneva Convention Relative to the Treatment of Prisoners of War* (GPW) begins with a definition of the POW as a person belonging to one of the following categories who have fallen into the power of the enemy:

1. Members of the armed forces of a Party to the conflict, as well as members of militias or volunteer corps forming part of such armed forces.
2. Members of other militias and members of other volunteer corps, including those of organized resistance movements, belonging to a Party to the conflict and operating inside or outside their own territory . . . provided that such militias or volunteer corps . . . fulfill the following conditions:
   a. that of being commanded by a person responsible for his subordinates;
   b. that of having a fixed distinctive sign recognizable at a distance;
   c. that of carrying arms openly;
   d. that of conducting their operations in accordance with the laws and customs of war.
3. Members of regular armed forces who profess allegiance to a government or an authority not recognized by the Detaining Power.
4. Persons who accompany the armed forces without actually being members thereof, such as civilian members of military aircraft crews, war correspondents, supply contractors, members of labor units or of services responsible for the welfare of the armed forces, provided that they have received authorization from the armed forces which they accompany, who shall provide them for that purpose with an identity card.

5. Members of crews . . . of the merchant marine . . . and civil aircraft of the Parties to the conflict, who do not benefit by more favourable treatment under any other provision of international law.
6. Inhabitants of a nonoccupied territory, who on the approach of the enemy spontaneously take up arms to resist the invading forces, without having had time to form themselves into regular armed units, provided they carry arms openly and respect the laws and customs of war.

Article 12 clarified the matter even further: "Prisoners of war are in the hands of the enemy Power, but not of the individuals or military units who have captured them. Irrespective of the individual responsibilities that may exist, the Detaining Power is responsible for the treatment given them."[40]

The Soviet Union and the nations under its control at the time signed with reservations.[41] This spelled trouble for the Americans and the other United Nations forces fighting the communist North Koreans, who had invaded South Korea on June 25, 1950.

By July 1950, initial reports of war crimes had filtered into United Nations command centers, and General Douglas MacArthur quickly established the War Crimes Division to investigate alleged crimes in the field as quickly as possible after the incidents were reported. This investigating body defined war crimes as those acts committed by enemy nations, or those persons acting for them, which constitute not only violations of the laws and customs of war but also the contravention of treaties and international conventions.[42] The War Crimes Division consisted of three general branches: the Case Analysis Branch, the Investigations Branch, and the Historical Branch. The Investigations Branch, perhaps the most important group, consisted of relatively small teams which conducted on-the-spot field investigations as well as in-depth interviews of friendly and captured enemy soldiers in order to produce evidence of war crimes for the Case Analysis Branch. The War Crimes Division presented its findings to the United States Senate in 1954. "American prisoners of war who were not deliberately murdered at the time of capture or shortly after capture, were beaten, wounded, starved, and tortured; molested, displayed, and humiliated before the civilian populace and/or forced to march long distances without benefit of adequate food, water, shelter, clothing, or medical care to communist prison camps, and there to experience further acts of human indignities."[43] The investigation concluded that massacres and wholesale extermination of United Nations POWs in Korea were part of the captors' vision of psychological warfare. North Korea flagrantly violated virtually every provision of the 1929 and 1949 Geneva Conventions and of the 1946 Nuremberg Principles.

When the Korean War finally ended in stalemate and armistice, no substantive retribution could be exacted from the North Korean and Chinese captors by the United Nations command. The United Nations in general and the United States in particular began to learn a hard lesson: regardless of the intentions of the creators of international agreements, for conventions to be effective both sides had to obey international law. Such conventions are usually called after an international conflagration by war-weary nations hoping to address problems of the previous war. Winners make the rules for the losers, and there are no guarantees that future warring nations will see any value in such rules or application of them to conflicts.

As the second Indochina war evolved into the American Vietnam War, the statutes of the Third Geneva Convention of 1949 were in place, but they were not universally applied by all the warring sides. This inconsistency became clear when the International Red Cross approached all the warring parties concerning mutual adherence to the provisions of the convention. The Democratic Republic of Vietnam (North Vietnam) and the National Liberation Front (Vietcong) refused to consider the request, citing Article 85: ''Prisoners of war prosecuted under the laws of the Detaining Power for acts committed prior to capture shall retain, even if convicted, the benefits of the present Convention.'' North Vietnam's reservation to Article 85 was as follows: ''The Democratic Republic of Vietnam declares that prisoners of war prosecuted and convicted for war crimes or for crimes against humanity, in accordance with principles laid down by the Nuremberg Court of Justice, shall not benefit from the present Convention as specified in Article 85.'' The Americans and the South Vietnamese affirmed all the provisions of the 1949 Geneva Convention with no reservations.

After the American experience of captivity in North Korea, the military, diplomatic, and political communities knew that the Geneva Convention was a useless document to POWs caught in battles between nonsignatories or between parties that had made major reservations. The soldiers, as usual, were caught in the middle. Consequently, from a practical and legal point of view, American POWs in Vietnam had no international law on which to base reasonable expectations; rather, they had only the idealistic Code of Conduct for Members of the Armed Forces of the United States, which was first promulgated as a guideline for Americans in captivity by President Dwight D. Eisenhower in 1954:

1. I am an American fighting man. I serve in the forces which guard my country and our way of life. I am prepared to give my life in their defense.
2. I will never surrender of my own free will. If in command I will never surrender my men while they still have the means to resist.
3. If I am captured I will continue to resist by all means available. I will make every effort to escape and aid others to escape. I will not accept parole nor special favors from the enemy.

4. If I become a prisoner of war, I will keep faith with my fellow prisoners. I will give no information or take part in any action which might be harmful to my comrades. If I am senior, I will take command. If not, I will obey the lawful orders of those appointed over me and will back them up in every way.

5. When questioned, should I become a prisoner of war, I am bound to give only name, rank and service number and date of birth. I will evade answering further questions to the utmost of my ability. I will make no oral or written statements disloyal to my country and its allies or harmful to their cause.

6. I will never forget that I am an American fighting man, responsible for my actions, and dedicated to the principles which make my country free. I will trust in my God and the United States of America.[44]

It encompasses four principal concepts in the relationship among the prisoner, the captor, and the country as a whole: individual responsibility, institutional trust, religious faith, and community faithfulness, each helping to form the cornerstone of a combatant's will to live and possibly his actual survival in wartime captivity. Nevertheless, special problems continued to surface, especially when the rules and codes that were designed to ameliorate the dangers of military captivity were openly flouted or, in some specific cases, did not apply.[45]

The United States Army teaches its soldiers to treat all captives, whether military or civilian, according to the law of war. The United States Army's *Field Manual FM 27-10; The Law of Land Warfare* (1956) and *Pamphlet 27-1; Treaties Governing Land Warfare* (1956) mandate how American soldiers should treat their prisoners and describe what they should expect from possible captors. According to the army's training publication, *Soldier's Manual of Common Tasks* (1990), civilians and soldiers who have surrendered are not combat targets and must be permitted to surrender. They must be protected from acts of combat, violence, intimidation, and sexual abuse and must be treated humanely. Collective punishment, reprisals, and the taking of hostages are all prohibited. Prisoners have rights to housing, clothing, enough food to remain in good health, medical care, religious practice, mail, representation by fellow prisoners, and the retention of personal property. Anything short of adherence to these procedures constitutes a criminal act punishable under American military law, the Uniform Code of Military Justice.[46]

Although the number of Americans forced into wartime captivity in the twentieth century has been relatively small when compared to the large number of European and Australian prisoners, living, suffering, dying, and surviving military and civilian captivities have been a significant part of the American wartime experience. And with each war, new efforts are made to address the issue of POWs. Chaos and atrocities that took place in the major wars of the late nineteenth and early twentieth centuries inspired the Hague and Geneva conventions. The Korean and Vietnam wars showed a startled American public that it was possible for captors consumed by political ideology, antiquated neocolonial influences, and vengeance to avoid adherence to or find loopholes in those conventions. Caught in the middle were American soldiers, sailors, and airmen who found themselves in the hands of captors who told them they were criminals, pirates, and enemies of the people.

Captivity Literature: Antecedents and the Context of American Colonial Narratives

Now, God makes room for a people . . . when He casts out the enemies of a
people before them by lawful war with the inhabitants, which God calls them
unto, as in Psalms 44:2: "Thou didst drive out the heathen before them."
John Cotton (1630)

In the context of colonial America, what was captivity literature? How
did it work? What did it mean? How was it connected to the culture and
experiences that generated it? The condition of captivity, real or imaginary, was expressed in what Moses Coit Tyler identified in *The History
of American Literature during the Colonial Period* (1878) as one of the
ten general classes of colonial literature: personal correspondence; state
papers; sermons; speeches; political essays in chapbooks, broadsheets,
newspapers, and pamphlets; political verse; lyric poetry; folksongs;
drama; and prose narratives of actual experience. For content, prose narratives of captivity relied solidly on the narrator's personal experience,
which took on significant meaning not only for the individuals actually
involved but for the captive's community. For expression, intent, and
structure, many narrators used the oral and biblical traditions of the European past combined with rich, immediate ethnological descriptions of
people, landscapes, and circumstances to create a readily understandable
depiction of the testing of human values through suffering.

In practically no other form of discourse of the colonial period and
beyond are human feelings more clearly expressed than in the narrative
of captivity, where we find the initial shock of captivity, sadness at being
taken away from family, home and friends, horror of and hatred for the
captor, resistance to the demands of the captor, and the joy of homecoming. The feeling that binds prisoners past and present to one another
and to the culture they came from, however, is the will to live—the one
characteristic that, for the most part, holds individual captivity narratives together thematically and simultaneously forms a vast community
of captives from the forest wars to Vietnam.

Beginning with the earliest captivity narratives in colonial times, former
prisoners discriminate between four essential attributes that insure the
will to live: the physical strength to withstand starvation, torture, and

sickness; the psychological ability to forgive oneself for surrender; the courage to ignore the captor's wants or demands; and the ethical and moral firmness to maintain an unswerving trust in the institutional relationships of family, home, church, community, and country. By expressing these commonalities, former prisoners managed to show how as captives, hostages, internees, or POWs they attempted to control a chaotic situation by using their physical, psychological, and moral assets to transform the catastrophe of captivity into the order that is necessary for survival.

Most successful prisoners are committed to some ideal outside themselves—personal religious, legal, community, institutional—that houses the essential force of resistance. No matter how simplistic such a commitment may seem, it is better to suffer for something rather than because of something. One must turn to Holy Scripture to find the wellspring of the captivity narrative as it first appeared in American colonial culture, especially to the books of Samuel, Chronicles, and Lamentations for the Puritans and other Protestants and to the Passion of Christ for the Jesuits.

No biblical precept demands that soldiers should spare an enemy captured in battle. Scripture provides the rule of the biblical battlefield in Samuel 15:3: "thus saith the Lord of Hosts . . . go and smite Amalek and utterly destroy all they have, and spare them not." If soldiers looked to Scripture for guidance, sparing lives after or during battle was the exception rather than the rule of military combat. Soldiers fighting holy wars were practical men; captives had to possess some intrinsic military, material, social, or political worth to be spared death on the battlefield or after the battle was over. However, the books of Chronicles and Lamentations show a different kind of battlefield, one consisting not of soldiers against soldiers in mortal combat, but of a battle between God and man in which the captors act as God's conduit for His trial of man's faith and His demand for faithfulness from individual believers.

In Chronicles, Jerusalem falls because the Hebrews "mocked God's messengers, despised His words, and scoffed at His prophets until the wrath of the Lord was aroused against His people and there was no remedy." The Lord sent the King of Babylon as His instrument of captivity and punishment. He destroyed the "young men with the sword . . . and spared neither young man nor young woman, old man or aged." After the slaughter, prisoners were carried into the kingdom of Babylon to become slaves of the king. Persia rose to power, and, fulfilling the prophecy of Jeremiah, God moved King Cyrus to "build a temple for Him at Jerusalem in Judah." Cyrus commanded that the Hebrews in captivity should be freed to return to Jerusalem and the temple.

Jeremiah wrote Lamentations in an age of crisis. The temple had been destroyed, ritual had been interrupted, national sovereignty had been eliminated, and his people had been taken into hostile captivity. Confessing

sin and expressing grief, humiliation, and hope, Jeremiah salutes his audience, "The Lord is righteous," and explains why the captivity took place.
"I rebelled against His command." He then asks his audience to look upon
his suffering. "He has made my skin and my flesh grow old and has broken
my bones. He has besieged me and surrounded me with bitterness and
hardship. He has made me dwell in darkness like those long dead."
Jeremiah explains why a captive resists a captor in terms of the eventual
unity with a God who is eternal, just, loving, and compassionate, a God
who brings His children into conflict unwillingly. "For men are not cast
off by the Lord forever. Though he brings grief, he will show compas-
sion, so great is his unfailing love. For he does not willingly bring afflic-
tion or grief to the children of men." Jeremiah then tells his audience
why this captivity was so terrible.

> Remember, O Lord, what has happened to us; look, and see our dis-
> grace. Our inheritance has been turned over to aliens, our homes to
> foreigners. We have become orphans and fatherless, our mothers like
> widows. We must buy the water we drink; our wood can be had only
> at a price. Those who pursue us are at our heels; we are weary and find
> no rest. We are submitted to Egypt and Assyria to get enough bread.
> Our fathers sinned and are no more and we bear their punishment.
> Slaves rule over us, and there is none to free us from their hands. We
> get our bread at the risk of our lives because of the sword in the desert.
> Our skin is hot as an oven, feverish from hunger. Women have been
> ravished in Zion, and virgins in the towns of Judah. Princes have been
> hung up by their hands; elders are shown no respect. . . . Why do
> you always forget us? Why do you forsake us so long?

In the end, he begs God to "restore us to yourself, O Lord, that we may
return; renew our days as of old, unless you have utterly rejected us, and
are angry with us beyond measure." Jeremiah's timeless lament was a
literary model for future prisoners. Into the collective mythic memory
of his people, and the Judeo-Christian tradition in general, Jeremiah introduced the idea that captivity will forever remain a burden, for it causes
nothing but loss.

Following the themes of Lamentations, *Foxe's Book of Martyrs* (c. 1580),
that great English Protestant polemic written by John Foxe (1516–1587),
starts where the Acts of the Apostles stops. Foxe recounts the experiences
of prisoners in the first Roman persecutions of the Christians, the martyr-
dom of the Apostles, and the death of Thomas Cranmer, Protestant Arch-
bishop of Canterbury, in 1556. Later editions include the persecutions,
captivities, and executions of Protestant martyrs up to 1820. *Foxe's Book
of Martyrs* reflects the interplay between religious and political issues

found in the religious captivity narratives of the New World. Foxe devotes considerable attention to the kind and degree of captivity and torture that penitents suffered for their faith, both at the hands of Roman emperors and later with the Roman Catholic inquisitors. Biblical captivity stories, *Foxe's Book of Martyrs,* and even the prison experiences of John Bunyan's main character, Christian, in *The Pilgrim's Progress* (1678) supplied moral inspiration and saintly models for the Puritans in the seventeenth century.

Richard VanDerBeets, in *The Indian Captivity Narrative: An American Genre* (1984), suggests that memoirs of colonial Indian captivity are presented as straightforward and generally unadorned religious documents.[1] Loaded with scriptural references, these narratives make it clear that a transmission of religious values takes place through the act of redemptive suffering. Captivity, as it is shown in the Bible, is always a test, sometimes a trial or ordeal of faith, and sometimes a punishment—a stern, wrathful God's way of revealing to the captive(s) indisputable evidence of divine providence and God's ultimate wisdom. Captives condemned and lost to death at the hands of evil and miscreant captors surrender not to fate, or bad luck, but to the manifestation of God's will. Captives who live through the ordeal and return home are redeemed by God for a higher purpose.

Folklore also holds a prominent place in the formation of colonial and later contemporary treatments of captivity. Folklorist Samuel P. Bayard suggests that the essence of folklore resides in the transmission of a common fund of traditional ideas. "The true field of folklore," writes Bayard, "lies in the realm of thought." The primary materials of folklore are categories of creative ideas recognized as common property to the degree that they reflect beliefs, actions, and emotions of the society.[2] Following Bayard's lead, the captivity theme in prose narratives and common artistic products forms a distinct category of creative idea. It is topical and long-lived and has generated social commentary and artifacts that reflect broadly held beliefs and emotions through actions. Folklorist Stith Thompson quantified the variety of general captivity folktales in *Motif-Index of Folk Literature* (1957) into 100 different types with further variations based on condition of captivity, rescue, escape, and pursuit.[3] The captivity theme is likewise strong in literature of the heroic age. The archetypal northern European heroic captivity is Saxo Grammaticus's description of Ragnar Lodbrok, Viking king of the Danes, in *Saga of the Volsungs,* a tale of brutal torture and revenge.[4]

Traditional ballads address captivity conditions and circumstances in stories that resemble folktales and legends. "The Turkish Lady," a version of "Young Beichan" or "Lord Bateman," Child #53, parallels the legend of Gilbert Beckett, and dramatizes the experiences of North African captivity that occurred from the late Middle Ages to the nineteenth century.

Bertrand Bronson points out in *Traditional Tunes of the Child Ballads* (1959) that at least 112 versions and variants of "Young Beichan" exist in regional collections.[5] According to folklorist Roger Abrahams and other ballad scholars, "Lord Bateman" has been one of the longest lasting and most popular of all those in the Child collection in America.[6] It tells the story of a nobleman seeking adventure on a dangerous voyage in Turkish North African waters. After a shipwreck, the hero is taken captive and imprisoned. Hopelessness shrouds the noble captive until the captor's daughter falls in love with him and volunteers to help him escape. The impasse of religion stops this union at first, but in several variants the religious impediment gives way to the material consideration of the captive's wealth. The Bateman story combines love and captivity in a way that synthesizes the immorality and evil of the captivity with the romance between unlikely lovers. The story centers on the "Turkish Lady," who tries to overcome her lover's captivity and impending slavery by facilitating his escape from her father's prison. The drama of this ballad is found at the point of escape and beyond. Some variants allow the former prisoner and the Turkish lady to marry; some do not. After freedom, the prisoner abandons his lover, breaks his bond of fidelity, and sails for home. Not to be abandoned so easily, she follows him after some years. It is no accident that the "Lord Bateman" ballad mirrors the step-by-step progression of the captivity narrative contour. The romance of this story requires the captive to be basically helpless and passive. Lord Bateman's mentor, lover, and future wife, the "Turkish Lady," enjoys freedom of movement, status in her native land, and freedom of choice. Although a union between a Christian and a Moslem in Turkish North Africa was a capital crime, she falls in love with Bateman anyway and makes her way, actively seeking not only her own happiness but also the fulfillment of the contract she made with Bateman for his release. Unlike the Norse captivity legends where captivity breeds vengeance, this ballad features the consummation of love and the adventures of illicit romance.[7]

In oral and biblical tradition, the twists of the tale reflect the art of the teller. The American captivity narrative follows suit, with authors adding a multitude of creative twists to a well-established, yet thoroughly migratory narrative contour. Audiences seem to understand and appreciate captivity literature as more than morality plays. What contextualizes the colonial narrative of captivity is a synthesis of religion, folklore, and wars with Indian tribes that flared up over a period of 150 years.

In 1630 John Cotton preached his sermon "God's Promise to His Plantation" to his Puritan flock before they boarded the *Arabella* to cross the Atlantic to American New England. Taking his text from II Samuel 7:10, Cotton told the congregation: "Moreover, I will appoint a place for my people, Israel, and I will plant them, that they dwell in a place of their own, and move no more." In that sermon John Cotton appointed the Puritans as God's new chosen people, and made the position very clear that Puritan claims for land and conquest would be based on the perception of their own Divine Right—God's will that they should inhabit the land. Cotton thundered, "Now, God makes room for a people . . . when He casts out the enemies of a people before them by lawful war with the inhabitants, which God calls them unto, as in Psalms 44:2: 'Thou didst drive out the heathen before them.' "[8] The moment in 1630 when John Cotton stepped down from his platform marked the day when the native tribes of New England—indeed, tribes throughout the entire North American continent—were doomed to defeat and, later, removal at the hands of land-hungry European settlers. The Pequot War (1637) was fought in New England when the Pequot tribe resisted Puritan expansion into their lands. The tribe was totally destroyed. Bacon's Rebellion (1676) was a civil insurrection among the English fought in Virginia over the low tobacco prices that impoverished small farmers. Under Nathaniel Bacon, the farmers sent an unauthorized army to attack the Indians and Jamestown. The colonial rebels were defeated by an alliance between Indians and British forces. In 1675, Metacomet, or "King Philip," of the Wampanoag tribe remembered the Pequot War and called for unified Indian resistance against any further expansion and land acquisition by the Puritan New England settlers. King Philip's War (1675–1678) ravaged New England, and the settlers lost one-sixth of their male population and twenty-five towns in brutal combat with the Indians. King Philip was captured and executed. King William's War (1688–1697) in New England continued the hostilities between the French and their Abenaki allies and the New England Puritans. Queen Anne's War (1702–1713) was the American version of the War of Spanish Succession in Europe. The Iroquois became English subjects and again fought the French. The Three Year's War (1722–1725) found the Abenakis once again warring with the English in New England over the French mission forts along the northeast Canadian border. King George's War (1744–1748) continued the Three Year's War between the French-Abenaki alliance and the New Englanders. The French and Indian War (1754–1763) was a trading and frontier war. In New England, French and English boundaries stirred bitter controversies. Although Nova Scotia was ceded to Britain in 1713, the French still claimed it as their own. To the west, the French built forts farther along the St. Lawrence and Mississippi rivers, and in Pennsylvania they attempted to contain the British trading and expansion efforts along the western frontier. As a major power, the British brought large forces to bear, and in the end the French were defeated and lost all claims to Canada. Pontiac's Rebellion (1763–1764) found the Ottawa tribes attempting to retain their traditional hunting and living areas from Erie to Detroit. Lord Dunmore's War (1774) cast the Shawnee tribe against the British and colonials in an attempt to assert control over its traditional hunting grounds along the Ohio River. The Shawnees were defeated by the British.

During the American Revolution (1775–1783), the major tribes in colonial America, especially the Iroquois nations in New York and Pennsylvania, allied themselves with the British. They knew that if the Americans defeated the British, they would lose their lands. The Ohio Invasions (1789–1794), when armies of the United States launched punitive expeditions against the tribes in eastern Ohio, proved the Indians correct. Anthony Wayne defeated the Indians at the Battle of Fallen Timbers in 1794. Shortly thereafter, in the Treaty of Greenville, the tribes surrendered southern Ohio to the United States. In Jay's Treaty of 1794, the British agreed to leave their outposts in the United States and ended the alliance between the northern tribes and the British in America. The Creek Indian War (1791) was fought to secure Kentucky, which became a state in 1792. The Indiana/Illinois Wars (1812–1814) were the frontier version of the War of 1812 between the United States and Great Britain. Looking for traditional allies and finding one in Tecumseh, the British secured Indian friendship and help, but it was too late; the Americans were becoming stronger, and Chief Tecumseh was defeated by William Henry Harrison at the Battle of Tippecanoe (1811). In the end, the Indiana and Illinois territories were opened up for settlement by Americans. So ended the forest wars.

As Americans advanced south and west, they fought many more wars with Indians over the land. The Wars of Removal included the Creek Indian War (1825), fought in western Georgia between the Creek tribe and the U.S. Army. It ended at the Battle of Horse Shoe Bend, and the Creeks were forcibly relocated in the Oklahoma Territory. The Cherokees followed suit shortly thereafter in "the Trail of Tears" ordered by President Andrew Jackson in 1829. Black Hawk's War (1832) began in 1825 when the United States government decided to continue removing the native tribes from their traditional lands. Through force of arms the government finally forced the southern tribes to surrender their hunting grounds. In return, the United States government gave them either annuities or reservations beyond the Mississippi. In effect, the government was compressing the eastern tribes into the western territories. The Indians of the Plains, and later the West, knew what was coming and resisted.

The Great Plains Wars were fought during and after the Civil War. The Cheyenne and Arapaho Wars (1861–1867) erupted when war parties attacked farmers and stagecoach stations. At the conclusion of hostilities all prisoners were returned, and the Indians thought that they were at peace. The Colorado Militia under the command of Colonel J. M. Chivington then massacred the remaining Indians at Sand Creek, an act which resulted in mass Indian distrust of the American government's intentions. The word "hostile" was invented to describe those Indians who refused to submit to government security-dependence or to live on the reservations as wards of the federal government. The Sioux Wars (1865–1868) were a series of brutal wars between the United States and numerous lines of the Sioux nation after which the Sioux were defeated and assigned to specific reservations. The Montana War (1875–1876) was fought against united Sioux tribes who rebelled against strict reservation life. This war culminated in George Armstrong Custer's defeat at the hands of Crazy Horse at the short Battle of the Little Big Horn, or, as the Sioux and Cheyenne call it, the Battle of the Greasy Grass, in June 1876.

As the second wave of European immigration began to exceed all expectations and the notion of manifest destiny became an obsession, new settlers moved West in greater numbers. The last Indian wars were punitive and bloody wars of removal, rebellion, and conquest. Beginning in 1868, the western tribes—Cheyenne, Arapaho, Comanche, Kiowa, and Apache—were hunted down and destroyed. The Apache Rebellion took place in 1885 when groups of warriors and their families rebelled against government treatment and the restrained life on a reservation. The rebellion was put down, and Geronimo was captured and jailed by the United States Army. The last Indian war, the Ghost Dance War of the Sioux (1890), was not really a war at all. After the slaughter at Wounded Knee, the Sioux believed that the ghosts of former warriors would protect them from the bullets of the soldiers and that a new spirit of united tribalism would force the onrushing Americans to abandon Indian lands. Again, the tribe was subdued, and a spirit of defeat and hopelessness gripped native American tribes throughout the land. It was not until 1924, thirty-four years after the last hostilities ceased, that the United States government granted citizenship to all native Americans.[9]

Dating from King Philip's War, New England produced most colonial captivity narratives because New England was the center of hostilities between aboriginal Indian tribes and the land-hungry English. The ravages of the forest wars informed the captivities of Mary Rowlandson, Hannah Dustin, John Gyles, and many other Puritans who found themselves captured by tribal enemies. New England was a fierce battleground. As masters of hit-and-run guerrilla tactics, small raiding forces focused on lucrative targets and rarely took prisoners. Those people not taken as prisoners in colonial times died in battle or in their homes. If they were unfortunate enough to be taken captive, they often died at the hands of their captors. Cotton Mather, in Article VII of his book *Decennium Luctuosum* (1699), crystallized the Puritan vision of the conditions of prisoners, "Truly the dark places of New England where the Indians had their unapproachable kennels were habitations of cruelty."[10]

The New England Puritans understood their captivities as acts of God's will in a strict Calvinist sense. Their captivity narratives triangulated the crusade against infidels, the religious mandate of Calvinist Christianity (the struggle between God and Satan for the possession of a person's individual soul), and the secular as well as religious European oral tradition. In the same way as they understood the books of Chronicles and Lamentations, or the Acts of the Apostles, or *Foxe's Book of Martyrs* (c. 1557), or even *Pilgrim's Progress,* Puritan audiences understood the intended religious meanings in their Indian captivity narratives. They could also plainly perceive the similarity of the captivity narratives to the ballads, legends, folktales, and heroic captivities of Europe. It is not surprising that these narratives became bestsellers. Mary Rowlandson's narrative, first published in 1682 as *The Sovereignty and Goodness of God, Together with the Faithfulness of His Promises Displayed: Being a Narrative of the Captivity and Restoration of Mrs. Mary Rowlandson,* was reprinted and reedited more than thirty times.[11] The Rowlandson narrative and many others simultaneously entertained their audiences in a way much valued in the European traditional past and instructed their readers in the Puritan faith. This instruction was based on three powerful forces of fear: the realistic horror of tribal warfare; the overwhelming influence of the Calvinist religious faith on everyday life; and the longstanding effects of a continuing secular and religious oral tradition.

Such narratives retained their extremely wide appeal for audiences in the seventeenth, eighteenth, and nineteenth centuries. J. Norman Heard suggests that fear formed a powerful motivation for frontiersmen and women to act as they did. Frontiersmen lived in constant fear of Indian captivity.[12] In all likelihood, they would be killed in unthinkable ways for the ritual entertainment of the captors. According to Heard and other commentators of the Indian captivity experience, the women faced another kind of sentence—lifelong bondage and possible assimilation into the captor's tribe. Heard observes that frontier people tried always to guard against Indian attack, but sometimes there was no way short of suicide to avoid falling into the hands of raiders.[13]

Since the Puritans and other dissenters in America were refugees from established European religions, individual settlers suffered nearly paralyzing, possibly atavistic, fears of any form of religious oppression in America. They established an offensive rather than a defensive religious, military, social, and economic strategy to make sure that they would never again be subjected to religious domination. When a person suffered capture by an enemy under these circumstances, little room existed for negotiation or compromise. Thus, the Puritans perforce adopted an all-or-nothing position in which the catastrophic act of military confrontation in battle—completely winning or totally losing—replaced the civil act of negotiation and compromise. To the frontiersmen, the Indian nations may have been allies from time to time against the French, but they were never really friends. Some individual members of various tribes were assimilated, converted to Christianity, disarmed, and harmless. If not allies, Indians were hostile enemies in total war. To the Puritans, who drew clear, dualistic distinctions between good and evil, right and wrong, civilization and savagery, godliness and hell, the Indian nations around them were evil incarnate, and they understood their own destruction of the Indians as an enactment of God's will.

When one considers the dangers in which the settlers lived, the contempt they had for the Indians, their devout dependence on the Bible for support, and the actual treatment they received in captivity, the experience of Mary Rowlandson and her fellow Puritan prisoners resolves into a test of individual faith, faithfulness in the Puritan community, and a personal trust in providence or God's will. Richard Slotkin suggests in *Regeneration through Violence: The Mythology of the American Frontier, 1600–1860* (1973) that the New England captivity narratives functioned as a myth, reducing the Puritan state of mind and worldview into archetypal dramas.[14] Describing the captivity myth in *The Indian Captivity Narrative: An American Genre* (1984), Richard VanDerBeets asserts that the captive takes a journey of initiation from death to rebirth consisting of three steps: separation, a symbolic death in the isolation from one's own culture; transformation, ordeals in passing from ignorance to knowledge and maturity in captivity; and return, a symbolic rebirth with a sense of moral and spiritual gain.[15] The Puritan preachers detailed the torments of Indian captivity as examples of God's ways of testing or punishing His creatures.[16] Former prisoners drew such powerful lessons from their experiences that they felt obliged to pass them along to others who might profit from moral instruction. Thus, the American captivity narrative not only joined its biblical and folkloric predecessors but was incorporated fully into an already popular, well-established Puritan sermon form, the jeremiad.[17]

One common theme in the Puritan jeremiad was retributive justice. To the Puritans, primary justice was the wrathful penalty exacted by God from his sinful children—the *lex talionis*—the traditional legal mandate that calls for justice in the form of "an eye for an eye," or retaliation. One example of the vengeance-justice theme is the story of the Puritan captive Hannah Dustin and how she wrought havoc upon her captors.[18] As told by Cotton Mather in *Decennium Luctuosum* (1699), the captivity of Hannah Dustin began in 1697 when a war party of Abenaki Indians captured her along with her week-old child and its nurse, Mary Neff, in a raid on Haverhill, Massachusetts. After their captors killed Dustin's child, the prisoners began a death march, or remove on foot, through the forest.

They were turned over to a large Indian family, and while their new captors slept, Dustin and Mary Neff found tomahawks and killed them in their sleep, one by one. Only an Indian woman and a small child escaped. The lesson that Cotton Mather wanted his readers to learn was this: in the spirit of *lex talionis,* rather than merely escaping once the opportunity presented itself, Dustin and Neff became instruments of the Puritan wrathful and vengeful God. Not only did they kill their captors prior to their escape, they scalped them as well. Then, taking advantage of the instruments of escape around them, Hanna and Mary stole a canoe and finally left God's battlefield completely victorious in His name. After Dustin and Neff arrived home, they presented the scalps to the Massachusetts General Assembly and received a bounty of fifty pounds.[19]

From this narrative of retributive justice, we can reasonably infer that the Puritan-Indian wars were, in part, "wars of attrition" in which "body count" functioned primarily as a physical representation of God's vengeful justice and secondarily as a manifestation of the transformation of the wilderness into property. On the other hand, the Puritans paid a heavy price of religious, social, and legal implosions for their anti-Indian fears. Although they won the military campaigns against the tribes and expanded European communities into the conquered Indian lands, they began to claw at themselves by placing blame and guilt on the victims of captivity.

The Puritans noted that former captives acted differently from "normal" people in their midst.[20] Today, psychologists use the term "posttraumatic stress disorder" to describe the symptoms; Cotton Mather called it witchcraft, and used one former captive, Mercy Short, as an example. Mercy was captured at her home in Salmon Falls when she was fifteen years old. Her parents and three siblings were murdered in front of her, and she was taken to Canada. Eventually she was ransomed from Canada. After returning home, Mercy showed forms of the illness that all returned prisoners experienced in one form or another: an inability to sleep, a perpetual watchfulness, an awareness of the power of God, and an understanding of the wilderness that alienated her from her kindred.[21] Coached by Cotton Mather, her spiritual mentor, protector, and savior, Mercy began to see visions—specters—of Satan's workers and familiars everywhere. Cotton Mather searched for a justification for Mercy Short's specters. Mercy had been infected by the devil and his power of witchery. To Mather, Satan had come from his dwelling place in the forest to possess the citizenry of Massachusetts through Mercy Short, and it was the duty of the Puritan communities to do something about it. The elect had to realize that the unseen threat existed, and then understand that it was God's vengeful curse on honorable and godly citizens to allow such an event to take place in their communities. Puritans believed that Satan's power knew no boundaries; he could manifest himself in members of their communities in the Massachusetts Bay as easily as in England. In order for the Puritans to exorcize themselves, they could not permit a witch to live among them. In other words, a radical shift took place in Puritan America, from an individual's psychological trauma resulting from the captivity experience to a dangerous form of group guilt manifesting itself through community norms.

The New England tragedy of 1692–1693—the hysteria of the witchhunt —in part represented a backlash against the experiences of former captives. According to George Lyman Kittredge, English legal tradition viewed witchcraft in two related ways: theologically as a sin and legally as a capital offense committed by an individual against a Christian community. Unlike usual criminal procedures, the witchcraft trials presumed guilt, and spiritual, or "spectral" evidence was acceptable. Victims charged that devilish "specters" of real people appeared to them.[22] This kind of spectral evidence violated the traditional English common law, which required the firsthand eyewitness account of wrongdoing. Former prisoners were suspected of having become witches, and later, as the hysteria spread through the colony like a fever, spectral evidence was manipulated in the theocratic New England court system to permit the arrest, trial, condemnation, and execution of innocent people for the crime-sin of witchcraft. Although critics of the Puritan theocratic system of justice ended the use of spectral evidence in American courts throughout the colonies and later throughout the nation, the root cause of the tragedy was the Puritan fear that in captivity the Indians "brainwashed" their prisoners into rejecting God and threatening His community of Calvinist saints.

The French Jesuits were as pious about the propagation of Catholicism in the New World as the Puritans were in establishing their Calvinist "City on the Hill" in New England. The French clergy-adventurers wanted converts. Beginning in Canada and making their way down the Mississippi River to the delta, the French Jesuits not only worked hard to spread their faith but also worked hand in hand with traders and explorers to compete with their enemies, the Protestant English, for land, influence, and trade with the Indians. Allies were important; tribal allies were necessities, and the French secured the friendship of the Hurons, Shawnees, Ottawas, and some tribes from the western end of the Iroquois Confederacy who normally allied with the English.

To the French in Canada, English expansion into their territory became intolerable. When the American extension of Europe's Seven Years' War broke out, it was known as the French and Indian War (1754–1763). The French built a chain of forts along the major rivers from Lake Erie to Ohio to defend New France against the English and to act as missions for Indian conversion. In a basically defensive frontier war, the French attempted to contain British trading and expansion efforts at and before Pennsylvania's western frontier. Benjamin Franklin in Philadelphia saw the French threat as an encroachment on the Pennsylvania colony and commissioned the English General Braddock, along with a mixture of British and colonial troops under George Washington, to march against Fort Duquesne (Pittsburgh). Braddock was killed along the way, and his defeated force retreated. In time, the French were defeated by the British, but there were legacies, one of which was an ever-increasing animosity between the colonial Americans and the Indian tribes that allied themselves with the French west of the Alleghenies.

Working with the Indians in French America, the pioneer Jesuits left exciting accounts of their adventures in the wilderness. When they suffered the pain of torture at the hands of their captors, they saw themselves repeating Christ's passion and death willingly. These priests were painstaking narrators, recording all the day's events and quitting their work only in death. In *The Jesuit Relations* (1644–1653), stories appear of the adventures and captivities of Fathers Isaac Jogues, Bressani, Goupil du Poncet, Breboeuf, Chaumont, Lelemont, de Noüe, Daniele, Lelande, Garnier, and others. Father Louis Hennepin of the Recollects tells of his own captivity of four months in 1680 among the Lakota people near the present city of Minneapolis in *Description de la Louisiane* (Paris, 1683) and again in *Nouvelle Decouverte* (Utrecht, 1697).

According to Roy Harvey Pearce, the English immigrants of the seventeenth century were intelligent, orderly, and organized. They strove for progress and felt no reluctance to solicit Indian help. Sustained by the idea of order in the world around them, "they were sure, above all, of the existence of an eternal and immutable principle which guaranteed the intelligibility of their relations with each other and to their world and thus made possible their life in society. It was a principle to be expressed in the progress and elevation of civilized men who, striving to imitate their God, would bring order to chaos."[23] James Needham and Gabriel Arthur were two of these immigrants. In 1673, with his indentured servant, Gabriel Arthur, Needham was sent by Colonel Abraham Wood to eastern Tennessee to explore the French Broad River area. Needham was killed in combat by the Cherokees, but Arthur was taken captive. In his Cherokee captivity of one year, Arthur was taken on war expeditions as far south as western Florida and well into the Carolinas. His capture was recorded later by Abraham Wood, who preserved it in a letter written on August 22, 1674.

And here Gabriel received shot with two arrows, one of them in his thigh, which stopped his running, and so was taken prisoner, for Indian valor consists most in their heels for he that can run best is accounted the best man. These Indians thought this Gabriel to be no Tomohitan by the length of his hair, for the Tomahitans keep their hair close cut to the end so an enemy may not take an advantage to lay hold of them by it. They took Gabriel and scowered his skin with water and ashes, and when they perceived his skin to be white they made very much of him, and admired at his knife, gun, and hatchet.[24]

Unlike later military prisoners, the people taken by the eastern woodland tribes were civilians who were caught up in the wars being fought between settlers and the neighboring Indians. The Europeans, especially the British, Scots-Irish, and Germans, were insatiably land hungry. There was no problem at first; there seemed to be room for everyone when John Smith landed in Virginia and later, in 1620, when the Calvinist Pilgrims landed in New England. The increase of non-Puritan narratives between 1700 and 1800 came at a time when Pennsylvania was a major wartime battleground of the French, Indians, British, and colonials. For the Lutheran and Reformed Germans, Scots-Irish Presbyterians, and other Protestant settler-colonists, the captivity experience became more than a jeremiad of Calvinist faith or reportage about the values of community faithfulness; it evolved into a partly factual, partly fictional genre that described the shocking price one had to pay for pioneering the frontier. The captors—symbols of blood, murder, and death—became villains, literally beasts, who purposefully attacked and murdered innocents, carried off women for sale to the Catholic French, or forced prisoners to assimilate into their tribes.

The narrative of two German girls, Barbara Leininger and Marie LeRoy, captured in 1755 in Union County, Pennsylvania, first appeared in 1759.[25] As an archetypal captivity narrative from this period, it contains all the major requirements of a captivity narrative: precapture biography, capture, remove, landscape, resistance, torture, escape, rescue attempts, liberation, and the lament after repatriation. The Marie LeRoy–Barbara Leininger narrative demonstrates which components of the colonial captivity story were necessary to elicit the audience's belief. Based on the traditional themes of determination and will to live, the LeRoy-Leininger narrative shows both the dangers of frontier life and the fruits of individual ingenuity. Their bravery in the face of mortal danger was inspired by their strong Lutheran faith and unceasing community loyalty. The LeRoy-Leininger captivity experience gave people something to reflect upon, something to fear, and something that could generate continued faith in themselves. A major change, however, occurred when the captive decided to remain with the captors.

There are two major kinds of assimilation to consider during the colonial period: Indian assimilation—from white to red—and religious assimilation—from English or German Protestant into French Catholic. The French clergy-adventurers wanted converts, and the Indians sold many of their prisoners to French Catholics for ransom. One example of the Puritan-to-Catholic assimilation experience is the story of Jemima Howe (1759) and her two daughters. Jemima remained a Calvinist; her daughters, however, were ransomed by a French family and put into a convent. One daughter became such a staunch Catholic that she never returned to her Puritan ways. She refused to leave Canada on her own volition, and only under the threat of force would she consent to go home even for a visit.[26]

To prisoners and their families, both kinds of assimilation presented serious physical and spiritual dangers. After the captive decided to assimilate into the culture of the captor, however, little could be done about it, as we learn from the narrative of Mary Jemison, the "White Woman of the Genesee," who along with Eunice Williams was seized in 1755 by the Seneca. According to R. W. G. Vail, Jemison was carried away from her Pennsylvania home when she was a little girl in 1755 and lived through the Revolution as the wife of a Seneca chief in the Genesee Valley for many years thereafter. Her narrative, published in 1824, painted an excellent picture of life among the Senecas and discussed the issues of the Revolutionary War from a tribal point of view. It was deservedly one of the most popular of all tribal captivities, and appeared in thirty-five editions and issues.[27] Shortly before she died, Mary Jemison told Dr. James E. Seaver the story of her capture, adoption, and marriage into the Seneca tribe. Taken as a child, Jemison was cherished by her Indian adopted parents, and she painted the picture of her captivity as a life of freedom and adventure. It is understandable why many assimilated captives not only lost their language, religion, and customs but also the desire to return to the grinding toil of a white family on the frontier.[28] The Jemison captivity is remembered today in legend and in some place names of the region.

The last distinct category of colonial captivity literature is the romance. The appearance of romance is itself a testimony to the popularity of "actual" narratives and forms a bridge between fact and fiction, usually more fiction than fact. Examining the love relationship between the captive and a central figure—sometimes a rescuer, sometimes even a captor—the captivity romance serves as a preview to popular, modern melodramas. One such narrative is the romance of Molly Finney, the "Canadian Captive." According to Emma Lewis Coleman's *New England Captives Carried to Canada* (1925), Molly's actual captivity was first reported in the *Boston Gazette* on May 24, 1756, simply as an Indian attack against the Thomas Means family of Flying Point.[29] Molly lived with the family and was captured in the attack. This romance captivity appeared in several parts in E. G. Cattermole's anthology, *Famous Frontiersmen, Pioneers and Scouts* (1888). In Cattermole's popular melodramatic prose, Molly's romance contains all the essential events: precapture freedom, attack and capture, removes, description of the prison landscapes, resistance to the desires of her captors, and her rescue. Instead of being held indefinitely or assimilated by her Indian captors, she is sold to a Catholic French family, who make her a house servant and offer religious conversion. Like a hero in a Horatio Alger story, Molly's virtue and goodness triumph over her ill fortune. "She . . . cast sunshine into the family where she lived, the reflection of which gladdened her own soul."[30] An English trader, Captain McLellen, enters the scene with the express purpose of rescuing Molly. In league with Captain McLellen against her French captors, Molly makes her fairy-tale escape like a "caged bird suddenly liberated."[31] Safely aboard the rescue ship, Captain McLellen declares his love and proposes marriage. Molly accepts. They leave Canada and sail south, the romantic captivity–love story ending with Captain McLellen and the "fair captive of Quebec" betrothed and bound homeward in freedom for a life of wedded bliss.

Beginning in the sixteenth century with the chronicles of European adventurers captured by Indians, early colonial captivity narratives are relatively simple documents. Narrators specialize in ethnological reportage rather than emotional reflections on personal experience and relations with the Indians.[32] Alvar de Vaca's *The Journey of Alvar Nunez Cabeza de Vaca and His Companions from Florida to the Pacific, 1528–1536* (1542) describes Vaca's adventures in Florida; *True Relation of the Gentleman of Elvas* (1557) narrates John Ortiz's adventures among the Indians of the American Southeast; and Hans Staden's *True History of His Captivity among the Tupi Indians of Brazil* (1557) chronicles the adventures of a German sailor who sailed from Seville in 1549 with the expedition of Don Diego de Senabria for Rio de la Plata. Staden's ship was wrecked on the coast of Brazil where he was captured by the Tupi Indians. After his rescue in 1557 by a French ship, Staden returned to Germany and published his thriller in Marburg. In English, the first popular non-Puritan captivity narrative was derived from Captain John Smith's adventures in North America and appeared in *General History of Virginia* (1624). Puritan narratives recorded life in the New England forest wars of the seventeenth century. Non-Puritan narratives between 1700 and 1800 proliferated when Pennsylvania became a major battleground in the forest wars between the French, British, colonials, and their allied native tribes.

For the Germans, Scots-Irish, and other Protestant settler-colonists, the captivity experience became more than the story of Calvinist faith or community faithfulness characteristic of the Puritans. Sometimes the narratives were religious epistlelike jeremiads; sometimes they reported the soldier's plight as a POW; others recorded adventure, and still others told how and why a captive preferred to assimilate into a captor's tribe. Regardless of the narrative category, audiences learned very powerful lessons about life on the edge of death from the real or fictional experiences of the prisoners. To pass the experience along to others, complete with its horrors and lessons, was required and expected of survivors. The legacy has been the longstanding tradition in America that demands narratives from those prisoners who return home.

No set rules regulated the relationship between captors and captives in the forest wars except for the whim of the captor, usefulness of the captive for ransom or assimilation, and the traditional ways of the tribes themselves. There is little doubt that the strong tradition of captive taking existed among the Indians of North America long before European settlers faced them in war. Prisoners were taken to replenish wartime losses and sometimes to augment a labor force that may have been depleted in warfare with neighboring tribes. Often, captives were taken to obtain victims for ritual torture and tribal revenge and sometimes to obtain ransom, wealth, or even degrees of prestige and political leverage with allies.[33] Sometimes prisoners assimilated into the captor's environment; more often they did not. Many prisoners were killed during long marches and first ordeals, and many were tortured to death on arrival in the captor's camp. Others were ransomed either by relatives or traders after they had been sold to the French. Some prisoners escaped; most did not. Some prisoners assimilated, as Mary Jemison did, into their captors' tribes and lived relatively peacefully for the rest of their lives. Some prisoners, like Simon Girty, became renegades; that is, they became either Catholics or white Indians and decided to bear arms for their cause against members of their former societies. To whatever degree a person survived captivity in the colonial period, the captivity experience changed a person's life significantly.

The sustained appeal of the captivity story rests on traditional ideas about the nature of stoic heroism. For the most part, traditional and popular defeated heroes die in battle. With his last breath Roland warns his comrades of impending danger; George Armstrong Custer dies as the last man standing in defiance of the overwhelming force of charging Sioux horsemen and infantry intent on his destruction. One can hardly imagine Custer being taken captive. He had the ethical responsibility to die with his men, just as the naval heroic tradition demands that a captain should go down with his ship. This theme has become a part of western traditional lore.[34]

Functionally, the colonial captivity narratives defined and described competing visions of American cultural diversity and expressed colonial sensibilities. For the Puritans especially, captivity experiences served as lesson-oriented good sermons, which used the experience as a firm warning: if you displease God, His wrath will be manifested in the form of personal captivity. Captivity narratives also rationalized military, social, and legal actions relative to immediate and long-range political relationships between European settlers and the Indians. From a literary and cultural point of view, captivity narratives formed an American literary genre that draws and shapes material images from the very wellspring of human experience.[35]

To the prisoners of the forest wars, the experience of captivity was both a spiritual and a physical catastrophe. The body was defiled, time was stolen, and a sense of community was assaulted by the captors. Worse, the captive's soul might be utterly lost. In the Puritan narratives especially, the experience was a personal way for a captive to discover the will of God. In Vaughan and Clark's study of captivity, *Puritans among the Indians: Accounts of Captivity and Redemption 1676–1724* (1981), the captivity narrative was a "spiritual autobiography." According to Cotton Mather's characteristic Puritan dualism, the captivity represented an encounter with God's greatest enemy—Satan—while at the same time it acted as the instrument of God for the chastisement of His guilty people. Thus, for Mather and the Puritan prisoners, particular interest in the wilderness other than the prison landscape was lost in the horrors the prisoners observed and experienced. The natural terrain of the forest became an abstraction of the captor, or the "depraved natural man" who attempted to destroy all the physical, emotional, and cultural ties to colonial civilization. As prisoners, individuals had little or no hope of being restored to the full life of the community; thus, deprived of family members, who in many cases were killed in captivity, the Puritan captive could rely only on God to sustain his will to live. Colonial captivity was a terrible experience, a world of darkness and chaos, a hell with its own peculiar characteristics of place, space, and time.

PART TWO

The Anatomy of Experience

Constructing the Narrative Contour: Time, Domains, Sequence, and Event-Scenarios

We are honored to have the opportunity to serve our country under difficult circumstances.

Admiral Jeremiah Denton (1973)

Clifford Geertz suggests in *The Interpretation of Culture* (1973) that scholars should consider approaching culture in terms of the organization of social activity, institutional forms, and systems of ideas. Here I follow this advice in my own attempt to define and describe what Admiral Denton meant by "difficult circumstances" and how captivity narrators have expressed them.[1] Through the development and use of a consistently repeated structure the literature of captivity has maintained a remarkably rich, extended vitality. Each captivity narrative is, of course, individual because each prisoner's experience is unique; however, after one examines a large number of these works, little doubt remains that prisoners from colonial times to Vietnam have styled their messages within a set of recognized, understandable, temporal, contextual, sequential, and categorical boundaries. The content and flow of events within these boundaries constitute the narrative contour, akin in part to the phenomenon of a melodic contour that signals a distinct and identifiable family of folk melodies.

Many POWs lived for months and years with a crushing sense of doom when they saw themselves and their comrades dying from disease, starvation, exposure, misdirected bombardments, lack of medical care, and murder by firearm, bludgeon, bayonet, and the beheading sword. They faced forced marches on bare subsistence rations or none at all. They were exposed to intense cold or heat, they were often brutalized; they were prodded by bayonets or attack dogs and left to die, especially if they were too injured or too weak to keep up. Americans in captivity have been victims of terrible crimes such as torture and mutilation, beatings, and forced heavy labor under inhuman conditions. Many prisoners of war who were severely injured in combat prior to capture had little hope of any but the most meager medical attention, and at times, none at all. Staring captivity in the face, Navy pilot Giles R. Norrington, POW in North Vietnam for nearly five years, explained how he developed and maintained his will to live.

81

When I arrived at my cell I was at the absolute nadir of my existence. Not only was I wounded, I was beginning now to feel the full emotional isolation of my captivity, the hopelessness of my situation, and the misery that attends being that most pitiful of all creatures—the prisoner of war. But one day at a time, one step at a time I began to try to pull together the pieces. I realized very clearly that I had just suffered a loss in a round, but this was not a one-round fight. I was going to continue to fight until the final bell rang, and I was, by God, going to emerge victorious.[2]

The questions remain: How do narrators translate the experience not only for themselves, but for a public that has no firsthand knowledge of captivity? and How do narrators step beyond the limited regions of annals, diaries, and chronicles? The answers lie in a process that creates a multifunctional narrative contour which blends factual personal experience with moral, legal, and ethical judgments of the individual and the community. The first step is to define the quality of "prisoner-ness," including distinguishing between elements of legal POW status as defined in international law, establishing the polemic intent, showing what actions individuals and POW communities took to defend or abandon their respective positions, and defining the extent and quality of individual and community belief systems. The second step redefines time, from chronological to narrative event time, and the third step requires the narrator to follow the natural flow of major events. By completing this process, narrators create a string of sequentially ordered event-scenarios that contain enough detail to make sense of the experience (see Appendix 1).

Prisoner Status. The first level of interpretive distinction prominently clarified in a captivity narrative is the status of the narrator. The term captive implies that a person has no legal status, and treatment relies solely on the whim of the captor. The captive is virtually a slave of the captor. If a captive remains alive, it is because as a prisoner the person may have some intrinsic value. If a captive is wealthy, a ransom might be negotiated. If a captive has political significance, some kind of cartel or exchange might be offered. A modern application of the status of captive is hostage. Prisoner, on the other hand, as well as other associated terms such as internee, evader, hostage, and even renegade—a prisoner who assimilates into the captor's culture to the point of joining the captor's armed forces—all imply a recognized legal status; hence, there exist rights and responsibilities between captors and POWs. A recognized process of hostility—war itself—creates captivity status in which there are international rules for the treatment of POWs and other prisoners. These rules are not mere utopian suggestions or guidelines for voluntary action; they are, like the 1949 Geneva Convention and other similar documents, international laws which must be obeyed by all the signatories, although it should be clear from the experiences of the American POWs that many captor nations have disregarded their obligations in favor of punitive captivity.

Narrative or Polemic Intent. The second level of interpretive distinction consists of five possible polemic intents: jeremiad, apology, propaganda, complaint, and romance. The jeremiad or sermon narrative focuses on the captivity experience as a curse or a trial imposed on an individual or even on a people by an angry God. Whether one examines the books of Chronicles or Lamentation, the Puritan narratives, or the Jesuit narratives, the captivity experience translates into a formula of spiritual redemption. The narrative apology functions as a statement of defense: why the narrator acted the way he did, or why a community of prisoners acted the way they did. The apologies focus on the exigencies of the experience and the means for physical survival in general without a deity acting as the central cause and effect figure. Most military or soldier narratives fall into this broad category. Apologies defend survival, resistance, vengeance, forgiveness, condemnation, assimilation, and escape. Some narrators explain how and why a prisoner or a community of prisoners survived through active or passive resistance; others describe the motivations that determined the need for escape; still others tell why a prisoner joined the captors and assimilated into the captor's culture.

The narrative of propaganda rails against the captor's behavior and ideology; more important, one finds in the propaganda narrative an implicit political, ideological, or military call to action. The narrative complaint is a statement of attack, usually against the captors, but sometimes against the community of prisoners. Some narrators are vengeful, others are forgiving, and most wish to discover the mysteries of their captors' culture. The captivity romance appears mainly in antique folklore, including folktales, ballads, legends, and in modern fiction and popular films.

Action. The third level of interpretive distinction offers an array of possible modes of action: "playing it cool" to survive the captivity; resisting the captors' efforts to convert or assimilate POWs; planning and executing escapes from the prison camp, deciding to partially or totally assimilate into the captor's culture, deciding or being forced to collaborate with the captor's demands for cooperation; or, in the case of evaders and raiders, committing some form of sabotage against enemy forces.

Heroics. War has a steady appetite for heroics, and the fourth level of interpretive distinction answers that need by describing six kinds of heroic actions directly or, in some cases, indirectly related to the captivity experience: the defeat hero, like Major James P. S. Devereux, USMC, who had to surrender Wake Island in 1941, or General Jonathan Wainwright, USA, who surrendered Corregidor in 1942; the stoic heroes, who continue to perform their duty in the face of varying levels of adversity, up to and including possible execution; the different types of escapers who decide to risk their lives to liberate themselves; the assimilator who makes a decision of conscience to join the captors; the passive survivors who force themselves to withstand captivity in order to tell the story to a disbelieving world; and the raider who, against all odds, attempts to free POWs from a camp during hostilities. In captivity, heroics translate into a force that generates a will to live. Resisting prisoners withstand enormous physical strains in interrogation and torture; others break down at the mere thought of physical abuse and collaborate to avoid pain. Stoic prisoners withstand what they have to withstand with a quiet sense of duty. Some POWs defy the odds and escape; others die trying. Some prisoners reflect on the situation and decide that joining the captors takes more courage than remaining in captivity. For the vast majority of prisoners, the currency of prison camp heroism has been resistance.

Beliefs. Prisoners bring their major belief systems with them into a prison camp. In the American experience, those beliefs include a passionate demand for success, a desire for material abundance, a reliance on the fruits of technology, a sense of the power of community over the desires of the individual, a sense of military duty to a war's just cause, a sense of individual fairness, loyalty to a POW community, and a dependence on the strength of international and military law. The ideals of success, abundance, technology, and community shatter upon entry into a prison camp. However, the narratives reveal that in time prisoners in a community rebuild values one by one until a community of POWs in many ways resembles the essence of the American small town.

Fears. The prisoner's fears include the passage of time, random bad luck, lawlessness, torture, collaborators and renegades, and circumstances over which they exercise little or no control, not to mention starvation, atrocities, solitude, personal weakness, and rejection by the POW community.

Faith. In everyday life, Americans tend to keep their religious faith to themselves. The American tradition dictates that religious faith is a private matter, requiring Americans to interact with one another based on a long continuity of accepted secular values and ideals. From the forest wars to Vietnam, American POWs have displayed six major categories of faith: faith in God as each POW understood God; faith in the idea and integrity of country; faith in the military and civil institutions they represented and in the strength of the community of prisoners behind the wire; faith in international laws and conventions that regulate the POWs and limit what the captors can do; faith in the family at home and in the individual prisoner to survive the experience. Typical domain combinations can be seen at a glance in Appendix 1A.

Having identified themselves within these qualitative domains, captivity narrators then undertake the deliberate restructuring of time. French novelist and former POW Pierre Boulle comments: "The memoir of a prisoner can scarcely be set down as a continuous narrative corresponding to the dreary procession of each hour, each day, or even each month. To follow this procedure would amount to imposing on the reader a boredom as unbearable as that suffered by the captive himself."[3] Therefore, Boulle, the narrator of *My Own River Kwai,* converts long periods of chronological time into synchronic, narrative time that orders long periods of uncertainty, boredom, hunger, danger, and fear. Like narrators before and after him, he expresses his experience as a series of patterned events that compress the chaos in captivity into understandable, expressive units of time. Chronological time is encased in distinct narrative event-scenarios, which contain examples of the narrators' personal drama.

The third step in creating a captivity narrative is to formalize those dramatic units of time into clear and distinct *event-scenarios* (see Appendix 1B). From the forest wars to Vietnam, captivity literature has shown a relatively consistent, highly repetitive common narrative contour, one that has been derived from the experience itself. Structurally, what John Cawelti calls "supertexts" and Northrop Frye calls "patterns of significance" take shape as seven important repeated event-scenarios that must be in place in varying degrees so that the narrative contour makes sense within the complex relationships of captor to POW, POW to POW, and POW community to prisoners and captors.[4] Beginning with a precapture autobiography, the captivity narrator shapes the story after the seven major events of the actual captivity experience—precapture autobiography, capture, remove (long march or death march), prison landscape, resistance, and release (escape, liberation, and subsequent repatriation)— and ends the narrative with the deep reflections that form a prisoner's lament. Whether former POWs happen to be resisters, survivors, escapers, or assimilators, as narrators, brevity, clarity, drama, precision, and the condensation of time culminate in the experience-structure-idea relationship found in the following event-scenarios.

Precapture Autobiography. The captive or POW tells the audience about himself. A military prisoner may explain what his concept of duty was and why he was placed in harm's way. He describes and contextualizes the frame of reference and initial point of view before going into captivity, including idyllic memories of home, family, happiness, freedom, and normalcy.

Capture. The capture describes how, where, and when a free person is taken into captivity by an aggressive enemy captor. The victim can be an individual soldier or sailor or an entire military garrison that may be forced to surrender as a unit. With the advent of airplanes as combat weapons, a new word has been invented, "shootdown," which describes individual capture after aerial combat or loss of the aircraft to a surface-to-air missile or concentrated ground fire. What is vital in this event-scenario is that the narrator lost the battle he was in and in the space of a moment lost his freedom as well. Comrades or, in the case of the tribal captivities, family may be dead at the hands of the captors. Whether in the air, on land, or at sea, the POW has to admit that surrender became a reality, and only the present moment matters. Death is close, and life hangs on a new captive's every move, every breath, and every passing moment. A radical transition, perhaps the first real transformation in the captivity experience, has been accomplished. In spite of the laws of war, international conventions, or military traditions that may be in force, the POW loses everything at the moment of capture. Life itself depends on luck; fate rests on the whim and will of the captor.

Death March/Remove. This event-scenario describes when and how the POW was taken from the place of capture to the place of permanent captivity. In the twentieth century, the term remove gave way to long march or death march. After the new POW is taken by the enemy, it is common practice to remove him from the battlefield toward a rear area specifically designed for the reception and processing of POWs. It is usually in this stage of captivity that the outer layers of the captive's cultural veneer begin to peel away. This dreadful event-scenario first reveals what can happen to the captive or prisoner. Comrades are killed (executed or murdered) by the captors for trifles: wanting water, walking too slowly, falling down, being hungry, or, in extreme cases, showing physical resistance to the captor. Next to capture itself, it is the most dangerous event of captivity because it marks the prisoner's first truly dangerous encounter with the captor's value system.

Prison Landscape. If POWs survive the death march, they ultimately arrive at a permanent prison facility. Regardless of the war or the century, memories of the prison camp or prison cells are branded into prisoners' consciousness. Time seems to stand still, and it is no wonder that prisoners describe each enemy prison facility in remarkably rich detail. Prisoners, especially bored prisoners, become expert ethnologists.

Resistance, Survival, or Assimilation. The experience itself creates a spiritual transformation in the individual through great physical and psychological pain. This stage of the captivity narrative describes how, where, and when captors apply physical torture, and/or psychological pressure on POWs in order to change their way of thinking or at least to change their overt behavior in the camp. In this event-scenario POWs understand the captors better. Faceless, stereotypic captors become real people with names, sometimes funny names which American POWs derived from cartoons or other popular culture sources. Captives understand what the captors want and what the enemy's expectations and weaknesses are. Reflection begins in earnest. POWs' feelings surface as they continue to undergo deep psychological transformations. Prisoners are confronted with some basic decision making. In this event-scenario they examine the nature of their fundamental cultural values as they surface as weapons against the captor. These values either support or destroy the prisoner's sense of self and community.

Release and Repatriation. Here the narrator describes his happy and sad repatriation and return—or attempted return—to the world from which he came. Release may come from advancing friendly forces who overrun the enemy and liberate the prison camp, or from friendly forces who raid the prison camp in a secret operation during hostilities, or even as a result of formal exchanges. In some cases parole or the payment of a ransom results in liberation. Most commonly, however, liberation and repatriation take place at the end of hostilities after a truce or after a treaty of peace between the belligerents. Tales of escape, perhaps the most naturally heroic event in captivity, are found in this part of the narrative. A small number of POWs escape, but most escapees suffer recapture and severe punishment for their efforts. In this event-scenario former POWs take the time to consider the ever-rising and ever-intensifying social, ethical, and moral conflicts over the efficacy of escaping, especially when the well-being of the prison community is at stake. Escape aside, this event-scenario focuses on the joy of release and the thrill of homecoming.

Lament. In the lament, the most introspective of all the event-scenarios in a captivity narrative, narrators express a strong, sometimes overwhelming, sense of loss. The lament gives them the opportunity to grieve for the time wasted in captivity, for the material opportunities that were lost over time, and for their dead comrades. Some former prisoners lament their captivity experience in poetry, some in song, some in written narrative, some in alcoholism, a few in suicide, and some in prayer. Characteristically, narrators insist that a permanent cultural transformation of values, insights, ethics, and morality took place in captivity. People, places, institutions, even circumstances in postcaptivity life are compared to those in captivity. Every day in freedom means a day not being a captive. The narrators' act of writing about their experiences of captivity serves not only as a catharsis for personal feelings and a way to tell the world what happened to them, but also as an ethical forum for expressing individual and collective outrage against willful, often illegal, acts of inhumanity.

This seven-point basic structure forms a step-by-step historical event-chronology of captivity. Relying on a relatively formalistic sequential synchronic event-structure as a replacement for chronological time, event-scenarios contain the thematic, dramatic, and interpretive elements needed to describe, explain, clarify, and evaluate the captivity experience.[5]

After each war, American soldiers returning from the enemy's dungeons and prison camps described their experiences for the public. Whether they appeared in the form of published diaries or full prose narratives, military prison memoirs would evolve into a major branch of captivity literature that, in part, resembles the Puritan narratives in structure, but that has a distinct mode of expressing fundamental values and feelings. From the materials of folklore through narrative to the movies, Americans have used the captivity theme to validate specific traditional perceptions that reinforce their most important beliefs.[6] Tested by capture, solidified in confrontation, and confirmed in resistance, escape, or rescue, the captivity experience affirms visions of the individual and collective stoic heroism, sacrifice, humility, resistance, success, and victory of ordinary people who found themselves thrust into very difficult circumstances.

(top) *"Prisoners Entering Andersonville Prison."* (bottom) *"Prisoner Shot for Dipping Water Too Near the Dead Line."* Source: *John Urban,* Battle Field and Prison Pen: Through the War and Thrice a Prisoner *(Philadelphia: Hubbard Brothers, 1882), pp. 248, 294.*

Libby Prison in Richmond, Virginia, was reserved for Union officers. Source: *National Archives.*

Gen. Benjamin Butler, USV, commanded victorious federal troops in New Orleans and was later appointed a Union Agent of Exchange. Source: *National Archives.*

(opposite, top) *Union POW prison pen for Confederates in Shenandoah, Virginia. From temporary Union prison pens close to the fighting lines, prisoners were transferred to one of the larger, more permanent prison facilities like Fort Delaware, Johnson's Island, Camp Morton, or Elmira.* Source: *National Archives.*

(opposite, bottom) *Three Confederate soldiers taken prisoner after the Battle of Gettysburg, July 4, 1863.* Source: *National Archives.*

(above) *Drawing of punishment and execution of American POWs by Japanese guards.* Source: *Stan Sommers,* The Japanese Story *(Marshfield, WI: American Ex–Prisoners of War Association, 1980), p. 55; reproduced courtesy of the American Ex–Prisoners of War Association.*

(opposite, top) *POWs starting the Bataan Death March, April 1942 (Japanese army photo). On the eighty-five-mile march, 7,000 to 10,000 died. Of that number, a little over 600 were Americans; the rest were Filipinos.* Source: *National Archives.*

(opposite, bottom) *POWs resting along the route of the Bataan Death March, April 1942, their faces showing traditional defiance toward their captors.* Source: *National Archives.*

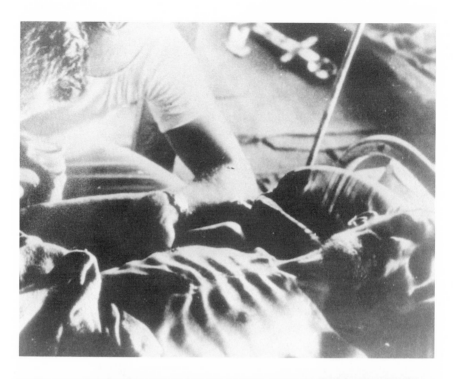

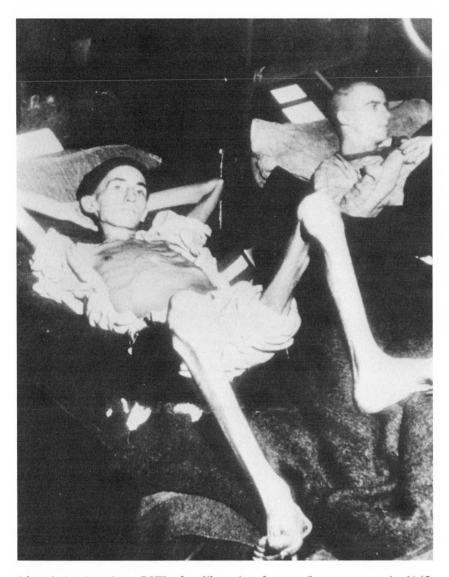

(above) *An American POW after liberation from a German camp in 1945.*
Source: *National Archives.*

(opposite, top) *An American POW dying from dry beriberi in the Bilibid prison hospital; the prison was used by the Japanese as a transient camp for receiving, searching, and assigning prisoners to permanent prison camps after the surrender of Corregidor.* Source: *National Archives.*

(opposite, bottom) *Red Cross parcel distribution in Stalag IX B, Germany. Kriegie life was hard, but food packages helped.* Source: *National Archives.*

(top) *Survivors of the Suncheon Tunnel massacre in Korea. In that incident, some American prisoners were not mortally wounded. Refusing to panic, they played dead beneath the bodies of their mortally wounded or dead comrades and waited for rescue.* Source: *National Archives.*

(bottom) *Five American POWs from Illinois in North Korea in 1952. Left to right: unknown; Ralph D. Moyer, Chicago; Archie Edwards, Arcola; Burrel Lauter, Matoon; and Paul Martin, Chicago. Photograph reproduced courtesy of Ralph D. Moyer.*

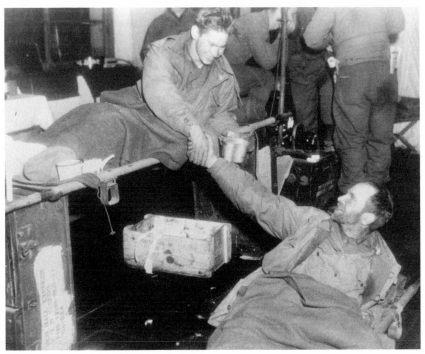

(top) *A POW camp in North Korea. Photograph reproduced courtesy of Ralph D. Moyer.*

(bottom) *Two freed American POWs in Korea.* Source: *National Archives.*

(above) *Col. Norman A. McDaniel, USAF (Retired), a POW in Hanoi from 1966 to 1973, was one of eighteen African-American POWs imprisoned in Hanoi during the Vietnam War. Photograph reproduced courtesy of Alisa Giardinelli.*

(opposite, top) *This drawing shows how Americans resisted North Vietnamese orders for silence by tapping abbreviated messages in what they called the "Smitty Harris Tap Code."* Source: *John M. McGrath*, Prisoner of War: Six Years in Hanoi *(Annapolis, MD: Naval Institute Press, 1976), p. 34. Reproduced courtesy of the Naval Institute Press.*

(opposite, bottom) *Called "the Ropes" by the Americans, this form of torture was a Vietnamese adaptation of a European method, called strappado, that was used until the eighteenth century.* Source: *John M. McGrath*, Prisoner of War: Six Years in Hanoi *(Annapolis, MD: Naval Institute Press, 1976), p. 79. Reproduced courtesy of the Naval Institute Press.*

Capt. Giles R. Norrington, USN (Retired), a POW in Hanoi (1968–1973), spoke about his personal ideals and vision of survival as he narrated his captivity experience to a class in October 1989. Photograph reproduced courtesy of Edward Palsa.

CHAPTER FIVE

Becoming a Prisoner of War:
Transformation and Initiation

I had always thought out the possibilities of being killed or wounded, but never of being captured, so I was unprepared. . . . I must confess that, when I found myself alone in my cell, I burst into tears like a child.

Harold B. Willis (1917)

Soldiers experience a process of transformation and initiation when they become prisoners of war. In captivity narratives, either before or soon after the capture is recounted, narrators take their readers back to the days of personal freedom, family, and what the narrator considered to be normalcy.

The components of the capture experience consist of an explanation of precapture status and circumstances; the moment of institutional or technical failure when control shifts to the enemy; the moment of individual personal decision whether to fight to the death or surrender; the first physical takeover by the enemy; and the first realization that as a captive a prisoner exercises little or no control over his environment. All five components shock the new prisoner into understanding that he lives by luck, military happenstance, international conventions if they apply, and, ultimately, by the whim, if not the pleasure, of the captor.

Mary Rowlandson set the tone and established the polemic intent in the forest wars for narrative descriptions of precapture freedom and capture. Captured by Indians on February 20, 1676, during King Philip's War, her description of capture forecasts the hundreds of similarly detailed accounts that would follow. The attack comes without warning; the fighting takes place in her own home. Her relatives die before her eyes, and she cries to God for help in her hour of sorrow, "Lord, what shall we do?"[1] Mary had little to do but try to escape the holocaust that appeared before her eyes. She took her children and left the house, but the attacking Indians continued firing a rain of bullets. With no escape possible and the fire ever increasing inside the house, Mary and those with her darted for freedom, but as they left the house her brother-in-law fell dead, and the Indians killed her nephew with a tomahawk. Her sister cried to God for her own death, "Lord, let me die with them," and she fell dead from a bullet. According to Mary, her capture followed the butchery. Her captors cry, "Come go along with us." Mary responds that she believed they would kill her, but they told her that if she would go along, they would not hurt her. Reflecting for a moment, Mary Rowlandson repeated Psalm 8, "Come behold the works of the Lord, what desolations He has made in the Earth."[2]

Framed during the French and Indian War in Pennsylvania, and published originally in German in 1759, the "Narrative of Barbara Leininger and Marie LeRoy" describes the captivity experiences of two German women who were taken prisoner in guerrilla raids into the Pennsylvania interior. Culminating in escape, the narrative contains all the essential elements of the captivity narrative: precapture identification, capture, removes, tortures and near-death experiences, cravings for food, resistance, prayers, escape, repatriation, and a short lament. Of all the ingredients in this narrative, Barbara's escape is the most significant: luck, wit, courage, and a commitment to escape can overcome even the most severe emotional effects of captivity.[3] The narrative begins with an attack on Marie LeRoy's home. Early in the morning of October 16, 1755, LeRoy's hired man went out to fetch the cows and heard the Indians shooting. Soon after, eight attackers came to the house and killed Marie LeRoy's father with tomahawks. Her brother defended himself desperately for a time, but was at last overpowered.[4] The Indians attacked Barbara Leininger's home next, and in a raid similar to the one that Mary Rowlandson described, the attackers shot her father, killed her brother, and took her and her cousin Regina captive along with the others already in tow. Writing in a manner characteristic of the day, she notes that "toward evening the rest of the savages returned with six fresh and bloody scalps, which they threw at the feet of the poor captives, saying that they had a good hunt that day."[5]

Rowlandson's and Leininger-LeRoy's captures are two of hundreds of recorded captivities during the forest wars. The captors were small guerrilla parties intent on destroying what they could, living off the land, and taking prisoners selectively. Narrators consistently were horrified by the gore of the fighting, especially when it was so one-sided. In the end, captives like Rowlandson, Leininger, LeRoy, and many others came to understand that their lives were spared for a reason; they had ransom or trading value.

Trading value continued to be an issue when the British and Continental armies began taking each other's soldiers prisoner. From the beginning of the Revolution (1775–1783), General George Washington attempted to reach some understanding with his British counterparts in America concerning the growing number of POWs on both sides. In one letter to Sir William Howe on November 9, 1776, Washington asserted that "it is not my wish that Severity should be exercised toward any whom the fortune of War has thrown, or, shall throw into our hands. On the contrary, it is my desire that the utmost Humanity should be shewn them. I am convinced the latter has been the prevailing line of Conduct to Prisoners."[6] Yet in fact severity was commonplace, whether capture took place on land or at sea. If the prisoner was obviously a soldier who surrendered after battle, as Colonel Ethan Allen did, then chances were good that the captors would treat him reasonably well, at least in the beginning. Unlike his civilian predecessors in the forest wars who were attacked by an overwhelming guerrilla force, Allen fought his enemy in the field until he was certain that any more resistance would have meant death for him and his men. He described the fight and the surrender.

> I had but about forty-five men with me, some of whom were wounded. The enemy kept closing around me, nor was it in my power to prevent it; by which means my situation, which was advantageous in the first part of the attack, ceased to be so in the last. Being almost entirely surrounded with such vast, unequal numbers, I ordered a retreat, but found that those of the enemy who were of the country, and their Indians, could run as fast as my men, although the regulars could not. Thus I retreated near a mile, and some of the enemy, with the savages, kept flanking me, and others crowded hard in the rear. . . . I agreed to surrender with my party, which then consisted of thirty-one effective men and seven wounded. I ordered them to ground their arms, which they did. The officer I capitulated with then directed me and my party to advance towards him, which was done. I handed him my sword.[7]

Ethan Allen's experience demonstrates one of the foundations of military captivity in war: front line regular soldiers treat their prisoners well after the shooting stops. They know they might be captured some day themselves, and the profession of arms dictates a tradition of dignity between actual combatants.

The American navy was in its infancy, and the new nation relied heavily upon armed private vessels—privateers—under letters of marque to patrol its coasts and harass enemy shipping. Success brought financial rewards, but capture by the British meant that passengers and crew would be imprisoned without any hope of release.[8] The captors seldom distinguished between crew and passengers. Most prisoners, military or civilian, found themselves in irons, dungeons, or prison ships either in America or England. General Washington complained bitterly to the British about the conditions of captivity imposed on American seamen. Writing to Admiral Digby about the reported terrible conditions in the British prison ships, Washington commented: "If the fortune of war, sir, has thrown a number of these miserable people into your hands, I am certain your excellency's feelings for the men must induce you to proportion the ships (if they *must* be confined aboard ships) to their accommodation and comfort, and not, by crowding them together in a few ships, bring on diseases which consign them by the half-dozen in a day to the grave."[9]

Diplomat Benjamin Franklin also addressed the conditions of American seamen in English prisons from his quarters in France. Franklin received many letters from former prisoners soliciting his help. One letter, written by Josiah Smith in 1777, told Franklin what it was like to be captured at sea and interned by the British. Like most American seamen, Smith preferred strongly to be imprisoned than endure impressment and sail aboard a British man-of-war.

> I was born in the State of Massachusetts Bay and educated in the University of Cambridge, where I commenced in 1774 from which time I applied myself to the Study of Physic & Surgery till January 1777, when I took passage in the Ship *Montgomery* of Newbury Port bound to Bordeaux. But on the 14th of March just as we were verging upon the Coast of Europe, we had the misfortune to be chased & taken by King George's Ship *Albion* of 74 guns; ours being a merchant Ship laden with Masts Spars &c: We were sent into Plymouth & there closely confined without the least distinction or difference to rank or title; and part of the time on short allowance. And after being divested of every thing (except our clothing) even to the little money which I had in my pockets and after much difficulty I obtained my liberty at the expiration of two months; and after this by virtue of my being a passenger, and their expecting that for this indulgence I should enter into their service. The ship's company after losing all their wages & adventures were turned over to other ships & compelled to do duty; and though they resolutely swore that they were subjects of the United States & beg[g]ed to be sent to prison with those of their countrymen taken in arms, yet were compelled to serve the king.[10]

Smith was a passenger, not a crewman. Thomas Andros, however, was a civilian who sailed against the British navy as an American privateer. He, too, described his capture.

> I entered a volunteer on board a new brig, called the *Fair American,* built on purpose to prey upon the British commerce. . . . We had not been long at sea before we discovered and gave chase to an English brig, as large as ours, who in appearance mounted as many guns. As we approached her she saluted us with her stern chases, but after exchanging a few shots we ran directly alongside, as near as we could and not get entangled in her top hamper, and with one

salute of all the fire we could display put her to silence. And thanks be to God, no lives were lost.

I, with others, went on board to man the prize and to take her into port. But the prize master disobeyed orders. His orders were not to approach the American coast till we had reached the longitude of New Bedford, and then to haul up to the northward, and with a press of sail to make for that port; but he aimed to make land on the back of Long Island. The consequence was, we were captured on the twenty-seventh of August by the *Solebay* frigate, and safely stowed away in the old *Jersey* prison ship at New York.[11]

Andros, along with thousands of American privateers in the Revolution and later in the War of 1812, was captured at sea by ships of the British navy. After the Revolution, American merchant ships were often captured, not by the British but by the Barbary pirates.

The merchants along the American coast had been active traders well before the Revolution created an independent United States. Colonial merchant ships traded freely with the Islamic states of North Africa under passports from Britain. But when British colonial America became the United States, the Americans carried no passports, were not protected by the British, and sailed at their own risk in the waters patrolled by the small but powerful navies of the Barbary states. On the morning of July 25, 1785, the American schooner *Maria* was sailing three miles east of the coast of Portugal with hopes of reaching Cadiz sometime in the next forty-eight hours. Portuguese fishing boats dotted the sea. In the distance, a small, strange-looking Algerian xebec stopped two Danish brigs, but the sight did not disturb the Americans, whose country was at peace with the world. The *Maria*'s commanding officer, Captain Issak Stevens, never changed course, and *Maria* proceeded, ignorant of the long captivity awaiting everyone aboard. The Algerian craft came closer, one man in European dress standing at the open helm; her decks were cleared for action, and guns bristled as they aimed at the deck of the *Maria.* Suddenly, armed Algerian sailors appeared. They launched a rowboat, boarded the *Maria,* and demanded the crewmen's nationality. The Algerian boarding party then ransacked the ship for two hours. The Americans were ordered into the rowboat face downwards while the Algerians loaded their booty into the longboat. When the Americans reached the xebec, they were told that they were prisoners of the Turkish state of Algeria and that Rais El-Arbi was the captain and their captor. The officers and men were taken below to the cargo hold and not fed until the next day. The xebec passed through the straits of Gibraltar and headed for its home port of Algiers. As they approached the city of Algiers, the Americans wondered what was about to happen to them.[12] They would become slaves.

The *Maria* was the first of many American merchant ships taken captive by the Barbary powers—Algeria, Morocco, Tunisia, and Tripoli—from 1785 to 1815. In Algiers, the *Maria* would be joined by officers and crews of the *Hope* from New York, the *Minerva* from Philadelphia, the *President of Philadelphia* from Philadelphia, the *George* from Rhode Island, the *Olive Branch* from Portsmouth, New Hampshire, the schooner *Jay* of Colchester, the *Jane of Haven Hill,* and the *Polly* of Newbury Port.[13] Captured in 1793 aboard the Boston brig *Polly,* John Foss narrated his capture in *A Journal of the Captivity and Suffering of John Foss* (1798).

> About one hundred of the Pirates jumped on board us, all armed, some with Scimitars and Pistols, others with pikes, spears, lances, etc. As soon as they came on board they made signs for us all to go forward, assuring us in several languages that if we did not obey their commands they would immediately massacre us all. . . . They then went below into the cabin, steerage and every place where they could get below deck and broke open the Trunks and Chests there, and plundered all our bedding, clothing, books, Charts, Quadrants and every movable article. . . . When we had been taken into [Algiers] we were conducted to the Dey's palace by a guard. When we were brought before the Dey he said he was determined never to make peace with the United States, adding, "Now I have got you, you Christian dogs, you shall eat stones." He then picked out four boys to wait upon himself and then ordered the rest of us to be conducted to the prison.[14]

The number of American civilian merchant sailors held in Algiers was rising, for the United States had no navy to speak of and rescue was impossible. Furthermore, the politics of North Africa was a mystery to Americans like John Lamb, who undertook a mission to free the American prisoners. Lamb made no impression on the Algerians, who were accustomed to large ransoms, and failed to accomplish anything other than mystifying them with his bad manners. For most Americans captured at sea by Algerian pirate entrepreneurs, life in the dungeons and prisons became dull, boring, and tedious. Some died quickly from disease, especially from the plague. A few American captives actually rose from slavery to prominence in Algerian society. James L. Cathcart had been a prisoner of war in the *Jersey* for two years during the American Revolution, and after being taken prisoner by the Algerians, he learned Swedish, Arabic, and Turkish. In *The Captives* (1899), a narrative that his daughter reconstructed from his personal papers, Cathcart revealed that eventually he became the senior Christian adviser to Dey Hassan Bashaw, the Turkish ruler of Algiers, and tried to explain to him that the United States possessed far fewer resources than the wealthy European powers. With his facility with languages and his flare for dynamic interpersonal relationships, he exercised some entrepreneurial and diplomatic skills to secure financial backing from the Swedish ambassador to open a tavern for Christians in Algiers. Cathcart left Algiers a wealthy man; however, as a group, the American prisoners experienced their government's sad inability to buy their freedom. In the end, civilian and, later, military prisoners throughout the Barbary States had to wait for diplomacy, tribute, and ultimately military operations to be launched in Tripoli by a fledgling American navy before significant actions could be taken on their behalf.

On land, America's war with Mexico saw only a few soldiers taken into captivity. The Kentucky cavalry marched from Louisville to Mexico in the spring of 1846 under the command of Colonel Humphrey Marshall. By the time the regiment reached Mexico, morale was low: half the men were sick, and the other half were barely able to nurse them.[15] Their horses were tired, their uniforms were tattered, and they scoured the Mexican countryside constantly for meager provisions. On January 15, 1847, a group of thirty men from the regiment scouted the hacienda of Encarnacion, about fifty miles from Saltillo, a city of about 15,000 inhabitants. It began to rain, and the commanding officer, Major John P. Gaines, decided to camp at Encarnacion for the night. The anonymous author of *Encarnacion Prisoners* (1848) describes their capture.

> Minon, who commanded the advance guard of the army of Santa Anna, had nearly reached the hacienda the preceding day. That night, having been informed that an armed force invested the place, he surrounded it. His command consisted of a fine brigade armed with lances and escopettas. On the next day the American scouting parties found themselves in a dilemma at once unpleasant and inextricable. They capitulated and became prisoners of war. When they had resolved to surrender, Major Gaines went out with Minon to agree upon the terms of their capitulation; and while Gaines was thus in the hands of his captors, a Mexican of equal rank was left in the hands of the Americans as a hostage.[16]

Two officers of the group, Lieutenant George Davidson, son of Kentucky pioneer Colonel James Davidson, and Captain Danley, urged battle with the Mexicans; the others voted for surrender. Major Gaines had asked Colonel Minon for a written document containing the terms of the surrender, but Minon refused, saying that his word would be carried out to the letter. Accepting the Mexican colonel's word of honor, all the Americans, with the exception of Major Gaines and Major Borland of the Arkansas cavalry, gave up their arms and horses. In a moment a contingent of the officers and men of the Kentucky cavalry became POWs and began their remove from the town of Encarnacion to Mexico City.

Meanwhile, Captain Heady, the senior captain of the regiment, along with Lieutenant Churchill, formulated a search plan for the missing group. Heady, Churchill, and seventeen of their men set out to find them. Instead they found 300 armed Mexican cavalrymen. According to the anonymous narrator, "As they drew near the steel of their lances seemed to flash fire; while on the staff of each was nailed a small flag, the banner of Mexico, that fluttered like a pennon in the breeze."[17] Captain Heady decided it was no use for seventeen men and two officers to be slaughtered by an overwhelming Mexican force and offered a flag of truce. A Mexican lieutenant rode up and demanded the party's immediate unconditional surrender. Heady refused and demanded to speak with the commanding officer, Colonel Valentinklus, who accepted the Americans as POWs and permitted the officers to retain their horses and sabers. From the point of surrender, the Americans were marched twelve miles to Minon's camp at Potosi hacienda, where he received them politely. Then Heady, Churchill, and the seventeen American prisoners followed the party of Gaines and Borland on a 300-mile march from Encarnacion to San Luis Potosi.

Another group of the Louisville legion surrendered to the Mexican army in April 1847 when they were traveling with 120 wagons from Monterey to Camargo. Mexican morale was high, and it became extremely dangerous for Americans to travel lightly armed from garrison to garrison with supplies. The Camargo train was attacked by General Urrea, and after the battle those who surrendered were made POWs and marched to Mexico City.

In April 1861, the United States declared a blockade of Southern ports. The British responded by proclaiming the belligerent status of the Confederacy, and shortly thereafter, on November 8, 1861, the United States Navy intercepted the British ship *Trent,* and took two Southern diplomats, James M. Mason, the former chairman of the Senate Foreign Relations Committee, and John Slidell, also a former member of the Senate, into custody. Their captivity was short-lived. The British government, whose cultural, political, and diplomatic sympathy leaned more toward the cavalier, cotton-producing South than toward the industrialized, Puritan North, was outraged that the United States Navy had violated the freedom of the open seas to seize these two Confederate commissioners. Queen Victoria considered Americans crude and vulgar, but the United States was not an enemy. Consequently, she directed her government to redraft the ultimatum in order to give the United States government a way out without any embarrassing loss of pride.[18] Nevertheless, Britain demanded the release of Mason and Slidell from Fort Warren Prison in Boston harbor, and under the threat of war with England, Canada, and possibly Mexico, the Lincoln administration realized that European intervention in 1861–1862 meant certain victory by default for the Confederacy. Mason and Slidell, the first prisoners of state in the Civil War, were freed on January 1, 1862, and an inopportune international war with England and possibly Canada was avoided.[19]

The first Northern noncombatant prisoner of state in the Civil War was Alfred Ely, a member of the House of Representatives from New York. He had received permission to visit the Bull Run battlefield on July 20, 1861, and was captured. He remained a guest of the Confederacy until his release in December of that year. While walking down a road toward the first formal fighting between the armies of the Union and the Confederacy, Ely noticed a large number of men standing in a field nearby. "I halted in the middle of the road. The striking of a rifle-ball near where I was standing admonished me of the danger of my position."[20] After Ely recognized that he was a target, he scurried under a tree for some cover and protection, to no avail. He wrote in his narrative:

Two officers then came forward to the tree and inquired who I was, and I told them my name was "Alfred Ely." "What State are you from?" "From the State of New York," I replied. "Are you connected in any way with the Government?" "Yes." "In what way, sir?" "A Representative in Congress." One of the officers, a captain, immediately seized me by the arm, and said that I was their prisoner, and took from me the pistol which I had that morning borrowed from Mr. Seth Green. He took nothing else.[21]

For Ely, however, the real shock of capture occurred when he was brought before the commanding officer of his captors. Sitting high on his horse, and very angry, the Confederate colonel wanted to know who this new Yankee civilian captive might be. His immediate captor, Captain W. S. Mullins, CSA, introduced him to Colonel E. C. B. Cash, CSA, of South Carolina. " 'Colonel, this is Mr. Ely, Representative in Congress from New York,' to which the colonel, in a most angry tone, replied, drawing his pistol, and pointing it directly at my head, 'God damn your white-livered soul! I'll blow your brains out on the spot.' The captain and another officer rushed before the colonel and prevented him from carrying out his threat, the former exclaiming, 'Colonel, colonel, you must not shoot that pistol, he is our prisoner.' "[22]

B. F. Nelson was a very young Confederate Kentuckian who fought under three famous Confederate cavalrymen: John Hunt Morgan, Nathan Bedford Forrest, and Joseph Wheeler. His narrative, a short oral history in *Confederate Veteran,* attempts to explain one of the real problems encountered by prisoners, especially members of the Confederate cavalry and irregular units taken captive in the Civil War.[23] Was the Confederate cavalry operating simply as guerrillas? At the time, if such a status were determined by the captor in the field, then the captives were not POWs at all; they were considered to be outlaws committing capital crimes against the federal government. The Confederate cavalry units commanded by John Hunt Morgan, John Singleton Mosby, J. E. B. Stewart, Nathan Bedford Forrest, and others, therefore, presented a problem. To the federal authorities, cavalry meant irregulars, and, since irregulars at the time often fought not only for a political cause but also for money, executing captured Confederate irregulars became a relatively standard procedure in the Union army. However, once the Confederates began to reciprocate, the Union field officers began to change their ways. Nelson was fortunate not to be hanged and was granted full POW status. He recorded his capture by what he called criminals.

> There were good horses in that region and each decided to pick out a fresh one before starting back. So on the night of our departure, each of us mounted a good horse and rode all night and the next day. Taking for granted that all danger was over, we stopped, fed, and rested, little aware of the proximity of a notorious family of robbers by the name of Underwood, who claimed to be Federals or Confederates whichever was the most convenient for their purpose. About twenty-five or thirty of them surrounded us and took us to Flemingsburg and then to the jail at Maysville for the night.[24]

John Urban served with the Union army as an infantryman and was captured three times. Once he escaped, and once he was rescued in a raid led by General George Armstrong Custer, USA, while he was marching under guard to the rear. His third capture was his last. Urban found himself in Andersonville, and in *Battle Field and Prison Pen, or, Through the War and Thrice a Prisoner in Rebel Dungeons* (1882), one of the most popular captivity narratives of the Civil War, Urban narrates his third and final capture.

> The Rebels had advanced rapidly . . . and were sending a shower of bullets into the struggling mass in the swamp. I stopped for a moment to survey the situation, and then ran to the right for a short distance, and made an attempt to cross. I jumped for what I believed to be a firm spot of ground, but it proved to be anything but solid, for I sank into the mire almost to my knees. Thinking I could not get across, I worked myself back, and ran still further up to the right, looking for a better place to get over. I had lost considerable time in extricating myself from the mire; and as the rebel line, which had

extended a considerable distance past our left, had advanced and
taken possession of the ground on the other side, I found my retreat
cut off, and I was taken prisoner. . . . I dropped my gun and was
entirely disarmed, when the cowardly scoundrel thrust his bayonet
almost into my face, and swore that he would [cut] the Yankee head
clean off me. A few moments [later] . . . we were taken to the rear.[25]

Urban's experience resembles the thousands of Civil War captures that
found their way into publication as full-length narratives or as newspaper
and magazine accounts. None was particularly embellished with glory;
they were more apt to be straightforward chronicles of soldiers who made
conscious decisions to allow other soldiers to live. For valor and bravado
in a capture, the American public had to wait for the adventures of Richard
P. Hobson's capture in the Spanish-American War.

Only a few American prisoners were taken during the three-month
Spanish-American War (1898). Admiral William T. Samson, commanding
officer of the American North Atlantic squadron, attempted to intercept
and destroy the Spanish cruiser squadron under the command of Pascual
Cervera off Puerto Rico and Havana, Cuba. Cervera had figured on such
a pursuit and entered port at Santiago, Cuba. The American commander
faced a terrible problem: although his forces were superior to those of
the Spanish, there was only one approach to Santiago, through a narrow
channel that at the time was heavily mined and dangerous. Lieutenant
Richard P. Hobson, USN, a young naval construction engineer, volunteered to take an expendable 333-foot collier, the USS *Merrimac,* into
the harbor under fire, scuttle it, and in effect render the Spanish naval
force impotent inside Santiago harbor. Under Spanish fire, they sank the
collier in the wrong place; in the melee, their lifeboat was destroyed,
and they were taken prisoner. When they were picked up by Admiral
Cervera's personal lifeboat, the Spanish Admiral said, "Valiente!" Six
weeks later they were exchanged for a Spanish officer. All seven enlisted
men received the Medal of Honor in 1899; Hobson received the medal
in 1933 by a special act of Congress. Postwar books like Marshall Everett's
Exciting Experiences in Our War with Spain and the Filipinos (1900)
and Walter Millis's *The Martial Spirit* (1931) glory and romanticize
Hobson's exploits and the war in general. Everett cites a verse, "Hobson
and His Chosen Seven," which expresses the spirit of the time:

> Come kings and queens the world around,
> Whose power and fame all climes resound!
> Come, sailors bold and soldiers brave,
> Whose names shall live beyond the grave.
> Come, men and women, come boys and girls,

> Wherever our flag to the breeze unfurls!
> Come one, come all, let none stand back,
> Come praise the men of the *Merrimac!*
> Out from the water, out from the fire,
> Out from the jaws of death most dire!
> Far up in the fame and light of heaven
> See Hobson with his chosen seven![26]

Hobson and his seven men became the sweethearts of an American press hungry for nonadmiral, nongeneral, plain-man American military heroes. That his exploit had been a military failure—Hobson bungled the assignment, and nothing was blocked at all—was completely overlooked. Instead, Hobson became a symbol of courage, defiance, action, and devotion to duty in the heroic imagination of the American public.

During World War I, Americans were fighting the forces of Imperial Germany in several ways: as airmen, as ground-pounders or "doughboys" in the infantry, and as sailors delivering war materiel and fighting the German submarine threat at sea. Compared to captivity prior to and after this war, the experience was relatively genteel. Danger, of course, was omnipresent in combat, but from the POW narratives little doubt exists that a strong sense of honor, even chivalry, prevailed on both sides, a condition that faded away as the twentieth century rumbled on.

According to the *Report of the Adjutant General of the Army to the Secretary of War* in 1919, American forces took 48,976 German soldiers prisoner, and 4,120 American soldiers were captured on the western front (see Appendix 3B).[27] Experience, however, was preceded by large doses of negative war propaganda. The Allied popular press painted the Germans as barbarians and vice versa. James W. Gerard was the American ambassador to the German imperial court prior to World War I and during the period when the United States was the protecting power for POWs in Germany. Filled with hate and indignation for what he believed were German atrocities against innocent civilians and prisoners of war, he wrote *Face to Face with Kaiserism* (1918), a book filled with hearsay likely created as propaganda to gain American political support for the Allied cause. The book included a letter supposedly written by a nameless Prussian soldier who describes the German execution of Russian prisoners after the Battle of the Masurian Lakes in 1914.

> It was frightful, heart-rending, as these masses of human beings were driven to destruction. Above the terrible thunder of the cannons could be heard the cries of the Russians: "Oh, Prussians! Oh, Prussians!" But there was no mercy. Our Captain had ordered: "The whole lot must die; so rapid fire."

As I have heard, five men and one officer on our side went mad from those heart-rending cries. But most of my comrades and the officers joked as the unarmed and helpless Russians shrieked for mercy when they were being suffocated in the swamps and shot down. The order was: "Close up at it harder!" For days afterward, those yells followed me, and I dare not think of them or I shall go mad. There is no God, there is no morality, and no ethics any more. There are no human beings any more but only beasts.[28]

Gerard presented another letter, one more outrageously damning than the first one, from an unnamed, probably fictitious German soldier from the eastern front in Russian Poland, dated December 18, 1914. In part it said, "Wounded Russians are killed with bayonet according to orders, and Russians who have surrendered are often shot down in masses according to orders in spite of their prayers."[29] A third letter cited by Gerard supposedly came from a German soldier on the western front writing directly to the American government:

Englishmen who have surrendered are shot down in small groups. With the French one is more considerate. I ask whether men let themselves be taken prisoner in order to be disarmed and shot down afterward. Is that chivalry in battle?

It is no longer a secret among the people; one knows everywhere that few prisoners are taken; they are shot down in small groups. They say, "We don't want any unnecessary mouths to feed." Where there is no one to enter complaint, there is no justice. Is there, then, no power in the world which can put an end to these murders and rescue the victims?[30]

With this kind of vicious propaganda flooding the American book and pulp market prior to America's entry into World War I, it was no wonder that youthful Americans were surprised when they were not executed after capture. Mike Shallin belonged to L Company, 308th Infantry, 77th (Rainbow) Division. His narrative, an oral memoir called "The Guest of the Kaiser," published in Henry Berry's *Make the Kaiser Dance* (1978), details his life at the front and his capture in the trenches during an unexpected enemy ground probe.

It all happened on September 5, a few weeks before my outfit moved into the Meuse-Argonne mess. I was in charge of my squad, a rifle grenadier one. You know, those are the ones that shoot out those small bombs like a grenade. The only problem was we didn't have any bombs, so we weren't stronger with firepower than the rest of the group.

Well, we're moving up through this tough terrain when we spotted some men in the distance who appeared to be running toward us. We had been told to be very careful who we shot at, as the area was loaded with our patriots. These men kept getting closer, and our lead man kept watching them.

"Don't shoot at those guys," he instructed us. "I think they're our scouts." But now we're all looking at them and getting concerned.

"The hell they are," I warned. "I think they're Germans."

Just then they opened up on us with everything they had, tearing us to pieces. It was horrible. I'm not as sensitive as I used to be about it, but I can still hear this badly wounded buddy of mine yelling for his mother in Yiddish.

Well, we're naturally looking around trying to find someplace where we can set up a defense, but the first thing we knew they were on top of us. My sergeant and several of us had jumped into this old trench where we could see that the Germans were all around us, with one of them yelling, "Komerouse, Komerouse." We didn't have a prayer, so they nabbed all thirty-two of us.

After the capture, a serious incident took place that could have cost the life of every prisoner. One of Shallin's comrades shot a German sergeant after the Germans accepted the white flag of surrender. More than a violation of chivalry, it was a crime against the traditional rules of war. After soldiers show the white flag or raise their hands to indicate surrender, shooting ceases, and the rules of captivity come into force. According to Shalin:

After we surrendered, as we were crawling out of the trench, one of our men takes a shot at a German sergeant, badly wounding him. Christ, all hell broke loose. We were lucky they didn't machine-gun all of us. As the German was lying on the ground, he's cursing the devil out of us, then he bawls out in German, "If you're not going to tell me who fired, I'll do away with all of you."

Fortunately for us, a German officer came over at this time, wanting to know what's going on. Now we can hear all the Heinies crowing in German a mile a minute, and we're scared to death. As for myself, I actually didn't know who fired, so there's not a darn thing I can say.

Finally, the officer tells the wounded man that he can pick out the one who fired; he can shoot him—no one else. Believe it or not, the sergeant points at our medic, the only one of our men who didn't carry a weapon. Then our sergeant gets into the act: "Wait a minute," he pleads, "that man couldn't have done it—he didn't even have a gun."

At this point the German officer has had enough: "Take them all back to the rear," he orders, "and don't shoot anyone." I've been thanking God for that officer ever since.[31]

Pilots were a special breed of combatants, the knights of World War I. Aviation was a new technology, and men became pilots for a variety of reasons. Some were incorrigibly romantic individualists who refused to submit themselves to the discipline of army life, preferring to joust against a personal enemy in the air rather than leading infantry in battle on the ground. For the pilots, most of whom were officers, combat was a "dog-fight," a one-on-one game of mortal combat that combined individual luck, skill, marksmanship, and courage in a regimen that focused more on the pilot's personal quest for victory than on the army's mission in the war. Pilots were special to each other too. On both sides they behaved as if they belonged to a mystical brotherhood. If they survived the shootdown, before they became guests of the Kaiser in a prison camp they became luncheon guests of the victorious enemy squadron. Such was the case with two American combat pilots, James Norman "Jimmie" Hall and Harold B. Willis.

Hall never learned to drive an automobile but proved to be an excellent pilot and one of the most spectacular American airmen in World War I. In *My Island Home* (1935), he narrates his perceptions of the chaos of combat, the hazards of shootdown, the kindness of a German infantry medic, and the pilot's international, unwritten code of chivalry.

On the morning of May 7, 1918, . . . German anti-aircraft batteries were firing steadily at me, and, as I could not change direction, they were putting their bursts closer and closer. Of a sudden my plane gave a violent lurch and I started falling out of control. I had about a thousand meters altitude at the time, and it doesn't take a falling plane long to cover that distance, although it seemed long to me. I saw the ground coming swiftly up to meet me at various angles, and just before it did I pulled back hard on my stick, with the happy result that my Nieuport hit at not too steep an angle. The landing gear was sheared off and the fuselage skidded along the ground right side up.

By sheer luck I fell in an open field surrounded by woodland. German troops had their dugouts in the wood and came rushing from all sides toward my plane. When they had lifted me out I asked one of them who spoke English to set me on my feet; but the moment I touched the ground I knew that one or both of my ankles were broken and grabbed for their shoulders for the pain was severe. They carried me into a dugout near the border of the wood, and a few minutes later a Medical Corps orderly came. He examined my feet and told me that my right ankle was badly broken but he was not certain about the left one. Both hurt badly so I told him to leave off further examination until I was taken to a hospital. He bound up my ankles and put a dressing on my nose which was broken again. Then I was given a drink of water and a German cigarette, and I thought: "This is not as bad as it might have been."

Presently an Infantry officer appeared and asked for my papers. Luckily, I had nothing in my wallet but 800 francs in money—it was near to the first of the month—and my pilot's identification card. At least, I thought I had nothing else, but later I found a typewritten combat sheet of squadron orders in my trousers pocket. In a moment of unguarded leisure I wadded this into a little ball, slipped it into my mouth, chewed and swallowed it, my stomach receiving the morsel not gladly, but in a co-operative spirit. The officer kept my identification card, returning my wallet and money, taking my word for it that I had nothing else.

About an hour later, several other officers—airmen—arrived. They were pilots of the squadron which had attacked that morning, and I met the man I had been diving on when the fabric burst on my upper right wing. He spoke no English, but I conversed with him through another officer who spoke it well. It gave me a strange feeling to be talking with this man who should have been dead, and, I believe, would have been dead except for the accident to my Nieuport. I did not try to analyze this feeling at the time, but later, in the hospital, as I lay gazing at a fly-speckled ceiling, I regretted, as a pursuit-pilot, that I had not shot him down, and was deeply grateful, as a human being, that the event fell out as it did. They told me that, as a result of our combat, one of the pilots had been shot down in flames. (This plane, as I learned afterward, was brought down by Eddie Ricken- backer. It was his second victory.) The "living dead man" then sug- gested that I have lunch with them at their squadron before being taken to the hospital. I was not in a company mood just then, but, of course, accepted the invitation. Then they went out to look for my plane. . . .

When the German airmen returned they brought with them an offi- cer of an anti-aircraft battery in the vicinity who was very happy be- cause, he said, his battery would get the credit for bringing me down. "How's that?" I said. "You saw what happened to my plane." "Yes," he said, "but that isn't what brought you down." Then he told me that in their battery they had a 37 millimeter gun which had been fir- ing at me, and that one of the shells had stuck fast in my engine with- out exploding. I remembered, then, the sudden lurch my plane had given just before I started falling. Nevertheless, I couldn't believe what he had told me until I was shown the engine with the shell stuck fast in it. It seemed incredible. I have said earlier, that anti-aircraft batteries in World War I almost never made a direct hit upon a plane. And that is true. . . . So my own missed rendezvous with death was even more remarkable than I had supposed it to be.[32]

Harold B. Willis was an American volunteer flying combat missions with the Lafayette Escadrille in 1917 when his aircraft engine began to disintegrate under fire. Pilots did not use parachutes during World War I; if the aircraft was shot down, they went down with it. Nothing can be more unnerving than to know that one is alone and helpless and about to face the enemy on his terms. Willis describes his shootdown.

On the 17th of August 1917 I was acting as escort to a group of bombing planes when two enemy machines dove down on us and attacked my convoy. I was flying a Spad monoplane, a chase machine. I fought the enemy planes off to the best of my ability, but before very long their fire put my motor out of commission and the machine began to dive. As I neared the ground, I had for a second the idea of nosediving and burying myself with my plane; but, seeing a wood, I instinctively cleared it, and landed on the top of a little hill. One of the German pilots, flying over me, waved his hand and landed close to me, followed by his comrades. They greeted me very politely. They were young men perfectly correct in their manners.

My plane was completely wrecked: thirty bullets in the fuselage, the motor and the radiator, half the cables cut through, the wings riddled. And so finished the career of a machine that had served me for many months.

I was glad that I was in the hands of the aviation officers, as we had a certain sense of camaraderie, of which there was never any among the other troops. They took me to their camp and gave me lunch. There I waited for an automobile which took me to the fortress of Montmedy.

When Willis finally had the time to reflect, he contemplated the impact of his captivity. "The first three days were terrible. It is at such times that one is sorry to be alive, especially on waking in the morning. Asleep, one dreams of one's country and of the front, and of one's friends. But when one is face to face with the reality, without hope, without news, it is terrible."[33]

At sea, terror came with the unexpected explosion of a submarine-launched torpedo disintegrating the hull of a ship. Far from being watertight below decks, most torpedoed ships of the period sank like stones. Crew members and passengers had only moments to jump from the relative comfort and warmth of the ship into a very deadly and cruel ocean. Cold weather and heavy seas made survival nearly impossible if a person were left in the water longer than a few minutes. Lifeboats were fragile craft, rarely in good working order, and certainly not seaworthy for a mean Atlantic. On May 31, 1918, the weather was cool and clear. The Atlantic was relatively calm for a change, and the USS *Abraham Lincoln,* a captured German merchant ship of the Hamburg-American Line converted for transport use by the American navy, was heading west from the coast of France toward the United States with virtually empty holds. A large ship capable of hauling eight thousand tons of cargo or five thousand troops, the *Abraham Lincoln* was running at twelve knots that morning until she was rocked by two explosions. General Quarters was sounded. The crew ran to their battle stations, but the *U-90*'s torpedoes had already done their worst. The force of the explosion crushed the No. 12 lifeboat, and threw it up on deck not ten feet from where Lieutenant Edouard V. Isaacs, USN, stood. When he reached the after control tower, all the guns and boats were manned, but at 0910 he received the report that holds 5 and 6 were flooded with water approaching No. 1 deck. He reported this to the captain, who ordered him to abandon ship. At 0915 all hands aft were off the ship in lifeboats and life rafts. The ship had been gradually settling since the third explosion, and the main deck was within a few inches of the surface of the sea. The USS *Abraham Lincoln* was sinking by the stern, and Lieutenant Isaacs would soon be taken prisoner, the only American naval line officer captured at sea in World War I. With waves washing over the deck, Isaacs jumped on a life raft with his messenger, and the old ship, turning over gently to starboard, put her nose in the air and went down.[34]

Isaac's capture was not random. The commanding officer of the submarine, Kapitän Leutnant Remy, a professional naval officer and German naval academy graduate, had been ordered to search for and capture the captain or senior surviving officer. The other ships in the convoy were far in the distance, and the submarine had time to scan the survivors' lifeboats for their officer prisoner. Although Isaacs lost his cap in the sinking, Captain Remy identified him as an officer; there was no way to hide the fact. Isaacs became a prisoner of war aboard the *U-90* for the remainder of its patrol. Isaacs records the event in his narrative, *Prisoner of the U-90* (1919).

"Come aboard." We pulled alongside, and I rose to step out of the lifeboat. The men, realizing that I was about to leave them, perhaps never to return, raised their voices in protest and tried to restrain me.

I turned to calm them, telling them not to worry, that it was only the fortunes of war, and stepping on the gunwale, I grasped the hands of those nearest me in a heartfelt good-bye and jumped on the deck of the submarine. . . .

As I walked along the deck a German sailor came behind me and took my pistol. I then gave him the whole belt. Going up to the conning tower I saluted the officer whom I took to be the captain. He addressed me in rather fair English as follows:

"Are you the captain of the *President Lincoln?*"

"No, sir," I replied. "I believe the captain went down with the ship, for I have not seen him since. I am the First Lieutenant."

"I am Captain Remy," he said. "My orders are to take the senior officer prisoner whenever I sink a man-o'-war. You will remain aboard and point out your captain to me. . . ." When Captain Remy finished speaking he offered me a glass of sherry, which I took with thanks, for the water had been rather cold and I was numb from my waist down. We then cruised slowly among the boats and rafts. . . .

The submarine then left the scene of the sinking and cruised up and down on the surface for the next two days. Early the following morning a radio message from an American destroyer was intercepted and Captain Remy gave it to me to read. It said: "*President Lincoln* sunk. Survivors saved. A few missing."[35]

Like his comrades flying against and shot down by the Germans in World War I, Isaacs would be the guest of his captors before he would be transferred to a prison camp as a POW. The relationship between combatants would be cordial and professional from the first day of captivity until his transfer to POW facilities deep in Germany.

Captivity for the more than 4,000 other American POWs would end in 1918 with very few deaths. The same cannot be said of the captivity experiences of World War II. In Europe and Asia during World War II, 130,201 American army, air corps, and marines were captured by enemy forces. Additionally, 7,300 American civilian men, women, and children were captured and interned in Asia and the Pacific Islands in 1941–1942.[36] Over 14,000 died, and by 1945, 116,129 had been returned to American military control.

When the war broke out, the United States had garrisoned many Pacific islands with a minimum of forces. Marine, navy, and army units were rushed to Wake Island, Guam, and the Philippines in 1941 in order to establish a "presence." Shortly after the strike on Pearl Harbor on December 7, 1941, the Japanese attacked and invaded many American installations in the western Pacific, and in less than six months every American in the region was either dead, a prisoner, or actively engaged in guerrilla warfare against the Japanese. The American strategy for defending the Philippines was called "War Plan Orange—3" and assumed that the Japanese would attack the island of Luzon and the capitol city of Manila. The American plan recognized Japanese military superiority and called for a tactical retreat to the Bataan Peninsula that protected Manila. Forces in place on Bataan were supposed to provide a defense perimeter for the fortress at Corregidor that in turn would play for time to permit the fleet stationed at Pearl Harbor to sail to the rescue.[37]

The strategy was fatally flawed. The fleet had been severely damaged in Pearl Harbor, and although General MacArthur had 120,000 men on paper, most of the force was made up of untrained Filipino reserve soldiers, many of whom had never fired a shot in combat. Although by December 1941 nearly 23,000 American soldiers had arrived in the Philippines to bolster the force on station, they were garrison troops who had no experience of combat. After the Japanese invasion and General MacArthur's departure for Australia, communications and logistics broke down in the American commands, turning what had looked to be a massive fighting force into a starved, munitionless, defeated, and retreating mélange of men. Major General Edward P. King, Jr., USA, commanding officer of the Luzon forces, officially surrendered to Colonel Motoo Nakayama on April 9, 1942. Although General Jonathan M. Wainwright on Corregidor ordered him not to surrender, he did anyway, claiming he had no choice. Approximately 17,000 Americans and 12,000 Filipino scouts were captured by the Japanese army when Bataan fell in April and Corregidor finally fell in May 1942. During the first year of captivity, 30 percent of the American prisoners, more than 5,000 men, and 80 percent of the Filipinos had died (see Appendix 3E).[38]

Wake Island is a tiny horseshoe-shaped speck in the Pacific ocean. Its airfield represented a threat to the shipping lanes the Japanese wanted to control. Major James P. S. Devereux, USMC, was the senior marine and second in command on Wake Island when the Japanese attacked on December 7, 1941, just hours after Pearl Harbor.[39] His command fought the invaders, but the defenders were quickly overwhelmed and forced to surrender on December 23. In all, 1,555 marines, navy men, and civilians were captured, of whom 100 died in captivity. Devereux, a consummate warrior, was angry with his Japanese captors but determined to uphold the rules of honor in surrender. His narrative, *The Story of Wake Island* (1947), told in the language of the time, complete with racial slurs against the Japanese, explains the very complicated event from a commander's point of view. Going beyond his own capture, Major Devereux describes the difficult and complex surrender of the entire garrison in great detail, beginning with, "Cease firing. Destroy all weapons. The island is being surrendered."[40] Unlike captures that are primarily personal events, the Devereux narrative shows how heavy the weight of command can become in captivity. Wake Island's surrender—the first to the Japanese army—shocked the American military, especially the Marine Corps, and a press report insisted that Devereux radioed defiantly, "Send us more Japs." After Devereux's release from captivity in 1945, he denied the report; nonetheless, the spirit of his defiance, real or fabricated, became legend in the United States military establishment during World War II and in the Marine Corps ever since.

In Europe, in the Second World War, no free lunch with the enemy squadron awaited the captured airman. Instead, the prisoner was transported to the *Durchgangslager-Luftwaffe,* commonly called the *Dulag-Luft,* a facility that served as a transient holding camp and interrogation center for recently downed Allied airmen. Although stays in the Dulag-Luft varied in duration, Americans received their first taste of intense interrogation with hidden microphones, false prisoners planted among their ranks, and real hunger. After the stay in the Dulag-Luft, the Kriegies were removed to more permanent Stalags or Oflags. Kenneth W. Simmons writes in *Kriegie* (1960) that after his shootdown: "I gathered my parachute and Mae West and stumbled onto the highway in my stocking feet. I tried to appear unafraid. Every muscle in my body ached, but I put on a calm face showing no sign of distress. At a command from the Lieutenant, a guard of six soldiers formed about me. We moved off in marching formation with the young officer out in front. As we started through the village scattered civilians gathered to observe me. I saw bitter faces and wild staring eyes."[41] Simmons describes one of the grimmest circumstances in World War II: the German civilian response to Allied bombings and the subsequent threat to Allied POWs that hatred posed. No war in Europe since the Thirty Years War (1618–1648) had disturbed the lives or caused the deaths of so many civilians. In effect, the soldiers who captured the Americans had to protect them against the wrath of the civilians.

The ground war was even more grim and lacked any degree of chivalry. Between December 16 and 25, 1944, 23,554 American soldiers were captured by German forces during the Battle of the Bulge in the Ardennes. The battle would have been a catastrophe for Allied forces but for a drastic shift in the weather that allowed Allied aircraft to interdict and destroy advancing German armored columns. In the midst of the battle, American infantrymen suffered the worst atrocity experienced in combat with German forces during World War II. The Americans were pushing toward their assigned positions in Luxembourg when they encountered Waffen SS troopers commanded by Colonel Jochen Peiper. "B" Battery of the 285th Field Artillery Observation Battalion surrendered after a brief battle near the town of Malmedy, Belgium. They were told to line up in a tight formation and wait for trucks to take them to the rear, and then a junior

SS officer ordered a nearby tank to open fire on the prisoners. Three machine guns began firing; some Americans broke and ran for their lives; most fell where they stood. After all the prisoners had fallen, SS officers and sergeants approached the scene with small arms to finish off the survivors. If they moaned they were shot; if they moved they were shot. Even after the foot soldiers left, tanks continued to spray the heaps of dead with machine-gun fire. But not all were dead. Several survived beneath the bodies by playing dead; others survived by running to safety when the shooting began. When the smoke cleared there were eighty-one bodies: forty-one were shot in the head while they were lying on the ground; three men got away and were rescued; twenty-six were finally pulled to safety by American troops who discovered them after the SS left. After the war, the American army charged Colonel Peiper and some of his officers with war crimes for the Malmedy incident. After his conviction, he was sentenced to death by hanging, but a lenient court later commuted the sentence to a short stay in prison. After his release, Peiper, who was known as "Blow Torch" to his troops, moved to France and finally died in a mysterious house fire.

American capture in Korea by the North Korean army began in 1950. Because the Korean War was fought mainly on the ground, the vast majority of American and United Nations POWs were infantrymen. Early in the war many Americans and United Nations soldiers were executed on the spot; to their credit, the Chinese Communists were more lenient. It was cold in Korea when Sergeant Lloyd Pate's commanding officer ordered him to fight no more. Although he retained the means and will to resist the enemy soldiers, his lieutenant realized that his unit was overwhelmed and surrounded. Any more resistance would have been a waste of lives. He ordered his men to lay down their weapons and surrendered the unit to the enemy. In his postrepatriation narrative, *Reactionary* (1956), Pate narrates his capture by the Chinese People's Volunteers:

> Before we knew it there were about two hundred Chinese all around us—in the ditch in front of us, behind us, on the banks on each side. There was a lieutenant with us and we held a quick conference to see what the majority wanted. A few of us wanted to fight it out and the rest wanted to surrender. The lieutenant gave a direct order to those of us who wanted to fight. He said to lay down our weapons and surrender for the benefit of the majority. . . . The guards they put on us came over looking for the stuff they could confiscate. They took my Lord Elgin watch, my Parker pen and pencil set, a ring I had bought in Japan, my cigarettes, and some chewing gum. They got watches and rings off practically everybody in the group.[42]

Beginning in 1963, American infantrymen, advisers to the South Vietnamese Army, began to be captured. James N. Rowe was a first lieutenant
in the United States Army's Special Forces who in 1963 fought a furious
but losing engagement with the Vietcong in the Mekong Delta region of
South Vietnam. Rowe was captured while aiding his wounded comrade,
Captain Humbert "Rocky" Versace, who, with Army Sergeant Kenneth
Roraback, would later be executed by his captors in reprisal for the Saigon
government's execution of a Vietcong terrorist. In his narrative *Five Years
to Freedom* (1971), Rowe describes his capture:

> I tied the bandage and slowly turned my head. There was the muzzle
> of an American carbine and behind it, the Vietcong. I stood up, the
> two VC pulled my equipment harness from my shoulders, grabbed
> my arms, and quickly tied them behind me, once at the elbows, once
> at the wrists.
> "God bless you, Nick."
> "God bless you too, Rocky."
> "Di!" [Go]
> They threw me down the path.[43]

Most prisoners in North Vietnam were airmen from the navy, Marine
Corps, and air force who were shot down by antiaircraft batteries, small
arms, or surface-to-air missiles during combat missions over North Vietnam. From time to time, aircraft would collide in combat, or pilots suffered misfires or equipment malfunctions, and, as one navy combat pilot
and POW, Richard Stratton, commented, they would in effect shoot themselves down. With the aircraft on fire and probably disintegrating rapidly,
each pilot had to balance the certainty of immediate death against the
fear of captivity; either eject into the enemy's hands or die immediately.

All pilots and navigators carried survival equipment: pistol, radio, flares,
compass, money, and personal effects, but none of these items did much
good when a parachute's passenger hit the ground with a broken leg,
injured back, or even more serious wounds. The downed aviator was a
rat in a maze. Regardless of the circumstances, every shootdown was a
traumatic experience. Injured or not, the airman's first thought was survival, his second thought was escape, and his third thought was rescue.
Most were rescued by Search and Rescue, or SAR, in North Vietnam; many
were not.

Howard Rutledge describes his shootdown and capture in 1965 as a
surprise. He was an old veteran fighter pilot of Korea and had not
expected to be shot down in Vietnam. Rutledge was hurt on impact and
in self-defense drew his pistol and shot an attacker. Fortunately his resistance to capture led to no reprisals. Robinson Risner, in *The Passing of*

the Night (1973), calls himself a victim of pure bad luck. Risner had been shot down and rescued once before; his capture in Vietnam seemed inevitable to him. After a successful ejection from his mortally damaged aircraft, Risner's parachute opened, and he fell silently to earth. On the ground and wounded, Risner saw angry armed North Vietnamese militiamen surrounding him. At that moment he faced his first cardinal decision: surrender himself and his freedom or die. Risner surrendered.

What was it like to capture an American pilot? Van Anh, a member of the People's Army of Vietnam (PAVN) in 1964, participated in the capture of an American pilot in Laos and narrates his experience in David Charnoff and Doan Van Toai's *Portrait of the Enemy* (1986). Stationed in Laos, Anh and his comrades responded to an alarm that signaled an air attack and fired all the small arms at the aircraft they could. After they destroyed the plane, the North Vietnamese soldiers captured the American pilot.

> The pilot came down into the jungle about three kilometers [almost two miles] away. We ran, struggling against time to get to the place where he fell before his comrades could get him. About fifteen minutes after he parachuted, the sky was full of jets, helicopters, and an L-19 spotter plane. We climbed the mountain, past the waterfall while they circled around, looking for him in the wrong place. It took us almost six hours to find and capture him, but by then the sky had clouded over, and the planes couldn't see anything underneath. . . . The battalion commander told another comrade and me to write down the interrogation. This was the first time in my life I had met an American.[44]

North Vietnamese soldiers would meet many more Americans before hostilities ended in 1973. Colonel Norman A. McDaniel, USAF, was an officer-crewman on a mission over North Vietnam in 1966, early in the war. His aircraft was struck by a missile and exploded into a fireball, and McDaniel faced his first decision: bail out or die. He left the burning aircraft for captivity in North Vietnam, which lasted from March 1966 to February 12, 1973. According to McDaniel:

> I went there not expecting to become a prisoner of war, but I knew that that possibility existed. And so as I flew my combat missions over North Vietnam, I was well aware of the perils and the possible dangers.
>
> On the morning of July 20, 1966 the EB-66C aircraft which I was flying—which is an electronics reconnaissance airplane—was hit by surface-to-air missiles. Fortunately, the detonation of the missile was not directly upon the airplane. Had it been, certainly, I would not be your speaker tonight. But fortunately, or unfortunately, the

missile detonated close enough to the airplane that some of the fragments punctured the fuel tanks and the plane caught on fire immediately. Within a matter of seconds, I moved from a position of relative security—expecting to complete my mission and return to my base to rest and prepare for the next mission—to a position of imminent danger and possible death. Because as the plane went out of control, began to lose altitude, lose oxygen, pressurization, communication, I had to make a decision to stay with the airplane or to eject.

There were six of us on the crew; four ejected downward, two ejected upward. I was supposed to be the first one to eject downward. Since we had lost communication I had to make that decision myself. And so I chose to eject.

When he landed, he met his enemy face to face.

As I descended, I saw holes being ripped in the parachute above me, and I heard the bullets zinging past my ear because the North Vietnamese were shooting at me as I descended in the chute. As soon as I hit the ground, the enemy converged upon me and captured me immediately. I had no chance to escape. I was stripped of my flight suit, flying boots, and clothing. My hands were tied behind my back, and I marched down the knoll of the little grassy hill to a hut. In the front yard of the hut was a pit which they began to force me into. I assumed at that time that this was the execution place, and for some reason I was not afraid. It might have been shock or it might have been the realization that it was my time. I thought to myself. "Well I have done my best, and I guess it's my time to go."

On the ground, McDaniel faced angry captors who made no bones about his status; McDaniel was a "war criminal" and an "air pirate." In a conversation with journalist Wallace Terry, McDaniel commented:

I could smell the hate. Some of them had pistols. Some guns. Some shook knives at me, shovels, even hoes. They motioned for me to stand up. Then they inched forward, about fifty of them, communist militia, like popular forces. . . . They made me strip down to my shorts and T-shirt. They took off my boots. They tied my hands behind me. . . . When I mentioned the Geneva Convention, they laughed in my face. "You're not qualified to be treated as a prisoner of war. You're a criminal. Black American criminal."[45]

Giles R. Norrington piloted a naval reconnaissance aircraft, an RA-5C Vigilante, from the USS *Enterprise* in 1968 when he was shot out of the sky over North Vietnam. As a professional military man, he includes in his oral narrative a description of his ship, which, essentially, signified his institutional community. As a deeply religious and moral man, Norrington took a moment to describe his thoughts and feelings that Sunday morning before his capture.

On the fifth day of May 1968 I was serving aboard the aircraft carrier USS *Enterprise*—a real speedboat. . . . She would do an easy thirty-five knots in the water, and that was impressive enough. . . . I might add she was a thousand feet long and grossed over eighty-nine thousand dead weight tons, and carried a combat complement of something like ninety-three aircraft. She was an awesome fighting machine. I had a great deal of pride in that ship, in the air wing that was embarked in her, and in my own squadron Reconnaissance Attack Squadron I [which was] flying the RA-5C Vigilante Aircraft.

I had arisen early that morning, not being able to sleep any more. I had my two hours of rest for the night . . . not atypical in combat operations at sea. I went top-side on the carrier . . . just to enjoy being outside and being with my God. It was, after all, a Sunday.

I walked the flight deck and watched a few sailors who were making the initial preparations for the organized chaos of flight deck activities that would begin several hours later. It was a grand day to be alive. I had a wonderful breakfast following my walk on the flight deck, and then I went to the air operations section, picked up my mission for the day and went to the integrated operational intelligence center and met my navigator, now Captain Richard Tangeman, who was then lieutenant, and we began to prepare ourselves for the mission that lay ahead. It was by no means an ordinary mission. Because no mission was ordinary over North Vietnam.

Norrington's shootdown happened in an instant.

It was no more than fifteen minutes into the flight [that] they blew the right wing off my aircraft. Now, for those of you who have experience in aviation, you have the intellectual knowledge that one-wing aircraft do not fly. . . . I am here as living proof, empirically, that I have proven scientifically in a laboratory environment that one-wing aircraft do not fly. . . . I had just entered a whole new realm of my life. For forty-five minutes I successfully evaded capture . . . [but] just as I made my last radio call to the aircraft that were flying air rescue overhead, I was captured . . . by a young man . . . who could not have been more than sixteen or seventeen years old. He was a young militiaman with an ancient rusty Czechoslovakian rifle. And you talk about the crazy thoughts that go through your mind in difficult circumstances? My first thought when I saw that rusty rifle was, "Oh my God, if he shoots me I'm going to die of rust poisoning."[46]

Capture extinguished Norrington's individual and institutional freedom and simultaneously introduced him to the catastrophe of survival in difficult circumstances. The only set of rules Norrington knew were derived from the international statutes he learned in professional studies and in survival school. Faced with an unknown future and the distinct possibility of no future at all, Giles R. Norrington joined the thousands of POWs who marched ahead of him into enemy hands, bound and sometimes blindfolded, wounded from battle, exhausted but grateful to be alive, captured.

Capture represents the beginning of the prisoner's descent into his own personal hell, there to survive or die, often at the whim of the captor. Capture itself is, perhaps, the dimmest, most frightful moment of the captivity experience. For the person involved, it is a radical, catastrophic shift in status: from freedom to captivity, from relative independence to total dependence, from institutional protection to personal vulnerability, from the assumption of the rule of law to the faint hope that some laws might be obeyed by the captors. Ultimately, capture means a shift from civilization as the prisoner knows it to an alien value system. In 1944, an army airman, Harold Longacre, remembered his shootdown in a short, simple verse he called "God's Minute," so titled because he had only a minute to leave his aircraft and to make his choice between certain death and capture. In Longacre's mind, the decision was clear; at least, in a stalag he might have a chance to survive.

> I had just a minute
> Only sixty seconds in it
> Forced upon me, couldn't refuse it
> Didn't seek it, didn't choose it
> But it's upon me to use it
> Give account if I abuse it
> Just a tiny little minute
> But eternity was in it.[47]

Nothing is worse for the military combatant than to have to lay down arms before the enemy. Although surrender is not considered dishonorable when a commander is no longer capable of fighting, it tarnishes a combatant's sense of personal honor. Universally, soldiers are taught that the objective of war and individual combat is to win. Surrender implies losing, and Americans in particular dislike losers, regardless of the context.

Treatment at capture depended on the respect of one combatant for the other, and ill treatment rarely began before the prisoners met the rearguard. Common to all POWs is the passage through the needle's eye, the small opening between life and death that guides them into a wholly new and different world. Capture in World War I showed that chivalry might be possible; most captivities displayed very little. The technology of World War II raised the level of hatred among the civilian populations as their homes were shattered by bombs. Capture in Korea and especially in Vietnam became an indefinite sentence, because no one knew how long the war would rage. But most important, capture meant the possibility of survival, and survival might be the first stage of victory for the prisoner of war.

CHAPTER SIX

Prisoners under Guard:
Removes and Death Marches

Inside the cattle cars, we had started a trip that would turn men into swine.
                                              Kenneth W. Simmons (1960)

In the forest wars, especially for Puritans, captivity was a ritual of redemption. For Puritan prisoners, removes represented the second phase of redemptive suffering in the captivity experience. Assuming that captivity was imposed by God as a test, trial, or ordeal of faith, some prisoners believed that the remove was a punishment for sins, and others believed it signified steps in the gathering of tangible evidence of divine providence and God's wisdom.[1]

According to the Puritans' narratives, small groups of Indian captors forced them over icebound streams and mountain passes. The weak and unfit died on the trail; others, including the children, were mutilated, beaten, and killed. Death was always close. Male captives, if not killed during the attack, were considered to have forfeited their lives if they surrendered. In some cases they survived captivity; in others they were taken to the captor's village and tortured to death.[2] The situation for women was different. In the forest wars, female prisoners were more highly valued; they could be bartered, traded, assimilated, sold to the French, or ransomed back to their people. Therefore, they were kept alive by their captors more often than infants, very young children, or men over the age of twelve.

Mary Rowlandson's intent was not only to show how Puritan life was a struggle between God and Satan for the possession of a person's individual soul but also to show the destructive nature of her captors. She reminded her audience that "it was their usual manner to remove when they had done any mischief, lest they should be found out, and so they did at this time. We went about three or four miles, and there they built a great wigwam big enough to hold a hundred Indians, which they did in preparation to a great day of dancing."[3]

For many captives in the forest wars and thereafter, hunger during the remove was a pervasive misery that dominated their lives, and Rowlandson made that fact clear. To her, captivity was indeed a fallen condition and a punishment for individual or collective sinfulness. She observed

117

the food her captors ate on the trail and perceived her captors to be inhuman beasts of the forest.

> The chief and commonest food was groundnuts. They eat also nuts and acorns, artichokes, lily roots, ground beans, and several other weeds and roots that I know not.
>   They would pick up old bones, and cut them to pieces at the joints, and if they were full of worms and maggots, they would scald them over the fire to make the vermin come out and then boil them and drink up the liquor and beat the great ends of them in a mortar and so eat them. They would eat horses' guts and ears, and all sorts of wild birds which they could catch; also bear, venison, beaver, tortoise, frogs, squirrels, dogs, skunks, rattlesnakes, yea, the very bark of trees, besides all sorts of creatures and provision which they plundered from the English.[4]

In nearly the same breath, Mary condemned her captors as enemies of God on one hand and instruments of God's wrath on the other:

> I can but stand in admiration to see the wonderful power of God in providing for such a vast number of our enemies in the wilderness where there was nothing to be eaten but from hand to mouth. Many times in a morning the generality of them would eat up all they had and yet have some further supply. . . . It is said, Psalm. 81:13,14, "Oh, that My people had hearkened to Me, and Israel had walked in My ways; I should soon have subdued their enemies and turned My hand against their adversaries." But now our perverse and evil carriages in the sight of the Lord have so offended Him that instead of turning His hand against them the Lord feeds and nourishes them up to be a scourge to the whole land.[5]

Peter Williamson was captured and made a prisoner during the French and Indian War. Unlike many male prisoners, he was allowed to live. His original narrative was titled *French and Indian Cruelty: Exemplified in the Life and Various Vicissitudes of Fortune of Peter Williams, a Disbanded Soldier* (1757); a later version was called *Sufferings of Peter Williamson, One of the Settlers in the Back Parts of Pennsylvania, Written by Himself.* In both he describes several removes, and like Rowlandson, comments that his captors fed him poorly. "They would sometimes give me a little meat, but my chief food was Indian corn." Then they traveled deep into the back country, and Williamson became a beast of burden for his captors.

As soon as the snow was quite gone, they set forth on their journey toward the back parts of the province of Pennsylvania; all leaving their wives and children behind in their wigwams. They were now a formidable body, amounting to near 150. My business was to carry what they thought proper to load me with but they never entrusted me with a gun. We marched on several days without any thing particular occurring, almost famished for want of provisions; for my part, I had nothing but a few stalks of Indian corn, which I was glad to eat dry: nor did the Indians themselves fare much better, for as we drew near the plantations they were afraid to kill any game, lest the noise of their guns should alarm the inhabitants.[6]

By contrast, some captives were not mistreated by Indians during their removes. Although she continued to fear her captors, Barbara Leininger comments that on her march she was treated relatively well.

The next morning we were taken about two miles further into the forest, while the most of the Indians again went to kill and plunder. Toward evening they returned with nine scalps and five prisoners. On the third day the whole band came together and divided the spoils. In addition to large quantities of provisions, they had taken fourteen horses and ten prisoners, namely, one man, one woman, five girls and three boys. We two girls, as also two of the horses, fell to the share of an Indian named Galasko. We traveled with our new master for two days. He was tolerably kind, and allowed us to ride all the way, while he and the rest of the Indians walked.[7]

What Barbara did not know during her remove was that her captors would later attempt to assimilate her into the tribe. What her captors did not know was that she would escape.

During the Revolution American soldiers captured by regular British, Hessian, or loyalist forces on land were removed from the battlefield and interned in dungeons, churches, or local jails. There were no military prison facilities set aside for them. The status problem—whether the Americans were rebels or bona fide soldiers of a sovereign nation—caught the captured members of the American Continental army and soldiers of state militias at their weakest point. The term "rebel" was popular, and the loyalist press constantly referred to them as rebels: the rebel army, a rebel officer, rebel troops, rebel horses, rebel ships, the rebel fleet, rebel currency, rebel newspapers, rebel houses, and even rebel cattle.[8]

Twenty-seven men taken by the British in 1775 after the American surrender at Bunker Hill became the first American POWs in the Revolution. In these early months, no one knew how the captured men would be handled, and Washington, mindful of the precedents to be set in 1775, tried to establish that the captured Americans were prisoners of war, not criminals or rebels.[9] If the prisoners were treated simply as rebels, they were vulnerable to any form of reprisal the British might wish to inflict. General Washington knew this and wished to forestall criminal procedures and possible executions if at all possible. Perhaps Washington knew it was going to be a long war. About 300 soldiers surrendered to the British at Quebec in 1776, including Ethan Allen. After General Howe's first offensive in America, more than 4,000 Americans surrendered. By 1780, thousands of American Continental soldiers were held as prisoners by the British in America, especially after the big captures of Continental troops on Long Island and the American defeats at Fort Washington, Camden, and Charleston, South Carolina.

At sea, when American privateers were captured, the prisoners were often put into holds for the trip to England or transport back to America. They knew full well that their destination would be either a prison hulk or a prison in England. The first American prisoners were confined in the British prison hulks in Plymouth and Portsmouth, but when this arrangement was found to be both dangerous and unsatisfactory, they were sent inland to Winchester. Forton Prison, originally built as a hospital for British seamen, held many Americans; Millbay or Mill Prison housed others. Deal Prison in Scotland and Kinsale in Ireland also held Americans. Regardless where Americans were held, the British regarded them as traitors and pirates and disqualified them generally from parole or exchange.[10] There were, however, exceptions to the exchange policy. Henry Laurens, the former president of the Continental Congress, was captured while sailing to Holland as the American Ambassador. He received special treatment in the Tower of London until he was exchanged for General Cornwallis after the surrender at Yorktown. Others found themselves imprisoned in Senegal, on the Isle of Guernsey, in Portugal, and even in Halifax, Nova Scotia. On the way to jail, the prisoners' initial shock at being POWs gave way to feelings of panic and despair. Deprivations of food and water took their toll. Meanwhile, the captors stripped the prisoners of all their valuables, including their pride, as the guards verbally taunted and physically abused them. From the narrative sources of Ethan Allen and others it is clear that what angered prisoners the most was the humiliation they received from members of the loyalist population.[11]

As in later wars, prisoners became an inconvenience during the Revolution. Sailors fared worse than soldiers in British hands. Thomas Andros explains in his narrative that after his ship took an English prize ship at sea, the prize master made the terrible mistake of heading for loyalist Long Island. There the crew was captured and transported to prison hulks off Brooklyn.[12] Colonel Ethan Allen describes his six-week remove in irons aboard the British ship *Gaspee.* First condemning his captors, Allen comments that, "All the ship's crew . . . behaved toward the prisoners with that spirit of bitterness which is the peculiar characteristic of Tories, when they have the friends of America in their power, measuring their loyalty to the English King by the barbarity, fraud, and deceit which they exercise toward the Whigs."[13] Allen describes his irons in great detail.

The handcuff was of the common size and form, but my leg irons I should imagine would weigh thirty pounds; the bar was eight feet long, and very substantial; the shackles which encompassed my ankles were very tight. I was told by the officer who put them on that it was the King's plate, and I heard other of their officers say that it would weigh forty weight. The irons were so close upon my ankles that I could not lay down in any other manner than on my back. I was put into the lowest and most wretched part of the vessel, where I got the favor of a chest to sit on; the same answered for my bed at night. I procured some little blocks of the guard, who day and night with fixed bayonets watched over me, to lie under each end of the large bar of my leg irons, to preserve my ankles from galling when I sat on the chest, or lay back on the same, though most of the time, night and day, I sat on it.[14]

Allen, characteristic of a resisting POW, describes confrontation with one of his captors while on his shipboard remove to England:

About the same time a lieutenant among the Tories insulted me in a grievous manner, saying that I ought to have been executed for my rebellion against New York, and spit in my face. Upon which, though I was handcuffed, I sprang at him with both hands and knocked him partly down, but he scrambled along into the cabin, and I after him; there he got under the protection of some men with fixed bayonets, who were ordered to make ready to drive me into the place aforementioned. I challenged him to fight, notwithstanding the impediments that were on my hands, and had the exalted pleasure to see the rascal tremble for fear.[15]

Charles Andrews was captured early in the War of 1812. First he was confined aboard the prison ship *Hector* at Plymouth, but due to crowding and a number of escapes, the prisoners were removed from the ship and ordered to the Dartmoor prison in the English back country about seventeen miles from Plymouth. In his narrative, *The Prisoners' Memoirs, or, Dartmoor Prison* (1815), Andrews describes his march from one prison to another.

Two hundred and fifty dejected and unhappy sufferers, already too wretched, were called, each of whom received a pair of shoes, and his allowance of bread and salt fish. Orders were then immediately given, for every man to deliver up his bed and hammock, and to repair forthwith into the different launches belonging to the ships of war, which were along-side the ship, ready to receive them. The prisoners entered, surrounded by the guards and seamen belonging to the *Hector* and *La Brave*. We were landed at New Passage, near Plymouth, and were placed under the guard of a company of soldiers, equal in number to the prisoners! Orders were then given to march at half past ten in the morning, with a positive injunction that no prisoner should step out of, or leave the ranks, on pain of instant death. Thus, we marched, surrounded by a strong guard, through a heavy rain, and over a bad road, with only our usual and scanty allowance of bread and fish. We were allowed to stop only once during the march of seventeen miles.

We arrived at Dartmoor late in the after part of the day, and found the ground covered with snow. Nothing could form a more dreary prospect than that which now presented itself to our hopeless view. Death itself, with the hopes of an hereafter, seemed less terrible than this gloomy prison.[16]

Thousands of Americans made the same march that Andrews and his fellow prisoners made from the prison hulks to Dartmoor Prison in Devonshire. Some died; most lived to bring their stories home to a disbelieving public. Long marches would continue, however, as new prisoners came under the command of new captors in the hot climate of Mexico.

After their capture, men of the Louisville cavalry, known as the Encarnacion prisoners, faced a long march of 300 miles from Encarnacion to San Luis Potosi. The first leg of the journey was a 130-mile march through desert interrupted by only a few ranches spaced about twenty to thirty miles apart. Fortunately, the ranchers had sunk deep wells to water their cattle, and there was no lack of water for the thirsty Americans. When they arrived at Metahuila, a town of about 10,000 people and the first town of importance along the route, they were fed, then they readied themselves for the next leg of the journey of 120 miles to San Luis. At Metahuila the Americans encountered General Santa Anna's main force, consisting of 5,000 infantry, a large body of cavalry, and Santa Anna himself, the "Napoleon of the South." The anonymous narrator describes General Santa Anna generously.

Santa Anna is a prodigious embodiment of the whole compass of Mexican character. In him we behold the polished mannerist, the expeditious leader, the proud dictator—and at the same time we see the groveling sensualist, the reckless gamester, and the inexorable tyrant, and these so blended and commingled as at once to excite our admiration, pity, and contempt. . . . He is just to a farthing, for if an enemy suffers pecuniary loss because of the recklessness of the men under his control, he would indemnify him out of his own pocket.[17]

By the grace of one of General Santa Anna's officers, Major Romero, the Americans were given some mules, horses, and donkeys for the next leg of the journey. In order to keep the donkeys moving on the trail, the prisoners sat backward so they could whip them readily. Although it may have looked ridiculous, the Americans were experienced cavalrymen and knew when and how to protect themselves from strong winds and sand blowing in their faces. After several days, the party finally reached San Luis Potosi, a city of about 60,000 people. As the American prisoners entered town, the populace gathered to see them as they were driven to prison. "Death to the Yankees," they cried. "Kill them," some cried out in patriotic fury, as they hurled stones at the prisoners. Major Romero, the Mexican officer in charge of the American prisoners, saw what was happening on the streets, and ordered his men to fix their bayonets to hold the angry civilians at bay.

After a short stay at San Luis, the Americans were removed to Mexico City, a march of 150 miles. Along the way, the Americans faced more angry civilians armed with knives and rocks. They stopped about ten miles from Mexico City, and were informed that a revolution was taking place. This event terrified the Americans.

When a revolution takes place in Mexico, the government swings from her moorings, the national compact is broken in pieces, responsibility is at an end, and matters of the highest moment are settled by the mob. The news of this rebellion was to us cause of serious alarm. The laws of nations had since our captivity been our only safety, and these were now forgotten amidst the ebullience of popular violence—we were the common enemies to all parties—and from ocean to ocean the whole nation was our enemy. We knew not at what moment some muddy current of the angry populace would sweep us away.[18]

Knowing that real danger existed for the prisoners, the Mexicans decided to march the Americans into the city at night. They halted at the city's gates, and an officer was dispatched to find out if any danger lay ahead for the prisoners. He returned and signaled the prisoners to proceed to prison. The enlisted men in prison suffered far more than the officers. Kept in close confinement, they slept on a damp floor and became infested with lice and disease. Their officers shared money and clothes with them, but it was difficult to avert boredom and low morale. Their officers petitioned General Santa Anna for their release, and as a result 180 enlisted prisoners were removed from Mexico City to the town of Tampico. The American army sent out a detachment of 120 men to raid Tampico and regain the prisoners, but they met Mexican forces instead. The prisoners were marched to the town of Tierra Caliente and remained there for one month. Finally, 180 enlisted POWs were released after making a promise (parole) not to bear arms against Mexico again. The officers remained in captivity.

Long marches in the Civil War found prisoners on both sides driven like cattle to their prison pens. While serving with his beloved "Arkansas Dixie Greys," Henry Morton Stanley was captured during the Battle of Shiloh in 1862. Immediately following his capture, he felt disgraced and shameful, much like prisoners before and after him. In Stanley's eyes his unit had deserted him, and, in an instant, he found himself a POW in the hands of the Union army.

> I became so absorbed with some blue figures in front of me, that I did not pay sufficient heed to my companions; the open space was too dangerous, perhaps, for their advance; for, had they emerged, I should have known they were pressing forward. . . . I rose from the hollow; but to my speechless amazement, I found myself a solitary grey; in a line of blue skirmishers! My companions had retreated! The next I heard was, "Down with that gun Seccesh, or I'll drill a hole through you! Drop it quick!" I was a prisoner! Shameful position! What would become of my knapsack, and my little treasures,— letters, and souvenirs of my father? They were lost beyond recovery![19]

Stanley's guard began to remove him immediately beyond danger, to the rear of the battle line. He found himself engaged in political conversation with his guards, those men who had taken him prisoner, enemies but also frontline soldiers. Then near-disaster struck. Stanley saw rearguard green soldiers who spoke with a German accent. They wanted to use Stanley for bayonet drill. "Drive a bayonet into the ——! Let him drop where he is!" Stanley perceived that these rearguard soldiers wanted the taste of blood with no risk before their own blood flowed in battle. As a prisoner, Stanley feared that he might become a target of opportunity. "I looked into their faces, deformed with fear and fury, and I felt intolerable loathing for the wild-eyed brutes! Their eyes, projected and distended, appeared like spots of pale blue ink, in faces of dough! Reason had fled altogether from their features, and to appeal for mercy to such blind, ferocious animalism would have been the height of absurdity."[20]

At that moment, when death at the hands of the rear guard seemed sure, Stanley's guards, two soldiers from Ohio, stepped forward bravely and stopped the coming slaughter. These men lowered their rifles, and, with the help of several officers who brandished their swords, turned the would-be assassins back to their duties. Further to the rear, Stanley joined other Confederate prisoners for a long trip upriver by steamer. He felt alone despite the presence of hundreds of other prisoners in the same situation. "We were a sad lot of men. I feel convinced that most of them felt, with myself, that we were ill-starred wretches, and special objects of an unkind Fate. We made no advances to acquaintanceship, for what value had any beggarly individual amongst us? All he possessed in the world was a thin, dingy suit of grey, and every man's thoughts were of his own misfortune, which was as much as he could bear, without being bothered with that of another."[21] After reaching St. Louis, Stanley and his compatriots were put on railroad cars and taken across the state of Illinois to chilly Chicago and the confines of Camp Douglas. Union prisoners would suffer similar fates, and many would be railroaded to Andersonville and other Confederate prisons to die, or, if they were fortunate enough to survive, to be exchanged.

During World War I, Americans and Germans obeyed two international agreements for the treatment of POWs: the Treaty of Amity, written and signed by the United States and Prussia in 1785, and the Hague Convention of 1899. Amelioration of the conditions of the sick and wounded was covered under the 1906 Geneva Convention, and most prisoners on both sides of the trenches survived their captivity experiences. Corporal Mike Shallin survived his trip by train to the prison camp. "Then they started to march us toward their lines. Remember, the Germans had been there four years or so—they had developed real little communities back there. After we reached a certain point, they stuck us on a single-gauge railroad train that was something similar to what we used to have at Luma Park on Coney Island. We rode this "Toonerville Trolley" until we reached the prison camp.[22]

Other POWs had quite different experiences on their way to the camp. In his narrative, *Heaven High, Hell Deep* (1935), Norman Archibald describes his train ride to the camp.

In a compartment with the guards in strategic seats in the four corners, Lawson, Foster, the officer and I sat down. Doors and windows were locked; revolvers were brought to light. "If you try to escape, we shoot you," one guard patted his gun. The train started.

Where were we going? What direction? Why the change? Long after dark the train jerked to a stop. We walked for several miles over fields and low rolling hills until we came to an enclosure. Two barbed wire fences, about ten feet high, six feet apart and turned over at the top, surrounded a low brick building and in the open, outside, was a wooden structure, presumably a guard house. Met by a German sergeant, we were led through gates cut in the double row of prickly meshing and into the brick building, which was but one room wide. Two beds, planks for mattresses, were built steamer fashion against the wall. Two others, boards nailed to posts, stood two feet from the floor. Inside, the door was shut. Four walls of solid brick and we were in total darkness but for a tiny window near the ceiling.[23]

For Harold Willis, the first remove meant a luncheon engagement with members of the squadron that shot him down. He recalled that the German squadron was quartered in a comfortable old house. American aviators were rarities on the German side of the lines at that time, and his captors knew not only that he belonged to an American squadron with a hat-in-the-ring insignia—for that was marked on his plane—but also that he had been a pilot in the Escadrille Lafayette. Willis "knew that the Germans were more than curious to learn the plans and the organization of our Air Force: how many squadrons were already at the front and the numbers soon to come. They were greatly interested in my Nieuport, Type 28, and I did not hesitate to say that it was a superb pursuit ship, far better than their Pfalzes and Albatrosses."[24] After the lunch and a short interrogation, Harold Willis began his second remove, this time to the POW camp where his real captivity began. "I was sent to the aviation distribution camp at Landshut, Bavaria. There I was subjected to a very severe search. My skin, mouth, ears, and hair were minutely examined. Acids were poured on my body to bring out suspected secret communications in invisible ink. My shoes and clothing were taken to pieces. Even the Croix de Guerre on my tunic was ripped off. A map and compass which I had were taken away from me." Then Willis was removed again, this time to his final destination, the German POW camp for officers at Gütersloh.

After my stay at Landshut I was sent to Gütersloh which is about 100 kilometers from the Dutch frontier. During my stay in Bavaria I observed that all the German States did not suffer the same privations. In some the people were well fed and in others nearly starving. At Gütersloh, we were reasonably well fed and had meat, enough bread and, in addition, beer.

I was the first American to arrive at Gütersloh, where there were about 600 French and 1,200 Russians. Every one was very kind to me and gave me food and clothing. The clothing I badly needed at the time. My stay at Gütersloh was the pleasantest in any of the many prison camps where I was imprisoned.[25]

James Norman Hall had a similar experience. After his shootdown and capture, his captors invited him to lunch with them at their squadron officer's mess. Hall was a little surprised at the courtesy. After lunch he was sent to the hospital for treatment of the wounds he received in battle. His recollections express his thanks to his captors in a way that indicates the chivalry of pilots in World War I.

I must not forget to mention another courtesy extended to me by the pilots of this German squadron. While I was in the hospital they brought me a snapshot of my Nieuport just as it fell, showing the tattered fabric hanging down from my upper right wing and the engine spilled out in front. I still have this photograph, which was taken by the pilot I had failed to kill. Although he did not say so, he may have thought that he owed me this memento of the day when, by the fortunes of war, we both missed death.[26]

Willis, Shallin, and Hall found something quite different from what they expected as POWs. The Civil War captivity experience was still within living memory, and it is no wonder that these men were surprised at the consideration they received from their captors. This is not to say that being a prisoner in World War I was easy for American and Allied prisoners. According to Carl P. Dennett in *Prisoners of the Great War* (1919), the conditions in the German camps were bad enough that Americans repeatedly risked their lives to escape and return to their own lines.[28] Nevertheless, captivity, at least in the remove event-scenario during World War I, seemed to be a respite from the terrors of combat rather than a precursor of what was yet to come.

The term "death march" came into common use in World War II. After hostilities between Japan and the United States began in December 1941, 61,000 Allied prisoners would be carted to Burma and Thailand to labor on the famous jungle railway. Nearly half were British, 18,000 Dutch, 13,000 Australian, and 650 American, of whom 320 were from the Second Battalion, 131st Field Artillery Regiment of the Texas National Guard, who had been captured in the Dutch East Indies. The other Americans were sailors who had survived the sinking of the cruiser USS *Houston* in the battle of Sunda Strait near Java on March 1, 1942.[29] One month later the death march of Bataan would add a new dimension to American POW history. The prisoners discovered quickly that Japanese captivity depended greatly on the whims of the guards, most of whom were transportation rather than line troops. On the march and thereafter in the prison camps, Americans witnessed unimaginable cruelty and callousness from individual Japanese soldiers, and in the end they held the Japanese leadership, from generals to sergeants, responsible for their actions as war criminals.

On a dusty little road along the Bataan peninsula, small numbered signposts in English mark the stops along the route of the Bataan death march. In the spring of 1942, all the operating American military units received orders to surrender to the Japanese army. Although the Americans were not badly outnumbered, they ran out of ammunition, fuel, food, medicine, and general military supplies. As an organized fighting force, they were finished. Never before in the history of American arms had an enemy caught an American military force so unprepared for war.

After the surrender, walking under a sizzling tropical sun, the Japanese denied their American and Filipino prisoners food and water. Those men who broke ranks and ran to the side of the road to scoop up a drink of water from one of the many springs were shot or bayoneted. Of the 75,000 Americans and Filipinos who surrendered to the Japanese army in the Philippines in 1942, 7,000–10,000 died or were killed on the march. Of that number, only a little over 600 were Americans; the rest were Filipinos. The march stretched about eighty-five miles, the final destination being Camp O'Donnell, a former American outpost just northwest of Clark Field. Death caught up to the Americans there, where 2,330 died in a few weeks from mistreatment, disease, and fatigue from the march. Harold R. Kipps, survivor of the Bataan death march, writes that

on the morning of April 11, 1942 we were taken over by the Japanese Army, or the "Nips," as we called them, and were herded together like a Western Cattle Drive, and started to hike to the rear of the Japanese Army, who were setting up beach heads for an attack on Corregidor. . . . I was one of the some twenty thousand American and about eighty thousand Filipino soldiers of the Philippine Army and Scouts who were assigned or attached to the Armed Forces on Bataan . . . who participated in the most infamous "Death March."

There were some small groups . . . taken to O'Donnell by trucks. My guess would be there were no more than 300 oficers and enlisted men. They arrived on April 11th and immediately made arrangements for the providing of food and water for those who were to follow. The first group of about 1,200 men arrived on the 12th, the second group on the 13th, and the third group on the morning of April 14, 1942, of which I was a member. Groups of various numbers arrived at O'Donnell nearly every day until all the prisoners were evacuated from the combat area (Bataan), before the attack on Corregidor. There was no attempt by the Japanese to classify or identify anyone by rank or organization during or on the March. You were just an enemy or a piece of captured material. You were at the pleasure and use of the Nips and to be done with as they saw fit.

The Geneva Convention was not recognized by the Japanese Army. The American prisoners were not recognized as such until about September 1945. We were just captives and had no rights as such, and no one received any pay for labor services prior to this time. . . . From Marvelis [Mariveles], Bataan, I, among hundreds of others, followed the road known as the "Zig-Zags" over mountains toward Manila. The road, or more so a trail, being used by the advancing Nips and us trying to get back of the Japanese lines, we were forced to hike along the side of the road but could not get out of sight of the guards who were escorting us. There were many men shot for just being a few feet off of the trail, and every time you came close to a Nip you were stopped, searched and beaten until you hit the ground, and many never got up to continue the march.

The Japanese were moving a tank unit over the road. Many men were run over and squashed in the ground which had about a foot of dust. The bodies looked like turtles or frogs that you have seen that were run over by cars on our highways. Also along the edge of the road were many of our soldiers, both American and Filipino, who had been bayoneted through their necks and stomachs, and some had been bludgeoned to death by the butts of the Nip rifles. After three or four hours of hiking under the above conditions and a 110 degree temperature we arrived at the Bavaca Area which the Nips had provided along the route from Bataan to San Fernando so they would be able to organize the captives into marching groups of about 1,200 for better control. The areas were like corrals for cattle. . . .

After arriving at the first bivouac area, I joined a marching group in about fifteen minutes and continued on the march through two more bivouacs for a distance of about fifty kilometers, where we were put into pens of a hog farm, about 11:00 pm. We left there about 3:00 am and arrived about 6:00 pm in a village where there were rice mills and storage bodegas or warehouses. Of the 1,200 in our group only about 700 or 800 could get into the bodega, leaving several hundred on the outside, which the Nips ordered inside or be shot. They machine-gunned the entire perimeter killing many. We stayed in the building until daylight. I saw a detail of about twenty-five men digging graves or trenches and rolling the bodies in.

About 600 Americans were told to form a single file and start toward the main road past a building where we would be given something to eat. We got a small scoop of rice that contained straw, bugs, worms, and all kinds of other dirt, but it was the first food I had on this trip, and it was welcome. We were marched on north and arrived in the city of San Fernando about 8:00 am. There about 800 were loaded into box cars, about 200 to a car, and taken by rail to Capas, arriving about 9:00 am, which was the rail head for Camp O'Donnell, located about nine kilometers to the west. We hiked for about two hours and arrived at O'Donnell about 11:00 am.[29]

Another Bataan survivor, Bill F. Gurule, describes his experience in *Fleeting Shadows and Faint Echoes of Las Huertes* (1987).

After the shelling stopped completely, we were moved by [the Japanese] to an open area, and we were there for a long time. . . . The next day . . . our trek . . . began. . . . This was truly a death march for thousands of those who had so courageously and valiantly defended Bataan. . . . Many, if not most, were bayoneted or shot by the Japanese without any provocation whatsoever as we staggered on. . . . Those who made it reached O'Donnell in a week or more. The effects of the rigors which we had just experienced and under the conditions of this place began immediately to take their toll. Daily, from fifty to sixty men on the American side and hundreds more on the Filipino side were being carried on open litters made of bamboo, then dumped in a common grave which was half-full of water.[30]

Not all Americans marched; 1,600 were in two field hospitals. According to Stanley Falk's study, *Bataan: The March of Death* (1972), several key conditions set the stage for the American tragedy. The first, and most important, was the horrid physical state of the Americans by April 9, 1942. They had run out of readily accessible food and medical supplies and had spread remaining supplies out in a series of hidden caches unknown to most troops. Consequently, many Americans began the death march in a run-down physical condition; a heavy death toll could be expected, especially when events found the Japanese unprepared for such large numbers of sick and starving POWs. American senior officers suggested at the surrender that the Japanese allow the Americans to take charge of themselves and use their own transport to the prison facilities. The Japanese refused and confiscated the American vehicles for their own use.[31]

As the war continued, the Japanese began to transport their Allied prisoners to Japan, Formosa, and Korea by sea. These journeys became particularly dangerous because the Japanese refused to paint "PW" on the ships' hulls. When the American submarines did their work, their captains and crews had no knowledge that the slow-moving, zig-zagging targets contained hundreds, if not thousands, of doomed countrymen. The prisoners called these old merchant hulks "hell ships" for good reason: treatment was maniacal, temperatures in the holds rose to more than 100 degrees Fahrenheit every day, water was scarce, and food was only a dream.

General Jonathan M. Wainwright, USA, the most senior officer POW in the Philippines, spent more than three years in captivity. In his narrative, *General Wainwright's Story* (1946), he describes a trip on one of the Japanese hell ships in which he and hundreds of prisoners were traveling from the Philippines to Formosa.

> General Edward P. King [Wainwright's second-in-command and commanding officer of the Luzon Forces who made the Death March] and I were taken to a cabin on the boat deck of the Japanese ship and were told that we must not leave the room during the trip. But it was a comfortable place, and for a time I believed that the Japanese general might well be telling me the truth when he intimated that happier days lay ahead of us. I soon found out, however, that King and I were the only Americans on the ship who were being treated as something more than cattle. All others were jammed in the hold in scandalous style. They slept on two long wooden shelves extending six feet out from the walls and arranged one over the other. Each man was granted two and a half feet of space on the shelves, with no bed clothing and the most primitive toilet arrangements.[32]

Hundreds of American POWs traveled to Karenko prison camp in the holds of this ship. According to General Wainwright,

> The 150 others in our party were similarly jammed into another hold. The hatches were immediately battened down and the temperature in the holds rose to far over 100 degrees. At dusk we were ordered to close the portholes and draw the blackout curtains, which made our black holes that much more suffocating. Our hold was alive with bedbugs. There seemed to be millions of them crawling over us the rest of that miserable night, and there was so little air in the place that many of us feared death by suffocation. It was eight o'clock the next morning before we were permitted to open the portholes to suck in some air and to gain enough light to see and pick the vermin from our bodies.[33]

After the surrender of Wake Island in 1941, the marines under the command of James P. S. Devereux found that transport by sea to a permanent prison facility was going to be a difficult passage. On January 11, 1942,

Devereux found the following "Regulations for Prisoners" posted by the Japanese commanding officer of the naval prison escort:

1. The prisoners disobeying the following orders will be punished with immediate death:
   (a) Those disobeying orders and instructions.
   (b) Those showing a motion of antagonism and raising a sign of opposition.
   (c) Those disordering the regulations by individualism, egoism, thinking only about yourself, rushing for your own goods.
   (d) Those talking without permission and raising loud voices.
   (e) Those walking and moving without order.
   (f) Those carrying unnecessary baggage in embarking.
   (g) Those resisting mutually.
   (h) Those touching the boat's materials, wires, electric lights, tools, switches, etc.
   (i) Those climbing ladder without order.
   (j) Those showing action of running away from the room or boat.
   (k) Those trying to take more meal than given to them.
   (l) Those using more than two blankets.[34]

According to Devereux, these twelve capital crimes were followed by five paragraphs of detailed instructions, ending on this grim note: "Navy of the Great Japanese Empire will not try to punish you all with death. Those obeying all rules and regulations, and believing the action and purpose of the Japanese Navy, co-operating with Japan in constructing the "New Order of the Great Asia" which leads to the world's peace will be well treated."[35]

For those left behind on Wake Island, the fate was far worse than that of those on the hell ship. According to Devereux, most of the Americans who surrendered to the Japanese on Wake Island were shipped to prison camps. On the night of October 7, 1943, using the excuse that the ninety-eight American civilians still on the island had established a secret radio communication with United States naval forces, the Japanese machine gunned down the Americans on the beach.[36] For this crime, the Japanese commander on Wake—Rear Admiral Shigematsu Sakaibara—and eleven of his officers were sentenced to hang after trial by an American naval court at Kwajalein following the Japanese capitulation.[37]

In Nazi Germany, American Kriegies experienced three types of removes: the train rides to the Stalags at the beginning of captivity, the death marches in the snow during the winter of 1945 when the Germans retreated from the advancing Russians, and the marches through towns when and where the prisoners were put on display for an angry civilian population. Kenneth Simmons was herded through a German village and saw the bitter faces of the people he had helped attack a few hours earlier. As the group of prisoners began marching through town the crowd grew larger. Then he heard several women screaming, "Luft Gangster, Schwein, Schwein." After his recapture following a failed escape attempt, another Kriegie remembered how dangerous it was for German civilians to help escaped Allied prisoners. Although he appreciated the food he received, he made no attempt to thank his benefactors, for that simple gesture could have cost the lives of innocent, humane people. "The Home Guard had seen us and were firing. They thought the stick I was carrying, which I needed at the time for my legs, was a gun, apparently, so I quickly threw it down. They came up, captured us, and paraded us through the town and watched us carefully to see if our eyes rested on any particular family because they saw the food. Finally, they didn't catch the family because we didn't let on, of course."[38]

Kriegie Ray Marcello recalls his march through a German village in a simple verse he called "A Little Burst of Flak."

> The farmers and soldiers come over the hill,
> With blood in their eyes & ready to kill.
> They lift you up and give you a smack
> And the cause of it all was a burst of flak.
>
> They gather the crew and march you through town,
> Where the people watch you with a frown.
> They lock you up in a filthy old shack;
> The cause of it all was a burst of flak.[39]

If walking through throngs of angry civilians did not create fear, the experience of a long remove aboard a cattle train did. Kenneth Simmons wondered where they were taking him. For Simmons and thousands of other POWs in Europe, it was time to board a train for a seventy-two-hour trip to a permanent camp. To Simmons's horror, fifty-odd men crowded inside a filthy cattle car. The smell was nearly unbearable.

Food packs were stacked against the walls, and individual packs were spread out in the crowded space. Four pasteboard boxes were placed in each of the four corners of the car—to be used for toilets or sickness. Our blankets were used to cover the hay and cow droppings. We didn't have to lie in the offal, but the smell was forever present. . . . Inside the cattle cars, we had started a trip that would turn men into swine. The commandant was wrong about the stale air. Cold air gushed about us through holes and cracks in the sides. We kept our overcoats on, pulled our caps down over our ears, and put our hands in overcoat pockets. The drafts of freezing air swept through the car, and most of us were coughing before the night was over. . . . When we finally stopped, we heard the word "Plauen" spoken by several guards. Two guards took up positions at each car, and the doors were opened. Toilet boxes were dumped and thrown from the cars, splattering about the railroad station, as we climbed out of the cars and fell in line for an Appell. The guards were shouting and cursing about the boxes being dumped all over the station, but we ignored them. Our hatred for the guards was at an all-time high, and we gave them absolutely no cooperation.[40]

In the winter of 1945, the American Kriegies waited for liberation. Camps in Prussia, Poland, eastern Germany, and Austria waited for the Red Army, and many could hear the roar of Russian artillery thundering in the distance. The Russians were coming! Hoping to use their prisoners as bargaining chips with the Allied powers, the Germans decided to move as many Kriegies as possible with them in their retreat west. The German Air Force no longer existed as a fighting force, and German trains ceased to roll. The German Army and Air Force took to the roads, and began to walk very long distances in the snow alongside their Allied prisoners. Robert J. Thornton was one of the Americans who walked from Stalag Luft IV west during the "Black March" of 1945.

We were evacuated from Luft IV in early February [1945]. This was a forced march that lasted 87 days. Actually it was a death march. The Red Cross followed us with food as long as it could. It wasn't near long enough, about 50% of the march. Dysentery was so bad that we gave up many times, but the "buddy" system saved us. The buddy system means that when we started on the march, we picked another man to be with, no matter what happened. When one reached the end of his rope, the other would tie a knot in it. This worked very well. Dysentery became most unbearable. The internal pressures would tear you apart. You was not allowed to get out of line to relieve yourself at any time, so you just turned to the side and let it fly. If you fell out of line, one of two things would happen. Either you got bayoneted or the dogs got you. Either way, your suffering would be over. Another method they used. German war machinery was being moved to the front. This was done primarily at night, but they made sure that the Allied reconnaissance plane seen this equipment going into certain barns at dusk. By the time that the strafing planes would come in, they pulled the machinery out of the barn and marched us in. Many died under these strafings. Many died from malnutrition, and many died because they lost their will to live. The column I was in started out at about six hundred strong. I was one of about fifty that survived.[41]

Charles Miller made most of the journey by boat, but there were four miles left to march. Had it not been for a fellow Kriegie, his friend Rufus, Charles Miller would have died. "Two guys were handcuffed together. So, whatever you had, you either carried it or lost it. They [the guards] told us, if you drop out, if the guy you're handcuffed to can't carry it, you're both going to be shot. . . . 'Rufe, I can't make it.' 'What?' I said, 'I can't make it. I'm going to fall down. I can't make it.' And here we are, handcuffed, and this guy, he turned to me and said, 'Jesus Christ, you sonofabitch, you get me shot and I'll kill ya.' "[42] Neither man was shot; they were liberated on May 5, 1945, by the Russian army.

In Korea, if a POW survived capture, then he had another deadly experience ahead, the march north to the permanent camps along the Yalu River and the Chosen Reservoir. The usual procedure was to march the prisoners from the point of capture to a temporary collecting point, usually a village, where they would remain for two to five months. The communists would remove the prisoners' heavy clothes and combat boots at the point of capture, forcing them to march barefoot even in the coldest weather. The average food ration was one rice ball per day with little or no water. In the name of humiliation and political propaganda, the North Koreans forced their prisoners to parade through towns on display for the local populace. Anyone not able to continue marching due to exhaustion, frostbite, illness, weakness from starvation, or wounds received in battle was executed on the spot.

Approximately 376 Americans began the Seoul-Pyongyang death march on September 26, 1950, after capture in Seoul. After walking more than 250 miles in three weeks, 296 tired and frightened Americans arrived in Pyongyang. More than one thousand American prisoners began the march from Kuna-ri to the permanent Camp #5 at Pyoktong. On that march, 300 died from the treatment. More than 700 Americans began marching from the Bean Camp, walking to the permanent camp at Changsong; only 100 survived to repatriation. Other death marches include the Pyongyang to Camp #3 March and the two-part march from the Chosen Reservoir to Kanggye to Camp #1 at Changsong. The United Nations War Crimes Division discovered that the North Koreans committed several massacres prior to or during the marches north, including the murders on Hill 303, inside the Sunchon Tunnel, at Taejon, and at Kaesong. In each case, by accident, some American prisoners were not mortally wounded. Refusing to panic, they played dead beneath the bodies of their mortally wounded or dead comrades and waited for rescue.

On August 14, 1950, twenty-six Americans were surprised and captured by units of the North Korean army. After capture, the men were stripped of their combat boots and personal belongings and their hands were tied behind their backs. After two days, more American prisoners joined the group, making the total approximately forty-six. On the third day of captivity, August 16, 1950, all the men were led to a ravine, still with their hands tied behind their backs, and shot. Of the entire group of American captives on Hill 303, four men survived; one was Corporal Roy Paul Manning with H Company, 155th Cavalry Regiment. Testifying to Congress in 1954, Manning described his experience to the senators present: "I guess they thought we was dead. As they left, a couple of minutes later, I heard a sound like somebody was coming back, so I managed to wiggle my body underneath the fellow that was next to me—was dead—and they come by and they started kicking and you could hear the fellows hollering, grunting, groaning, and praying, and when they kicked me they kicked my leg and I made a grunting sound and that's when I caught it in the gut, got shot in the gut at the time."[43]

The Sunchon Tunnel massacre took place after the Seoul to Pyongyang death march in October 1950. The North Koreans loaded about 180 American prisoners into railroad cars for transport north to permanent camps. They were en route for several days, and late in the afternoon on October 30, 1950, the train arrived at the Sunchon Tunnel. The train stopped, ostensibly so that the North Koreans could issue rations to the Americans. The hungry and weary POWs assumed mistakenly they were going to be given some kind of meal, the first in days of traveling. Instead, they were taken from the railroad cars in groups of about forty to some nearby ravines and shot. Most of the victims, 138 POWs, died instantly. Others were rescued. Surviving this incident was Private John E. Martin, 29th Regimental Combat Team. In his testimony before Congress, he stated: "I just sat down when they started to fire and I fell forward on the embankment. . . . Then they went down and kicked somebody, and if they groaned they shot them again or bayoneted and kicked somebody else."[44]

Between September 23 and 27, 1950, from 5,000 to 7,000 people, including civilians and South Korean soldiers, were massacred in the town of Taejon. Approximately sixty American prisoners were taken from the Taejon prison. In groups of fourteen, they were bound together with wire, forced to sit in ditches, and shot. Of that group, only two men survived. Sergeant Carey Weinel, a member of the 23rd Infantry Regiment, 2nd Division, testified to a startled Senate committee: "Toward the last they was in a hurry to leave Taejon . . . so they took . . . the last three groups pretty close together. I witnessed the group right in front of me shot. . . . After they was shot we was taken to the ditch and sat down in the ditch and shot."[45] Sergeant Weinel added a footnote in his testimony: there was not a man that begged for mercy, not a man that cracked under the fatal ordeal at Taejon. He was struck by three bullets but, luckily, not in a vital spot. In the heat of the moment, Weinel kept his wits, fell into the ditch, and played dead. He was buried alive for approximately eight hours.

Massacres and war crimes took place throughout the Korean War. Thirteen American prisoners were murdered at Kaesong. Twelve prisoners were shot at Naedae on October 13, 1950. Twenty wounded Americans were made prisoners by the North Koreans and executed in July 1950, with only their surgeon surviving. Others continued north on the death marches. Again, like Bataan in 1942, any prisoner not able to keep up was shot. One prisoner recalled that about ten days after capture, two American jets strafed his hut, wounding a close friend with a .50-caliber bullet. "He was in the next room. He called out for my help, but the Chinese guard would not let me go to him. In dying breaths, he asked me to go to his home and tell his folks how he died. Soon after (about 5 minutes) the guard ordered us to go on a hillside close by. Then soon after, another guard came up to me, pointed to the building and pointed his rifle toward the ground and went bang, bang, telling me he had mercy killed my friend."[46] These prisoners, like thousands of others, paraded through North Korean towns on display to the civilian population. American and other United Nations prisoners died from malnutrition, dysentery, pneumonia, wounds, and maltreatment by the Korean guards.

Sadly, the American captivity experience in North Korea would not end in 1953; another incident would take place fifteen years later when the USS *Pueblo* was captured. After their ship was halted on the high seas, boarded, and captured in international waters off the coast of North Korea on January 23, 1968, the officers and men of the USS *Pueblo,* AGR 2, were taken ashore in Wonson harbor and interrogated. Once that process was complete, they began their trip to the internment facility. Before their captors permitted the officers and men of the *Pueblo* to board the train, they were taken by bus to a railhead, then crowded onto a concrete platform beside the railroad tracks. According to Stephen Harris in *My Anchor Held* (1970), the North Koreans took an immediate advantage of a propaganda opportunity. "Movie lights glared in our face. They ordered us to put up our hands, then to put them down again. One of these propaganda pictures later appeared on the cover of *Newsweek.*"[47] Then the *Pueblo* prisoners were blindfolded and herded on board a train. According to Lloyd Bucher's *Bucher: My Story* (1970), he was the last to board the prison train. "My feet were guided up the steps of a coach, led on by my tied hands down an aisle and thrust on to what seemed to be an old style coach seat. I could sense the presence of my men, but the beatings had momentarily ceased and they were very quiet. I must have been the last one brought aboard the train, because as soon as I was seated, it lurched forward with a shriek of the locomotive's whistle and started moving toward—God knew where!''[48] Bucher's captors had him in one of the most vulnerable positions a POW can experience: captured, beaten up but not disabled, exhausted from the beginning of the captivity experience, without sleep, initially interrogated, and along with the crew, completely dependent on the intentions of the captor. Bucher recalls his situation as one in which his "whole being was numbed by shock and weariness, yet remained acutely conscious of every mental and physical pain. . . . The Koreans were not about to give me any rest.''[49]

Bucher's shock at his removal was no less than that experienced by American airmen fighting in Vietnam at the same time. The pilots shot down in North Vietnam were initially put on trucks and taken eventually to the French-built Hanoi city jail, the Hoa Lo Prison, which the Americans called the "Hanoi Hilton." Directly after shootdown but before the trip to Hanoi, the local North Vietnamese militia often seized an opportunity to turn the event into a propaganda exercise. Again, prisoners would suffer the wrath of outraged civilians. Many were tied and beaten as they were dragged through villages. For many downed fliers, the truck ride itself was dangerous. Tied, bound, and sometimes gagged, and often in shock or wounded from the bailout itself, the pilots bounced around the truck's cargo bay for the whole trip while drivers pounded potholes and swerved to miss huge, gaping bomb craters. Often the wounded pilots arrived in Hanoi in terrible shape, not a good omen for the rest of their long captivity. Some prisoners remained in Hanoi; others were moved around the whole North Vietnamese prison system.

In South Vietnam, when Americans became prisoners, the Vietcong conducted dangerous long marches from the point of capture to their jungle sanctuaries. South Vietnam was a war zone full of mines and booby traps that took the lives of Vietcong as well as American soldiers as they walked the jungle trails. The Vietcong understood how valuable their prisoners were; they feared discovery and tried to avoid American attacks. They knew that the Americans searched for their POWs on the ground and by air. The Vietcong knew too that if they were sighted in possession of one or more prisoners by the Americans, raiding operations—"brightlight operations" in the parlance of the Vietnam War—would be launched very quickly.

In addition to short but steady series of marches through the jungle from one camp site to another, Vietcong guerrillas sometimes imposed long marches on their prisoners, trips by foot overland from prison camps in the South to North Vietnam by way of the Ho Chi Minh Trail. The captured German medical volunteers, Monika Schwinn and Bernhard Diehl, coauthored *We Came to Help* (1976) and documented their march north to Hanoi. After they were safely within the borders of the Democratic

Republic of Vietnam, the captors put their prisoners in trucks for the final leg of the journey.

Colonel Fred V. Cherry, USAF, a fighter pilot and the first African-American POW in North Vietnam, was a member of the 35th Tactical Fighter Squadron, U.S. Air Force, Karot (Thailand) Air Force Base. He was shot down in May 1965 and was shuffled between various prison camps near Hanoi until his release on February 12, 1973. In Wallace Terry's *Bloods* (1984), Cherry narrates his remove and reflects on the length of time he would have to spend in captivity. He had little notion that it would last eight years: "Now they got me dressed the way they want me, and they are going to walk me three miles to this village. I didn't know my ankle was broken, too. I was dusty, hot, sweaty, and naturally, pissed off 'cause I was shot down. Didn't wanna be there. I'm thinkin' about two, three, four months. I'm not thinkin' 'bout years. I'm not even thinkin' six months." Cherry was brought into the village and encountered violently angry civilians: "And this guy jumps on me, straddling my back. And he puts his automatic weapon right behind my ear with my nose pretty much in the dirt. And I said to myself, you know, this man might even shoot me." Then Cherry began to resist his captors: "When we got to the vehicle, they had a cameraman there. And he wanted to take pictures of me walkin' toward him. I wouldn't do it. I'd frown up and fall on my knees and turn my back. Finally, they quit. They never took any pictures. And they got me in the jeep." Finally, Cherry was interrogated for the first time: "The first place they tried to interrogate me appeared to be a secondary school. And they put me in this hut. I did what I was supposed to do. Name, rank, serial number, date of birth. And I started talking about the Geneva Convention. And they said forget it. 'You a criminal.' "[50]

Colonel Norman A. McDaniel, USAF, author of *Yet Another Voice* (1975), tells how he was shuffled between camps and how in confinement he was denied the opportunity to communicate with his fellow prisoners. "Eventually, they took me to another camp called the Zoo which was a more permanent camp, and between the Zoo and the Hilton over the period of time that I was there, I moved between those two camps and different cell blocks and different buildings within those camps. My first ten months were in solitary confinement, isolation, not being able to communicate or talk to the other prisoners overtly."[51]

Removes and interrogations were not restricted to flight officers shot down in North Vietnam. Sergeant James Jackson, Jr., of Talcott, West Virginia, was a Green Beret medic captured in South Vietnam on the morning of July 5, 1966. Sergeant Jackson was wounded in the battle before capture and could not be moved very easily. He knew that the Vietcong shot wounded prisoners on the spot or shortly after their capture, and because his captors spared his life and removed him to a prison pen, Jackson was thankful for his life. Released in 1968 as a political gesture, he narrated his eighteen-month ordeal of captivity to *Ebony*'s managing editor, Hans J. Massaquoi. Typical of narrations published before the war's end, his polemic intent focuses on describing his personal experience, while he carefully avoids specific descriptions of mistreatment at the hands of the Vietcong.

> Since I couldn't walk because of my injury, I expected to be shot on the spot. But instead, my captors dragged me away from the immediate battle area. I was beaten and kicked and generally treated quite rough. At first I was taken to a small village and from there, after dark fell, I was moved to a Vietnamese POW camp for interrogation. It was early morning when I arrived there, anyway after midnight. The interrogation started soon after daybreak. The methods need not be described. All I can say is that it was quite agonizing. . . . Eventually, I was moved to another camp that contained Americans, with no Vietnamese prisoners. Being in the company of other Americans definitely lifted my spirit.[52]

Supporting Sergeant Jackson's narrative account, Neil Sheehan writes in *Bright Shining Lie* (1988) that the Vietcong treated their military and civilian prisoners variously depending on military and political circumstances. Because of limited medical facilities, the Vietcong guerrillas shot seriously wounded POWs at the point of capture. If prisoners were unharmed or lightly wounded, they would be marched off and separated into two distinct groups: those who the Vietcong thought would or could convert to their side and those who opposed them. Those who opposed them were usually executed early in the captivity experience.[53]

Although the intensity of the suffering varied somewhat from one war to another, the hardships of the march are chronicled consistently as the third narrative event-scenario. Next to the moment of capture, the march is perhaps the most dangerous phase of captivity. The new POW suffers the first seriously dangerous encounters with the captor's value system. Signs of the first terrible things that can happen to the prisoner arise as violence becomes commonplace and even ritualized, and it becomes ever more clear that the captive state is far from safe. Prisoners witness the murder or execution of comrades for such trifles as wanting water, walking too slowly, falling down, complaining of hunger, or, in extreme cases, showing physical resistance to the captor. Narrators consistently characterize the march as a one-way journey to hell. With each step toward an unknown destination, the prisoner leaves more and more of his own civilization behind.

After capture, the long march is the first complete act performed under the captor's direction. Prisoners observe the captors' values and their individual and collective attitudes toward their prisoners. The march introduces real hunger, sustained physical injury, and pain. During a single march or in a series of marches, the seeds of a captive community are planted. Prisoner accounts and testimonies reveal that during the march they begin to accept the fact that they are prisoners and gain a clearer vision of the meaning of captivity. In this initiation the prisoner begins to square off against the captors and may meet members of the civilian population who, moments before, were within the cross-hairs of his gun sights and may even have been the victims of his weapons. He feels their wrath and learns to understand their fears and resentments. After the march is complete, the subsequent event-scenarios describe how prisoners solidified sets of traditional survival values that surface when they live in community, how prisoners come to decisions to escape, or how captors offered new political and social values to assimilators and collaborators.

CHAPTER SEVEN

A Sense of Place:
The Prison Landscape

Thou, *Scorpion,* fatal to the crowded throng,
Dire theme of horror and Plutonian song,
Requir'st my lay—thy sultry decks I know,
And all the torments that exist below!
                                        Philip Freneau (1780)

After surviving a death march, the prisoner arrives at the permanent prison facility. Ethnological precision marks descriptions of the prison landscape, the fourth event-scenario; exact memories of the POW camp or the prison cells seem to be permanently engraved into a POW's consciousness. Time stands still, and with boredom to fight, POWs become expert observers of their surroundings.

Surviving the remove or a series of removes meant that new challenges—new food, new people, and the welcome ritual or gauntlet—awaited prisoners in the captor's camp. In the forest wars the landscape of captivity was the Indian village. Mary Rowlandson commented on her captors' food and believed that God strengthened them to be the "scourge of His people."[1] In the French and Indian War, after Barbara Leininger and Marie LeRoy were brought to the Indian village of Kittanny (Kittanning in western Pennsylvania), all the captives were required to run a gauntlet. For some prisoners, the gauntlet meant death; for Barbara the gauntlet consisted of three blows on the back. She commented that "they were, however, administered with great mercy. Indeed, we concluded that we were beaten merely in order to keep up an ancient usage, and not with the intention of injuring us. The month of December was the time of our arrival, and we remained at Kittanny until the month of September, 1756."[2] Hunger, not violence, struck Barbara and Marie most bitterly in captivity: "The want of provisions, however, caused us the greatest sufferings. During all the time that we were at Kittany we had neither lard nor salt; and sometimes we were forced to live on acorns, roots, grass and bark. There was nothing in the world to make this new sort of food palatable excepting hunger itself."[3] Similarly, after surviving the gauntlet, Peter Williamson settled down to life in his prison, a remote Indian village called Alamingo.

At Alamingo I remained near two months, till the snow was off the ground. . . . I contrived to defend myself against the inclemency of the weather as well as I could, by making myself a little wigwam with the bark of the trees, covering it with earth, which made it resemble a cave; and, to prevent the ill effects of the cold, I kept a good fire always near the door. My liberty of going about, was, indeed, more than I could have expected, but they well knew the impracticability of my escaping from them. . . . Seeing me outwardly easy and submissive, they would sometimes give me a little meat, but my chief food was Indian corn.[4]

Rowlandson, Leininger, LeRoy, and Williamson set the precedent for full, rich description of the prison landscape, including details of the gauntlet, their captors' villages and customs, and the relationships they had with them. Indeed, military and civilian POW narratives from the Revolution to Vietnam would follow their example.

During the American Revolution, no description of a British prison ship quite equaled Philip Freneau's account of the *Scorpion.* Freneau, a civilian passenger on the armed American ship *Aurora,* was captured at sea by the British in May 1780. Following his release, he wrote "The British Prison Ship: A Poem," which was first published during hostilities early in 1781. Freneau became a great favorite of revolutionary war prison survivors, and selections from his long and artfully composed poem appear as chapter headings in many captivity narratives, especially those written about life in the British prison hulks. He begins with a stanza damning his British and Hessian captors:

> Amid these ills no tyrant dared refuse
> My right to pen the dictates of the muse,
> To paint the terrors of the infernal place,
> And fiends from Europe, insolent as base.

Freneau then describes life and landscape:

> The briny wave that Hudson's bosom fills
> Drained through her bottom in a thousand rills:
> Rotten and old, replete with sighs and groans,
> Scarce on the waters she sustained her bones;
> Here, doomed to toil, or founder in the tide,
> At the moist pumps incessantly we plied,
> Here, doomed to starve, like famished dogs we tore
> The scant allowance, that our tyrants bore.
> Remembrance shudders at this scene of fears—

Still in my view some tyrant chief appears,
Some base-born Hessian slave walks threatening by,
Some servile Scot, with murder in his eye,
Still haunts my sight, as vainly they bemoan
Rebellions managed so unlike their *own*!
O may we never feel the poignant pain
To live subjected to such fiends again,
Stewards and *Mates,* that hostile Britain bore,
Cut from the gallows on their native shore;
Their ghastly looks and vengeance-beaming eyes
Still to my view in dismal visions rise—
O may we ne'er review these dire abodes,
These piles for slaughter, floating on the floods,—
And you, that o'er the troubled ocean go,
Strike not your standards to this venomed foe,
Better the greedy wave should swallow all,
Better to meet the death-conducting ball,
Better to sleep on ocean's oozy bed,
At once destroyed and numbered with the dead,
Than thus to perish in the face of day
Where twice ten thousand deaths one death delay.[5]

In the text, Freneau renders a perfect example of the complete prison landscape event-scenario. He describes the prison ship itself, his guards, the surroundings and cells, the terrible food, and the vermin. For thousands of POWs in the hands of British soldiers, American loyalists, and Hessian mercenaries, the result of these conditions was death.

Unlike Philip Freneau, Colonel Ethan Allen was a soldier, and he expected soldierly treatment, if not the customary respect for his rank, from his British army captors. He had no expectation of the filth he found in his church-cellar jail. Allen expresses his outrage in his narrative.

The filth in these churches . . . was almost beyond description. The floors were covered with excrement. I have carefully sought to direct my steps so as to avoid it, but could not. They would beg for God's sake for one copper, or morsel of bread. I have seen in one of these churches seven dead at the same time, lying among the excrements of their bodies. I have gone into the churches and seen sundry of the prisoners in the agony of death, in consequence of very hunger, and others speechless and very near death, biting pieces of chips; others pleading for God's sake for something to eat, and at the same time shivering with the cold. Hollow groans saluted my ears, and despair seemed to be imprinted on all of their countenances.[6]

Charles Herbert, a young civilian privateer sailing under letter of marque on board the *Dalton,* was captured on November 15, 1776. He returned to Newburyport August 23, 1780, having spent two years as a POW in England. Herbert's diary describes the sufferings of this period: hunger, cold, sickness, and privation. After his release by an exchange of prisoners arranged by Benjamin Franklin, the American minister to France, Herbert joined the crew of the *Alliance,* a frigate commanded by Captain Landais and part of the squadron commanded by John Paul Jones.[7] He left no narrative, but he did bequeath a diary to his wife, who published it after his death. "Our allowance here in prison," he writes, "is a pound of bread, a quarter of a pound of beef, a pound of greens, a quart of beer and a little pot-liquor that the beef and greens are boiled in, without any thickening—per day." The bread was moldy, the beef was spoiled, and the greens were rotten, so Herbert and the other prisoners decided to take advantage of the permission granted to local vendors (sutlers) to sell prisoners some fresh food. But they needed money, so he seized upon what looked to him to be a unique opportunity to turn some profit with a charity box. In his diary for June 11 and 12, 1777, he wrote:

Having so lately had the small-pox, and being so long physiced afterwards, I require more victuals now, than I ever did before; and our allowance is so very small, and having only seven pence left of what little money I had when I came to prison, I had a continual gnawing at my stomach; and I find that unless I take some method to obtain something more than my bare allowance, I must certainly suffer, if not die, and that soon. As necessity is the mother of invention, I am resolved to try to get something, and to-day when a carpenter came to put in a window at the end of the prison, I entreated him to bring me some deal, and I would make him a box, which he did. . . . To-day we have made a charity-box, and put it up at the gate. There is written upon it, "Health, Plenty, and Competence to the donors." I have finished the box for the carpenter, and he likes it so well that he wants more made, and he brought me some more wood for that purpose,—some for him, and some for myself.[8]

Herbert and his comrades placed their hopes in this charity box, but soon discovered that the prison guard, conspiring with the turnkey, had put up a box of their own and were taking the money that generous people intended for the American prisoners. Herbert and his friends removed their box from public view and resolved to put it out no more.

Herbert's experience of kindness from British citizens was not unique. Many Britons were unhappy about the Admiralty's treatment of the Americans in captivity. Whether they were considered rebels or prisoners, there was no reason to kill them in captivity by starvation or by the willful imposition of vile prison conditions that led too often to disease and death. A letter written to the Lords Commissioners of the Admiralty on August 29, 1777, by an anonymous Englishman from Plymouth using the name "Humanitas," complained about the conditions inflicted on American POWs inside Mill Prison. "My Lords," he wrote, "Being persuaded of your Lordships' tender feelings, flowing from those truly humane principles which have ever distinguished Britains from the more barbarous Nations; I cannot but flatter my self with hope of your Lordships immediate interposition in behalf of the American prisoners, who are now actually perishing with hunger."[9] He called Mill Prison "a horrible Inquisition & infernal Slaughter house of American Victims."[10] As a result of the complaint, a Commission investigated the charges made against the warden but found no fault, and he remained the keeper as late as 1782. Throughout the Revolution, British prisons kept Americans as pirates and criminals.

During the Barbary wars, Americans discovered the bagnios of Algiers and Tripoli. Captured American sailors who had skills were sold as chattel slaves to a master's household. Those without special skills remained the property of the bashaw or Turkish governor. Life became a drudgery of endless work and constant danger. The prisoners enjoyed only those privileges granted to them by their jailers. Confined to a slave prison, a bagnio, the slave would be expected to fulfill two requirements: to be productive in his work and to give no trouble to his masters. According to H. M. Barnby, Christian slaves in Algiers were accepted as a part of Algerian society, because their slavery was considered the will of Allah. Discipline was rigorous and arbitrary. A Christian overseer need only report an infraction of the rules to a Moslem captor, and the prisoner would receive the bastinado, weeks in chains, or beheading if the infraction was serious enough. The slaves had their own hospital staffed by Catholic priests, chapels, brothels, and even taverns which were owned by other, more successful slaves. Every morning the slaves marched to work; every night they returned to the bagnio. To the Barbary powers—Algeria, Tunisia, Morocco, and Tripoli—prisoners signified cash, either as cheap labor or ransom. Few died in captivity.[11]

During the War of 1812, prison conditions in England saw some substantive change. The British no longer considered American military prisoners criminals, because the North Act of 1777 was repealed. The British Transport Board retained the prison hulk system used in the American Revolution, but there were so many French and Spanish sailors captured in the English wars in Europe and America that the British housed them in large prison facilities as well. In 1813 many Americans were moved from the hulks to the gruesome military prison at Dartmoor. Chosen for its location near the sea and the consequent inclement weather, Dartmoor prison was constructed in 1806–1809 to hold 5,000 men. Thirty-six acres were enclosed by stone walls; the outermost was about twelve to sixteen feet high. There were barracks for 400 soldiers and officers. Located in Devonshire, Dartmoor became known as Britain's national dungeon and was described by Charles Andrews in his narrative, *The Prisoners' Memoir, or, Dartmoor Prison: Containing the Complete History of the Captivity of the Americans in England* (1815). When Andrews arrived, his first look around convinced him that surviving his stay at Dartmoor would be difficult. "Death itself, with hopes of an hereafter, seemed less terrible than this gloomy prison."[12]

For the Encarnacion prisoners of the Mexican War, the prison landscape was less gloomy. They were taken to a large convent where two groups of Americans taken at Encarnacion were brought together for the first time. The Mexican captors were forced to use the local convent to protect their prisoners from angry civilians, and in Querataro, then a city of 4,000 people, the Americans dined on dog and cat. The officers were confined together in a room near a garden, where they often walked to pass the time. In confinement, the officers were allowed thirty-seven and a half cents a day; the enlisted men received eighteen and three-fourths cents. Both officers and men were forced to live upon this sum as well as they could.[13]

In Mexico City, the Americans were confined in a prison along with a chain gang of 300 Mexican felons. As the war progressed in favor of the United States, treatment improved. After the Battle of Buena Vista, for example, they were permitted to walk around in an open lot surrounded by the high walls of the jail. If they became sick, they were given medical treatment by Major Borland, and if hospitalized, they were cared for by the Sisters of Charity whom the anonymous narrator called, "angels of mercy in whatever nation or clime they may be found."[14] They were permitted visits by other Americans, including Midshipman Robert C. Rogers, also a POW, who had the liberty of the city and kept the Americans apprised of what was happening around town. Rogers later escaped and reported conditions of captivity to General Winfield Scott.

Prison landscapes in the Civil War consisted of fields, fairgrounds, converted warehouses, civilian jails, and former armories. Since neither side had any idea of how many prisoners it would take and no idea how long hostilities would last, few camps were built as prisons from the ground up; rather, they were adapted for use as temporary prison pens by the respective governments (see Appendix 2B and 2E for site locations of the major Union and Confederate military prison camps). Soldiers of the American Civil War in Northern and Southern captivity hated their prisons and took great pains to be accurate in their descriptions.

Confederate cavalryman and raider General Basil W. Duke, CSA, rode with his brother-in-law, General John Hunt Morgan, CSA, until their capture by Union forces and removal to the Ohio State Penitentiary, a maximum security prison in Columbus. In the language of the time, Union captors called the members of the Confederate cavalry "horse thieves" and treated them as felons rather than as POWs. In his heroic narrative praising Morgan's exploits, General Duke sketched the jail where he and Morgan were incarcerated.

> Let the reader imagine a large room (or rather wing of a building), 400 feet in length, forty-odd in width, and with a ceiling forty-odd feet in height. One half of this wing, although separated from the other by no traverse wall, is called the "East Hall."
> In the walls of this hall are cut great windows, looking out upon one of the prison yards. . . . In the interior building the cells are constructed—each about three feet and a half wide and seven feet long. The doors of the cells—a certain number of which are constructed in each side of this building—open upon the alleys. . . . At the back of each, and of course, running the whole length of the building, is a hollow space reaching from the floor to the ceiling, running the whole length of the building. . . . This space is left for the purpose of obtaining more thorough ventilation, and the back wall of every cell is perforated with a hole, three or four inches in diameter, to admit air from this passage.[15]

Morgan would later execute a daring escape from the prison, and Duke would later be transferred to Fort Delaware, near Delaware City, Delaware, where he would wait for exchange along with Generals Basil W. Duke, M. Jeff Thompson, Joseph Wheeler, and other prominent Confederate officers.

Johnson's Island prison camp for Confederate officers was on a small, desolate, privately owned island in Lake Erie just north of Sandusky, Ohio. It is about a mile and a half long and 400 to 500 yards wide. According to Decimus et Ultimus Barziza, in 1863 it consisted of eight acres, much of which was taken up by a "block" of thirteen numbered buildings. The blocks were arranged in two rows, with a broad street between them. According to Barziza: "We were permitted to walk in this street. . . . Outside the 'bull-pen,' as our prison-yard was universally termed, were the barracks for the guards, and the horses and families of the officers in command and on duty there."[16] Colonel Buehring H. Jones, CSA, of the 60th Virginia Infantry, remembered the busy cemetery on Johnson's Island in his narrative, *The Sunny Land* (1868): "Our cemetery, containing about a fourth of an acre, enclosed with a neat and substantial plank fence, white-washed, and the graves carefully sodded, all the work of our own hands, is located at the eastern extremity of the Island. There reposes the dust of some 300 of our countrymen. We bury our own dead, and on such occasions, like our working parties, we are always attended by a sufficient guard. The idea of dying and being buried on this lone Island is especially distasteful to us all."[17] The hospital, more a place to die than to live, was "a large building, about 200 feet in length, forty feet in breadth, and two stories in height . . . is divided into four wards and is always crowded with patients. . . . The patients are treated by none by Confederate physicians, of whom there are quite a goodly number in prison."[18]

Point Lookout federal prison camp for enlisted POWs was situated in the heart of Confederate-sympathizing Saint Mary's County, Maryland. Located at the point where the Potomac River joins the Chesapeake Bay, it held the largest number of Confederate POWs throughout the war, about 52,000 from June 1863 until July 1865, with an average prison population of about 20,000. Official government reports of camp deaths indicate that mortality reached 2,950 by the war's end, due, in part, to wounds received in battle, damp weather conditions, diet, and terrible overcrowding. When prisoners fell ill, the supply of medicine and the hospital facilities were not quite sufficient to meet their needs. One Confederate prisoner reports:

> I have seen men brought from camp on a litter, when they had been lying ill for days upon the floor of their tents, with only one thin blanket; and after getting to the hospital, they were put on the floor of the ward, instead of in a bed. Frequently, while they were making room for a patient, the poor wretch would lie shivering from cold, outside the tent; and once, I saw the litter set down upon the snow, and remain there some minutes, with a very ill man upon it. The dead were placed in a large tent, and I have gone there and found the tent almost blown away, and the bodies half buried in snow.[19]

Another Confederate POW describes his arrival at Point Lookout: "We were stripped of our clothing and our persons were strictly searched. Our money, watches and little valuables were taken from us. We were then marched into the camp enclosure and initiated in prison regulations. We were placed in small tents, capable of holding five men with great discomfort. Most of the men who came in with us slept on the ground. When it rained our situation was truly deplorable."[20] This prisoner then tells his readers about the lack of good water, one of the most difficult problems he and his fellow prisoners encountered in Union captivity at Point Lookout: "The salt meat created intense thirst, which we had no means of slaking. There were about thirty wells within the encampment, but all the water was strongly impregnated with copper and other minerals, and the surgeons pronounced it poisonous. We were advised by them to drink as little of it as possible. It turned the teeth and tongue, in many instances, perfectly black.''[21]

Complementing Johnson's Island, a camp reserved for Confederate officers, Camp Douglas, in Chicago, Illinois, was a prison facility reserved for Confederate enlisted men. One of the more notable Confederate prisoners incarcerated there was a young English immigrant, Henry Morton Stanley, who would later "discover" Dr. Livingstone in Africa. Eventually Stanley renounced his American citizenship and left the United States for his native England (where he became Sir Henry Morton Stanley), but during the Civil War, Stanley served briefly as a member of the Arkansas Dixie Greys. He was captured at the Battle of Shiloh in 1862 and interned at Camp Douglas.

> Our prison-pen was a square and spacious enclosure, like a bleak cattle-yard, walled high with planking, on the top of which, at every sixty yards or so, were sentry-boxes. About fifty feet from its base, and running parallel with it, was a line of lime-wash. That was the "dead-line," and any prisoner who crossed it was liable to be shot. . . . [There were] buildings allotted to the prisoners, huge, barn-like structures of planking, each about 250 feet by 40 and capable of accommodating between 200 and 300 men. There may have been about twenty of these structures, about thirty feet apart, and standing in two rows; and I estimated that there were enough prisoners within it to have formed a strong brigade—say about 3,000 men—when we arrived. I remember, by the regimental badges which they wore on their caps and hats, that they belonged to the three arms of the service, and that almost every Southern State was represented. They were clad in home-made butternut grey. . . . We were led to one of the great wooden barns, where we found a six-foot wide platform on each side, raised about four feet above the flooring. These platforms formed continuous bunks for about sixty men, allowing thirty inches to each man. . . . Several bales of hay were brought, out of which we helped ourselves for bedding. Blankets were also distributed, one to each man.[22]

An anonymous, less notable Confederate prisoner than Stanley describes New Year's Eve at Camp Douglas: ''We arrived at Camp Douglas [and] many of us were without blankets, and all without overcoats. Although the nights were already cold, the authorities refused to furnish either blankets or overcoats. In December we were stripped of the overcoats we had procured, the officers stating as an excuse that they might assist us in making our escape. . . . On New Year's Eve snow fell and the cold became intense. . . . Our own sufferings can hardly be imagined."[23]

Fort Delaware sits on Pea Patch Island in the middle of the Delaware River near Delaware City, Delaware. Its total area consists of 178 acres; the fort itself is a pentagon and consists of six acres. Its walls are thirty-two feet high, built of solid granite from seven to thirty feet thick. At its peak in 1863, it housed about 12,500 Confederate officers and political prisoners. Approximately 2,700 prisoners died there during the war, and there were more than two hundred escapes. Fort Delaware was unusual in several respects. It served as a Union political outpost in a sea of Southern sympathy. Its primary mission was to guard the strategic position of the Delaware River—the passage from the Atlantic Ocean to the ports of Wilmington and Philadelphia. Keeping Confederate prisoners was an afterthought. Delaware was a slave state in 1861, and Union authorities knew that its southern half teetered on secession. At the very least, there was a great deal of sympathy for the Southern cause in towns like New Castle, Delaware City, and even Wilmington itself.[24] As a prison camp, Fort Delaware housed both officers and enlisted men. The officers, including such Confederate notables as General Joseph Wheeler, CSA, General M. Jeff Thompson, CSA, and General Basil W. Duke, CSA, lived inside the fort; the enlisted men were housed in barracks outside. The fort also housed political prisoners seized by Union authorities for openly displaying Southern sympathies. Among these were Judge Richard B. Carmichael of Easton, Maryland, who was dragged from his courtroom by federal troops; Isaac C. W. Powell, the clerk of Carmichael's court; Stephen Joyce and Francis A. Richardson, editors of the Baltimore *Republican;* Madison Y. Johnson of Galena, Illinois, a personal friend of Abraham Lincoln but a man who advocated peace in time of civil war; Warren J. Reed of Kent County, Delaware, an active Democrat who was never told what the charges were; and Reverend Isaac W. K. Handy, a Virginian, who was caught preaching the Southern cause from the pulpit.[25] Describing the conditions of the fort in 1862, one British seaman, captured in a blockade-runner, wrote: "The granite walls are wet with moisture, the stone floors damp and cold, the air impure. The prisoners have no beds, but must sleep on the floor, they have no water to wash with and are surrounded by filth and vermin."[26] The British consul in Philadelphia visited Fort Delaware, then wrote to Secretary of State William H. Seward in January 1863. He secured the release of all the British seamen in Fort Delaware, but in 1863 it began filling up again after the Battle of Gettysburg. One Confederate reported that when he arrived at the fort his valuables were taken and then he was moved into the prison compound "with curses and kicks." There he discovered 8,000 fellow Confederates, many of whom were sick, and all of whom were suffering from hunger. "The sick were examined every morning. . . . The hospital arrangements were wretched. Men died there rapidly from want of care, unwholesome food and bad water. . . . Many prisoners died in the barracks during the winter. Many of them were frozen to death."[27] At the end of the war about 300 Union convicts remained on the island, tasked with dismantling the barracks. By June 1866, there were no more Confederate POWs, military or civilian, and Fort Delaware was back on a peacetime footing.[28]

Elmira Prison Camp, in Elmira, New York, was a large army barracks constructed in 1861 to serve as a depot for the Empire State Volunteers. It served its designed function until May 1864, when the federal government decided to use the Elmira facility as a prison camp. Under orders from Colonel William Hoffman, the federal Commissary-General of Prisoners, Lieutenant Colonel Frederick Eastman converted Barracks B into a prison facility.[29] In its brief career as a prison camp, Elmira, or "Hell-Mira" as it was known to the inmates, held a total of 12,123 Confederate prisoners. Suffering mostly from cold, malnutrition, and diseases, 2,963 men died, a death rate of 25 percent, significantly higher than the 11 percent death rate in most other Union camps.[30] Between September 1863 and February 1864, 1,848 Confederates died. The official records point out that the number of sick and dead rose sharply when the Confederate treatment of Union prisoners at Andersonville began to come into full view (see Appendix 2C for Elmira and 2D for Andersonville).[31]

One of the strangest, most demeaning events of the Civil War took place at the Elmira prison camp; it became a tourist attraction. The local Elmirans were terribly curious about what real rebels looked like. As a response to the citizens' curiosity, local entrepreneurs built a raised boardwalk between the guard towers that enabled the local population to spend a Sunday afternoon eating snacks and strolling around the camp perimeter while looking at the starving Confederates. No other Union prison camp commandant ever permitted local citizenry to humiliate Confederate POWs in this manner.[32]

Up to 1864, the Confederates planned on reasonably swift exchanges so that they could return their own men to duty quickly. Thus, a suitable Confederate prison facility was a spot isolated from the civilian population and accessible by train for large consignments of prisoners taken after large engagements. Nearly anything that could hold a large number of men would suffice as a prison camp. Warehouses, islands, old forts, hospitals, and fairgrounds were used initially with some success. Later in the war, when the Confederacy ran out of room for the large number of Union prisoners taken in battle, it resorted to using open fields, where the prisoners had to build their own quarters.

Belle Island, also known as C.S.M. Prison, Richmond, Virginia, housed

Union enlisted prisoners. Situated in the James River opposite Richmond, it was used as a military prison for most of the war. The lowest part of the island was the prison proper, surrounded by an embankment three feet high and ditched on either side. Up to ten thousand prisoners were housed in this facility. There were tents and barracks, but never enough to go around, and the death rate rose to extreme levels, especially during the winter of 1863–1864. Testifying under oath before Congress in 1868, one witness, Dorrance Atwater, the Confederate quartermaster's clerk for seven or eight months at Smith's tobacco warehouse in Richmond and later in Andersonville, offered the following sworn testimony:

> The island contained about 100 acres. The present camp at the southern end of a sandy plane contained about ten acres. A mound of earth inside, three feet high, constituted the dead-line; water was readily obtained from barrels sunk in the earth, but was impregnated with human filth from the camp. Ten thousand men were confined here in August, 1863; prisoners were allowed to go to the sinks only in the daytime. The men were without shoes, stockings or shirts, and lay upon the bare ground. The prisoners went several days in the severest weather without any food.[33]

Libby Prison—also in Richmond—was reserved for Union officers. This facility was a converted tobacco warehouse near Twentieth and Cary streets, not far from the Lynchburg Canal and the James River. One of the first sights an officer-prisoner would notice was the large sign saying, "Libby & Son: Ship Chandlers and Grocers." According to Captain Bernhard Domschke, USV, the Libby landscape consisted of three floors.

> The first consisted of the office together with the so-called supply room (a room without supplies) and a place for the sick. The second and third had been storage areas for ships' goods, each about fifty feet wide and sixty deep. Both floors had three such areas. . . . Under the first floor something of a cellar served various purposes. There the terrible cells—tiny dark holes infested by rats and other vermin—horrified everybody so maligned as to be locked in them. . . . Even a short stay in those dungeons amounted, without a doubt, to an eon of agony. . . .
> The Middle Rooms, having lower ceilings, were darker than the Upper. Higher ceilings under the roof with skylights brightened the Upper. Windows occurred sufficiently in the Libby but were nothing but openings; panes and sashes had long since disappeared. Wooden stairs connected the floors, without landings, steep—typical for warehouses. Here and there the roof leaked. Wooden bedsteads, so-called

bunks, filled the Upper and Lower West. Every other room offered only empty walls. Except, in each, the wooden trough for washing. Water piped in from the nearby canal served for drinking, cooking, and bathing—lukewarm in summer and (especially after a rain) laced with yellowish soil. . . . People accustom themselves but slowly to misery, gradually with reluctance accommodating the fact of being Fate's choice for torment. With humor one can endure even extended misfortune; the pain will not damage the mind. Some minds surrender, however, and remain scarred. Misery that can purify and ennoble may also consume and leave a person in ashes.[34]

Camp Sumter—located in the 29th district of Sumter County, Georgia, near the town of Plains—was better known in the North as Andersonville. The Confederate government leased the land from two farmers; Benjamin B. Dykes received fifty dollars and Wesley W. Turner received thirty dollars rent per month. In December 1863, the first attempt to construct a major facility for POWs began when Captain Richard B. Winder, CSA, received orders to proceed to Andersonville and supervise construction of a stockade and facilities to confine 6,000 men and to accommodate a large number of guards. The design for this facility was relatively simple; it consisted of 16.5 acres of open ground with a stream.[35]

As happens in war, especially in the American Civil War, what may have begun as a good idea turned into a catastrophe for the inmates. Andersonville was an innovation gone sour, an idea for a large centralized military prison facility established to relieve the field commanders of some of their burdens, and a place to keep thousands of Union prisoners in one place at one time. Originally, Andersonville Prison was constructed to house a high concentration of Union prisoners, who, during the first years of the war, overcrowded the small prisons and warehouses in the South. Moving prisoners from facility to facility taxed the limited Southern transportation system and increased the demands on Confederate field commanders to release fighting soldiers for duty as prison guards.

In 1864, General U. S. Grant ordered a cessation of prisoner exchanges, a move which was designed to challenge the Confederacy's ability to exist. As Grant and Sherman advanced in their campaigns, they lost more and more soldiers to retreating yet combat-ready Confederate armies full of fight and defiance. As a result, the Confederacy was bursting at the seams with Union prisoners and had no place to put them and little to feed them, and it seized on the idea of Andersonville without first thinking through the logistical problems. As a result, prisoners started dying shortly after they arrived in camp. Andersonville became synonymous with hopelessness, disease, maltreatment, atrocities, and death. One prisoner remarks despairingly in his diary, "What can the government be thinking of to let their soldiers die in this filthy place?"[36] John Urban, a member of Company "D," First Pennsylvania Regiment, offers a clear and detailed portrait of the landscape of Andersonville in *Battle Field and Prison Pen, or, Through the War and Thrice a Prisoner in Rebel Dungeons* (1882).

Andersonville prison, where the climax of rebel atrocity was reached, is located in Sumter county, Georgia, about one mile from Andersonville, a small station on the Georgia Central Railroad, sixty-two miles southeast of Macon, Georgia, and about fifty or sixty miles from the Alabama state line. . . . The general appearance of the place, however, is wild and desolate. It is very thinly settled, and was well calculated for the purpose it was intended for. . . . The extent of ground enclosed by the stockade has been a subject of considerable difference of opinion, as it was somewhat difficult to form an opinion, owing to the crowded state of the prison; but I suppose after the enlargement of the pen in July, it contained about twenty-five acres. Of this, four or five acres were swampy, and could not be occupied. A small stream of water, about five or six inches deep, and several feet wide, entered the east side of the prison, and ran through it. This stream had its origin in a swamp a short distance from the stockade, and the water was warm and impure. To add to its natural filthiness, the rebels had built their cook-house directly across the stream on the side where it entered the prison, and the water was often covered with filth and grease. The rebels also washed their dirty, lousy clothes in the stream. On almost every clear day we could see dozens of them sitting along its banks for that purpose; and thirsty as the poor prisoners were, they could hardly make use of the water. The entire prison was enclosed with a high stockade made of pine logs. These logs were about sixteen feet long, and were put into the ground about four feet, thus making a fence twelve feet high. As some of the prisoners succeeded in tunneling out, the rebels built a second stockade a short distance from the first one, and the intervening space they kept lit up during the night with large fires, to prevent the prisoners who might succeed in getting out from escaping. Sentinel boxes were built on top of the stockade; these were about fifty feet apart, and were reached by steps from the ground on the outside. On the inside, about thirty or thirty-five feet from the stockade, was a small railing, fastened on stakes about two feet high. This was called the "Dead Line," and woe to the poor prisoner, whether ignorant of its terrible meaning or not, who crossed, or even reached under it, for instant death was sure. . . . The earth, with the exception of the swamp, was of hard, red clay, with a slight covering of soil almost as light as sand. Lying and starving on this unmerciful, unyielding earth; dying from exposure, hunger and thirst; the sun beating on them until in many cases the hands and neck were burned to blisters—what would not these suffering and dying men have given for the tempering shade of the trees, which the rebels so cruelly and ruthlessly cut away? . . . How can I ever expect to live in this horrible place? After the gates closed on us, we stood around for a short time, dumbfounded, and did not know what to do. . . . One of my comrades, with a groan of despair, exclaimed "My God, can this be hell?"[37]

For Urban and the thousands of Union POWs in Andersonville, the amount and kind of rations were as bad as the place. According to Urban, "Tuesday we received our first day's rations in Andersonville, which consisted of one pint of cornmeal, a small piece of pork, and about a spoonful of cooked rice."[38] Cornmeal and rice were not received well by Northern palates.

Camp Oglethorpe near Macon, Georgia, served as the officer-equivalent of Camp Sumter at Andersonville. Created from the remnants of a fairground, it operated from 1863 to the fall of 1864. More a transient than a permanent prison camp, Camp Oglethorpe was situated about three-quarters of a mile east of Macon. The stockade was built of boards that enclosed an area of about three acres. A picket fence stood about three yards inside the stockade marking the dead-line. The only building in the camp was the prison hospital; otherwise the prisoners were completely exposed to the elements and suffered exposure, starvation, and brutal treatment.[39]

C.S.M. Prison, Cahaba, Alabama, called "Castle Morgan" after John Hunt Morgan, the famous Confederate cavalryman and escaper from the Ohio State Penitentiary, was reserved for Union enlisted prisoners. About ten miles south of Selma, Alabama, it stood in the middle of a riverside town where the Cahaba and the Alabama rivers joined. Like many other Confederate military prisons, Cahaba was a converted agricultural warehouse. Established in the spring of 1863, it was a collecting point for men on the way to Andersonville.[40] Its population was never great, but when Andersonville overflowed in 1864, Cahaba served as a regular Confederate military prison for eight or nine months until the war ended. Cahaba's brick walls stood fourteen feet high and measured 193 feet by 116 feet on the outside, enclosing 15,000 square feet. Surrounding the wall was a stockade of two-inch planks, set three feet into the ground and standing twelve feet high. A plank walkway at the top gave guards an elevated position from which to watch their captives. In 432 wooden bunks, the Union enlisted prisoners slept under the roofed portions of the warehouse without straw or bedding of any kind.[41] The sadness of Cahaba was not so much in its landscape, but in the fact that so many of its former inmates died on their way home aboard the doomed *Sultana* in 1865.

Camp "Sorghum" was C.S.M. Prison, Columbia, South Carolina, for Union officers. Camp "Sorghum" consisted of four or five acres with poor water, a few scrub pines, and no sanitary facilities. One Union POW, Colonel John Fraser, USV, of the 140th Pennsylvania Volunteers, would become the president of the Pennsylvania Agricultural College (later Penn State University) in 1866, and, later, the chancellor of the University of Kansas. The conditions in Camp Sorghum outraged Fraser, and not believing that the Confederacy wanted to murder its Union POWs, he petitioned Lieutenant General William Joseph Hardee, CSA, the Commanding General of the Department of South Carolina, Florida, and Georgia, for better treatment. Fraser's genteel document, though brief, drives home the problems suffered by the officers and enlisted Union prisoners held in the Confederacy. Without adequate food, clothing, and shelter, there would be no hope of survival for any of them. In desperation, Fraser stated his case to Hardee.

> We the undersigned in behalf of the Federal officers confined in this prison, hereby respectfully submit to you our protest against the treatment which we have received at this place.
>
> As Union prisoners of war we have had heretofore almost uniformly good reasons to complain of rations short in quantity & very inferior in quality, of an extremely inadequate supply of cooking utensils & of very long detention of letters, monies & boxes from home, but never before we were placed in this prison have we had reason to complain that the confederate authorities had aggravated these standing grievances ten fold by exposing us as they have done here to the inclemency of the weather in a camp in which not a structure of the humblest kind has been erected for our accommodation. . . . We have been left for more than five weeks to shift for ourselves the best we could. . . . Our government has already found it necessary to retaliate in behalf of Union prisoners of war by reducing rations allowed to your compatriots. We deprecate the necessity of inflicting additional retaliation by turning 1,400 Southern officers out of their prison shelters & subjecting them to treatment as nearly as possible identical with that which we receive.[42]

Fraser told Hardee that he might not know or realize fully how bad the conditions were in camp. In Fraser's view and in the view of the Northern postwar court that ultimately tried Henry Wirz of Andersonville, a commanding officer cannot shed his responsibility to tend to his prisoners. Fraser wrote: "In justice to you we will state we do not believe that you fully realize our condition in this camp. For your undoubted bravery & great experience & ability as an officer assure us that the generosity of the tried soldier would long ere now have moved you to grant us the redress which we have a right to expect at the hands of the authorities of a civilized people."[43]

In the North, former prison camps rest quietly in the cradle of time. The cemeteries containing Union and Confederate dead are the property of the federal government of the United States. Each year, the United Daughters of the Confederacy ensure that the graves of the Confederate war dead are decorated and honored. In the South, Libby Prison is gone; gone too are all the rest of the prison pens, except for Andersonville. After the war, the site was confiscated by the federal government, and the cemetery was administered by the United States Army. As the wooden grave markers wore away, they were replaced by marble. Andersonville today is an active national cemetery. With a large monument from the state of Georgia to all American POWs, the old Camp Sumter, administered by the National Park Service, is the site of the National Prisoner of War Memorial. Johnson's Island is in private hands, except for the Confederate cemetery. Fort Delaware, part bird sanctuary, part museum, belongs to the state of Delaware and admits visitors; Point Lookout, now a park, belongs to the state of Maryland. The others are gone, their memories preserved only by regional historical associations.

German prison camps during World War I were large facilities. Each side knew that in a large war there would be thousands, possibly millions of prisoners, and the German army had developed an efficient method for dealing with them. After capture, prisoners were housed in temporary camps near the lines. Individual Allied POWs experienced confusion, adjustment, suffering, bad rations, and no packages from the American Red Cross. A prisoner lost his clothing and shoes before being sent to a large prison camp in Germany operated by the army corps that took him prisoner. For example, an Allied soldier taken by the 17th Army Corps, whose headquarters was in Danzig, would be sent to Tuchel Prison in East Prussia.[44]

By and large, most American officers were housed in the southern German prison camps in Villingen, Karlsruhe, and Landshut. Some officers and most of the enlisted prisoners were housed at the large facilities at Güstrow, Holzminden, Brandenburg, Rastatt, Stralsund, Parchim, and many other places throughout Germany. Once inside the camps, the prisoners augmented their vocabularies. Working *Kommandos* were parties sent out from the main camp to smaller outlying camps. Single men might be sent out to a farm or, less frequently, to a small factory. Groups might also be sent out to factories. The worst fate was an assignment to work in a mine. Early in the war when the United States acted as the protecting power for Allied prisoners under the Hague Convention, Albert J. Beveridge visited some German camps and came away satisfied, perhaps duped into believing that the Allied prisoners were being treated well. Beveridge reported that "of the many thousands of prisoners personally inspected, all but one appeared to be in robust health. You were surprised at their rosy cheeks, well-nourished condition and general fitness."[45]

Although the United States was neutral and the protecting power for British prisoners until 1917, after America entered the war, American POWs found themselves in the same fix as their allies. Mike Shallin describes his camp as a hellhole.

> Our barracks had one door with a little window for the guards to look in—nothing more. The ventilation was dreadful, particularly as our only place to relieve ourselves was this big wooden bucket near the door. You can imagine what the smell was like. We had to sleep on the floor, which knocked the hell out of our kidneys and bowels. The result was that all night the men were going over to the bucket to take a leak or a crap. Naturally, the damn bucket would frequently overflow—you can imagine what that was like. Then there were the fleas; they were everywhere. And the flies were just as bad. You'd spend all night relieving yourself, smelling, scratching and swatting—with very little sleep.[46]

Norman Archibald points out that food, sleep, and air were vital to the POW's survival. He writes in *Heaven High, Hell Deep 1917–1918* (1935): "Food, ill-tasting and unwholesome, must be eaten and we would eat all we could get. Sleep, on boards and in our uniforms, was difficult but sleep we must. Air, except for my delightful recess, was denied. This manner of living, we knew, could not be withstood for long."[47] Navy Lieutenant Edouard V. Isaacs contrasts the cuisines of two landscapes: shipboard and POW camp. At sea, while he was a POW in the *U-90*, he dined in the wardroom with the ship's officers. Captain Remy reminded Isaacs that food in the German navy was the best in Germany and begged him to eat while he had the opportunity. "God knows," writes Isaacs, "he spoke the truth."[48] Isaacs discovered soon that the camp had fleas so numerous that they made life miserable. It was impossible to get any disinfectant from the Germans, although Isaacs asked the commandant and finally the doctor for some. According to Isaacs, it would have been a small matter to fumigate the barracks, but the Germans did not consider it necessary for mere prisoners. After he became a POW in the Landshut Oflag in 1918, life became even more challenging:

> I quickly became accustomed to life in the camp. We had no breakfast. At noontime we had a plate of soup made out of leaves. This was

followed usually by a plate of black potatoes (the good potatoes were saved for the German Army) or horse carrots or some similar vegetable. At 6 p.m. we had another plate of soup and sometimes there was a dessert: a teaspoonful of jam. It was terrible tasting stuff and for a long time we could not tell what it was made of; but a few months later we saw peasants gathering the red berries of the mountain ash and they told us they made them into jam. That accounted for the taste.

That was our ration from the Germans with the exception of the black bread. Once a day we were given a piece of this bread about as big as a man's fist . . . the small size of this half pound is easily understood. . . . We tried to analyze it one day and this is what we found: First, water and potatoes; second, sawdust and chaff; and third, sand.

As for the soup, . . . it never changed. It looked and tasted like water; and the leaves with which it was filled were, of course, not edible. . . . The canteen sold cider and so-called wine, and once in a while some dried fish. No other foodstuffs could we buy. They had . . . "ersatz" cigarettes and tobacco at exorbitant prices . . . [which] must contain seventy-five percent hops by order of the Government. It looked like wheat chaff, but we bought it just the same, rather than have nothing to smoke.[49]

In spite of the complaints POWs express in their narratives, military captivity for Americans remained relatively humane during World War I because of the existence of camp help committees elected from among the prisoners themselves. Throughout the German prison system, three major issues occupied the camp committees: food, spies in camp, and reprisals. American committees communicated directly with the American Red Cross, and together they provided food and clothing to all the American POWs, who would often share their bounty with their allies. Not only did the committees investigate problems and present complaints to the camp commandant, but sometimes they actually negotiated with him concerning food, clothing, mail, and other issues, the idea being that they could forestall problems for their fellow prisoners and anticipate the needs of new arrivals.[50]

In spite of occasional political reprisals, American prisoners in Germany during World War I were not subject to any systematic or authorized physical abuse. That their clothing and personal effects were stolen upon capture was part of a common experience. The Germans considered most of a POW's personal effects the booty and spoils of war until these practices were banned in the November 1918 POW treaty between Germany and the United States. The American POWs had not starved in German captivity. They received more than twenty pounds of food and clothing a week, better food and clothing than the German population had seen for two years.[51] The Americans would have starved, however, without packages of food and clothing sent to them by the American Red Cross in Berne, Switzerland. In effect, during World War I, the United States made the conscious decision to guard its POWs in enemy hands. Consequently, American POWs in German hands were able to maintain their health, dignity, military communities, and individual self-respect.

When World War II began for the United States in December 1941, Camp O'Donnell was a partially completed airfield about eight miles west of the Manila railroad line at Capas on the island of Luzon in the Philippines. A high barbed-wire fence surrounded the camp, and wooden gun towers gave the Japanese guards a complete view of their prisoners' activities. The Japanese decided to put their first American prisoners in Camp O'Donnell, and here the survivors of the Bataan Death March would learn that no international agreements would protect them.[52] According to William Wallace, one of the American POWs who spent time in Camp O'Donnell, "The further we went into captivity, the worse it became. It gets to the place where it's unbelievable to the imagination of a person who was not there. . . . I learned the human body can suffer nearly everything and still survive."[53] The General Headquarters *Weekly Summary* (No. 104) of 29 October 1943 summarizes the debrief of Major William E. Dyess, USA, who had escaped from the Davao penal colony, another camp used by the Japanese to house Americans taken in Bataan and Corregidor. Dyess was held prisoner in Camp O'Donnell for two months. The summary comments on the treatment at Camp O'Donnell.

The principal diet in all camps was rice, with occasionally about a tablespoon of camote, the native sweet potato, often rotten. The Japs issued meat twice in two months, in portions too small to give even a fourth of the men a piece one inch square. [According to Major Dyess] abundant food supplies were available in the countryside, and the Japs deliberately held prisoners on a starvation diet.

Many of the prisoners at O'Donnell had no shelter. The death rate among Americans from malnutrition and disease increased rapidly from twenty daily during the first week to fifty after the second week. The death rate among the Filipinos was six times greater. Hospital and sanitary facilities did not in any real sense exist. Medicines were promised but never supplied. Prisoners lived in filth, and died in large numbers of malaria, by dysentery and beriberi.

The Japanese nevertheless constantly insisted on work details. By 1 May 1942 only about twenty out of every company of 200 were able to work. [Major Dyess states] that 2,200 Americans and 27,000 Filipinos died at O'Donnell Prison Camp.[54]

When Corregidor surrendered in late May 1942, the prisoners were marched through the streets of Manila on their way to Bilibid Prison. This facility was used by the Japanese army as a transient camp for receiving, searching, and assigning prisoners to the permanent prison camps in Formosa, Korea, Manchuria, or Japan. Cabanatuan was a prison camp located about 100 miles north of Manila and had been an American agricultural experiment station before the war. It consisted of three sites (Camps 1, 2, and 3): Camp 1 contained most of the transferred Camp O'Donnell prisoners; Camps 2 and 3 were filled with the men who surrendered after the fall of Corregidor in May, 1942. In a space of 100 acres with the usual guard towers and a high barbed-wire fence, each area consisted of a large wooden dispensary building, a guardhouse with a cell at one end, a long shelter used as a garage, and a number of nipa-thatch barracks about sixty feet long to house 120 men.[55] Describing his experience, Hubert Gater told Donald Knox that after the first week of working day and night he was so exhausted that he fell into his bunk. "The next morning four men from my section were dead. That really shook me up. O'Donnell. Cabanatuan. Death followed us."[56]

Davao remains a Philippine federal prison today in a jungle clearing on the island of Mindanao. Beginning in 1942, about 2,000 American POWs grew food for the Japanese garrisons throughout the Philippines. The prison barracks were made of lumber with large corrugated steel roofs and mahogany floors.[57] Tacloban prison camp, a smaller facility on the island of Leyte, was shaped roughly like a trapezoid with evenly spaced thatch-roof huts housing mostly British and Australians. One American confined in Tacloban with the British and Australian prisoners was Douglas Valentine. In *The Hotel Tacloban* (1984), written by his son and published in England, Valentine describes the "doghouse," the place of solitary confinement, "Placed squarely in the center of the prison yard in the empty space between the last two British huts on either side and the Japanese billets. . . . Made of durable wood resembling teak, unventilated and only four feet cubed, it was there that POWs were sent for punishment. Our cemetery was located in the area between the guards' billet and the last British hut on the north side of camp."[58]

In Karenko prison camp (also known as Kwarenko) in Formosa (Taiwan), the Japanese army housed some of the most distinguished British, Dutch, and American officers and civil officials captured early in World War II. Discipline there was extremely harsh, and the guards humiliated their prisoners by punishing them for trifles or for disobeying ridiculous orders. For example, the commandant ordered Allied senior officers to bow to Japanese privates and corporals. In order to induce noncompliance, the guards often hid from view, then jumped out among unsuspecting officers on their way to the latrine. The prisoners, unaware of the guards' presence, would pass them by without the bow. The guards would then beat the prisoners for not showing the required respect.[59] When orders came for a further removal, the prisoners were delighted to leave Karenko. General W. E. Brougher, USA, comments in his diary about starvation in Karenko and his arrival in the Japanese prison camp in Mukden, Manchuria.

April 8 Thin food. Starvation rations. Very cold weather, colder than Karenko. Everybody miserably cold and hungry. . . .
April 10 Letters returned for revision and enclosure in envelope. . . . Food situation getting desperate. Everybody ravenously hungry—no vegetables in soup—no sugar. Red Cross supplies belong to us and in hands of Nipponese—will not let us have them. Will not buy sufficient food for us to sustain life. Unless something is done soon we will starve to death —and it won't be long.[60]

Finally, some Red Cross packages arrived at the camp. Brougher was elated; food meant life.

April 14 There is a Santa Claus after all! This morning we were issued 1 individual package—1 lb. sugar, 8 oz corned beef, 4 oz cocoa, 1 lb salt. The individual package was just like a Christmas stocking—15 or 16 different items in it. Mine contained: 1 bar chocolate candy, small package lemon drops, 2 small packages sugar, 1 pineapple and plum jam, 1 small cheese biscuit, tongue and liver paste, steak and rice, margarine, marmalade pudding, bacon, 1 can tomatoes, 1 can ham paste and gelatin, soap and tea. . . . My, my, my! And how good the chocolate bar tasted! I guess I've missed candy more than anything else. It is understood now that we'll get 1 lb of sugar a week and 3 lbs meat a week. That will supplement the mess in fine style and we will begin to live again.[61]

James P. S. Devereux, taken with the marines at Wake Island and the North China Marines, was interned at Woosung prison camp in Korea. The prisoners' quarters were seven barracks, each a long, narrow, one-story shack into which the Japanese crowded 200 men. At one end of each barracks was a wash rack and toilets. Facing the toilets, and much too close for sanitation, was a galley where food was prepared. The camp was surrounded by an electrified fence; and later, inside that fence, another electrified fence was erected around the barracks and the toilets. Devereux writes of the desolation of that prison landscape.

The prisoners slept on wooden platforms and each man was given a straw tick and four blankets for his bedding, but four of those skimpy blankets were not half as warm as one ordinary American blanket. The jerrybuilt barracks gave little protection against the intense cold, and during the bitter winter we were soon pooling our blankets and sleeping four in a bunk to keep from freezing to death. The North China Marines who joined us at Woosung had winter uniforms, with overcoats, fur hats and gloves, but the rest of us had only the thin tropical uniforms we had brought from Wake. During the whole time of our captivity, the cold was our bitterest hardship and our suffering was made worse because we never had enough to eat.[62]

After their early glimpse of the landscape, the Americans began to learn what the code of Bushido—honor, obedience, and valor—was all about for Japanese soldiers and their prisoners. The prison facilities, regardless of location—Philippines, Korea, Formosa, or Manchuria—matched the Japanese view of retributive justice against the soldier who surrendered. Perceived as having disgraced themselves for surrendering, the American prisoners in the Pacific learned that their captors believed they were cowardly, soft, and materialistic. If ever there were a conflict of cultures that cost thousands of lives, it was in the prison camps in the Pacific during World War II.

In Europe, the prison system for Kriegies was patterned after the one developed by the German army during World War I (see Appendix 3D for the major German prison camps). Germany had at least ninety POW camps; Italy had twenty-one camps that were taken over by the Germans in 1943 when Italy changed sides.[63] Rarely, if ever, were American POWs confined in the concentration/death camps operated by the SS, although there were sections in some of these large camps set aside for other Allied prisoners. Auschwitz, for example, had a section set aside for British, French, and Russian POWs.[64] Committed escapers, after they were identified, were often confined together. One section of Stalag Luft III in Sagan, Silesia, from which the "Great Escape" was made in 1944, and Oflag VII in the Colditz Castle were two of these escaper-concentrated compounds.

Some prisoners were separated from the mass of Kriegies in the large camps and put into small work camps, or *Arbeitskommando*. Bill Watkins recalls his *Arbeitskommando* quarters: "Camp was an older two story house, with an exercise yard. Main floor was latrine, eating area, sleeping room. The second floor contained three sleeping rooms and guard room. Except for injury on the 'job,' we worked at assigned jobs. The freight yard group worked under civilian direction while the working group was sent out under guard to the woods. . . . Most days off were spent filling bomb craters and removing snow from ice rinks."[65] Another Kriegie, Warren Fencl, remembers his receiving camp in remarkable detail:

> We reached our new home, a POW Receiving Camp near a rail center where POWs are sent to France, then Germany. The camp was a modified barnyard, either a sheep or a cattle shed, from the smell, I'd say sheep shed. From our pacing the yard and remarks from the Germans, the lot was 100 × 200 meters with tree trunk poles 8' to 10' with three coils of accordion barbed wire attached to cross pieces and a guard tower 12' high opposite the shed. The shed was about ninety meters long. The center of the building was two stories high where feed and grain were kept, now it's the office, it's about ten meters and the rooms on each side were the sheds. We POWs stayed in one room and the guards stayed on the other side.[66]

Stalag Luft IV was a noncommissioned officers camp, mostly airmen with the rank of sergeant. Located about two and a half miles south of Kiefheide, in Pomerania, south of the Baltic Sea, Stalag Luft IV was activated in April 1944 but was never actually completed, despite German effort. The dense foliage and underbrush served as an added barrier to escape. Two barbed wire fences, ten feet high, completely surrounded the camp. Between the two fences was another fence of rolled barbed wire four feet high. An area 200 feet deep, from the fence to the edge of the forest, was left clear, so that any one attempting escape would have to traverse this area in full view of the guards. Fifty feet inside the wire fence was a warning wire similar to Civil War "dead-lines." A prisoner could expect to be shot first, then questioned, if he stepped over it. At close intervals around camp were towers, with powerful spotlights and machine guns, enough to deter anyone from trying to escape. Stalag Luft IV contained four compounds: lagers A, B, C, and D with ten barracks in each, a kitchen, an outside hand pump, and a building used for a toilet. Each had a shed to store potatoes, carrots, and the like. The kitchen had a couple of large steam-type boilers used to cook potatoes, barley, carrots, cabbage, and broth. Outside the lager there were buildings for German storage, office, and barracks, one of which was used as a hospital for the sick POWs.

Orvis C. Preston of Northlake, Illinois, observes that "this was a new camp, not nearly finished, named Stalag Luft IV. I arrived on June 20th, 1944 and [was] assigned to Lager A, Barracks 10, Room 1. . . . [It] had seven triple bunks, twenty-seven men. There were six slats, (boards three feet long by three to four inches wide) and a burlap type mattress, partly filled with grass or straw. We had one table, two benches, two stools along with a stove, little coal or rubbish to burn in it. At times we would get five lumps of coal in cold winter.''[67]

Charles Miller was shot down over Wilhelmshaven in May 1943. After more than thirty-six hours in a life raft in the North Sea, Miller and his crew were rescued by a German patrol boat and taken prisoner. In *Remembering War: A U.S.–Soviet Dialogue* (1990), Miller recalls life in Stalag VII A, a huge camp located about fifty miles from Munich that housed American, Russian, French, English, and other Allied prisoners. Had more food been available, the death rate among non-Russian prisoners would have been even smaller than the mere one percent it was. For the Russians, however, there were no Red Cross parcels; the Soviet Union was not a signatory to the 1929 Geneva Convention, and Charles Miller knew that the Russian prisoners ate the dogs. ''Some nights you'd get locked in your barracks, and just for the hell of it, a couple of German guards would come up and take the police dogs and let them in. . . . One time they did it with the Russians. And the dogs didn't come out. . . . The Russians had actually eaten those two police dogs!''[68]

These narratives indicate life was hard but generally not lethal for most of the American Kriegies in Europe. Fortunately, the German military experience with vast numbers of prisoners in World War I paid off in World War II. The camps were designed for efficiency and were guarded by experienced soldiers rather than political forces or rearguard reserves with no combat experience. Rank was respected for the most part, as was the 1929 Geneva Convention. Kriegies received some medical attention; some sick and wounded prisoners were exchanged. Aside from the 1 percent who died in captivity, mostly from wounds received in battle, most of the vast number of American Kriegies in Europe, although debilitated by hunger, abnormal weight loss, and sickness, made it home alive. The prisons of Korea and Vietnam, however, were far less humane.

The Korean landscape, although beautiful in peace, was deadly in war and presented a different and difficult challenge to United Nations soldiers who found themselves prisoners of the North Korean and Chinese armies. After the long marches north to the camps in the winter, the prisoners were extremely tired, often debilitated to the point of exhaustion. United Nations POWs in Chinese captivity discovered that they were "students" in an ideological, winner-take-all game of tug-of-war. John W. Thornton found himself captive of the Chinese and was chosen to attend what his captors told him was "a great school of communist learning" in Pyoktong, North Korea.[69] The Chinese called it "Pyoktong University"; Thornton and the other POWs called it "PU": "Pyoktong University was a high-powered interrogation center, and an exclusive one at that—P.U.

was reserved strictly for non-Korean captives. It was an all-business college. The faculty quickly informed us that they *meant* business and would *give* the business to anybody that didn't learn their lessons properly."[70] At school, Thornton's cell was a cubicle about six feet by eight feet with a light bulb hanging from the ceiling. Touching the bulb brought one or several severe penalties: solitary confinement in any one of the "holes" available in the camp, or beating, or both. According to Thornton, "We were six men in a six-by-eight cubicle in the warmth of spring with flies and lice for company."[71] Thornton left Pyoktong in October 1951 for Ping-chong-ni, an all-officer camp where he would remain until repatriation in September 1953.

Ralph D. Moyer recalls that the Chinese told his group of prisoners that the permanent camp had running water, electric lights, and warm rooms. Upon arrival, they discovered the village was the same as all the others in North Korea, drab and forlorn-looking, cold, and gray. Once in camp, men began to die. Moyer remembers that in June 1951 the Chinese refused to let the prisoners bury their dead, and he could look across the Chosen Reservoir about a half mile away and see Korean hogs feeding on their remains.[72] In camp, sergeants were separated from privates, corporals, and the officers; likewise, all the black prisoners were separated from their white comrades. The French, British, and Turks had their own areas as well. Once in a great while the prisoners were allowed to mix. After July 1951, however, the general conditions improved. According to Moyer: "We were cleaned up, given Chinese summer blue jacket and pants, tennis shoes, underwear, soap, and were given hair cuts. Our own men did the barbering. Food was never close to being good, but there was some improvement over that long winter of 1950 and early 1951. We got a Red Cross package once, about two weeks before release."[73]

Eighteen years later, captivity in North Korea remained unchanged. The crew of the USS *Pueblo* in 1968 were treated no differently from the earlier POWs in Korea. According to Stephen Harris in *My Anchor Held* (1970), he and his fellow prisoners had to conform to what the North Korean communists called the "Rules of LIfe," which included heavy doses of propaganda, or what the North Koreans called "culture." A prisoner was punished if he committed any of the following "crimes": making false statements, refusing questioning, or hinting to others to do so; attempting to signal other rooms by any means of communication including unauthorized written communication; or showing disrespect to any North Korean guards or duty personnel.[74] The American prisoners found it nearly impossible to conform, and according to Harris and Bucher, the officers and crew suffered greatly from the beatings they received for their disobedience.

Special Forces Sergeant George Smith served in South Vietnam during the pre-1965 period when most military activities were confined to advising and training units of the South Vietnamese Army. Captured during an unsuccessful operation with that army, Smith had the training and experience to judge the terrain as a POW if necessary. In his narrative, one of the few to appear before the large POW repatriation in 1973, *P.O.W.: Two Years with the Vietcong* (1971), Smith describes the camp he called "Auschwitz" and the countryside he thought of as "virgin territory."

Auschwitz wasn't primarily a prison camp. It was a guerrilla base camp, a supply center. . . . Base camps supply all the guerrilla units operating in an area. It's a wagon-wheel type of thing: . . . the hub, the guerrillas operate all around it, and they come in and get resupplied and go back out. And they have a main supply route that they supply the hub with. . . . Keeping prisoners there was a sideline. There were all kinds of people coming and going. The camp's company would carry in rice on their backs, poles for building the houses, wood for the fires; they operated the rice mill and supervised the prisoners. Fishermen would go out at night with their tackle and come back the next morning with a mess of fish, and they had a hunting party out most of the time. The jungle is very thick—it's like virgin territory—brambles and twigs and briars and bamboo. It's just impossible to go through unless there's already a path cut. But the hunting parties knew where to go. They'd go out with their rifles over their shoulder and come back with whatever was available, deer, boar, maybe a monkey.[75]

Whereas the Vietcong guerrillas housed their American POWs in base camps and makeshift prison camps, the North Vietnamese kept prisoners in an extensive system that consisted of eleven prisons, including what POWs called the "Plantation," the "Zoo," "Alcatraz," and the escape-proof "Hilton" in Hanoi, plus six other prison camps within a fifty-mile radius including the "Briarpatch," Son Tay, "Faith," "Skidrow," D-1, the "Rockpile." The camp the Americans called "Dogpatch" after the newspaper cartoon "Lil' Abner" was located in the mountains in the northernmost part of North Vietnam five miles from the Chinese border.[76]

American POWs were kept in bamboo cages in the south; in the north they stayed in cells that captured pilots measured in minute details. In *A POW's Story: 2801 Days in Hanoi* (1990), Larry Guarino describes what the American prisoners called the "Heartbreak Hotel" section of the "Hanoi Hilton."

I was shoved into the cell. I looked around me. It was about seven feet wide by sixteen feet long. Against the far wall was a wooden bench with a set of rusty old iron leg stocks set up to hold four people. . . . There was one arched-shaped window seven feet from the floor, with a double set of iron bars across it. I could see out by climbing up on one of the benches, but there was nothing to see but another wall, six feet away. It was about sixteen feet high, topped with broken glass. Steel angle irons, strung with barbed wire, protruded from the top of the wall.[77]

When Howard Rutledge and other Americans in the "Hilton" were uncooperative, they were placed in a tomblike building in tiny individual cells, six feet by six feet. Each cell held two concrete bunks, one on each side, with barely enough room to walk between them. The bunks were about two feet wide and at the bottom of each, embedded in cement, was a set of iron stocks, what Pierre Boulle described as the "Justice Bar." A prisoner would put his feet in place, and another iron bar was forced down across the top with an iron pin to lock them.[78] "The enemy knew that the best way to break a man's resistance was to crush his spirit in a lonely cell," says Rutledge. "In other wars, some of our POWs after solitary confinement lay down in a fetal position and died. All this talk of scripture and hymns may seem boring to some, but it was the way we conquered the enemy and overcame the power of death around us."[79]

Like the thousands of prisoners before them, POWs in Vietnam adjusted to the environment or died. Camp regulations were posted periodically by captors to make sure that the prisoners understood the nature of their status in the camp. According to John M. McGrath's *Prisoner of War: Six Years in Hanoi* (1975), the camp regulations were weapons of terror used by their captors to justify inflicting punishment (torture) upon, "the blackest criminals in the D.R.V.N." (Democratic Republic of Vietnam).[80] There was no way that the American POWs could obey these regulations; however, in time they did come to terms with them through acts of resistance.

Two major narrative motifs appear in varying degrees within the prison landscape event-scenario: the physical description of the prison including the cell, ship, or camp and the reinforcement of the emotional will to survive through the physical acquisition of food. The cell is the prisoner's immediate world, and nearly every narrator measures it in minute detail. POWs had to learn how to come to terms with jail, how to accept it, and how to manipulate it to their best advantage. The guards were either lauded or damned: lauded for protecting them against the wrath of civilians, or damned for outrageous behavior against them. Most POWs saw only ugliness, dirt, and filth, with only their imaginations to create fantasies of the beauty of home. James N. Rowe, however, saw the U Minh

Forest from his cage as offering a paradox between Vietnam's natural beauty and the ugly loneliness of his close confinement.

> Rest there, stranger, and enter not
> the green canopied world of progressive decay.
>   From afar you viewed this land of trees,
> standing straight, leafy green,
> and thought to yourself in a pleased, human way,
>   "how tall they stand, how thick the leaves. How
>   alive that world of trees must be."
>   For from afar it so appears. The trees reveal
> their gift of Nature, but hide from view the world
>   within.
> So you approached while the sun was high,
>   thinking of the shade and the cool relief
> from the sun's burning rays.
>   I watched you come and knew your thoughts,
> for there are those who have entered before.

In Rowe's poem, the world extends beyond the cage. Rowe was fortunate to have the strength to develop his vision since he spent so much time in solitary confinement.

There is little doubt that a great amount of time in captivity generates extreme boredom. One method to fight it lies in observing every possible detail in the surrounding landscape, including the cells, walls, guards, prison routine, and especially the food. There is nothing more common in captivity narratives from colonial times to Vietnam than prisoners' descriptions of food; it becomes an obsession, not only because food and life are inextricably related, but because the act of eating becomes an event—something to anticipate, something to do. POWs learn quickly to eat anything. Dogs, cats, rats, snakes, and insects go on the menu. The rule in captivity is eat or die.

In capture, the individual separates from his primary culture and begins the journey into a world of chaos. The prison landscape is the body of that chaos; it represents a place of evil, a place so horrible that only the most graphic terms can describe it. However, a hidden agenda lurks beneath descriptions of individual prison landscapes, an individual and collective recognition of the *we*ness of the captivity experience.

CHAPTER EIGHT

The Prisoner's War:
Resistance and Torture

If I had a thousand lives, I would lose them all here before I would betray my friend.

Sam Davis (1863)

In military prison camps, captives who choose to resist their captors have had three distinct choices: active or hard resistance, when prisoners resist their captors' demands to the point where anything that hints at cooperation or collaboration will be rejected; passive resistance, when prisoners either shun their captors or decide to deceive them into mistakenly thinking they are cooperating, and avoidance, when prisoners attempt to dodge a captor's attentive focus, what the POWs of the Korean War called "playing it cool." In the first case, hard-resisters learn early in captivity that simple acts of striking back might be a pathway to oblivion. Passive resisters learn to use deception; avoiders simply evade physical contact with their captors whenever possible.

Like escapers, many resisters narrate their experiences soon after repatriation. They have a story to tell. Passive resisters often wait years, sometimes decades, before they take up the pen, often because specific incidents are painful to confess or remember. Many avoiders have yet to narrate their experiences. Many hard resisters, including escapers, are executed outright by their captors, or, in some cases, tortured into passivity. In any case, the choices of resisting and surviving are hard to make, and narrators have shown conclusively that decisions to resist, regardless of the degree, incur high prices both during and after captivity.

After capture and the long march, prisoners begin to understand their captors better. In general, in the resistance event-scenario, captors become identifiable personalities whose task is to destroy their prisoners' sense of community. In the process, POWs faced basic choices: cooperate and survive, or resist and die. From a sense of duty, personal pride, religious faith, or institutional code-based mandates, the resisting POW can not allow himself to cooperate fully; hence, the war between captors and POWs continues unabated from the battlefield to the prison pen. How that war is fought, however, has changed significantly.

Resisting enemy captors is never easy when the enemy holds absolute

171

life-and-death power. As prisoners expanded the basis of the will to live from the individual to the community, several narrators point out that a distinct intellectual, if not spiritual, metamorphosis occurred, from perceiving the prisoner as individual to seeing him as a member of a captive community. Leading the community were hard-resisters for whom a quality of single-minded, inner stubbornness became the essence of the captivity experience and the inspiration for subordinates. When captors decided to inflict torture, the hard-resisters were first in line.

Torture is the act of inflicting injurious pain and suffering on another for a specific reason. The third-century Roman jurist Ulpian defined judicial torture as the *quaestio,* that is, the torment and suffering of the body in order to elicit the truth.[1] In the thirteenth century, the Roman jurist Azo defined torture as a legal procedure that inquired after truth by means of torment. The law of torture as it developed during the Renaissance is best seen in two primary works: the *Constitutio Criminalis Carolina,* the criminal procedure ordinance promulgated for the German Empire in 1532, and the treatise by Joost Damhouder of Bruges, *Praxis Rerum Criminalium* (1554), which appeared in Latin, Dutch, French, and German and circulated for at least 150 years among the magistrates of western Europe.[2] Both these codes limited the use of judicial torture as a legal means to gain acceptable testimony in a court of law. For example, torture could be used only in the cases of capital crimes and only as a last resort. Certain classes of persons, such as aristocrats, clergy, high public officials, lawyers, and physicians were exempt from torture, and it never took place on Sundays or Catholic holy days of obligation.[3] Evidence given in or after judicial torture was designed to supplement or even replace the evidence given by two witnesses. Judicial torturers used the strappado, rack, thumbscrews, and legscrews, all of which were designed to inflict great pain without permanently damaging the victim. These devices also allow the torturer to regulate the pain so that when the victim answers correctly, pain can be reduced or removed. Conversely, if the victim resists questioning, the torturer can apply more pressure and cause more pain. John H. Langbein points out that the process of torture used in the sixteenth century consisted of five basic steps: threat, questioning, verification, repetition of torture, and voluntary confession.

1. *Threat.* The victim must know that he can and will be tortured if the proper answers are not forthcoming. The sight of the torture chamber usually confirms the reality of the threat in the victim's mind. At this point many potential victims will gasp at the thought of the systematic application of pain and lose their determination to resist the captor.

2. *Suggestive Questioning.* During the torture session, the operatives will stop from time to time to question the victim. The torturer is supposed to elicit answers, not supply them.

3. *Verification.* If there are several victims related to one crime or incident that generated the imposition of torture in the first place, the torturer will attempt to verify the information received from the suggestive questioning of previous victims.

4. *Repetition of Torture.* If the victim or victims resist the torture, the operatives continue to apply it in increasing doses until a confession is obtained.

5. *Voluntary Confession.* Once the torture session is over and the confession is rendered by the victim at the place of torture, it is imperative for the torturer to make it look as if the victim rendered it voluntarily. The victim will be asked to repeat the confession in public, in a courtroom, possibly for radio or through a loudspeaker, or even for visiting outsiders such as journalists. Regardless of the setting, the victim must know that the public performance is part of the process. The torturer will make sure the victim knows that the process can begin again.[4]

Preliminary torture, or *torture prealable,* of the convicted was common in Europe. The criminal convicted of a captial crime had already forfeited his life and could be forced into giving evidence concerning his accomplices. Codified in France by an ordinance of 1670, it was accepted practice until 1788, when Louix XVI abolished it.[5] Despite its prohibition in France, the *quaestio* and *torture prealable* were exported to Indochina and remained there even after the French left. According to American captivity narratives of the Vietnam War, the traditional rationale behind the *torture prealable* was used extensively by the North Vietnamese as a pretext for torturing their American POWs.

The criminal status of POWs was abandoned formally in 1648 with the Treaty of Westphalia, but only within contemporary historical memory has torture itself been abandoned as a legal means of soliciting information. Being a prisoner is not in itself a criminal act; a POW cannot be treated as a criminal except as punishment for a crime of which he has been convicted by due process. Article 1 of the Declaration against Torture adopted by the United Nations General Assembly on December 9, 1975, states:

For the purpose of this Declaration, torture means any act by which severe pain or suffering, whether physical or mental, is intentionally inflicted by or at the instigation of a public official or a person for such purposes as obtaining from him or a third person information or confession, punishing him for an act he has committed, or intimidating him or other persons. It does not include pain or suffering arising only from, inherent in, or incidental to lawful sanctions to the extent consistent with the Standard Minimum Rules for the Treatment of Prisoners.[6]

The first group of these definitions is concerned with the old Roman law of torture; the last concerns itself with the acts of nations against their prisoners since World War II, not only against their own prisoners but against POWs who have come under their control. Some tortures were homegrown, especially those of the American forest wars; some evident in the American Civil War were based on punishment rules internal to armies; others were the result of neocolonial influences and were corroborated in narratives and other imaging.

Resistance, especially hard resistance, extends the soldier's act of war from the battlefield to the prison camp and, as a result, places the POW in extreme danger. It is axiomatic too that POWs of higher rank experience greater pressure to cooperate with the captors. In the colonial Indian wars, torture was understood by narrators to be a kind of entertainment at the prisoners' expense; in the national wars, including the Civil War, it was understood as punishment or punitive neglect, and in the Pacific prison camps it was seen as a manifestation of the "Yellow Peril." In the ideological wars of the twentieth century—Korea and Vietnam—the North Koreans, communist Chinese, the Vietcong, and the North Vietnamese all wanted their prisoners to produce propaganda. When the Americans refused to cooperate, they suffered varying degrees of torture, for three reasons: as punishment for acts of defiance; as an inducement to cooperate at least minimally; and as a threat to a captive's person so intense as to generate limited cooperation through a blinding fear of physical pain. The North Koreans learned the ways of military Bushido from the Japanese, the communist Chinese learned the ways of Marxist political reeducation from their experiences after victory over the Nationalist Army in 1949, and the Vietnamese learned the *quaestio,* including the "justice bar," strappado, and bastinado, from the French.

Torture at the hands of Indian captors was understood as part of a captive's journey of initiation.[7] After captives are separated from the culture and complete the long journey, they must undergo a series of excruciating ordeals that symbolize transition from ignorance to knowledge. Captives of the Indians had first to run the gauntlet prior to suffering other kinds of indignities. The narratives from the forest wars of the American colonial period, especially King Philip's War and the French and Indian War, indicate that the captives believed the torture inflicted upon them was simply a traditional form of ritual entertainment for their captors. It infuriated them, and they express varying levels of resentment. Peter Williamson describes one torture experience of his captivity.

At day break, my infernal masters ordered me to lay down my load, when tying my hands again round a tree, they forced the blood out at my fingers' ends. And then kindling a fire near the tree to which I was bound, the most dreadful agonies seized me, concluding I was going to be made a sacrifice to their barbarity. The fire being made, they for some time danced round me after their manner, whooping, hollowing and shrieking in a frightful manner. Being satisfied with this sort of mirth, they proceeded in another manner; taking the burning coals, and sticks flaming with fire at the ends, holding them to my face, head, hands, and feet, and at the same time threatening to burn me entirely if I cried out: thus tortured as I was, almost to death, I suffered their brutalities, without being allowed to vent my anguish otherwise, than by shedding silent tears; and these being observed, they took fresh coals, and applied them near my eyes, telling me my face was wet, and that they would dry it for me, which indeed they cruelly did. How I underwent these tortures has been a matter of wonder to me, but God enabled me to wait with more than common patience for the deliverance I daily prayed for.

At length they sat down round the fire, and roasted the meat, of which they had robbed my dwelling. When they had supped, they offered some to me: although it may easily be imagined I had but little appetite to eat, after the tortures and miseries I had suffered, yet I was forced to seem pleased with what they offered me, lest by refusing it, they should reassume their hellish practices.

Williamson was to undergo yet another torture session, however, though not directed toward him but toward one of his fellow captives.

Here they lay for eight or nine days diverting themselves, at times, in barbarous cruelties on the old man: sometimes they would strip him naked and paint him all over with various sorts of colours: at other times they would pluck the white hairs from his head, and tauntingly tell him, "He was a fool for living so long, and that they would shew him kindness in putting him out of the world." In vain were all his tears, for daily did they tire themselves with the various means they tried to torment him; sometimes tying him to a tree, and whipping him; at other times, scorching his furrowed cheeks with red-hot coals, and burning his legs quite to the knees.[8]

Barbara Leininger's captivity narrative from the French and Indian War makes explicit the kind of torture common during the forest wars, in this description of the retributive and vengeful torture of a recaptured escaper:

> Three days later an Englishman was brought in who had likewise attempted to escape with Colonel Armstrong and burned alive. His torments, however, continued about three hours, but his screams were frightful to listen to. It rained that day very hard, so that the Indians could not keep up the fire. Hence they began to discharge gunpowder at his body. At last, amidst his worst pains when the poor man called for a drink of water, they brought him melted lead, and poured it down his throat. This draught at once helped him out of the hands of the barbarians, for he died on the instant.[9]

Should one attempt to escape from such captors or not, especially when the prisoner knows in advance that, if retaken, he will be roasted alive? He must weigh two evils: either remain among the captors as a prisoner forever, or die a cruel death. Witnessing the kinds of torture common during the forest wars did indeed make a lasting impression among the American colonials, and, in part, as propaganda, escalated the level of fear and hate that was to culminate in the total destruction of the native American tribes by 1890.

Historian Howard H. Peckham claims there were 18,182 American POWs in the Revolution of whom 8,500 died in captivity, most aboard the prison hulks (see Appendix 2A). Other estimates put this figure much higher.[10] In 1808, twenty large containers of bones were collected from the shores of Wallabout Bay in Brooklyn, and as late as 1841 bones of the victims of the prison ships there were still to be found in and around the Brooklyn Navy Yard. While digging, some workmen in 1841 found a quantity of human bones, among which was a skeleton with a pair of iron manacles still upon the wrists.[11] These remains leave little doubt that some torture took place aboard the hulks in the Wallabout Bay.

One of the most notorious British jailers in the hulks was Captain William Cunningham, a man who proved to be a genuine killer. Under the cover of midnight darkness he marched about 260 American prisoners to the gallows and the grave, executed without cause or judicial process.[12] One plausible reason for Cunningham's wrath may have been personal vengeance; in 1774, the Sons of Liberty forced him under arms to kiss the Liberty Pole in New York City. In England after the war, Cunningham became a thief. He was caught, tried, and executed in 1791 for a forgery of 300 pounds. In order to free his conscience just before his hanging, he asked forgiveness for the murders of the American POWs in his charge during the Revolution. Cunningham's confession bore witness to his misdeeds.

When the war commenced, I was appointed Provost Marshal to the Royal Army, which placed me in a situation to wreak my vengeance on the Americans. I shudder to think of the murders I have been accessory to, both with and without orders from the government, especially while in New York, during which time there were more than 2,000 prisoners starved in the different churches, by stopping their rations, which I sold. There were also 275 American prisoners and obnoxious persons executed, out of all which number, there were only one dozen public executions, which chiefly consisted of British and Hessian deserters.

The mode for private executions was thus conducted: a guard was dispatched from the Provost, about half past twelve at night to the Barrack street, and the neighborhood of the upper barracks, to order the people to shut their window shutters, and put out their lights, forbidding them at the same time to presume to look out of their windows and doors on pain of death. After which the unfortunate prisoners were conducted, gagged, just behind the upper barracks and hung without ceremony, and there buried by the black pioneer of the Provost.[13]

Cunningham ended his confession, "I beg the prayers of all good Christians, and also pardon and forgiveness of God for the many horrid murders I have been accessory to."[14] After writing these words, he was executed.

Clandestine murder, however, was not the only form of torture in the Revolution. David Sproat, the loyalist Commissary of Naval Prisoners, believed that the American privateers in his charge were private citizens who had sought to profit financially from rebellion and, therefore, deserved no sympathy. Under Sproat, the forms of cruelty shifted more toward acts of punitive neglect rather than the active process of the *quaestio*. Ethan Allen relates incidents of starvation and neglect in his narrative.

The private soldiers who were brought to New York were crowded into churches and environed with slavish Hessian guards, a people of a strange language who were sent to America for no other design but cruelty and desolation, . . . whose mode of communicating ideas being intelligible in this country, served only to tantalize and insult the helpless and perishing; but above all was the hellish delight and triumph of the Tories over them, as they were dying by hundreds. This was too much for me to bear as a spectator, for I saw the Tories exulting over the dead bodies of their murdered countrymen.[15]

Reprisals—inflicting vengeful injury on innocent persons—were among the accepted methods of making a prisoner's life miserable. As long as each side held POWs, reprisals were used to make the enemy conform to the accepted rules of international law, or, perhaps in some cases, to punish prisoners for the enemy's misdeeds. General Washington knew that prisoners in the hands of the British were vulnerable to any form of reprisal the British might wish to inflict, an eventuality that he wished to forestall if at all possible. In the War of 1812, the British army had sent thirty-three Irish-American POWs to England to be tried for treason, claiming that they were rebellious British subjects rather than American citizens. Congress authorized the president to retaliate, and thirty-three British prisoners were placed in close confinement. The British upped the stakes to sixty-six and even threatened severe measures against American civilians and villages. The Americans responded by closely confining sixty-six English prisoners in irons under threat of execution. When Winfield Scott was released in 1813 he urged the Congress to pass a bill validating reprisals against British prisoners for deeds done against the Irish-Americans in captivity. The United States responded by taking the same number of British prisoners and putting them in close confinement. The British were outraged and threatened death for some prisoners. The stalemate was broken when the British decided to parole the Americans, and the incident subsided.[16] Of the Irish-Americans taken hostage by the British, all but two lived through the experience.

Reprisals continued into the Civil War—each side hanging members of the other's partisan cavalry until it was generally agreed that cavalry troopers would be treated as POWs. In the world wars, reprisals were intended to send a clear message to the enemy government to improve POW conditions. To individuals in captivity, reprisals were imposed without cause; among warring powers, the threat of reprisals had always brought its rewards.

Hard resistance begins as a personal response to the demands of a captor. One of the most famous episodes of pure, stubborn resistance took place during the Civil War, with the capture and execution of Sam Davis of Tennessee. Davis, a Confederate scout for General Braxton Bragg, CSA, was sent on a dangerous mission to find out what he could concerning General Grant's troop strength around Chattanooga. After scouting Grant's lines and learning that the entire Sixth Army Corps under the command of General G. M. Dodge, USA, was poised to attack Confederate lines, Davis tried to make his way back to deliver this valuable information to General Bragg, but he was captured by federal forces. In a replay of the John Andre–George Washington espionage confrontation during the Revolution, Davis had concealed a map of federal fortifications in Nashville in his saddle, and his boot hid a letter written by his commanding officer addressed to General Bragg that contained information concerning the federal troop movements. Although he was captured in uniform

(Andre had worn civilian clothes), Union officers charged Davis with espionage. Found guilty with the documents in his saddle and boot, he was sentenced to die. While the trap was being adjusted, one of Dodge's officers renewed a previous offer made to Davis—information for his life—but Davis refused the offer saying, "If I had a thousand lives, I would lose them all here before I would betray my friend or the confidence of my informer." Without any force from his executioners, he stepped on the trap himself and died a few moments later.[17] Like Major Andre for the British and Nathan Hale for the Americans, during the Revolution Davis would become a symbol of selfless duty, resistance to a captor, and soldierly determination not to give in, regardless of the consequences. As a classic captivity defeat hero, Davis, like Nathan Hale, attracted a following. Hale's statue stands in the CIA's rotunda in Langley, Virginia; Davis's memory has attained nearly cult status among those interested in the Civil War's Southern cause.

Captain Bernhard Domschke, USV (United States Volunteers), and his fellow officers in Macon Officers Prison were holding religious services in camp. As a group or community act of resistance, part of the service consisted of prayers for the president of the United States. The Confederate assistant camp commander attempted to dissolve the service and informed the prisoners that "I can no longer allow prayers for the President of the United States in these services." The chaplain then stepped forward and in a loud voice prayed for the president, his cabinet, the Congress, and generals Grant and Sherman. According to Domschke, the assistant camp commander stood thunderstruck.[18]

Punitive neglect was taken to extremes in the Civil War. Captors on both sides starved their prisoners into debilitating physical condition and then neglected to treat them for disease or wounds. The results were inordinately numerous deaths by starvation and gangrene. Where the camp was far to the north, such as Johnson's Island in Ohio, or Elmira in New York, the Union captors refused to house their Confederate prisoners properly, and the Confederates died from the effects of the cold weather. In the winter when the Potomac River flooded at Point Lookout, the prisoners suffered terribly.

In the South, in addition to providing improper or insufficient food, the captors would jam thousands of Union prisoners into small areas with no sanitation or suitable housing, thus causing their deaths indirectly from disease. Describing the neglect he experienced at Andersonville, John McElroy comments that the suffering in the hospital was a form of torture in itself.

The most conspicuous suffering was in the gangrene wards. Horrible sores spreading almost visibly from hour to hour, devoured men's

limbs and bodies. I remember one ward in which the ulcerations appeared to be altogether in the back, where they ate out the tissue
between the skin and the ribs. The attendants seemed trying to arrest
the progress of the sloughing by drenching the sores with a solution
of blue vitriol. This was exquisitely painful, and in the morning, when
the drenching was going on, the whole Hospital rang with the most
agonizing screams.[19]

Starvation and deprivation were forms of cruelty by punitive neglect,
but prisoners would frequently receive direct forms of punishment as
well. Drunkenness was a vice almost unknown in a Civil War prison camp.
The prisoners were deprived of liquor for the duration of their stay in
prison. Often bottles of claret, champagne, or bourbon were sent to Confederate prisoners, but the liquors were considered contraband by the
Union authorities. Chances were excellent that such contraband would
be consumed by the guard force. At Elmira, one Confederate soldier had
his thumbs tied behind his back, with the ropes drawn in the *strappado.*
Refusing to tell where he had obtained some whiskey, he was gagged and
struck in the face and his front teeth were knocked out. He was let down
with his face covered in blood.[20] Captain J. J. Geer's narrative *Beyond
the Lines, or, A Yankee Prisoner Loose in Dixie* (1864) describes what
he believed was a common form of punishment among his Southern captors: "The person was thrown to the ground, either face or back down,
according to the whim of the punisher, and while in this position, a
number of stakes or wooden pins are driven in the earth around him,
in such a manner as to bind him immovable to the ground." Geer describes
the application of this form of torture to one Union prisoner named Flood.

Flood was a large man, and possessed of immense strength; and the
first time he was thus pinned down, he tore himself loose from his
fastenings. Upon seeing this, his captors again seized him. But he
struggled manfully, and it was not until six or eight powerful men
attacked him simultaneously, and with weapons, that he was secured.
This done, however, they obtained stakes that an ox could not have
broken, and with these they fastened their victim down so firmly,
that it was impossible for him to move half an inch. And in this position, he lay face down *for twenty-four hours,* during which time a
heavy rain fell. In consequence he took a fatal cold, and, four days
later, he was laid in the grave. This punishment was quite common
among the rebels.[21]

During the Civil War, only the work of the relief societies ameliorated
the sufferings of the prisoners. In the North, the United States Sanitary

Commission reported on conditions in the Southern camps. In the South, the Sisters of Charity attempted to help Union prisoners from Charleston to Andersonville. Cruelty nonetheless remained the prisoner's fate at the hands of commandants and guards who understood such treatment to be part of their duties. At Libby Prison in Richmond the general order was given to the guards by the commandant to shoot any head that appeared in the window. At Belle Isle, also in Richmond, there was one Confederate guard, a Sergeant Hiatt, who liked to arrange small planks in the gable shape of a house roof. The ends would be on the ground, and the peak would be three or four feet high. He would cover them with a slippery, gooey substance, then tie his victim's hands behind him and compel him to try to walk up the planks, urging him on with the bayonet. Time after time the victim would fall on his face, causing blood to gush out from his nose, mouth, and ears.[22]

Before World War I broke out in Europe, Americans had few reasons to regard Germany as hostile. By 1914, many Germans had been to America either as temporary immigrants or visitors. There was an active permanent German culture in America, from the Mennonite immigration in Pennsylvania to entire German communities in Pennsylvania, Minnesota, Iowa, Texas, and Wisconsin. America was an immigrant country, and many Americans were accustomed to interacting with Germans on a personal, social, and cultural basis. But after the sinking of the *Lusitania* at sea on May 7, 1915, with the loss of 1,150 people, including 114 Americans, and the interception of the Zimmerman Notes to Mexico, Woodrow Wilson's progressive, neutral America entered the war on the side of England and France. The long-standing cultural relationships between the United States and Germany withered. Negative propaganda against Germany and popular stereotypes of Germans found their way into the American press. War was declared, and beginning in 1917, Americans fought Germans on the battlefields and in the prison camps.

Before the United States entered World War I, when Senator Albert J. Beveridge inspected German camps, he noticed that the English were especially hostile to their German guards. He reported that one camp commander said, "The English are very difficult. . . . We can't get along with the English. They won't work. They object to everything."[23] Beveridge asked one British prisoner, "Would you rather be here or in the trenches?" The answer came with a snap, "In the trenches, sir. I'd like to get a crack at them, sir! Anything is better than this."[24] In general, the resistance of the English prisoners to the Germans was apparent and unconcealed, open, and bold. The dislike of the German officers and guards for their stubborn wards was no less manifest.

According to some former World War I POWs, the Germans attached great value to obtaining military information and spared no pains, tricks, threats, or expense to make the prisoners talk. James Norman Hall found himself in a position of having to resist his captors, but it was a genteel resistance. His interrogator questioned him for some time, wishing to confirm certain items of military intelligence. According to Hall:

> He professed to know a great deal about the movements of our troops and the organization of our Air Force. Some of his information was quite accurate, but of course I made no comment one way or the other. When he showed me some superb aerial photographs of our flying fields, among them one of our field at Toul, I successfully registered only polite interest. This cost some effort. I had seen that view of our field many times when going out on and returning from patrol, and the thought that I might never see it again was a gloomy one.[25]

When efforts failed to gain military information from American prisoners through direct interrogation, the Germans hid microphones inside prisoners' living quarters and placed friendly English-speaking Germans in the cells as active spies. One prisoner reported that after eighteen days confinement in a fortress the Germans conducted him to the place that came to be called "Microphone Hotel," a rather pleasant experience by POW standards. The Germans installed microphones in specific rooms where the prisoners gathered or lived, hoping to gain military information from casual conversations. As dramatized in the World War II play and film *Stalag 17,* the Germans also ordered spies who spoke perfect English to mix with the Americans. The idea was that after a good meal the Allied captives would talk to each other freely, exchange experiences, and discuss matters which might yield valuable military information.[26] Having been tipped off about the microphones by British POWs, the Americans maintained silence.

Lower-ranked POWs who possessed little military information never saw "Microphone Hotel"; instead, they worked as forced laborers in factories or farms. There, they exercised forms of passive resistance against their captors by working as little as possible. Clifford Markle, an American medic captured in the Battle of Seicheprey in 1918, found himself assigned to work in a wire factory in Cologne. He comments that "there was not one of us who would not have given ten years from his life to have been back in the trenches with the American Army."[27]

Prisoners honed their resistance to the prison camp system and camp rules to a finer edge with the publication of camp newspapers. At Libby Prison, Union officers published the *Libby Chronicle;* Confederate officers at Fort Delaware published several editions of a handwritten, four-page newspaper, *Fort Delaware Prison Times.*[28] In Germany, one such newspaper, *The Barbed Wireless,* was published by Americans, "spasmodically" as they put it, at Ukrainerlager, Rastatt, and Baden camps by the "American Overseas Publishing Company, Incarcerated." With some humor, the editors stated that their purpose was "to keep its readers as thoroughly misinformed as possible on all events of no importance whatsoever":[29]

The Barbed Wireless is a periodical appearing irregularly and on the rare occasions the editors feel themselves animated by a desire to work. It is published solely in the interests of the American soldiers who find themselves temporarily the guests of the enemy in the delightful community of Rastatt, formerly a summer resort, but now open to Americans throughout the entire year.

The purpose of this embryonic journal is to keep alive the spirit of Americanism, to drive away any gloom and depression that might take root from time to time, and to set down in durable form a record of all events and happenings among us which may prove of interest later on when our life at Rastatt is but a dim memory—a passing flash in the kaleidoscope of life.

In order that we may secure the best possible results in making the paper of interest and value to all, we earnestly request the co-operation and assistance of every American in camp. Contributions of any nature whatever are acceptable. If not printed, they will be thrown out, thereby keeping our office boy busy and out of trouble. Everyone can write, draw, or rhyme something or nothing—funny stuff or deep stuff, jokes, limericks, or sporting dope; no matter what.[30]

The British published a newspaper at Camp II in Münster, *The Rembahn Review,* and used prison humor in much the same way: not only to pass information to inmates but to form a basis for solidarity and resistance. This practice of publishing camp newspapers as resistance tools continued into World War II. Allied POWs intercepted BBC war news on contraband radios and circulated information bulletins in many of the stalags.

According to narratives and other reportage, the harshest treatment took place in the *Dulag-Luft,* or *Durchgangslager Luftwaffe,* the transient camp for captured airmen operated by members of the German air force intelligence service near Frankfurt am Main. There were over sixty English-speaking interrogators assigned to the camp, built to handle the growing number of Allied flyers shot down over Germany. It was in the Dulag-Luft that the "cooler" was first used and threat of torture imposed when skilled German interrogators attempted to gain intelligence data from the Allied prisoners. Interrogations and intelligence-gathering operations inside the Dulag-Luft became harsher when Luftwaffe pilot Franz von Werra escaped from his prison train in Canada, crossed to the United

States, and returned to Germany. According to postwar studies, Captain von Werra influenced the Luftwaffe's decision to keep the Allied airmen in solitary confinement.[31]

In resistance, the Kriegies created systems of observations teams, or "stooges" to watch for patrolling German "goons" or for roving "ferrets" who sought to seek out and destroy Kriegie attempts to tunnel or hide contraband. The Allied Kriegies developed sophisticated resistance networks and makeshift codes to continue their battle against the Germans. "Stooges" created a vast nonverbal communication system network in the camps consisting of shuffles, knocks, hand signals, whistles, songs, and body movements that signaled warnings of imminent danger to tunnelers, forgers, traders, "goon tamers," and those Kriegies involved in intelligence-gathering or escape activities that potential trouble was near. Universally, the British and American Kriegies called their German guards and other prison camp personnel "goons," a term borrowed from popular prewar comic book characters. As a form of resistance, German-speaking Kriegies would often be ordered to communicate with, if not entertain, targeted German camp officials. Called "goon-tamers" by the Kriegies, these Allied prisoners would trade favors, acquire contraband, and, perhaps most importantly, gather intelligence for X, the camp's intelligence and escape organization. On the negative side, perhaps from boredom or contempt, many Kriegies enjoyed "goon-baiting" and treated pushing a Luftwaffe guard or "goon" to the limit of his patience as a sport. Experienced "goon-baiters" knew when to back off and become conciliatory, if not overtly friendly, before they earned a trip to solitary confinement in the "cooler."

In Germany during World War II, few American Kriegies encountered the professional torturers of the Gestapo. Had they been subjected to their ways, Americans in wartime Germany would have confronted a very different experience. In 1944, the encounter at Malmedy during the Battle of the Bulge taught the Americans a severe lesson. The Waffen SS murdered captured Americans as they stood in a field waiting to be removed to the rear. The threat, however, existed from time to time in the stalags and oflags. Although the SS remained tasked with POW oversight until the end of the war in May 1945, the stalags and oflags were staffed by members of the legitimate German armed forces rather than by German politicos intent on destroying their prisoners.

Captivity in Asia was far more punitive than in Europe. According to Laurens Van der Post's *Night of the New Moon* (1985), the Allied POWs suffered slow deaths, never just shooting. Bayonet practice was conducted on live POWs who were tied between bamboo posts. Executions took place when a POW showed a spirit of "willfulness" or did not bow correctly in the direction of the rising sun.[32] Atrocities against resisters started during the death march on Bataan and continued until liberation in 1945. By 1943, the Japanese placed one supervisor and ten guards in charge of farm work details of 100 men. Each supervisor carried a short club and used it at will. Commonwealth prisoners recall with horror the atrocities in Singapore, New Guinea, and Thailand. For the Americans, the atrocities in the Philippines and particularly on Palawan Island became the stuff of epic.[33]

Palawan Island is a narrow strip of land running southwest in the South China and Salu seas near the Negros Islands in the Philippines. The Japanese seized it early in the war, and in 1942 they decided to build an airstrip. A detail of approximately 400 American prisoners was sent from Cabanatuan in August 1943. The Japanese later decided to enlarge the airfield, and the Americans were forced to labor with little water in blazing heat. At first, according to reports, food and shelter were better than they were in other camps, but in 1944 treatment changed radically. A new camp commander, Captain Kinoshita, took charge, and in spite of the continued heavy work, he lowered the food ration by one-quarter. On December 14, 1944, air-raid sirens sounded, and the guards hurried the Americans into shelters. A second and, later, a third, alarm sounded. Meanwhile, the camp staff poured gasoline into the shelters, set them on fire, and began firing rifles and machine guns through the flames to block any egress. Only ten men survived. One of the ten, Marine Sergeant Willie Smith, who had been captured on Corregidor in 1942, provides this account. "Presently a group of Jap guards accompanied by two or three officers entered the compound yard. They told us to stay in our shelters and not to look out. . . . I saw the Japs throw gasoline in each end of the biggest shelter and toss torches in after it. They did the same thing immediately after at two other shelters. Men screamed. Men moaned. Men broke from the shelters, their clothes, faces and hands aflame. Japs shot them down."[34]

Major James P. S. Devereux, USMC, sums up the predicament of the American POWs in Japanese hands: to resist was not only a fight for life, but also a fight to maintain self-respect.

Hidden behind the routine, under the surface of life in the prison camp, was fought a war of wills for moral supremacy—an endless struggle, as bitter as it was unspoken, between the captors and the captives. The stakes seemed to me simply this: The main objective of the whole Japanese prison program was to break our spirit, and on our side was the stubborn determination to keep our self-respect whatever else they took from us. It seems to me that struggle was almost as much a part of the war as the battle we fought on Wake Island.[35]

Struggle to keep one's self-respect was not only the key phrase for the Wake Island marines, but also for the American and Filipino death marchers of Bataan, the prisoners of Corregidor, Wake Island, and Guam, and all the Allied POWs and internees held in Asia from 1941 to 1945. Indeed, subtle resistance activities often found their way into camp newspapers. POW newspapers had never been permitted in the Japanese POW camps; however, they permitted them in civilian internee camps. *Santo Tomàs Internment Camp Internews* and *Camp Health* (1942) were the first internment camp documents from World War II. Russell Brines of the Associated Press created *Internews,* which, with *Camp Health,* acted as a window into civilian wartime internee-captivity. Both papers were restricted to Santo Tomàs, but when internee Jennifer White was returned by the Japanese in 1942 to the United States, she managed to hide a large number of the newspapers in her luggage. Published in the United States by Relief for Americans in the Philippines, it featured illustrations, cartoons, advice, weather reports, and announcements of activities including barn dances, talks, Easter celebrations, boxing matches, and softball tournaments. It even had want advertisements and solicitous messages from the Japanese commandant.

Five years after the end of World War II, Americans found themselves having to resist two more captors in Asia, the North Koreans and the Chinese. General William F. Dean, USA, the highest-ranking American POW taken prisoner by the North Korean Army, noted the idiosyncrasies of his captors concerning what they wanted from him and how he resisted. Dean thought the North Koreans wanted military information. He was surprised that they wanted political propaganda.

> Pressure on me was greatest to agree to perfectly obvious falsities: that the United States was an aggressor; that we had exploited the people of South Korea or wished to do so; that General Douglas MacArthur had ordered Syngman Rhee to start the war. On questions of real significance—our defense plans for Japan, commitment of troops, infantry strategy or organization—they gave up when met with boldfaced lies or simple refusal to answer. . . . There was also an almost pathological insistence on getting something signed. I would not broadcast on the radio, therefore I must sign a paper saying that I would not go on the radio. I would not sign a proposed letter, then I must sign a letter saying why I would not sign a letter.[36]

Lloyd Pate was no general; he was an infantry sergeant who had little knowledge of grand strategy but considerable knowledge about how average American soldiers respond to leadership in a prison camp. In his narrative he reveals that he and other enlisted men faced interrogation goals similar to those faced by General Dean. His manner of resisting began by watching those members of his camp he called "in-between" prisoners, those who were more concerned about surviving than resisting. "The Chinese got most of their information about what went on in the camp from this group. Not all of these men were bad. They had some damn good men in there, but some of them would denounce the Chinese to your face and sell you out behind your back."[37] Pate chose to be a member of what the Chinese called reactionaries, those prisoners who would resist their offers of better treatment for cooperative propaganda production at every turn. "I was a reactionary because I was stubborn. I didn't like a guy to stand over me and preach things I knew were a pack of lies."[38] Along with some other reactionaries, Pate took resistance one step further; he began a program of active resistance by way of sabotage.

We started taking nails up to the road at night and burying them with the points up. Then when the Chinese trucks and convoys would come through they'd have flats. We held several small convoys up for a few days. I remember one poor bastard who had eleven flats in a hundred feet. As fast as he'd fix one and ride a few feet, he'd blow out another tire. . . . Then we started making gadgets out of nails and wire. These things didn't have to be planted. We'd just drop them and they always landed with three points down and one point up. Every morning when we went for our trot, someone would scatter a few of the gadgets on the road. . . . They [the Chinese] didn't know what in hell had happened or who was behind it, but they knew they didn't have their old control over our company and they didn't like it. They had a general idea that the reactionary squad was to blame but they couldn't prove a thing.[39]

One has to ask why nothing was done to Pate and the others involved. Perhaps the answer lies in the fact that the United Nations forces, specifically the Americans, held thousands of Chinese and North Koreans prisoner on Koje-Do Island. Reprisals were always possible.

Torture, resistance, and survival continued in North Korea with the capture of the USS *Pueblo* in 1968. According to the ship's communication and intelligence officer, Stephen Harris, in *My Anchor Held* (1970), his captors threatened him constantly with execution. They put an unloaded gun to his head, pulled the trigger, and attempted to debilitate him psychologically. Harris comments: "I always expected to be shot, but when the slide was drawn back . . . I did not hear any bullet hit the floor. I know it was a game they were playing with me, and they weren't going to kill me."[40] Harris describes the beatings he and his shipmates suffered at the hands of their captors. "The colonel said I wasn't worth a bullet, and I would be beaten to death. . . . They beat me to the floor, and I lost consciousness after a few minutes. Then I was carried out to my room and thrown on the bed. . . . I asked permission to go to the bathroom. . . . All I could urinate was blood. . . . They asked me if I knew I was responsible for the lives of my crew and I answered yes, . . . and told them they had murdered one of my men. . . . I received a blow that sent me across the room for that statement."[41]

While Captain Lloyd Bucher, his officers, and crew were in prison in North Korea, other Americans were in captivity in North and South Vietnam. Instead of feeling the neocolonial effects of the Japanese military code of Bushido the Americans experienced in Korea, POWs in the Vietnam War felt the stinging backlash of hundreds of years of French colonialism in Vietnam. Pierre Boulle, author of *Bridge Over the River Kwai* (1954), was a French colonial and a second lieutenant in the French army in Indochina during World War II. After the French government capitulated to the Germans in 1940 and established the Vichy regime, he declared himself to be a member of the Free French army in Indochina. After spending one year in China and Thailand he returned to the Red River Delta in disguise. He was captured by the Vichy French authorities and taken to the "Hanoi Hilton" for two years and four months. Boulle describes the torture devices the Americans would face later, especially the "justice bar" used by the French navy and then the French security service for recalcitrant Vietnamese under the sentence of death.

> It consisted of two parts. There was a fixed section, embedded in the cement with two cylindrical cavities . . . in it like humps of a camel in reverse. A second half, cast iron, pivoted on a hinge round the fixed section and was equipped with two similar cavities which when the contraption was clamped down fitted exactly over the first two so as to form two perfect cylinders equal in diameter to that of the ankles of the average man. The result was that a prisoner lay flat on his back on a concrete floor with his head turned to the ceiling and his feet extending beyond the bar, unable to turn on the side and forced to indulge in extraordinary acrobatics in order to use the latrine pail placed beside him by the benevolent administration.[42]

Some American prisoners in Vietnam would not live long enough for the "justice bar." Their resistance began by evading capture itself. Such was the case of Lance Sijan. Shot down over Laos on November 9, 1967, he suffered a bad head wound, a shredded right hand, and a compound fracture of the left leg. Sijan began to crawl through the jungle and evaded his captors for forty-six days. Finally, he died trying to escape. Robinson Risner, in his narrative, *The Passing of the Night* (1973), writes, "In my wildest imagination I had no idea American POWs would be treated as inhumanely and cruelly as we were.'' He describes the American prisoners' position as a captive community, one which the North Vietnamese fought nearly to the last day of captivity in 1973. ''We believed the American people were behind us. . . . We were told continuously that demonstrators were representative of the true Americans. We knew this was an out and out lie. . . . Everything bad in our society was pointed out on a day to day basis—the inequities, crime, inflation, dirty politics and any dirt under the rug. . . . We were not a select group. We represented America and the American people.''[43] Risner considered himself a member of a unified prisoner community, a concept clearly understood by the North Vietnamese and most of the American POWs. According to James B. Stockdale, effective resistance was not built so much on desperate stands or on heroic displays of high thresholds of pain; it thrived on a unified, timely, persistent, committed group of signals to the Vietnamese: they must punish one and all, day after day, to get what they wanted.[44] As senior ranking officer, Stockdale issued to the prisoners clear and prohibitory orders: ''You were required to take torture, forcing the Vietnamese to impose significant pain on you before acceding to those specific demands.''[45] Howard Rutledge's modern jeremiad, *In the Presence of Mine Enemies* (1977), observes that the enemy knew that if they could isolate a man—make him feel abandoned, cut off, forgotten—they could more easily destroy resistance and break down an individual POW's morale. To win the war against nerves, boredom, starvation, and pain, prisoners had to devise all kinds of ingenious systems to communicate with their fellow prisoners. Thus, in Rutledge's view, the Americans in North Vietnam learned to think like criminals, to devise ways to lie, cheat, and deceive.[46]

In Hanoi, as Larry Chesley points out in *Seven Years in Hanoi: A POW Tells His Story* (1973), the North Vietnamese tried to preempt the POWs' need for information by replacing it with propaganda. They prepared an English-language newspaper, the *Vietnam Courier,* to supplement news broadcasts from the *Voice of Vietnam:*

The *Courier* was a Vietnamese newspaper written in English which we received at irregular intervals—every month or two. The strictly party line written in the sterile political style and without the softening preface of pleasant music had no power to persuade. Nevertheless many of us read it so that we could find out, by reading between the lines, what was really going on in the world. Here again the North Vietnamese stimulated us to read it by starving us of all other kinds of literature. Until about the last month or two communist propaganda material (either North Vietnamese, Chinese or Russian in origin) was the only literature we had to read during our entire prison stay.[47]

The North Vietnamese went further than prohibiting POW-written newspapers; they forbate even interpersonal communication between their prisoners. Eugene "Red" McDaniel's resistance narrative, *Scars and Stripes* (1975), notes that there were times when the prisoners beat the system by taking advantage of the Vietnamese custom of the midday snooze:

> From 11:30 am to 1:30 pm was siesta, and during this time we did our serious communicating. The guards were relaxed, knowing we would be napping anyway. At this time we would write notes . . . by mixing the brick dust that collected under our beds with water and using a bamboo stick from our brooms, we could write fairly well on the stiff onionskin toilet paper. We stuck these notes to the indented place in the underside of our toilet bowl. . . . We called this our "pony express" system, and it worked well. . . . There were other ways to communicate too: pounding on the walls, thumping the signals in the dirt with our brooms, and using coughs, hand signals, and clothes snapping.[48]

The "pounding on walls" took the form of an old system of tapping a code; the prisoners called it the "Smitty Harris tap code" after the prisoners who introduced it. The first set of taps was a preparatory question. When the question was answered in the affirmative, the conversation would continue in a series of taps.

1. Question: Are you ready to receive? Tapping "Shave & a Haircut."
2. Answer: Yes. "2 Bits" or 2 Taps.

Then, each prisoner began tapping words in abbreviated forms and acronyms, using the following table. The first digit corresponds to the row; the second digit to the line:

	1	2	3	4	5
1	A	B	C	D	E
2	F	G	H	I	J [K = C]
3	L	M	N	O	P
4	Q	R	S	T	U
5	V	W	X	Y	Z

At night before everyone retired, the walls would come alive with taps. "God Bless You," was the good-night tap, with "Don't let the bedbugs bite" as a response. One would strike the wall:

$$2 - 2 = G$$
$$1 - 2 = B$$
$$4 - 5 = U$$

Toward the end, the North Vietnamese relented on the prohibition against communication and began permitting the Americans to gather for group meetings. Some meetings were religious services, common in captivities during past wars but not common in North Vietnam. From 1970 on, the North Vietnamese allowed prisoners to wander around the compound and talk in quiet conversations, but as James B. Stockdale points out, a single American standing before a group leading a prayer or singing a hymn was a "provocative act." For the hard resisters, Stockdale notes, group meetings presented perfect opportunities for expanded resistance.

We staged the provocative act in Building 7 on a Sunday in mid-February 1971, about six weeks after we had been put together. On that afternoon, we quietly assembled for religious services. Even those among us who would normally never have gone to church gladly took seats up front in the interest of unity. The prayer was led, and the trio assembled, and then in burst the waiting Vietnamese guards, rifles drawn. Those churchmen who had addressed the group were quickly dragged off to solitary confinement in Heartbreak Hotel next door.

That triggered what became known as "the church riot of 1971." Building 7 burst into a standing, shouting rendition of "The Star Spangled Banner" that could be heard over much of downtown Hanoi. Each of the big cellblock buildings around the circle picked up after us in turn, and then they all vied for militancy and loudness in a one-after-another rendition of American patriotic songs.

The next day . . . leg irons . . . Hanoi officials and citizens who had heard the ruckus the day before . . . were being shown "the iron fist of righteous Vietnamese vengeance." To us, the whole exercise was in the category of a lark.[49]

The Vietnamese had been under French colonial influence too long not to have learned the practices of systematic judicial torture, either as *quaestio* or as *torture prealable*. Narrative descriptions of torture techniques make it clear that the North Vietnamese knew both very well. Why should prisoners take torture? They looked to their senior ranking officers for guidance. James B. Stockdale understood that this question was too important not to address, because each prisoner needed something solid to fight for when the captors held nearly all the cards in their favor. Stockdale understood that in captivity a clear conscience is as important as life-sustaining food. POWs need both to maintain a will to live and strive for victory. Fear and guilt were the tools of the captor. Stockdale writes: "It is they that beat you down, particularly when you are lonesome and despondent. All of this torture seems to me a mere acceleration of the basic process of unhinging a victim with fear and polarizing him with guilt. Only the prisoners' comradeship and loyalty to each other could effectively deter this repeated tearing down of a man."[50]

At home, there were some Americans who refused to believe that POWs were tortured. Others believed that their torture was somehow justified. In 1973, shortly after the American POWs were repatriated, antiwar activist Jane Fonda, after hearing reports of Americans tortured in the camps in North and South Vietnam, commented to *Newsweek* reporters: "There was most probably torture of POW's. Guys who misbehaved and treated their guards in a racist fashion or tried to escape were tortured. Some [U.S.] pilots were beaten to death by the people they had bombed when they parachuted from their planes. But to say that torture was systematic and the policy of the North Vietnamese government is a lie."[51] Narratives, debriefs, and sworn public testimonies suggest strongly how little Fonda knew. Apart from commentary from antiwar prisoners, few captivity narratives from this war lack detailed descriptions of torture. In Hanoi, torture was used to punish prisoners who broke camp rules and as a device to get valuable propaganda information from prisoners by having them fill out what appeared to be a simple questionnaire. Stockdale was amazed at the legalism of his captors. "I marveled in amazement at the effectiveness of the little device of always basing the infliction of punishment on the technical legalism of having violated one of their written documents."[52] Ralph Gaither's *With God in a P.O.W. Camp* (1973) describes the torturous ordeal brought about by his refusal to fill out such a biographical questionnaire.[53] Larry Chesley's *Seven Years in Hanoi* (1973) shows that the lack of medical care imposed its own tortures, some of them long sustained.[54] Colonel Fred Cherry, USAF, had to endure surgical procedures without anesthetics. In interrogations, or "quizzes" as they were called in Hanoi, Cherry noted that his captors would cup their hands and hit him over the ears. If that technique did not work, then the torturer might kick the stool out from under him, and he would fall tied and wounded to the floor. If he still refused to answer the questions in quiz, he might be made to stand on his knees with his hands in the air, and, like most other prisoners, he would be subjected to the fanbelt treatment, that is, a severe beating with rubber hoses.[55]

Rabbi Abraham Feinberg, an antiwar activist from Toronto, Canada, visited Hanoi early in 1967. As an integral part of his visit, he insisted that the North Vietnamese officials include interviews with American POWs as part of his itinerary. Reflecting on the totality of his visit, he wrote, "I shall always remember what happened there."[56] Not knowing exactly what to expect, Feinberg was startled when a "clean-shaven, clean-cut, plump man, close to thirty-five, in blue dungarees, leather or chamois jacket, canvas shoes" entered the meeting room.[57] Even more startling, the prisoner bowed from the waist with "more than a hint of elaborate deference." According to Rabbi Feinberg:

We had never seen a deep bow from the waist. Suddenly a newspaper clipping someone had sent me in Toronto whisked back before my eyes. It said POWs purposefully perform the bow, as though briefed in a military manual, in the presence of visiting journalists to substantiate allegations of humiliating sadism, or of brain-washing in case they make statements injurious to the United States. (It seems to me now, ex post facto, reasonably convincing that the Vietnamese military would surely not order POWs to bow under the eyes of three clergymen whose championship they want to secure. Also why would supposedly brain-washed or brow-beaten men seek to hector and annoy their captors by unauthorized bowing? Very puzzling indeed!)[58]

Rabbi Feinberg knew that bowing was foreign to westerners and seemingly accepted the propaganda that POWs bowed as deception to cover injurious antiwar statements. He had no idea, however, that North Vietnamese prison policy forced the Americans to bow under the threat of torture. In the past, the Japanese army had initiated POW bowing, forcing officers to bow to any Japanese soldier regardless of rank; the Chinese in Korea also used it as a tool to demean nonbowing westerners. In effect, this nameless POW used the deep bow not only as a form of forced respect, but also as a form of passive resistance designed to tell Feinberg that what he was about to see and hear was a smokescreen.

In the interview, Rabbi Feinberg asked the prisoner, whom he does not name in his book, what, if anything, he could do. Responding to the kindly Feinberg, the prisoner exercised his second option to resist; he asked Rabbi Feinberg for a King James Version of the Bible saying, "My wife will know what books to send."[59] Feinberg was moved at the request and at the POW's religious fervor. In his religious and moral fervor to help end the war by participating in the peace movement, he could not have known that 1966–1969 was the most brutal period of American incarceration in North Vietnam, nor could he have known that the North Vietnamese would never have permitted an American POW to read a Bible. By asking Rabbi Feinberg for help, the POW bypassed the North Vietnamese refusal to fill out Red Cross prisoner cards in accordance with the 1949 Geneva Convention. Consequently, in many cases, visits like Rabbi Feinberg's with direct promises to contact spouses, served in a roundabout way to confirm the fact that a missing soldier was alive in captivity, a vital piece of information not only to his wife and family, but also to his branch of the service and the United States government.

In the resistance event-scenario POW narrators describe how, where, and when captors apply physical torture and psychological pressure as punishment or motivation to change the prisoner's way of thinking or resistance behavior. They also describe their own response. In the national wars, military captors attempted to destroy a POW's sense of community with the other prisoners, sometimes through torture, solitary confinement, starvation, and punitive neglect. However, POWs have a military code that mandates resistance. Threats, torture, and privation always remain secondary to the soldier's mission behind the wire: to remain a soldier rather than a passive survivor, or worse, a collaborator or renegade.

Narrators spend a great deal of time reflecting on the inner changes that take place, both individually and in terms of the evolution of the captive community. This transformation is a step toward the "we" of the POW experience. Individually and collectively, beliefs in success or failure are reformulated by the requirements and sanctions imposed behind the wire. Stockdale points out that effective resistance is not related so much to heroism as to a pattern of behavior based on a personal commitment to community values. One might conclude that from Leininger to Stockdale, the powerful web that binds prisoners together is spun from the quality rather than the intensity of the resistance.

From Jeremiah's Lamentations to James B. Stockdale's *In Love and War* (1984), former prisoners have made it clear that strong reasons exist for resisting the captor. In the end, resisting means going home with some personal dignity. Either from a sense of duty, personal pride, religious faith, or institutional mandate, resisting POWs challenge captors to a duel of ideas and ideals. However, few prisoners have been successful in resisting their captors totally; those who try, die. The art of resistance lies in the balance between defiant stubbornness and degrees of cooperation. Those prisoners who decide to cooperate willingly take the risk of subjecting themselves to the permanent damage of illegal collaboration for which a high price might have to be paid upon repatriation. Those who resist strongly suffer at the hands of the captors but become heroes, like Lance Sijan, James B. Stockdale, and others in Vietnam. If resistance becomes public, as it did with Richard Stratton's famous bow in Hanoi and with televised images of prisoners during the Gulf War in 1991, resistance can become a public as well as a military issue. For the individual POW, however, public reaction at home remains a mystery until repatriation. Survival is the issue, ranges of physical and psychological survival learned by balancing principles of liberty, freedom, and military codes with the realities of a captor's demands for cooperation. The resister's dilemma, first understood as "damned if you do, damned if you don't," becomes a question of how much, when, against whom, and for what. With their bodies, resisters deny the captors' political, military, social, and legal values, and, in the end, uphold those values developed and held collectively by a resisting captive community.

CHAPTER NINE

The Line of Least Resistance:
Assimilation and the Renegade Captive

Let all our soldiers professing the Catholic religion remember the fate of the deserters taken at Churubusco.

General Winfield Scott (1847)

This chapter examines issues in the second major dimension of the resistance event-scenario, assimilation, or the line of least resistance. One should not mistake the act of assimilation for passivity, described by narrators as temporarily cooperating with a captor in order to be left alone. Assimilation is an active process undertaken by prisoners by their own free will. In some cases, active assimilation begins when prisoners decide not to remain incarcerated because life in a prison camp is actually a death sentence. In other cases, it begins with an opportunity to leave a prison camp and observe the captor's culture. For a few prisoners, it begins with observation and acceptance of the captor's cause, that it might be more just, legal, moral, or more popular than his own. In any event, according to what assimilated prisoners reveal in their narratives, some aspects of captivity are so completely repulsive to them that life in their captor's culture looks far better than death in a prison camp. Assimilating prisoners shun their captive community to a point where they abandon the first culture and enter into a citizenship relationship with their captors. They learn their captor's language and sometimes accept new personal, political, religious, and institutional values in order to blend into the captor's society.

In their narratives, hard resisters oppose assimilators and consistently deplore that the line of least resistance happened among their ranks at all. Anything more than forced cooperation is synonymous with collaboration, which they block whenever they can. The terms they use reveal their feelings clearly: traitor, deserter, turncoat, collaborator, "progressive," anti-war prisoner, and in the worst case, renegade, when prisoners actually changed sides to fight their former comrades on the battlefield. Considered to be far more dangerous than former prisoners who just want to live their lives peacefully in the adopted society, military renegades are political, ideological, or cultural converts who know why and how their former comrades fight, including the use of tactics, weapons, vulnerabilities, and

195

weaknesses. They know too that if they are recaptured, the status of military renegade would warrant criminal proceedings and, in wartime, the death penalty.

Assimilation depends on the relationship between captor and prisoner.[1] Time is the most important factor: the longer a prisoner remains with the captors, the better freedom within the captor's society looks. Because no one wants to be treated badly for long, acculturation eases communication barriers and improves chances for better treatment. Associations with other prisoners, particularly one's own countrymen, can keep a prisoner loyal to the first culture; if captivity brings with it prolonged isolation or even torture, then chances improve that a prisoner will consider assimilation as an attractive pathway to survival. Depending on the kind and degree of ideological or religious proselytizing he encounters, the new prisoner may well consider various forms of assimilation to survive a limitless period of incarceration.

Assimilation began to play a significant role in captivity culture as early as the first American prisoners in the forest wars. Captivities during the French and Indian War showed that the process of assimilation was understood, feared, and indeed hated by the prisoner's first culture. Never was this fact more clearly demonstrated than in November 1764, when Colonel Henry Bouquet invaded the Indian stronghold on the Muskingum River in eastern Ohio after the Battle of Bushy Run in Pennsylvania. In their treaty of peace, Bouquet required the Indians to release hundreds of white captives.[2] Among this large group, there were fully assimilated captives whom Bouquet forced back into a Eurocolonial culture. Two English and twelve German girls slipped away almost immediately to rejoin the Indians. Of the returned female captives, a few had devoted Indian husbands. One Mingo warrior was so attached to his assimilated wife that he risked death by following Bouquet's party all the way from Muskingum, Ohio, to Fort Pitt. Others refused to return freely, and the Shawnees had to deliver them forcibly to Bouquet's camp. The Bouquet mission ended on November 18, 1764, and the British and American colonials learned a valuable lesson: there were some captives sufficiently assimilated into their tribes that they preferred to remain with them and live as Indians. Taken at an impressionable age, somewhere between seven and twelve years, cherished by Indian adopted parents, and introduced to a life that seemed to be full of adventure, many captives simply lost the desire to return to the grinding toil of a white colonial family on the frontier.[3]

The assimilation process continued until the 1880s, when the North American Indians ceased to be a military force and captive taking halted. Young women were assimilated into tribal life more often than men. With few exceptions east of the Mississippi, most infants and male prisoners over the age of twelve were killed outright; many were sold or ransomed to the French in Quebec or to the British in Detroit. Mary Jemison and many other captives found the ways of Indian life so appealing that they assimilated readily. Feelings of hate and contempt between captors and captives disintegrated, and abundant evidence shows that many prisoners accepted the Indians as their own people and eventually regarded the European colonists as enemies. Mary Jemison was taken by the Seneca tribe in a raid upon her Pennsylvania home in 1755 during the French and Indian War. Unlike other prisoners who resisted their captors, Mary was welcomed into the tribe and later assimilated to the point where she was known as the "white woman of the Genesee." Her narrative was published in 1824 and remains one of the most popular and genteel of all the Indian captivity narratives of the period. After she arrived at the village of her captors, she was given new clothes and a new name, Dicke-wamis, or "pretty girl," a name she would keep for the duration of her stay with the Senecas.

> At night we arrived at a small Indian town . . . where the two Squaws to whom I belonged resided. There we landed, and the Indians went on; which was the last I ever saw of them . . . [T]he Squaws . . . went to their wigwam . . . and returned with a suit of Indian clothing, new and very clean and nice. My clothes . . . were torn in pieces, so that I was almost naked. They first undressed me and threw my rags into the river, then washed me clean and dressed me in the new suit they had just brought, in complete Indian style; and then led me home and seated me in the center of their wigwam.
>
> I was made welcome among them as a sister to the two squaws before mentioned, and was called Dickewamis . . . [meaning] pretty girl, or pleasant good thing. That is the name by which I have ever since been called by the Indians.[4]

Some male children, like Simon Girty, who were not killed during the initial raid, were often adopted outright. Although little is known of Girty other than what legend and regional lore provide, he is remembered as one of the first American renegades of the colonial period.[5] Born and raised in frontier Pennsylvania, Simon and his brothers George, James, and Thomas were able outdoorsmen as children. By 1755, Girty's father, also named Simon, had been killed in a brawl, and his mother remarried quickly to John Turner. The family lived along the Juniata River, near Lewistown, Pennsylvania, when the French and Indians struck east from Ohio and began raiding the region. The family sought refuge in Fort Gran-ville, but the French and Indians defeated the fort's defenders and took the Girty/Turner family prisoner. The first stop was the Indian town of Kittanning, about 100 miles northwest of Lewistown. In captivity, Girty's stepfather was killed quickly by tomahawk, but three of the four boys—Simon, George, and James—were adopted by various regional tribes. The Senecas adopted Simon, calling him Katepacomen. The Delawares adopted his younger brother George; James was adopted by the Shawnees; and Thomas escaped.

Simon Girty's life with the Senecas took him to Ohio, where he became one of the unwilling prisoners returned to European colonial society by the agreement between the Ohio Indians and Henry Bouquet in 1764. As a mature young man, Girty began a career as a go-between and agent among settlers and the regional tribes, but war again interfered with his relatively pastoral aspirations. By 1776, the American colonials had raised arms against the British and their Indian allies, and Girty had to take sides. At first, he attempted to secure a commission in the colonial forces, but the Americans in Pittsburgh refused his request. Along with Alexander McKee and Matthew Elliott, Girty decided to cast his fate with the British and the tribes he had known well as a young man. From then on, the Americans regarded Simon Girty as a renegade with a reputation for treachery, second only to that of Benedict Arnold.

Girty's reputation as a renegade took final shape when he was linked with the capture and execution of Colonel William Crawford after the Battle of Sandusky, June 4–5, 1782. Colonel Crawford had been a prisoner twice during the Revolution. When he served with the 5th Pennsylvania Regiment, he was taken captive at Fort Washington on November 16, 1776, and was exchanged on December 18, 1780.[6] His second captivity found him in the hands of the Delawares led by Simon Girty, a short captivity that cost Crawford his life. The incident was recorded in two escape narratives published in 1783, one written by Surgeon John Knight and the other by John Slover, Crawford's guide.[7] Crawford's execution was commemorated by a broadside ballad, "Crawford's Defeat by the Indians, On the Fourth Day of June, 1782," most probably published shortly after the battle, when Crawford's fate quickly became public knowledge.[8] In each of the versions popular at the time, Simon Girty was introduced as the white leader of the Indians who tortured Colonel Crawford to death.

> There was brave Colonel Crawford upon his retreat,
> Likewise Major Harrison, and brave Doctor Knight,
> With Slover their pilot and several men
> Was unfortunately taken on the Sandusky plain.
>
> Now they have taken these men of renown,
> And has drag'd them away to the Sandusky town,
> Where in their council condemn'd for to be,
> Burne'd at a stake by most cruel Girtee.[9]

According to the ballad and Dr. Knight's narrative, Girty perpetrated Crawford's execution, laughing as his former friend, Colonel William Crawford, was roasted alive in red-hot coals. As a result, Simon Girty had a price on his head. By war's end, he had married Catherine Malott, said to have been herself a captive among the Shawnees.[10] Although he is remembered in place names like Girty's Notch, along the Susquehanna River north of Harrisburg, and Girty's Run, north of Pittsburgh, Simon Girty emigrated to Canada and died in 1819, an American renegade whose notoriety was firmly entrenched in the popular mind and the oral tradition of the Pennsylvania and Ohio frontier.

As the Indian wars continued west of the Mississippi, the tribes of the Great Plains and Southwest took male captives and attempted to assimilate them. One German captive, taken as a young boy in 1866, was remembered in Texas simpy as "Kiowa Dutch." When he matured, he took up arms against the encroaching American settlers in central Texas. Hundreds of black people lived with Indians in the South, most of them runaway slaves or their descendants who joined the tribes voluntarily. In Florida some assimilated former slaves became tribal leaders. In Ohio and Kentucky, the Shawnees and Wyandots held a few black captives who had assimilated and retained the use of English well enough to serve as interpreters. In Texas and the Southwest, Indians developed the practice of stealing slaves for ransom or selling them to slave traders in Arkansas and the Indian territory. One black child was photographed with Geronimo's Apache Raiders at the time of his final surrender.[11]

From the forest wars on, countless nameless souls died during the long marches, the gauntlet, or the first ordeal of torture in camp. The more fortunate captives were ransomed by relatives or traders; many were sold to the French in Canada for religious conversion to Catholicism, and a large number escaped. However, hundreds of captives assimilated into their captor's cultural environment.[12]

During the Revolution, the Barbary wars, and the War of 1812, very few prisoners intentionally defected to the enemy camp. Early in the Revolution American army commanders lacked manpower and were anxious to recruit British deserters and POWs into the ranks of the Continental army and state militias, but General Washington and the Continental Congress refused to permit their subordinates to recruit enemy soldiers for fear of espionage and disloyalty. In August 1776, however, manpower needs overrode Washington's fears of espionage, and the Continental Congress authorized the raising of German battalions and granting of land bounties to deserters who would fight for the American cause. This policy was reversed in 1778, when Congress and Washington decided active recruitment of POWs was "impolite." By 1782, Washington and the Continental Congress reversed themselves again and openly recruited Hessians who expressed a desire to join German units of the Continental army. Washington thought that the German veterans would strengthen the military skills and experience of the army.[13] In 1782, to induce Canada to join the American resistance to England, a proposal was made in Congress to establish a regiment composed of Canadian prisoners who were willing to enlist.

Insisting that American colonials loyal to the Crown had been coerced into Continental service by a small number of political rebels, and believing that captured Americans were in fact British subjects, British authorities attempted to *impress,* that is, forcibly enlist, captured Americans into the British navy. They had some success during the Revolution because morbidity aboard the prison hulks in America was high and life in the military prisons in England was not especially promising. Naval impressment was so widespread that it became a war issue in 1812; in the meantime, Americans at sea faced adversaries other than the British, namely, the Barbary pirates of North Africa.

The American experience with shipwreck captivities and piracy started when the American colonies began trading in West and North Africa under British passports before the Revolution. Capture for enslavement or ransom in that region can be traced from the eighth century into the nineteenth, during which time hundreds of thousands of Europeans were captured and subsequently enslaved by Moslem captors, especially Turks and North Africans. When a pirate vessel attacked a merchant ship carrying European passengers, the prisoners were beaten and stripped of their clothing and were confined during transfer in a hot hold where they received scant food or water. In port, they were formally stripped of their citizenship, designated legally as slaves by an admiralty court, and finally sold at auction. Thus a thriving business in ransom was generated, estimates of Europeans in captive slavery ranging between 500,000 and 1 million persons.

Because they were "infidels," European prisoners suffered what John Blassingame calls the "inhumanity of captivity," a deep depression from the shock of enslavement, especially from the constant stream of insults, whippings, tortures such as the bastinado (whipping the feet), and branding.[14] European slaves who even brushed against a Moslem might be summarily beaten or killed because they were considered unclean. Consequently, a large number of European prisoners began the process of assimilation simply to save their lives. In the cultural exchange that followed, assimilated European prisoners taught their captors specific technological skills by developing a verbal patois, a combination of Arabic and the prisoners' native languages. Prisoners learned a new diet of boiled rice, roasted snails, milk, and even the blood and entrails of camels. They developed new behavioral patterns that focused on physical strength instead of social rank. In a world where guile was more important than wealth, some prisoners were so completely acculturated that they never readjusted to European society.[15]

After the Revolution, the United States merchant fleet sailed under its own flag and discovered that the Barbary powers demanded tribute to use the high seas for trade. In effect, the Barbary powers had declared war against American ships and seamen. America was a new country in 1794, and the Americans were a new source of income for the ransom-seeking powers. Barbary captivity ended only in 1815 when the United States signed treaties with the four Barbary powers of Morocco, Tunis, Tripoli, and Algiers. Until that time, sailing the waters of the Mediterranean remained very dangerous. In the war with Tripoli, when the frigate *Philadelphia* was captured by the Barbary pirates on October 22, 1800, 307 Americans were taken prisoner and held for nineteen months and three days. Of that group, five men died, and five assimilated into North African culture.

Never had large numbers of Americans defected to an enemy, except in the Mexican War (1846–1848) when more than 200 Americans deserted and called themselves the Saint Patrick Brigade. Mexican military leaders realized that a considerable amount of friction existed among the American troops on three major issues: slavery, regional animosities between the North and the South, and the conflict of religion between the native-born Protestants and the immigrant Catholics. There were about 3,000 Catholics in General Winfield Scott's army, mostly Irish and German immigrants who suffered terribly from the anti-Catholic prejudice of the native-born, mostly Protestant, heavily Southern troops. The Mexicans seized the initiative and attempted to recruit these men, hoping that they might be unhappy enough to join the Catholic Mexicans. General Santa Anna issued a proclamation in which he offered $10 and 200 acres of land, plus bonuses for weapons, to any American deserter. Concerning religion, General Santa Anna wrote: "Can you fight by the side of those who put fire to your temples in Boston and Philadelphia? Come over to us! May Mexicans and Irishmen, united by the sacred ties of religion and benevolence, form only one people."[16] Of the 200 men who deserted to the Mexican side, not all were active deserters. A few men who were captured while drunk and impressed into the brigade were afterward pardoned by General Scott.[17] The Brigade of Saint Patrick (San Patricio)—called the "Irish Deserters" by the Americans—was named for a Mexican town honoring the patron saint of Ireland and consisted of two companies of infantry in the Mexican army.[18] After a desperate battle against American forces at Churubusco, about eighty members of the San Patricios were captured in the convent of San Angel. After trial by court-martial, fifty men were condemned to death by hanging. Thirty were executed in a most bizarre way. They were kept standing upon an elevated gallows while Chapultepec Castle was assaulted by American troops. Told that the trap would be released when the American flag flew victoriously over the castle, the condemned men stood rigidly for hours in the heat while the battle raged. Finally, when the Mexican flag came down, and the American flag was raised, the men dropped to their deaths. On November 12, 1847, General Winfield Scott issued General Order 340 in the *American Star:* the lucky ones whose death sentences were commuted would receive "fifty lashes on the bare back well laid on, . . . have the letter "D" (for Deserter) indelibly branded on the cheek with a red-hot iron, to be confined at hard labor, wearing about the neck an iron collar having three prongs each six inches long, the whole weighing eight pounds, for six months, and at the expiration of that time . . . have the head shaved and be drummed out of the service."[19]

Not to be outmaneuvered by General Santa Anna, General Scott, a Queenston prisoner in the War of 1812, did some POW recruiting of his own. When Scott reached the town of Puebla in July 1847, he decided to muster the inmates of the town jail, mostly murderers and cutthroats, promising freedom to all those who would ride with a group called "Dominguez's Scouts," led by a man known to be a condemned murderer by the Mexicans. Scott's efforts came to nothing. What angered Scott and the American command was the reasonably effective Mexican pro-Catholic, anti-American propaganda. In order to put a halt to it, Scott used the executed deserters from Churubusco as an example and issued General Order 296, published in the *American Star* on September 23, 1847. "The conspirators have also the services of several false priests who dishonor the religion which they only profess for the special occasion. Their plan is to . . . entice our Roman Catholic soldiers, who have done honor to our colors, to desert, under the promise of lands in California which our armies have already acquired and which are and forever will remain a part of the United States. Let all our soldiers professing the Catholic religion remember the fate of the deserters taken at Churubusco."[20]

Thus ended the incident of the Brigade of Saint Patrick. It was a stern lesson to immigrant Catholics in the American army that deserters and renegades would be treated as capital offenders. Another valuable lesson was that the right kind of critical, issue-oriented propaganda can be a very useful weapon in war, especially in the hands of a captor whose ideology can form a powerful appeal to a small, sometimes zealously oppressed segment of the opposing army. This lesson would be learned again in a different ideological context during the Korean and Vietnam wars.

The Civil War would present new challenges to civilians and soldiers who found themselves in the enemy's prison camps. President Lincoln was faced with the problem of what to do with political prisoners, those citizens of the Union, especially those from the border states—Kentucky, Missouri, Maryland, and Delaware—called "Copperheads" in the North, who supported the Confederate cause. Using the principle that martial law superseded civil law in areas of insurrection, President Lincoln ordered civilian Confederate sympathizers incarcerated without trial. Few political prisoners ever took the Oath of Allegiance to the United States during the war and, as a result, they languished in prison without the benefit of habeas corpus, sometimes for the duration. After the war, the Supreme Court considered the action and ruled in *ex parte Milligan* that all the political prisoners had been held illegally and that a president could not declare martial law outside a combat area.[21]

Changing sides was not common among POWs in the Civil War, but it occurred regularly, albeit on a relatively small scale. As in the Revolution, political policies toward POWs wavered on both sides. In 1862, after New Orleans fell to the Union forces, General Benjamin "Beast" Butler, USV, began to urge Confederate prisoners to change sides and fight with the Union. He referred to them as "repentent rebels"; they were later referred to as "white-washed" rebels. As former soldiers of the Confederacy, they were required to take the Oath of Allegiance to the United States. Between September 1864 and November 1866, volunteer units of "galvanized" or converted Confederate prisoners were sent to the western frontier to fight Indians and keep the peace. As the frontier corps of the United States Volunteers, they were known as the "galvanized Yankees," and as Indian fighters in America's outback they would risk their lives in battle for the Union but never against their former comrades.[22]

Not all of them went west; one "galvanized Yankee" who stayed in the east was Henry Morton Stanley. Born in England and an immigrant to the United States before the Civil War, Stanley decided that switching sides was preferable to remaining loyal to a doubtful cause. He states in his autobiography that his resolve to be a POW was undermined for several reasons. "These were the increase in sickness, the horrors of the prison, the oily atmosphere, the ignominious carnage of the dead, the useless flight of time, the fear of being incarcerated for years, which so affected my spirits that I felt a few more days of these scenes would drive me mad. Finally, I was persuaded to accept with several other prisoners the terms of release, and enrolled myself in the U.S. Artillery Service, and, on the 4th June, was once more free to inhale the fresh air."[23] After he took the Oath of Allegiance he was released from prison, but shortly thereafter came down with dysentery and fever. After his release on June 4, 1862, he served in the Union army until June 22, when he was discharged. Out of work, Stanley joined the U.S. Navy, where he learned the journalist's trade. After Stanley left the navy, he became a newspaperman and explorer and left the United States in disgust. He died Sir Henry Morton

Stanley, an immigrant in a foreign land, a former Confederate soldier, a "galvanized Yankee," journalist, explorer, celebrity, and finally an American expatriate.

Becoming a "galvanized Yankee" was not an especially easy task for a native son of the South. Angry, betrayed comrades and messmates would harass him. Colonel Buehring H. Jones, CSA, described an experience that occurred while he was a prisoner at the federal prison camp for Confederate officers at Johnson's Island. One officer decided to take the Oath of Allegiance to the United States rather than remain a POW. After his messmates discovered what in their view was treachery, they began to "kick him out" of their midst, physically kicking him until the Union guards came and forced them to stop the violence. Then, as a result of the decision to change sides, the young man was shunned.

> His former friends will not speak to him, nor allow him to speak to them. Every hand will be against him; every tongue will hiss at him; every heart will loathe him. Even the Federals, whom he seeks to propitiate, will regard him with ill concealed scorn and contempt. . . . Because they believed, he had not the manhood to endure imprisonment, with its privations and suffering, for a cause, that, in his heart, he believes is just; but chose rather to take a solemn oath—an oath that he is too cowardly to perform—to support a cause that he believes is wrong.[24]

Regardless of treatment in camp by former comrades in arms, the "galvanized Yankees" freed needed Union troops for the battlefields of the Southeast to confront the Confederate legions. At first, these men were received with skepticism, suspicion, and even dislike, because few federal field commanders believed that the Confederates would make good soldiers. The skeptics were wrong. When the former Confederate troops confronted the fury and military skill of the native American tribes on the Great Plains, the "galvanized Yankees" fought with distinction, a sense of duty, and discipline admired by their Union commanders and feared by their enemies.

After the American army and navy defeated Spanish forces in Cuba and the Philippines, trouble began to erupt in earnest in the Philippine Islands. In the press of the time, the Spanish-American War was known consistently as the "splendid little war." By contrast, the fighting between Filipino insurgents and the Americans—known in the popular press as the "Bamboo War"—with a casualty rate at 5.5 percent and a price tag of nearly $400 million was neither splendid nor little. About 126,000 Americans were assigned to the Philippines between 1899 and 1902, many of whom saw a great deal of action in tropical conditions nearly identical to those of South Vietnam. American losses totaled 1,037 men killed in action, 3,179 dead from disease, and 2,818 wounded. Filipino casualties can only be approximated at 16,000–20,000 killed or wounded in action, and worse, approximately 200,000 civilians dead from famine, disease, and other war-related causes.[25]

Filipinos under the leadership of General Emilio Aquinaldo, and later the Islamic Moro tribesmen on the large island of Mindanao, demanded political freedom from the United States. President William McKinley declared the Philippine Islands a colony of the United States. This guerrilla war had no fronts, and the Filipino insurgents raised no large units. Hot weather bred disease, and racial animosities between the Americans and the Filipinos were high. In an insurgent or "small war," taking prisoners is inconvenient, and few soldiers other than renegades lived past capture. The 24th Infantry Regiment, an all-black unit of "Buffalo Soldiers," fought the Filipino insurgents and suffered high casualties. In *Smoked Yankees and the Struggle for Empire* (1971), historian Willard B. Gatewood, Jr., describes the activities of the renegade Corporal David Fagan, who deserted the 24th Infantry Regiment to accept the rank of captain in the Filipino guerrilla army. Fagan wrought havoc upon American forces for two years until he was killed and beheaded by Filipino bandits.[26]

The war became so unpopular at home that the United States decided to withdraw its main forces, especially from Mindanao, and left a relatively small police force in its wake. Antiwar and anti-imperialist feelings were high due to the activities of the Anti-Imperialist League, and when the veterans finally arrived in San Francisco, they were not well received, in spite of President Theodore Roosevelt's official thanks for their courage and fortitude.

World War I was not a war of conflicting ideologies; it was a war of nationalism, colonialism, and militarism. There was an abundance of spies, but changing sides in captivity was rare. Only two American POWs assimilated into German culture. Both soldiers were Central European by birth, and assimilation was a simply matter of returning home. One was Private Halas, 18th Infantry, 1st United States Division; the other was Private Harry Nicholoff of the 23rd Infantry, 2nd United States Division. Nicholoff, whose real name was Nincheff, was a Bulgarian by birth who bought American citizenship from a man named Nicholoff. Austrian by birth, Halas asked German officers to return him to Austria in return for the information he provided them inside the prison camp.[27] By contrast, World War II was a "holy" war of ideology and conquest. Although there were very few incidents of POWs changing sides, some narrators recall incidents of collaboration. In a diary published as *Bilibid Diary: The Secret Notebooks of Commander Thomas Hayes, POW, the Philippines, 1942–1945* (1987), Commander Thomas Hayes, USN, condemns a certain Sergeant Provo, captured on Corregidor in 1942, whom he believed caused the disappearance and subsequent death of an American officer in Bilibid Prison. He writes of Provo: "If I have anything to do with it, Provo will never reach the States alive. . . . He has American blood on his hands to answer for. He's a mutinous, disloyal, traitorous sergeant . . . and must be remembered by every one of us."[28] In Europe, the Germans recruited a minuscule group of Englishmen for a renegade British "Free Corps," approximately thirty British POWs who, after being lured by unlimited supplies of alcohol and sex, volunteered for German service.[29] The Germans made some attempts to recruit American POWs for an American "Free Corps," but the efforts came to nothing.[30] In his novels *Mother Night* (1967) and *Slaughterhouse-Five* (1969), Kurt Vonnegut, Jr., created Howard W. Campbell , Jr., one of the three American prisoners who Vonnegut says were members of the American Free Corps. Vonnegut's fictional Campbell in *Mother Night* is not really a renegade but an American agent, recruited before the war and exploited by American intelligence. Campbell was caught in the web of cold war espionage and he forced the Israelis to take him prisoner for war crimes. In the end he hanged himself in his cell.

Political proselyting efforts in Korea, conducted primarily by the Chinese rather than the North Koreans, would change a page of history in the American captivity experience. Shortly after their arrival in the camps along the Yalu River, American soldiers were introduced to the Russo-Chinese method of political reeducation. The Chinese referred to their United Nations prisoners not as POWs but as "students.' Whereas American reeducation of German prisoners had been kept secret during World War II, the issue of major and minor collaboration including outright assimilation—the twenty-one American cases—became a public issue during and after the Korean War. In *Reactionary* (1956), Sergeant Lloyd Pate writes: "There were the men who went along with the Chinese and agreed with everything they had to say. They stood up and publicly denounced their country, their government, all that America stood for, and their God. The Chinese called these men peace fighters and later they became known as progressives."[31] The Chinese urged the small community of "progressives" to persuade fellow prisoners to study United Nations war aims and to circulate peace petitions among their fellow prisoners. To support these efforts, the Chinese began holding special courses in the political economy of Maoism and Marxist-Leninism. The successful "progressive" became an informant for the captors against the camp's hard-resisting "reactionaries." The rewards were numerous: sufficient food, adequate medical attention, no torture, reasonably good treatment, and, as in the case of Clarence Adams, an appointment as camp librarian. Adams remained in China after the general repatriation in 1953. In 1965,

Adams would deliver propaganda broadcasts on the *Voice of Vietnam,* directed against American and allied forces in South Vietnam.

Other assimilated "progressives" assisted their captors in publishing two propaganda books that attacked the United Nations cause in Korea, United Nations treatment of North Korean and Chinese POWs, and American culture in general. The first polemic, *Shall Brothers Be* (1952), attempts to portray prison camp life for Americans, British, and Australians in North Korea in "progressive" terms. The second and last polemic coming from reeducated Allied POWs, *Thinking Soldiers* (1955), was edited by Andrew M. Condron, an ex–British Marine, Richard Cordon, and Larance V. Sullivan, two Americans who eventually returned quietly to the United States. The book consists of anonymous essays that attack American lifestyles, with special venom directed toward poverty and American racial discord. One essay, "Pages in My Life," by a "Negro Sergeant" is typical.

> I learned to walk into restaurants and cafes, sit down, and, if I didn't get served within a half an hour, to get up and leave. Once, while sitting in a theater in Louisville, Kentucky, in my brand-new army uniform, there came to my ears a hissing whisper: "You msut leave the theater. Negroes are not allowed." He, the manager, was "very sorry because the woman at the box office was new on the job. . . ." Driven into the army because I could not provide myself with the necessities for school and home life, I was now confronted with this. There seemed no end to this vicious circle. Before joining the army, my naive mind had told me that my uniform would make a difference.
>
> But here I was . . . the government sends me to Korea to defend my RIGHTS as an American citizen![32]

Some "progressives" became deserters; ultimately they decided to remain with their captors when the others were repatriated. After prisoners identified themselves as "progressives," much like the "galvanized Yankees" of the Confederate Army nearly a century earlier, they segregated themselves from the community of resisting prisoners emotionally and psychologically.

Although in Korea no reported renegades carried arms against their former comrades, such was not the case in Vietnam. The model of assimilation for prisoners in the Vietnam War resembled that used by the Chinese in the Korean War. The terms "progressives" and "reactionaries" were used by the captors to designate friendly or unfriendly prisoners. At home, partially assimilated POWs were known as "antiwar POWs." In Hanoi, a "Peace Village" appeared, operated by the "Peace Committee," a group of American "progressives" who sympathized openly with the North Vietnamese cause. The process began when the North Vietnamese denied American prisoners the freedom to communicate with one another under their exception to Article 85 of the 1949 Geneva Convention. The North Vietnamese maintained that the Americans were war criminals rather than POWs and could be legally punished. When prisoners were caught trying to communicate, they were "punished," that is, tortured. After months of solitary confinement, hard interrogations, starvation, and torture, the Americans were forced to make tape recordings of antiwar propaganda, some of which were broadcast on the camp public address system and others on the *Voice of Vietnam.* Prisoners were forced to write letters home stating their belief that the United States could never win in Vietnam. Home meant more than letters to the family; it meant letters addressed to the American government, including the president, stating that the United States government should listen to what the antiwar movement was saying and accept whatever terms were being offered by the North Vietnamese at the Paris peace talks.

During the Vietnam War, it became common practice for American antiwar activists to visit Hanoi. David Dellinger, Susan Sontag, Mary McCarthy, Oriana Fallaci, Cora Weiss, and Jane Fonda are only a few names in a long list of antiwar visitors who crossed the Pacific to Hanoi. Visiting with American prisoners became a high priority, and the North Vietnamese seized these events for propaganda purposes. Although most American flight officers in captivity had little desire to speak with these people, some did. These officers, members of the "Peace Committee" for the most part, looked relatively healthy in captivity and would willingly give antiwar statements to the visitors. Upon repatriation, many of these men left the service and continued their antiwar activities.

After torture sessions and months of solitary confinement under the "justice bar," even the hardest resisters eventually signed letters, made broadcast tapes, or cooperated in some way. There was no way out, and in this sense, cooperation should not be understood as a form of collaboration. At first, some prisoners yielded because they could not bear any more torture. Others yielded because they heard a few senior officers broadcasting antiwar statements on the camp public address system. According to John G. Hubbell, the Vietnamese discovered that a handful of senior officers imprisoned in the "Desert Inn" section of the "Hanoi Hilton" had antiwar feelings and convinced them to broadcast regularly. Hard resisters, including Jeremiah Denton, ordered these officers to stop broadcasting, but there was no response.[33]

In 1968, during and after the Tet Offensive, American POWs began to arrive in Hanoi from South Vietnam. As a group they were quite different from the host of pilots and airmen shot down, captured, and imprisoned in North Vietnam. The incoming arrivals consisted of army and marine enlisted soldiers and some officers who were captured in ground warfare. Some had been held in lonesome, solitary captivity, sometimes in bamboo "tiger" cages for months. Some had been able to form small POW communities; others were loners. Several men who either believed in the North Vietnamese cause from the start or adopted it as prisoners established a "Peace Committee" that held antiwar sentiments and expressed them openly. Incensed, some hard-resisting officer POWs attempted to file charges of collaboration against members of the "Peace Committee" after repatriation, but each respective service ordered prosecutions to desist. After repatriation in 1973, the antiwar prisoners of the "Peace Committee" were released without charges. The government policy of not charging anyone with collaboration under the Uniform Code of Military Justice held until Robert Garwood left Vietnam in 1979.

Private Robert Garwood, USMC, disappeared from his unit in late 1965. Captured by a Vietcong guerrilla unit while he was standing casually next to his vehicle, Garwood would spend fourteen and a half years in captivity, first as a resister, later as a collaborator, and finally as an assimilated defector and renegade. His father received the following message from the Marine Corps in 1965: "Regret to confirm that your son . . . has been reported missing . . . in the vicinity of Headquarters Battalion Motor Pool where he departed in a Mighty Mite vehicle to report to the Division G-2 section. He was discovered missing during bed check and further investigation reveals that he failed to report to the Division G-2 section. Extensive search operations are now in progress and every effort is being made to locate him."[34] Word went out to marine and army combat units to look for Garwood. Shortly after his capture, area soldiers began picking up Vietcong propaganda leaflets signed by Garwood. In May 1967, *Liberation Radio,* the voice of the Vietcong in South Vietnam, announced that Garwood had been freed, but he failed to appear. In July 1968, Garwood was photographed by a Marine reconnaissance patrol, and his father was notified that his son might be a defector. Among American forces, rumors began circulating that there was an American Vietcong "running" with the enemy. In October 1969, three Americans released by the Vietcong provided American intelligence officers some more data concerning Garwood. Then he disappeared from view until 1979.

In February 1979, Robert Garwood entered a bar in a Hanoi hotel, and quietly put a short note identifying himself into the hands of a Finnish diplomat. He stated that he was in a forced labor camp and said simply, "I want to come home." Shortly thereafter, the world knew for certain that there was at least one American still alive in Vietnam. Garwood left Hanoi for Thailand and freedom, but freedom was not to be Robert Garwood's fate. He met his Marine escort in Bangkok, and was quickly informed that the Marine Corps planned to file charges against him under Article 82 of the Uniform Code of Military Justice for "soliciting American combat forces to throw down their weapons and refuse to fight." According to prisoners familiar with Garwood's proselytizing work, he used a megaphone to shout: "I am an American. I am a deserter. I recognized the injustice of American intervention in Vietnam. Now I am fighting with the Liberation Front. Come and join us. You will be well treated. The Liberation Front guarantees that any man who voluntarily lays down his arms will be returned to his own country as soon as possible, or given a passport to travel to any country he chooses."[35]

Charges of treason and collaboration with the enemy in time of war carry a maximum penalty of death. Although the Marine Corps had not ordered anyone's execution since the Civil War, the army had executed one man, Private Edward Slovik, a member of the Pennsylvania National Guard, during World War II. In the eyes of the Marine Corps, Garwood was a defector and renegade. At Garwood's court-martial his community of prisoners stepped forward and told their survivor-witness stories about life with Garwood. Zalin Grant reports in *Survivors: American POWs in Vietnam* (1975) that Warrant Officer Frank Anton, who had been in a Vietcong prison camp with Garwood in 1968, believed that Garwood had been so cooperative with his captors that he had been promoted to the rank of "cadre," something like a lieutenant in the Vietcong political organization. Garwood, like Simon Girty in Indian captivity, received a new name, "Huynh Chien Dao," or "Brave Liberation Fighter." In political indoctrination sessions, according to Anton, Garwood criticized his fellow prisoners in public and made life in captivity even more miserable than it had been already. According to Grant, another prisoner, David Harker, said that the Vietcong urged him to behave like Garwood. Harker maintained that Garwood struck him once after he and other prisoners killed and ate the camp cat.[36] Finally, an international NGO (nongovernmental agency) prisoner testified against Garwood. Monika Schwinn, a West German volunteer nurse with the Knights of Malta, was captured in 1968 in South Vietnam along with four other German medical volunteers working with civilian casualties. Of the five West Germans imprisoned by the Vietcong, three died in captivity; only Monika Schwinn and her colleague, Bernhard Diehl, survived. Schwinn remembers the Robert Garwood she knew in camp in *We Came to Help* (1973): "When I think of Bob, I always picture him the way he looked the first and last times I saw him, dressed as a liberation fighter in a water-lily hat and rolled-up trousers. I have always wondered what he was fighting for. Money? Glory? A Soviet watch? His own survival? I'll never know."[37]

Schwinn's colleague, Bernhard Diehl, commented that after their removal to Hanoi he inquired after Garwood's whereabouts from one of the Americans he knew in South Vietnam. The American replied, "I have nothing to do with Bob. He's a deserter!"[38] As a result of formal testimonies from these POWs and others, the United States Marine Corps convicted Robert Garwood on the following specifications: he served as interpreter during Vietcong indoctrination sessions; he informed the enemy about complaints and feelings of fellow prisoners; he interrogated POWs about military matters, including escape plans; he indoctrinated POWs as part of a political course and suggested that they cross over to the enemy; he served as a guard in the prison camp, and he assaulted a fellow prisoner, hitting him with the back of his hand.[39] For these crimes under Article 82 of the Uniform Code of Military Justice, the jury ordered Garwood to be reduced to the lowest rank and to be given a dishonorable discharge, including the forfeiture of all pay and allowances. The Marine Corps owed Garwood $147,000 in back pay; all that was lost. Garwood would be free from the Marine Corps, penniless and dishonored. No one ever heard Garwood's story; he never took the stand, and he never wrote his own captivity narrative.[40]

Garwood may have been the only POW convicted, but he was not the only confirmed American military renegade in the Vietnam War. Between 1962 and 1975, a steady flow of information came into the hands of American intelligence services concerning the existence of former American soldiers, possibly POWs at one time, who helped the Vietcong conduct military operations.[41] One reported renegade was code-named "Pork Chop" by army intelligence because sighting reports indicated that he wore long, full "pork chop" sideburns. Between 1969 and 1972, "Pork Chop" operated in Binh Dinh Province and liked to pose as an American army officer in order to flag down South Vietnamese military vehicles for Vietcong ambushes. A two-man propaganda team known as "Salt and Pepper," one white and the other black, operated in Quang Ngai Province, south of the city of DaNang. Reports of other Americans operating with the Vietnamese army continued to filter through the intelligence system even after the cessation of hostilities. One man, PFC McKinley Nolan (sometimes reported as Nolan McKinley), was thought to have defected to the Vietcong in captivity, but no evidence ever surfaced showing that he assisted them with military operations against American forces. On June 5, 1979, the director of the Defense Intelligence Agency, Lt. General Eugene F. Tighe, reported to the House Foreign Affairs Subcommittee that he believed Nolan remained in Vietnam after 1975 to fight with the Khmer Rouge in Cambodia but returned again to Vietnam disillusioned. General Tighe commented, however, that all the reports he had seen were simply too vague to be verified.[42]

Assimilation should not be a surprise. In every war, some prisoners are loners and castaways from the consensus culture of the captive community. For the captors they represent not only living symbols of success but also the correctness of their own just cause and methods of incarceration. On the other hand, assimilators, especially if they become renegades, receive their victims' hate and contempt for life. Most renegades understand that fact and choose to remain in their adopted culture. Mary Jemison returned late in life; Simon Girty never returned. Many "galvanized Yankees" found a hostile welcome on their return home from the frontier wars. Two of the twenty-one "progressive" Americans of the Korean War who defected to China in 1953 remained there. Except for Robert Garwood, it is reasonable to believe that the American renegades in South Vietnam who operated with the Vietcong, the North Vietnamese Army, and the Khmer Rouge all opted to remain somewhere in communist Southeast Asia after American–North Vietnamese/National Liberation Front hostilities ceased in 1973.

Acculturation may take place in varying degrees from the first moments of captivity to the moments of repatriation. Nearly every prisoner collaborates to a limited extent because personal survival often depends on small passive accommodations and compromises made with the captors. Bowing or saluting, trading with guards, learning simple courtesies, or using specified forms of address do not constitute assimilation. Leaving one's POW community to live or to take up arms does. From the forest wars to Vietnam, few American POWs decided to desert to the captor's side, take up arms as renegades, or willingly perform aggressive propaganda duties. If they were the exceptions, what might be the rule? Can the number of prisoners who will assimilate be predicted? Based on a very rough sense of the numbers—of assimilated Indian captives, Americans who assimilated into North African culture during the Barbary wars, the 200-plus members of the San Patricio Brigade, the many "galvanized Yankees" and Confederates in the Civil War, the "progressives" in Korea, and the antiwar POWs in Vietnam—there seems to be a rule of thumb: an army should expect from one to two percent of its POW population to assimilate into or collaborate willingly with a captor's demands.

CHAPTER TEN

The Line of More Resistance: Committed Escapers

A Committed Escaper! It is for his benefit that window bars are set in cement, that the camp area is encircled with dozens of strands of barbed wire, towers, fences, reinforced barriers, that ambushes and booby traps are set, that red meat is fed to grey dogs.

Aleksandr I. Solzhenitsyn (1979)

Because of the obvious risks and likely subsequent punishments inflicted by the captor, the act of escape has always been considered heroic, even romantic. In the past, few escapers succeeded; most were recaptured. This chapter presents a sampling of the prisoners who chose escape as a final option; some made the decision out of duty, some out of boredom, some because they could no longer bear the confines of captivity. In each case, regardless of success or failure, freedom from captivity was deemed worth the risk.

Puritan captives abhorred the thought of either years in a remote Indian village or forced incarceration in Canada. Not only did they fear for their lives among the Indians, they feared relentless pressure by the French to convert to Catholicism if they were taken north to Canada. With these two powerful motivations in mind, some Puritans opted for escape. According to Cotton Mather in *Decennium Luctuosum* (1699), Hannah Dustin, along with her week-old child and her nurse, Mary Neff, was captured in 1697 during an Abenaki raid on the Puritan town of Haverhill, Massachusetts. After the raiders killed Dustin's child, they turned over both women to a large Indian family for safekeeping and further removal. While their new captors slept, Dustin and Mary Neff found tomahawks and killed them one by one in their sleep. Taking further advantage of the instruments of escape, Hannah and Mary stole a canoe and finally left their captivity.

Early in her captivity during the French and Indian War, Barbara Leininger attempted an escape, but she failed. After her recapture and condemnation to be burned alive, her captors gave her a German Bible, that she might prepare for death. Thereupon they "made a large pile of wood and set it on fire, intending to put her into the midst of it."[1] Then, according to the narrative, a young Indian begged so earnestly for Barbara's

213

life that her captors pardoned her after she promised not to escape again. Another escaper was not so fortunate as Barbara and suffered a torturous death, what Barbara dreaded the most.

> There we had the mournful opportunity of witnessing the cruel end of an English woman, who had attempted to flee out of her captivity and to return to the settlements. . . . Having been recaptured . . . and brought back to Kittanny, she was put to death in an unheard-of way. First, they scalped her; next, they laid burning splinters of wood, here and there, upon her body; and then they cut off her ears and fingers, forcing them into her mouth so that she had to swallow them. Amidst such torments, this woman lived from nine o'clock in the morning until toward sunset when a French officer took compassion on her and put her out of her misery.[2]

Contemplating her escape, Barbara analyses the risk. "Does he attempt to escape from the savages, he knows in advance that, if retaken, he will be roasted alive. Hence he must compare two evils, namely, either to remain among them a prisoner forever, or die a cruel death. If he is fully resolved to endure the latter, then he may run away with a brave heart."[3] Following her brave heart, Leininger tried again. Along with two men and two women she fled the captors' village. With stealth, luck, some minimal organization, and cunning, the group traveled on foot through the forest from the backwoods of Ohio to Pittsburgh and freedom.[4] Each person knew that recapture meant certain death.

In America, imprisoned sailors languished below decks in the dreaded hulks of Wallabout Bay; captured American soldiers were cast into criminal confinement in church cellars and local jails.[5] In England, captured American privateers found themselves in four British military prisons: Millbay in Plymouth, known simply as "Old Mill" Prison to the Americans; Fortune, or Forton Prison in Portsmouth; Deal Prison in Scotland, and Kinsale Prison in Ireland.[6] As criminals, American naval officers and seamen had little to forfeit if and when they escaped.[7] Continental privateer Captain Gustavus Conyngham was told that the gallows awaited him in Mill Prison. Conyngham scoffed when his captors brought him in irons to Pendennis Castle. "Then not contented, they manacled my hands with a new fashioned pair of ruffels fitted very tite [sic]. In this condition I was kept there 15 or 16 days, then brought to Plymouth and lodged in the black hole for eight days, before they would do me the honour of committing me on suspicion of high treason on his majesties [sic] high seas; then put into Mill prison."[8] Faced with the threat of certain death, he began tunneling. Twice his tunnels were discovered and destroyed. Conyngham finally succeeded on his third effort and got away on November 3, 1779, with fifty-three other prisoners.[9] As Conyngham asserts, "We committed treason through his earth and made our escape."[10]

Some resourceful individuals devised unusual methods for their escapes. American prisoners in Kinsale often seized small boats to make the passage to France. A communication from the Sick and Hurt Commissioners dated June 2, 1779, stated that the Americans were relatively well treated in British prisons because they received monetary support from American commissioners as well as assistance in their escapes from dissenting Englishmen.[11] Tunneling was, by far, the most common cooperative method used for mass escapes, and exits like Conyngham's were made regularly from the Mill and Forton prisons, where prisoners reported that guards were susceptible to bribes and where walls could be dug under or scaled. In response, the British offered a reward of five pounds for the return of escaped Americans, and it is conceivable that some prisoners faked escapes to share the reward. However, during the Revolution, most escaped to gain their freedom and fight another day. At Forton Prison, thirty Americans broke out, of whom eleven made passage to France. In 1778, the local British militia found French and American prisoners climbing through a hole in the outer wall. In that incident, twenty-five prisoners escaped. Later that year, fifty-seven Americans dug a tunnel from the Black Hole to a point beyond the prison walls.[12] Even in April 1782, when a general release was imminent, large numbers of Americans continued to escape, especially from Forton.[13]

In America during the Revolution it was nearly impossible for American prisoners to escape from the British army. They were too well guarded in small groups. A young surgeon, Elias Cornelius of the Connecticut militia, was an exception; he made his escape during a snowstorm while his sentry's attention was distracted. Cornelius perched on a tombstone in the yard and jumped over a fence. He satisfied other guards by posing as a drunken civilian and eventually reached a safe house near the edge of town.[14] Few American prisoners found a way to escape from the poisonous floating British prison hulks.[15] In a relatively short time, the Americans grew too sick or weak to escape. However, some prisoners remained healthy, and, if the conditions were favorable, some escapes were successful. Christopher Hawkins was taken on board the *Jersey* in 1781, made his way quietly down the side of the ship without arousing any suspicions from the guards, and swam to shore. Unfortunately, Hawkins was recaptured and temporarily housed in a private room. Luckily for him, his guards were more interested in a girl who was preparing food, and Hawkins seized the moment to slip away again, this time to freedom.[16]

Another *Jersey* prisoner, Thomas Andros, was obsessed with thoughts of escape. "While on board almost every thought was occupied to invent some plan of escape, but day after day passed, and none presented that I dared to put in execution. But the time had now come when I must be delivered from the ship or die. It could not be delayed even a few days longer; but no plan could I think of that offered even a gleam of hope. If I did escape with my life, I could see no way for it but by miracle."[17] Andros looked about the *Jersey* and the local terrain. "Intent on the business of escape, I surveyed the landscape all around. I discovered at the distance of half a mile what appeared to be a dense swamp of young maples and other bushes. On this I fixed as my hiding place. . . . When the complete darkness of the night had shut in, and while rain fell in torrents, I began to feel my way out. . . . I reached the dry land, and endeavored to shape my course for the east end of Long Island."[18]

The British continued to use prison hulks in England during the War of 1812, and with memories still fresh from the Revolution, American sailors were terrified by the prospect of confinement in them. The greatest number of American prisoners were sent to the *Hector* and *La Brave,* both hulks moored by chain about two miles from Plymouth. From the autumn of 1812 to April 1813, there were 900 Americans at Chatham Prison, 100 at Portsmouth, 700 at Plymouth. On April 2, 1813, the Transport Board ordered everyone to Dartmoor.[19] By 1814, Dartmoor was overcrowded, and two escape attempts were made by American tunnelers. Digging was accomplished in three barracks simultaneously. Captain Thomas George Shortland, RN, the interior commandant, halted the effort. Soon after Shortland's discovery, the Americans had nearly completed their second tunnel, but the war ended. They left the tunnel unfinished, only to be discovered in December 1911, when British authorities were excavating Dartmoor's foundation for a new building inside the prison. Dartmoor Prison remains in use today.

Daniel Drake Henry, captured during the Mexican War (1846–1848), was the interpreter for the Louisville cavalry. He was a Texan who had been a prisoner of the Mexican army in the Texas war of 1836, and knew that if the Mexicans discovered his identity, he would be executed immediately. Seizing a moment's opportunity after the unit's capture, Drake mounted one of the officer's horses and broke for freedom. Chased by five Mexican cavalrymen, Drake escaped. Returning empty-handed, the Mexican soldiers reported that Henry was gone, and the Mexican commander, Colonel Sambranino, was furious. He drew his pistol and held it against the American commander's chest, but hesitated to take his life. At that moment, another officer ordered his men to the ground and told the Mexicans they would not escape. Yet another officer said, "Shoot and be damned."[20] It was a tense moment, after which the Mexicans tied the Americans together for the long march to Mexico City.

Most of the American soldiers held POW by the Mexican army were kept in Mexico City until it became obvious that the city itself would come under siege. General Santa Anna then ordered their removal to areas away from the fighting. Some officers gave their word as parole and could not escape; those who refused, could. Midshipman Robert C. Rogers, captured with a small naval party surveying the coast two miles from Vera Cruz, refused to give parole. Foolishly, the Mexicans allowed him the run of the city. The prisoners knew that the American army was in Puebla and knew too that with the confusion of having an enemy army at their doorstep, the Mexicans would not be as careful as usual about guarding prisoners. Rogers and one other prisoner stole a hack and drove it to a nearby canal. Then they stole a rowboat and rowed to Lake Chalco where they found some horses. Finally, both men reached safety and reported their adventures to their commanding officer, General Winfield Scott, a former POW himself in Canada during the War of 1812.

During the Civil War, there were hundreds of successful escapes on both sides. Decimus et Ultimus Barziza, a product of William and Mary College, practiced law in Texas before the war and became a Confederate infantry officer in 1861. Captured during the Battle of Gettysburg in 1863, Barziza escaped from a train while it stopped in Huntingdon, Pennsylvania. Through cunning, wit, luck, good humor, and his ability to speak with a distinctly New England accent, he convinced rural Pennsylvanians and other unsophisticated Northerners that he was a discharged soldier from Maine on a business trip. In time he managed to travel north and crossed the Canadian border. Later, Barziza traveled aboard a blockade-runner to Wilmington, North Carolina, and freedom.[21] A Confederate sergeant named Womack used simpler means: he walked out the front gate of the Union prison camp at Elmira, New York, to freedom on October 26, 1864, using a set of forged identity papers.[22] In addition to Barziza and Womack, hundreds of escape stories demonstrate the desire and skill of Confederate soldiers to seek freedom in Dixie, such as the elusive cavalryman John Hunt Morgan, who escaped his close confinement in the Ohio State Penitentiary.[23]

Union prisoners at Andersonville found escape difficult. Some prisoners attempted to dig tunnels in the soft Georgia sand, but only one was successful. There was no wood readily available for shoring, and far too many prisoners lived in the compound to keep an escaper's secret. In Andersonville, 329 Union prisoners did, however, manage to escape from work details and paroles. And a large number of Union prisoners managed to plan and conduct a relatively successful great escape from Libby Prison in Richmond. It was without a doubt one of the most daring, well planned, and well executed mass escapes in American military history.

Under the direction of Colonel Thomas E. Rose, USV, groups of fifteen men clawed at the loose, wet soil below Libby with penknives and crude tools they fabricated from supplies inside the prison. Rose's plan called for diggers to link up with the Richmond sewer system; however, as they burrowed, water began to seep, then gush, into the tunnel. Rose and company decided on a new plan: they would dig under the street along the side of the prison and surface in the yard of a warehouse near by. At least it would be a dry route. More important for the escapers' morale, they tunneled under the very noses of their captors. After the tunnelers surfaced, twenty-five officers emerged early in the evening and took their leave of Libby. Posing as Confederate uniformed personnel, the Union escapers walked along the Richmond canal. A total of 109 Union officers made their escape on the night of February 9, 1864, and forty-eight succeeded in reaching the Union lines. One who did not succeed was Colonel Rose himself. Only about two miles away from the Union lines, Rose abandoned precautions, thinking that he was safe from any further pursuit, and talked with two men whom he thought were wearing Union uniforms. Unfortunately for Rose, they were Confederate scouts looking for escaped prisoners from Libby. After a short scuffle, a very unhappy Thomas Rose surrendered and returned to prison.[24] After his exchange he returned to his unit and fought again, this time suffering a severe wound while in combat against the Confederates in Georgia. Rose survived his wound and was mustered out of the army in 1865 as a brevet brigadier general.

Other escapers, especially those men traveling in groups, were recaptured after some bizarre circumstances. One party stole a boat on what they thought was the James River and followed the stream hoping to reach Hampton Roads. Unfortunately, they traveled the Appomattox River by mistake, upset their craft, and swam to shore for their lives. After nearly freezing to death, they were discovered the next morning by some Confederate soldiers and recaptured.[25] Another group was hunted down by dogs and recaptured. Fortunately, the recaptured officers received no unusual punishment, although after they returned to Libby, the Confederate prison commandant, Major "Dick" Turner, CSA, made it clear to them that he would not tolerate another prison break. He increased the number of roll calls to a point where most of the day was taken up by counting and recounting. By keeping the prisoners busily distracted with head counts, Turner began conducting close room searches and managed to discover caches of tools, knives, and sundry objects with edges that could be used to dig tunnels.[26]

The Libby officers knew that working in large, secret groups produced big results. On the other hand, failure was costly for everyone: the guards became surly; the commandant, whose position was always threatened by an escape, became more inquisitive about the slightest thing out of place; the food rations diminished in quantity or quality, and suspicious or misbehaving prisoners were put into solitary confinement for long periods of time for the slightest offense. Escapers learned that their non-escaping comrades, as members of a captive community, became innocent accomplices in the escape whether they had participated actively or just passively cooperated. The innocents were considered just as guilty as the escapers, and for the freedom of a few, many suffered. Both armies had to wait until 1863 for a definitive set of rules for land warfare that set down what was legally acceptable behavior toward POWs who attempted escapes. The Union army's *Instructions for the Government of Armies of the United States,* later the *Law of Land Warfare,* drafted by Francis Lieber, stated: a "prisoner of war who escapes may be shot, or otherwise killed in flight; but neither death nor any other punishment shall be inflicted on him for his attempt to escape, which the law of order does not consider a crime."[27]

During World War I, the first American POW to escape from Germany into Switzerland was Everett Buckley of Chicago, who served with the French Escadrille N-65.[28] The second American escaper was Thomas Hitchcock, Jr., of New York, also a flier with the French. He escaped from his train while it sat in the station at Ulm on its way to the prison camp, walked seventy miles out of Germany, and never saw an enemy soldier during the entire time on the road. Frank Sovicki of Shenandoah, Pennsylvania, was the first American private to escape from Germany. Captured at Chateau-Thierry on July 13, 1918, Sovicki was interned on a farm near the Swiss border and escaped on October 8, 1918. Robert A. Anderson, a flight lieutenant in the American army air force, was captured on August 27, 1918. He escaped from a German prison camp in Fresnes, France, and reached Holland on October 23, 1918. John Owen Donaldson, a pilot, also escaped from the German prison camp in Fresnes and fled to Holland on September 26, 1918.[29] No less committed to escape, but less fortunate, was Navy Lieutenant Artemus L. Gates. One of the Yale pilots flying Spads over Belgium, "Di" Gates was shot down, captured, and sent to an officer's camp in Germany. While he was riding by train toward the oflag in Villingen, Gates eluded his guards and made his escape through a window while the train chugged slowly through a tunnel. Gates hit the ground hard, but when he regained his composure he ran as fast as he could into the woods. In his pockets were bits of food he kept for traveling and a rudimentary map which told him where the railroad went. Determined to find the German border with Switzerland at Constance, Gates bypassed towns, stole food, and traveled at night. Finally, he arrived at the border crossing, but after so many hungry days, traveling on foot, and sleeping on the ground in frigid weather, energy seeped from his body, and he surrendered at the very last moment. The border guards recognized him as an escaped POW, and offered him some coffee and bread. Silent as the German soldiers put him into the guard-house, Gates was sent back to Villingen without reproach or reprisal.[30]

The premier American escapers of World War I, the men who received the most attention for their daring escape, were Harold B. Willis and Edouard Victor Isaacs. Willis was an adventurer and ambulance driver turned combat pilot in the Lafayette Escadrille. Shot down on March 1, 1917, and sent to the officer's prison camp in Villingen close to the Swiss border, Willis met Navy Lieutenant Edouard Isaacs, the only American naval officer taken prisoner at sea by a German submarine. Together, they planned and executed their escape from Villingen to Switzerland. Rather than just contemplating what he wanted to do, Willis began collecting and hiding provisions and quietly gathering information about the best route to Switzerland. One of the French prisoners hid a map in the sole of his boot, and while the Frenchman kept watch, Willis copied the map labori-ously for the first chance to break out. In preparation for his role in the escape, Isaacs cut through the bars in the windows in the various rooms and constructed three bridges made out of pine boards taken from the cases of food sent them by the Red Cross.[31] For his part in the escape, Willis received the French croix de guerre and returned to combat flying duty.[32] Isaacs returned to duty on October 13, 1918, less than a month before the Armistice, and later received the Medal of Honor. His citation reads:

> When the U.S.S. *President Lincoln* was attacked and sunk by the Ger-man submarine *U-90,* on 21 May 1918, Lt. Izac was captured and held as a prisoner on board the *U-90* until the return of the submarine to Germany, when he was confined in the prison camp. During his stay on the *U-90* he obtained information of the movements of Ger-man submarines which was so important that he determined to escape, with a view to making this information available to the U.S. and Allied Naval authorities. In attempting to carry out this plan, he jumped through the window of a rapidly moving train at the imminent risk of death, not only from the nature of the act itself but from the fire of the armed German soldiers who were guarding him. Having been recaptured and reconfined, Lt. Izac made a second and successful attempt to escape, breaking his way through barbed-wire fences and deliberately drawing fire of the armed guards in the hope of permitting others to escape during the confusion. He made his way through the mountains of southwestern Germany, having only raw vegetables for food, and at the end, swam the River Rhine during the night in the immediate vicinity of German sentries.[33]

Escaping from German and Italian prison camps continued a common European military tradition, respected and practiced on all sides. In

England, MI-9 (Military Intelligence) recruited old escapers from World War I to develop pathways or lines for both escapers and evaders. MI-9's officers lectured flight and ground officers, developed codes and escape kits, and created a spy network throughout occupied Europe. MIS-X, the super-secret American escape agency and equivalent to British MI-9, acted on the three major assumptions in the British POW model: (1) POWs remained responsible soldiers in captivity; (2) the prison camp remained a battleground; and (3) it was a soldier's duty to escape or assist in an escape whenever possible. Beginning in 1942, MIS-X developed a relatively sophisticated method to brief selected flight and ground officers on the use of a POW message code. With the code, POWs could send intelligence information concerning camp life, observations of German troop movements, and escape plans back to Washington. Then MIS-X developed two cover agencies—the Serviceman's Relief and the War Prisoner's Benefit Foundation—to develop and send escape and evasion materials, including maps, radios, money, and surgical saws, to be sent in relief packages. MIS-X believed that by using the regular mail and carefully avoiding sending these things in Red Cross packages, they avoided problems with the Geneva Convention regulations.[34]

Officers were expected to escape, or at least to plan and, if possible, lead escapes. Two heralded escapes took place from Stalag Luft III in Sagan, Silesia: the "Wooden Horse" in which two British officers used a vaulting horse to decoy the guards while they tunneled under the barbed wire, and the 1944 "great" escape. Paul Brickhill, an Australian airman and POW in Stalag Luft III, states clearly in *The Great Escape* (1950) that the breakout was the most meticulously planned mass exodus from a prison camp in the military history of the twentieth century. Brickhill describes "X," the organization led by Roger Bushell that planned and executed the mass breakout on March 24, 1944. Bushell wanted to send 200 men from the tunnel he called "Harry"; eighty got out; seventy-six made it to the woods while four were held at gunpoint at the exit hole. Only three POWs, two Norwegians and a Dutchman, managed their return to England; the others were recaptured in less than two weeks. Some were returned to Stalag Luft III; others were put into other special camps for committed escapers. Fifty men were executed by the SS/Gestapo under the illegal, anti-escaper *Kugel Order* issued in March, 1944. As a result of the murders, the senior American officer in Stalag Luft III prohibited any more escapes.[35]

With less bravado, and far less organization, other escapers, mostly individuals and partners, escaped and made their way from the many prison camps in Germany, Italy, Austria, and Poland as the German army crumbled before the advance of the Russians in the east and the Anglo-American armies in the west. During the war, most escapes were kept secret;

however, according to MI-9's August 31, 1945, summary, 28,349 British, Commonwealth, and Allied (Greek, Polish, French, Dutch, Czech, and Russian) soldiers and 7,498 Americans either escaped from prison camps or evaded capture in World War II. How many Kriegies fearing the wrath of the SS and Hitler's maniacal propensity to issue last-ditch orders broke camp for Allied lines just before liberation may never be known exactly.[36]

Escape from prison camps in Asia was especially dangerous.[37] Much like Barbara Leininger's evaluation of the escaper's dilemma during the forest wars, the stakes were the highest imaginable. A failed escape meant death and only death. Despite draconian reprisals, the first American escapers were among the first Americans captured at Bataan in April 1942. When Corregidor fell to the Japanese army on May 7, 1942, 11,000 American and Filipino prisoners were herded into an area about the size of two city blocks with Japanese guards posted around them. Who would try to escape from an island? It was a long swim to freedom. One night, however, two American officers, Edgar D. Whitcomb and William Harris, seized the moment, slipped into the water, and escaped.[38] More frequent were periodic, opportunity-oriented escape attempts from work details. Such was the case with several officers, including Second Lieutenant William E. Dyess, author of *The Dyess Story* (1944), Sam Grashio, who records his exploits in *Return to Freedom* (1972), and Captain Mark Wohlfeld and Second Lieutenant Hadley Watson, who had survived the Bataan Death March and were interned together in the Japanese camp at Davao.[39] Determined to escape into the jungle, Watson assaulted his guard and killed him with a shovel. Other guards were shot and killed as the Americans tried to escape their grasp. Wohlfeld explains that his escape was "more or less a spontaneous affair" rather than a planned event. "The actual fight at the squash-field," wrote Wohlfeld in a letter, "took less than sixty seconds, but once it was started it couldn't be stopped."[40]

In response to escaping Americans, Australians, and other Allied soldiers, the Japanese army amended its prisoner of war regulations on March 9, 1943, to permit recaptured Allied escapers to be punished in the same drastic way as its own deserters were punished. "The leader of a group of persons who have acted together in effecting an escape shall be subject to either death, or imprisonment for a minimum of ten years. The other persons involved shall be subject to either the death penalty or a minimum imprisonment of one year."[41] In practice, the Japanese formed what they called "shooting squads," groups of ten prisoners held responsible for a possible escape by any one of them. If one or several escaped from a "shooting squad," those left behind would be executed.[42]

Beginning in 1950, captivity at the hands of the North Koreans paralleled captivity at the hands of the Japanese during World War II. Atrocities were commonplace.[43] The will to escape, however, ran high, especially among pilots. After being shot down early in the war, Air Force Captain William D. Locke devised his escape at an opportune time during a North Korean retreat. He hid under the floor of a schoolhouse in Pyongyang where he had been interned and waited there until United Nations forces advanced on his position. Another air force pilot, Captain Ward Millar, author of *Valley of the Shadow* (1955), broke his ankles bailing out, then spent three months in relatively tame medical captivity with the Chinese. Millar knew that when he was fit, the Chinese would send him to a POW camp somewhere in North Korea. As a result, he stalled as long as he could by lying to his interrogators about his mission and general knowledge concerning military matters. He learned some Chinese and Korean, bartered with his captors for food and medicines, and managed to survive the initial weeks in ankle and leg casts. After Millar's broken ankles healed to the point where he enjoyed some mobility, he seized the opportunity to hobble out of a Chinese field hospital. With the help of a defecting North Korean, Millar managed to signal a friendly aircraft, and both men were rescued. Air force pilot Melvin J. Shadduck was shot down in April 1951, and spent thirty-four days in captivity near the Imjim River. He was sent on an errand by his captors and kept on going. Like other escapers in other wars, Shadduck found that he had to depend on the kindness of the local country people for his survival. Korea had been a Japanese colony from 1905 until the end of World War II, and many Koreans spoke Japanese. Shadduck also spoke Japanese and was able to communicate with some ease.[44] With the help of a young boy, Shadduck headed toward friendly lines where he finally found a detachment of Greek soldiers and freedom.

In contrast, escape from the Chinese camps in North Korea proved to be impossible even for the most determined. Security was rigid, and the camps were positioned along the Yalu River in a way that afforded the Chinese easy recovery of any Americans determined enough to leave. In *Reactionary* (1956), Infantry Sergeant Lloyd Pate describes the adventures of some who tried but failed. "None of the escapes was successful, but at least we could say we tried. It wasn't too hard to get out of camp, but from then on it got rough. The Chinks would search the immediate vicinity and then they would put out an alarm. The North Koreans would keep their eyes open because there was a reward for every prisoner they brought back."[45]

Experiences like Pate's repeated themselves in Indochina. The record of successful escapes is small in South Vietnam, Cambodia, and Laos, and nonexistent from the prison facilities in North Vietnam. Yet there were significant escape and rescue attempts throughout the war. First to escape were two navy pilots shot down and captured in Laos. In separate escapes, Lieutenant Charles F. Klusmann and Lieutenant (jg) Dieter Dengler overpowered their guards and fled their prison camps. On June 6, 1964,

Klusmann flew from the USS *Kitty Hawk* to photograph Pathet Lao installations in central Laos between Khang Khay and Ban Ban, a dangerous area known as "Lead Alley" because of the heavy concentration of anti-aircraft fire.[46] When Klusmann flew a low pass to get clear photographs, his aircraft was hit, and he was forced to bail out. In spite of American efforts to conduct a rescue, Klusmann was captured by the Pathet Lao and remained with them for eighty-six days of solitary confinement. After being coerced into signing a propaganda document denouncing the policies of the United States government in Southeast Asia, Klusmann was integrated into a small prison-camp population of Laotians and Thais. He formed an alliance with five prisoners and began planning to escape. They left the prison camp together on August 21, 1964, and after three days of evasion in the jungle, Klusmann found a friendly Meo village and freedom. Dieter Dengler was shot down on February 1, 1966, and was finally picked up by a helicopter on July 20, after five months in captivity.[47] Like Klusmann, Dengler planned for prisoners to steal the guards' weapons during siesta time, then use them to escape. Dengler executed his plan, shot his way out of the camp, and began a long and dangerous trek through the Laotian jungle. His Thai group members left him and headed toward home. One American disappeared, and the other was killed in a chase by enemy soldiers. Only Dengler survived the escape. He told his story to Congress and the *Saturday Evening Post* in 1966, thirteen years before he published *Escape from Laos* (1979). For his heroism, Dieter Dengler was awarded the Navy Cross; the citation in part reads:

> For extraordinary heroism during an extremely daring escape from a prisoner-of-war stockade on 30 June 1966. Playing a key role in planning, preparing for, and developing an escape and evasion operation involving several fellow prisoners and himself, Lieutenant (jg) Dengler, keenly aware of the hazardous nature of the escape attempt, boldly initiated the operation and contributed to its success. When an unplanned situation developed while the escape operation was being executed, he reacted with the highest degree of valor and gallantry.[48]

Dengler and Klusmann escaped from the Pathet Lao; twenty-four other POWs escaped from the Vietcong between 1968 and 1969. Army Special Forces Lieutenant James N. Rowe was captured and held prisoner by the Vietcong in South Vietnam from 1963 to 1968. Throughout his captivity, Rowe insisted he was just another American adviser, never revealing his true identity as a member of the Special Forces. In 1968, he was condemned to execution by the Vietcong for lying to them about who and what he was. Fortunately for Rowe, the Vietcong political authorities decided that he had to be moved to their central headquarters for execution. While the party was marching through the jungle, opportunity presented itself. Rowe's party came under attack by American B-52 aircraft. In the confusion during the heavy bombing, the guards became disoriented; the group dispersed, and Rowe seized the opportunity to escape. He killed the guard he called "Porky" and quickly signaled nearby low-flying attack helicopters. Judging from his clothes, the helicopter crews thought Rowe was a Vietcong, and made a swift pass with machine guns firing. Fortunately for Rowe, they missed him. Not until the second pass did they see his beard, identify him as a captured American, and rescue him.[49]

Several air force and navy officers matched the kind of prisoner described by Aleksandr I. Solzhenitsyn in *The Gulag Archipelago Three 1918–1956* (1976): "It is for his benefit . . . that red meat is fed to grey dogs."[50] They were George Day and Lance Sijan, both winners of the Medal of Honor, George Coker, George McKnight, and John Dramesi. Day won the medal in 1976 for his 1967 escape attempt and subsequent resistance in North Vietnamese captivity up to his release on March 14, 1973. His narrative, *Return with Honor* (1990) explains how he was shot down by flak eighteen miles north of the DMZ in an F-100. After his capture, he realized that he could escape, and aided by a B-52 strike near his position, he managed to evade recapture until he was two miles from the Marine base at Con Thien.[51] Air Force Captain Lance Sijan was shot down on November 9, 1967, and captured by North Vietnamese soldiers after forty-six days of evasion in the jungle. After a few days in a prison compound, Sijan escaped his captors, but within a few hours he was recaptured and beaten severely. As he lay nearly unconscious, he asked his cellmates about the chances of escaping again. Sick with pneumonia, Sijan began digging into the earthen floor, intent on escaping. Finally, Sijan, the escaper who could not be contained, died in captivity on January 22, 1968. He received the Medal of Honor posthumously.[52]

Navy Lieutenant (jg) George Coker and Air Force Captain George McKnight escaped from the "Dirty Bird Annex" on September 14, 1967. They jimmied the locks, escaped, and jumped into the Red River for an eight-mile swim downstream to the South China Sea. To their chagrin, they were discovered by a startled old Vietnamese woman who called the local militia. According to James B. Stockdale, *In Love and War* (1984), they were not ill-treated upon recapture.[53] After Lieutenant Colonel John A. Dramesi, USAF, was shot down in his F-105, he thought about escape from the moment of capture. After entering the North Vietnamese prison system, he formed a partnership with Edwin Atterberry, and, together, they planned their escape and struck out for freedom. Before their escape from the "Zoo," one of the outlying camps in the North Vietnamese system, the two men stole clothing that would hide their identities while they traveled the Red River to the sea. Like that of Coker and McKnight earlier, the Dramesi-Atterberry attempt failed. In contrast to Coker and McKnight's relatively benign treatment upon recapture, the North Vietnamese killed Edwin Atterberry in a torture session. John A. Dramesi's *Code of Honor* (1975) reflects on the ethos of escape and is dedicated to Atterberry.

Although unsuccessful, one raid had a positive effect on POW life in North Vietnam. The most exacting full-fledged prison raid planned and executed in enemy territory during the Vietnam War took place in 1970 against the Son Tay prison camp in North Vietnam. In the Pentagon, perhaps as early as 1966, the United States Air Force realized it was losing significant numbers of pilots over North Vietnam. Ranking military officers joined forces with the intelligence community—the Central Intelligence Agency, Defense Intelligence Agency, and National Security Agency —to initiate a show of force against the North Vietnamese in a real effort to free Americans from enemy hands. Led by Colonel Arthur "Bull" Simons, USA, the raiders struck North Vietnam on November 12, 1970. One HH-3 and five HH-53 helicopters carried fifty soldiers to the Son Tay prison camp. After landing, the raiders scrambled around the camp for twenty-seven minutes looking for American prisoners. No Americans were present; the North Vietnamese had moved them. American intelligence had suspected the removal of the Americans from Son Tay, but it was too late to stop the raid. Benjamin F. Schemmer points out in *The Raid* (1976) that American intelligence used a North Vietnamese deep penetrant, "Alfred," a senior Hanoi official, to procure a head count of the American prisoners. "Alfred" reported that there were no American prisoners in Son Tay; they were moved to "Dogpatch," the Dong Hoi Prison Camp near the Chinese border.[54] On the ground, the raiders smashed doors, searched cells, and entered into a brief combat with enemy soldiers on the site. Finding an empty camp, they boarded the escape aircraft and left. First Lieutenant George Petri, one of the raiders, commented, "When we realized that there was no one in the compound, I had the most horrible feeling of my life."[55]

In spite of its failure, the Son Tay raid had positive internal effects on prison conditions in North Vietnam. The North Vietnamese realized that outlying camps were vulnerable to American raids. Immediately following international press attention on the raid, the North Vietnamese began quickly moving prisoners to Hanoi. Inside the POW community itself, the raid served as a powerful morale booster. Few narratives fail to mention the effects of Son Tay inside the compounds. After repatriation, 320 prisoners were asked to take part in a survey conducted by the Monroe Corporation. Responding to questions concerning what aided their morale during their long captivity, most commented that the Son Tay raid played a significant role. In addition to the Son Tay raid, the Christmas bombing of 1972, known as "Linebacker II," also built morale among the Americans in the Hanoi prisons.[56] At home, the humanitarian goal of the Son Tay raid was ignored by many editors and television commentators who decried the resumption of large-scale bombing over North Vietnam. Antiwar activists condemned the raid as well; however, military communities, especially the families of the prisoners in captivity, understood Son Tay to be more a humanitarian than a purely military operation.[57] Despite the raid's failure to recover any prisoners, at least the government and the military services in general were showing some courage and determination in responding to reliable information concerning North Vietnamese mistreatment of Americans in captivity.

Frustrated with the state of affairs, the American Joint Chiefs of Staff proposed in 1972 that a force consisting of 3.5 divisions—57,500 men—be deployed solely to rescue the Americans in Hanoi. The plan called for simultaneous airborne, amphibious, and air mobile strikes to surround Hanoi with American troops. Small Special Forces teams would seize Hoa Lo (the "Hanoi Hilton"), the Plantation, and the outlying camps. The tactical problem, that more raiders would die than there were prisoners, ultimately defeated the planners. More importantly, by 1972, any overt American invasion of North Vietnam for any reason would have caused political chaos in the United States. Consequently, the Joint Chiefs of Staff scrapped the plan, and the alert was never issued. Nonetheless, all the forces were in place and ready to go if the president chose to order the operation.[58]

By 1972 peace talks promised an end to hostilities, and thoughts of escape from the rigidly monitored confines of the Hanoi Hilton and other prison camps in North Vietnam were largely abandoned. The 1973 peace accords between the United States, the Democratic Republic of Vietnam, the National Liberation Front, and the government of South Vietnam brought a temporary halt to the war and returned 651 American POWs from the region. The question of the soldiers and sailors who were known to have been captured alive but who were never returned still lingers.[59]

Escapers are POWs who reject captivity as a way of life or the fortunes of war and take the risk to seek freedom. Functionally, there have been four dominant, consistently repeated experiential patterns among escapers: (1) committed "natural" or "rogue" escapers described by Aleksandr I. Solzhenitsyn and dramatized by those relatively few prisoners who, for reasons known only to themselves, reject being in captivity regardless of any risks to self or to a community of fellow prisoners; (2) individual opportunity escapers, like Christopher Hawkins, Decimus et Ultimus

Barziza, Sergeant Womack, Sam Grashio, Mark Wohlfeld, Ward Millar, and James N. Rowe, who seized a fleeting, opportune moment to make one all-or-nothing dash for freedom; (3) small group escapers, like Dustin and Neff, Barbara Leininger, Willis and Isaacs, Coker and McKnight, Dengler, Klusmann, and others who decided to form small ad hoc partnerships or groups to plan and execute their escape; and (4) the great escapers, mostly tunnelers like Conyngham's group from Mill Prison, Rose's group from Libby, and Bushell's "X" organization of British, Commonwealth, and American prisoners in Stalag Luft III, who formed extensive secret organizations for detailed planning, hard and dangerous work underground, selection, and precise execution. Mass escape requires an organized matrix of selected escapers and nonescaping accomplices with one goal. Everyone has a rank, a job, and a place in the organization. Escape organizations create a hierarchy of responsibilities, weigh the risks, and share the rewards and retributions.

Without exception, the question of motivation is addressed in narratives, biographies, and reports. Some escapers claim they became angered or humiliated, fearful that despite any accommodation with the captors, there was ultimately little or no hope of anything more than misery or death. Some, like Barbara Leininger, claim to have based their commitments to escape on atrocities and concluded that if a captor committed crimes against others, chances were excellent that the same or more horrendous crimes would be committed against oneself. It is one thing to witness pain, quite another to suffer it. Boredom too has played a significant role in the decision-making process. During the Civil War one Confederate officer, a POW on Johnson's Island, saw little or no hope of exchange. He wrote about "the terrible ennui of prison life . . . an infallible sign of surrender when the men became listless and no longer cared for the things that had hitherto been either their work or their recreation."[60] Extreme ennui combined in some cases to force some prisoners into suffering what Kriegies call "wire fever," or "barbed wire disease." With no counteracting influences, it shows as utter listlessness, an opium-like lethargy of dull resentment, heartache, and feelings of oppression.[61] Saying, "I can't stand it any more," hopelessly embittered prisoners made direct and usually fatal charges against the wire in full view of the armed guards. Not escapers at all, they knew full well that fatal oblivion awaited. These suicides only conceded victory to a punitive captor and devastated group morale and the spirit of resistance among the living.

Some prisoners must escape; some escapers consider escape a duty; others see it as the only pathway from a humiliating circumstance. In addition to the *Law of Land Warfare* used by the American army from the Civil War to the present and the protection given to individual soldiers by the international conventions, the United States government issued

Order 207 in 1953, a pre-Code of Conduct, which stated that the American soldier is duty-bound to try to escape.[62] After President Dwight D. Eisenhower approved the Code of Conduct in 1954, the American POW had a set of simple, understandable rules to go by: "If I am captured I will continue to resist by all means available. I will accept no parole nor special favors from the enemy." In effect, not only did the code mandate resistance and restrict the POW from seeking even partial freedoms, between the lines, it provided an institutional mandate for escape. In spite of international laws to the contrary, captors have made reprisals directly against recaptured escapers, and in some instances against nonescaping members of a captive community. Escapers have received high praise and decorations by their institutional hierarchies, but they are not necessarily praised by their comrades, especially by those left behind to take the captors' punishment. In escapers' narratives, biographies, testimonies, and memoirs, one discovers a wealth of reflections on the many specific variables that activated the escape: the evolution of the commitment, the planning process, the unsuccessful attempts, the final escape from the prison camp, the adventures on the trail to freedom, and often the final success. Whether propelled by boredom, torture, personal humiliation, or as Solzhenitsyn suggests, simply a total disgust with life in captivity, some POWs consider the risks of retaliation irrelevant to themselves or to the comrades they left behind.

Each American military service operates a survival school—often called SERE, survival, evasion, resistance, and escape—dedicated to teaching officers and enlisted personnel how to survive captivity. The schools' curricula use lessons from the past to force students to face the realities of the captivity experience. One by one, as they try to work themselves through an evasion course, the students become POWs. After capture, the enemy interrogates them, often violently, for military information. Then they are removed or marched to a POW collecting area. Finally, they enter a simulated POW camp, there undergoing more interrogations, simulated political indoctrination, incarceration in doghouses, threats of torture, very little food, and abundant psychological stress. Some students escape; others take the punishment stoically; some give in to the physical and mental stress, and others begin the process of personal and community resistance. For the military services, SERE simulates captivity and helps to define individual stances in future wars and the inevitable instances of captivity. Soldiers learn that a POW needs self-discipline and determination, although brutal treatment may either render a committed escaper passive or a passive prisoner opportunistic. One need not be an obsessive escaper to acquire, as soon as possible, some of the necessities for survival—stealth, cunning, evasion, hand-to-hand combat, and field survival—after an opportunistic escape. Keeping one's powder dry is not an obsolete adage.[63]

The history of escape is the history of the gamble for self-liberation. Ultimately, there is no way to predict who will or who will not make an escape from a prison camp. The committed escaper plays not only for time but for the right time. Sometimes waiting for release or exchange is more prudent than acting on the notion that POWs, especially officers, are duty-bound to escape. For committed escapers, from the forest wars to Vietnam, there have been no ''how-to'' rules written in stone, only the necessity to obey the call of duty and personal integrity, even at the price of life.

CHAPTER ELEVEN

Final Pathways to Freedom: Release, Repatriation, and the Prisoner's Lament

It was the age that was brutally senseless, and heedlessly cruel. It was lavish and wasteful of life, and had not the least idea of what civilized warfare ought to be, except in strategy.

Sir Henry Morton Stanley (1909)

Prisoners of war gain their freedom generally in one of four ways: escape or self-liberation; rescue by raiders who enter hostile battle zones and withdraw captured soldiers; liberation by a large military operation against a POW camp during hostilities; or release by an agreement or contract including cartel-exchange, ransom, parole, armistice, or treaty of peace. Treaties of peace or agreements of armistice end hostilities and free all prisoners of war. In an exchange, belligerents trade their POWs, usually in equal ranks, or establish a rank-worth structure that frees POWs to fight again. In ransom, POWs are purchased for money or goods, and in parole, prisoners are released after giving their oath or word of honor not to bear arms against their former captor. Although the pathways are different, the result is freedom for the individual POW. As a two-part narrative event-scenario, release and repatriation reveal the components of each individual's pathway to freedom. The act of repatriation brings the POW home, where he expects to begin a new life. When bondage ends, the spirit of the newly freed prisoner is high, and the prisoner returns to family, friends, and familiar institutions.

When time finally heals some of the wounds of the prison camp, POWs may begin to reflect on the experience and lament the cost. As a concluding narrative event-scenario, the lament expresses grief and moderates the euphoria of finally being free. In lament, captivity narrators evaluate the cost of wasted time, reflect upon their lost material opportunities, and purposefully grieve for their dead comrades. The lament functions too as an ethical forum for former prisoners to express individual and collective outrage against willful, and often illegal, acts of inhumanity.

As an act of closure, narrators have recounted what the captivity experience cost emotionally as well as physically, what was gained, and what was lost, much as the prophet Jeremiah narrates the sacrifices made by the ancient Hebrews during their biblical captivity in the books of

Chronicles and Lamentations. To the biblical Jeremiah and the colonial narrators of the Indian captivity experience who followed his lead, the experience was not complete until the considerable emotional residue was addressed in the narrator's lament. After her repatriation in 1677, Mary Rowlandson, the consummate Puritan, explains the nature of tangible loss and spiritual gain at the hands of her captors. She recounts her loss of time and her joy at being given God's trial of faith.

> I have seen the extreme vanity of this world. One hour I have been in health and wealth, wanting nothing, but the next hour in sickness and wounds and death, having nothing but sorrow and affliction. Before I knew what affliction meant, I was ready sometimes to wish for it. When I lived in prosperity, having the comforts of the world about me, my relations by me, my heart cheerful, and taking little care for anything, and yet seeing many whom I preferred before myself under many trials and afflictions, in sickness, weakness, poverty, losses, crosses, and cares of the world, I should be sometimes jealous lest I should have my portion in this life, and that scripture would come to mind, Hebrews 12:6, "For whom the Lord loveth he chasteneth and scourgeth every son whom He receiveth." But now I see the Lord had His time to scourge and chasten me. The portion of some is to have their afflictions by drops, now one drop and then another, but the dregs of the cup, the wine of astonishment, like a sweeping rain that leaveth no food, did the Lord prepare to be my portion. Affliction I wanted and affliction I had, full measure (I thought) pressed down and running over. Yet I see when God calls a person to anything and through never so many difficulties, yet He is fully able to carry them through and make them see and say they have been gainers thereby. And I hope I can say in some measure, as David did, "It is good for me that I have been afflicted."
>
> The Lord hath showed me the vanity of these outward things. That they are the vanity of vanities and vexation of spirit, that they are but a shadow, a blast, a bubble, and things of no continuance. That we must rely on God himself and our whole dependence must be upon Him. If trouble from smaller matters begin to arise in me, I have something at hand to check myself with and say, why am I troubled? It was but the other day that if I had had the world I would have given it for my freedom or to have been a servant to a Christian. I have learned to look beyond present and smaller troubles and to be quieted under them, as Moses said in Exodus 14:13, "Stand still and see the salvation of the Lord."[1]

The sense of loss not only pervaded Puritan narratives but extended to the recollections of soldiers and non-Puritans as well. After his civilian captivity with the Indians, Peter Williamson became a soldier and was captured by the French at the fall of Oswego. In contrast to the redemptive threat of Rowlandson, Williamson expresses his hatred of his tribal captors bitterly in his lament: "From these few instances of savage cruelty, the deplorable situation of the defenseless inhabitants, and what they hourly suffered in that part of the globe, must strike the utmost horror, and cause in every breast the utmost detestation, not only against the authors, but against those who, through inattention, or pusillanimous or erroneous principles, suffered these savages at first, unrepelled, or even unmolested, to commit such outrages, depredations, and murders."[2] After his repatriation and unsuccessful search for his wife, Williamson expresses his feelings over her death while he was held captive: "Upon inquiring for my dear wife, I found she had been dead two months! This fatal news greatly lessened the joy I otherwise should have felt at my deliverance from the dreadful state and company I had been in."[3] Imprisoned first in Montreal and later in England and Scotland, he died a prisoner in Edinburgh in 1799.

By the close of 1776, the Americans held about 3,000 British prisoners in confinement, but between 1776 and 1778, there were numerous ad hoc exchanges made by the opposing armies, most of which were accomplished after a battle under the authority of the respective field commanders. The Continental Congress wanted to establish a general exchange for officers, sailors, and soldiers of equal rank. General Sir William Howe, as the senior British officer in America, was eager to establish a liberal exchange policy. General Washington was not nearly so eager, since such action would favor the combined British-Hessian army far more than his own. Washington favored a more closely guarded cartel arrangement where exchanges were negotiated on a one-for-one basis. Politics and military necessities interfered. The British were loath to admit that the United States was a sovereign country, and refused to yield what they considered their own sovereign rights. By April 6, 1776, negotiations for a general national prisoner exchange ceased.[4] Negotiations were attempted again in 1779 and 1780 between generals George Washington and Sir Henry Clinton, but those efforts also failed. Clinton wanted a large exchange, but Washington refused, knowing full well that a general prisoner exchange would benefit only the British. In 1782, Benjamin Franklin tried to arrange an exchange of British prisoners held in France for Americans held in England but came up short against the North Act, which declared the Americans to be criminals. Officers were generally exchanged, but most common soldiers and privateers remained in captivity until the war's end. The lesson learned in the Revolution was that generals can conduct individual negotiations and reach compromises for the exchange of individual prisoners, but nations cannot, especially when international rules do not exist, or, as in the case of the American Revolution, when one nation refuses to acknowledge the sovereignty of the other.

Ethan Allen, captured on September 24, 1775, in Montreal, believed that the British conspired to kill their prisoners when he wrote in his lament, "I was persuaded that it was a premeditated and systematical plan of the British council to destroy the youths of our land, with a view thereby to deter the country and make it submit to their despotism."[5] Other POWs of the Revolution would write their respective laments about lost time, opportunities, and comrades. Christopher Hawkins wrote about the "sufferings of my youth in my memory."[6] In addition to the prose laments that conventionally conclude captivity narratives, some poems written during captivity resemble the lament in tone and content. No one wrote a more literarily sparkling verse about the deaths that he and many other prisoners witnessed aboard the hulks in Wallabout Bay than Philip Freneau in his poem, "The British Prison Ship."

> Each day, at least six carcasses we bore
> And scratched them graves along the sandy shore,
> By feeble hands the shallow graves were made,
> No stone, memorial, o'er the corpses laid;
> In barren sands, and far from home, they lie,
> No friend to shed a tear, when passing by;
> O'er the mean tombs insulting Britons tread,
> Spurn at the sand, and curse the rebel dead.[7]

According to Freneau and other POW narrators who lament captivity in the Revolution, the British and Scots prison guards were harsh, whereas the Hessians were relatively humane. What angered prisoners most during the Revolution, seemingly, was the treatment they received from American loyalists, whom they cursed as mean-spirited, vindictive, dangerous, and intolerable. No wonder, then, that postwar American feelings turned against the loyalist population, who forfeited citizenship, homes, and property and, ultimately, abandoned America for new homes and lives in Canada. In that sense, the Revolution was very much a civil war, precursor to the protracted vindictive treatment Americans would impose on one another between 1861 and 1865.

The United States did not resort to ransom except in dealing with Indians during the Revolution and with the Barbary states thereafter.[8] In 1842, the Republic of Texas appropriated $20,000 for the redemption of Indian captives, and fixed the redemption price at $300 per captive.[9] After the Revolution, the United States expanded its merchant marine rapidly with an eye to competing with the French and British for North

African and Mediterranean trade. In 1792, the Senate suggested that a treaty should be made with Algiers, Tunis, and Tripoli providing $40,000 a year for the ransom of captives. In 1793, the American consul was given funds to support Americans in Algerian captivity. In the 1786 agreement with Morocco, Article 16 stated: "In case of a war between the Parties, the Prisoners are not to be made slaves, but to be exchanged for one another, Captain for Captain, Officer for Officer, and one private man for another; and if there shall prove a deficiency on either side, it shall be made up by the payment of 100 Mexican Dollars for each Person wanting; and it is agreed that all Prisoners shall be exchanged in Twelve Months from the Time of their being taken, and that this exchange be effected by a Merchant or any other Person authorized by either of the Parties."[10]

The treaty remains in force today. By January 1787, after the successful Moroccan negotiation, the American State Department believed that the United States should pay only $300 rather than the asking prices of the other Barbary powers: from $6,000 for sea captains down to $1,500 for seamen.[11] John Hay wrote to Thomas Jefferson that he believed the government should spare no reasonable expense to ransom its citizens. One American naval officer in captivity at this time was the USS *Philadelphia*'s surgeon, Jonathan Cowdery. His narrative, *Captives in Tripoli, or, Dr. Cowdery's Journal* (1806), records his impression of the relationship between cruelty and ransom: "I was informed that through the influence of many Turks, the Bashaw had given orders to Sarcy, our master, to treat the American prisoners with utmost cruelty, in order to induce the United States the sooner to make peace. He was impatient for his money."[12] The American Congress grew impatient as well and decided to end the money exchanges and captive taking in North Africa. After naval and land engagements in 1803 and 1804, an agreement was concluded on June 4, 1805, stipulating that prisoners captured by either party should not be made slaves but should be exchanged rank for rank. It further stipulated that any deficiency on either side should be made up by the payment of 500 Spanish dollars for each seaman. Most important, this treaty put a limit on the period of incarceration of twelve months after capture.[13] This treaty with Tripoli notwithstanding, ten years later Algiers declared war on the United States again over the same issues, captive taking and ransom. On March 3, 1815, Stephen Decatur, Jr., engaged the Algerians at sea, defeated them, and ended the issues of tribute and ransom with the Barbary powers.

During the War of 1812, from April 3, 1813, when the first Americans were imprisoned, until April 1815, the American POW population—American sailors, mostly young officers and crews of merchantmen and privateers—increased to 5,542 inmates. During that period, there were at least 252 deaths, and the Americans became increasingly embittered.[14] Captain Jeduthan Upton, the master of the privateer *Polly,* catching the spirit of the time, composed his poetic prison lament in Ashburton on January 23, 1813:

> Far from my native land in solitude I sigh
> In prison strong confined, in misery I lie;
> No friend—no partner dear, I call my own;
> A stranger here—unknowing and unknown!
> Alas! In vain I strive my liberty to gain,
> Use lawful means in hope I may attain,
> But hard as adamant is every soul.
> They will not even grant a short parole.
> The reason given why I am thus confined here
> Is because I was caught on board a privateer
> Whose guns at time of capture were not seen
> To amount to the lawful number of fourteen.
> Although so far renowned in history and story
> Is British justice, humanity and glory,
> Yet prisoners, who are strongly here confined,
> Are forced almost to live upon the wind.
> Sunday our allowance of bread and beef
> Would not tempt even the smallest thief;
> Monday the same is given, about,
> And wonderful to tell, our jaws hold out; . . .
> If such my cruel fate should chance to be
> I'd curse the hour when first I put to sea.[15]

His poem of lament cursing the hour he first put to sea reflects a consensus of feelings expressed by other prisoners in Ashburton and Dartmoor. Prisoners particularly feared incarceration in Dartmoor. One prisoner, James Hart, died, and his shipmates placed the following epitaph over his grave:

> Your country mourns your hapless fate,
> So mourn we prisoners all;
> You've paid the debt we must pay,
> Each sailor great and small.
> Your body on this barren moor,
> Your soul in Heaven doth rest;
> Where Yankee sailors one and all,
> Hereafter will be blest.[16]

On April 20, 1815, 263 Americans left Dartmoor; 5,193 followed a few days later. Still resisting the British, they carried a large white flag on which was represented the goddess of Liberty lamenting over the tomb of their killed compatriots, with the legend, "Columbia weeps and will remember!"[17] By December 1815, Dartmoor military prison was empty, and the naval component of the War of 1812 was over.

After engagements on the American continent, POWs were removed from the battlefield quickly and quartered either in private homes or in prison camps.[18] There was no formal program to enlist native-born American citizens in British forces, but prisoners were used as instruments for exchange. In the fall of 1812, Lieutenant Colonel Winfield Scott was taken prisoner with his small force after the British victory in Canada at the Battle of Queenston. Known as the Queenston Prisoners, the militiamen and their officers were immediately paroled and sent home; however, Scott and his regulars were imprisoned as POWs in Canada. The British put them aboard the *Duke of Gloucester* and the *Prince Regent* for the trip from Queenston to York. The group was then transferred to the twenty-our gun *Royal George* for the trip to Kingston. At that point the Queenston Prisoners took to open boats for the long trip down the St. Lawrence River to Quebec. On the trip, British commanders treated their prisoners well. At Ogdensburg, Scott and the prisoners encountered Lieutenant Colonel Thomas Pearson, the garrison commander. Pearson had himself suffered capture at sea when the transport on which he and his wife traveled to Canada was taken by an American privateer. In captivity, Mrs. Pearson experienced premature labor, and the American captors gave her such aid as needed. Generously and respectfully treated at the time by the Americans, Pearson was happy to reciprocate when Scott and the Queenston Prisoners came under his jurisdiction.[19]

Upon their arrival at Montreal, however, conditions changed for Scott and the Queenston Prisoners. The Governor General of Quebec, Lieutenant General Sir George Prevost, according to Scott, "behaved like a renegade in causing the prisoners to be marched, on their arrival at Montreal, along the front of its garrison, drawn up in line of battle, and by slights and neglects which excited contempt and loathing."[20] On November 20, 1812, the Queenston Prisoners were paroled and embarked on a ship for Boston. As a result of this experience, on May 14, 1813, the United States and Great Britain tried to establish the Mason-Barclay Cartel, an agreement that not only provided for the exchange of prisoners but delineated how captors on both sides would treat them. Although the provisions of the cartel were applied in practice, Great Britain never signed. On April 15, 1814, another agreement was formulated in Montreal that outlined formal prisoner exchanges. Finally, the United States and Great Britain signed the Treaty of Ghent on December 28, 1814, ending the war. Ratified by the United States Senate on February 15, 1815, Article II, the POW provision, stated: "All prisoners of war, taken on either side, as well by land as by sea, shall be restored as soon as practicable after the ratification of this treaty, as hereafter mentioned, on their paying the debts which they may have contracted during their captivity. The two contracting parties respectively engage to discharge, in specie, the advances which may have been made by the other for the sustenance and maintenance of such prisoners."[21] The War of 1812 remained essentially a stalemate. The British had important and threatening problems on the European continent to worry about, and the United States and Great Britain would not face each other again as enemies. Canada remained loyalist and British, and the United States would never again raise the issue of unification or Canadian conquest. Great Britain retreated from her fortifications in the United States and dropped the assumption that it could impress naturalized American citizens into naval or military service.

The issue in the Civil War was not so much the existence of parole or exchange but the condition of each side's prisoners upon release. The United States Sanitary Commission, the forerunner of the American Red Cross, sent representatives to tend to such men when they returned North from Southern prison camps. One member of the commission, Anna Holstein, was present in Annapolis for a prisoner exchange in 1864. She was horrified at what she saw:

> In one arrival of 460, only 60 were able to walk ashore; the 400 were carried; half of these died within a few days; one third of the whole number imbecile. They appeared like a wretched bundle of bones, covered with a few filthy rags. . . . Though coming from different prisons, all agree in this one fact: they were starved, without shelter, and wearing only the scantiest clothing—the rags which remained from the time they were captured—when their coats, blankets and valuables were all taken from them. Many, after conversing about it, will say: "You never could imagine such horrors."[22]

Another member of the Sanitary Commission, Lydia G. Parrish, whose husband was a physician, worked in the Philadelphia branch. In December 1863, she was accompanying her husband on a tour of Southern hospitals in Virginia and North Carolina when she heard that there was going to be a prisoner exchange. She obtained permission to go to the exchange under a flag of truce in order to give what aid she could to the exchanged prisoners. In December 1864, Parrish found herself in Annapolis, the location of the Sanitary Commission Home, and wrote the following in the *Bulletin of the United States Sanitary Commission:*

> No human tongue or pen can ever describe the horrible suffering we have witnessed this day. I was early at the landing, eight and a half

o'clock in the morning before the boat threw out her ropes for security. The first one brought 200 bad cases which the Naval surgeon told me would properly go to the hospital nearby, were it not that others were coming, every one of whom was in the most wretched condition imaginable. They were therefore sent in an ambulance to Camp Parole Hospital. . . .

In a short time another boatload drew near and oh! such a scene of suffering humanity I never desire to behold again. The whole deck was a bed of straw for our exhausted, starved, emaciated, dying fellow creatures. Of the 550 that left Savannah, the surgeon informed me not 200 would survive. . . . I saw five men dying as they were carried on stretchers from the boat to the Naval Hospital. . . . The stretcher-bearers were ordered to pause a moment by Surgeon D. Vanderkieft, that the names of the dying might be obtained. . . . Some had become insane . . . others were idiotic . . . a few lying in spasms. . . . When blankets were thrown over them no one would have supposed that a human form lay beneath, save for the small prominence which the bony head and feet indicated. . . . One in particular was reduced to the merest skeleton, his face, neck, and feet covered with a thick green mold. A number who had Government clothes given them on the boat were too feeble to put them on and were carried ashore partially dressed, hugging their clothing with a death grasp that they could not be persuaded to yield.[23]

Lieutenant Colonel F. F. Cavada, USV, attempted to understand the starvation inflicted on Union prisoners by the Confederacy, not so much as a policy of war but as a result of the North's success in defeating the South on the field of battle. In his lament he states: "The Confederate authorities assert that they are doing all they can for us! If unavoidable this system of starvation would be frightful enough; if intentional, it is too revoltingly cruel to ever meet with its full punishment upon earth."[24] On the Confederate side, lamenting his prison experience in Camp Douglas, Henry Morton Stanley blames the times rather than his Union captors. "It was the age that was brutally senseless, and heedlessly cruel. It was lavish and wasteful of life, and had not the least idea of what civilized warfare ought to be, except in strategy. It was at the end of the flint-lock age, a stupid and heartless age, which believed that the application of every variety of torture was better for discipline than kindness, and was guilty, during the war, of enormities that would tax the most saintly to forgive. . . . We were simply doomed!"[25] Lamenting captivity in song, an anonymous Union soldier composed "Union Prisoners, From Dixie's Sunny Land" and set the words to the popular tune, "Twenty Years Ago." In this post-repatriation lament, he recounts the captivity experience and assures the audience that he, along with all the other surviving Andersonville prisoners, will eventually take righteous vengeance against the Confederates in "Dixie's sunny land."

Dear friends and fellow-soldiers brave, come listen to our song,
About the Rebel prisons, and our sojourn there so long;
Yet our wretched state and hardships great no one can understand,
But those who have endured this fate in Dixie's sunny land.

When captured by the chivalry, they strip't us to the skin,
But failed to give us back again the value of a pin—
Except some lousy rags of gray, discarded by their band,
And thus commenced our prison life in Dixie's sunny land.

With a host of guards surrounding us, each with a loaded gun,
We were stationed in an open plain, exposed to rain and sun;
No tent or tree to shelter us, we lay upon the sand—
Thus, side by side, great numbers died in Dixie's sunny land.

This was the daily "bill of fare" in that Secesh saloon,
No sugar, tea or coffee there, at morning, night or noon;
But a pint of meal, ground cob and all, was served to every man,
And for want of fire we ate it raw in Dixie's sunny land.

We were by these poor rations soon reduced to skin and bone,
A lingering starvation—worse than death! you can but own,
There hundreds lay, both night and day, by far too weak to stand,
Till death relieved their sufferings in Dixie's sunny land.

We poor survivors oft were tried by many a threat and bribe,
To desert glorious Union cause and join the Rebel tribe,
Though fain were we to leave the place, we let them understand,
We had rather die than thus disgrace our flag! in Dixie's sunny land.

Thus dreary days and night rolled by—yes, weeks and months untold,
Until that happy time arrived we were all paroled.
We landed at Annapolis, a wretched looking band,
Glad to be alive and free from Dixie's sunny land.

How like a dream those days now seem in retrospective view,
As we regain our wasted strength, all dressed in "Union Blue."
The debt we owe our bitter foe shall not have long to stand;
We shall pay it with a vengeance soon in Dixie's sunny land.[26]

In a pre-repatriation, romantic lament, an anonymous Confederate officer imprisoned on Johnson's Island, seizes the moment to consider home-sickness and the loneliness of prison life in his poem, "The Prisoner's Lament":

> My home is on a desert isle,
>   Far away from thee,
>   Where thy dear smile I never see,
> Your voice I never hear.
> I rest beneath the Northern sky.
>   A sky to me so dreary,
> I think of thee, dear one, and sigh,
>   Alone upon Lake Erie,
>   Alone upon Lake Erie.[27]

Confederate Captain Sidney Lanier, one of the postwar South's premier men of letters, was captured aboard the blockade-runner *Lucy* by the USS *Santiago-de-Cuba* in 1864. He was taken first to Fort Monroe near Norfolk where he was imprisoned with criminals. Then he was transferred to Point Lookout prison camp. Released in 1866, Lanier walked home a bitter and angry man. In 1867, he published *Tiger-Lilies,* a novel in which he attempts briefly to discuss the prison experience. Bitterly, he writes: "To go into a prison of war is in all respects to be born again. For of the men in all prisons of the late war, it might be said, as of births in the ordinary world—they came in and went out naked."[28]

One cannot forget the tragic misery of the *Sultana* disaster. On April 21, 1865, the ship arrived at Vicksburg, Mississippi, with about 200 pas-sengers, and there embarked 1,965 Union enlisted soldiers and thirty-five officers just released from Confederate military prisons, mostly from Cahaba (Castle Morgan), Macon, and Andersonville. There were also two companies of infantry under arms that raised the total to 2,300 passengers on board. While the *Sultana* was steaming in the middle of the Missis-sippi River en route to Cairo, Illinois, the ship's boilers exploded, prob-ably because of the silty river water used to make steam. In an instant, the ship's light, dry wood above the waterline caught fire and caused a floating inferno. Lifeboats were burnt beyond use, and hundreds of people jumped into the cold waters of the river only to drown after their limbs cramped. Nonswimmers grabbed swimmers in panic; both drowned. Many healthy people survived by clutching debris and floating downriver, but others panicked and died. Freed prisoners, emaciated from their captivity, had little or no chance. Reverend Chester D. Berry col-lected and published some of the survivors' testimonies in *Loss of the Sultana and Reminiscences of Survivors* (1892). One survivor, POW Ira B.

Horner of Weston, Ohio, a former member of Company K, 65th Regiment, Ohio Volunteer Infantry, told how vindictive his captors were up to the end. "When we were to be exchanged and were passing out of the prison grounds, the monster who had presided over our prison tortures said by way of parting, 'I had rather shoot every one of you than see you exchanged.'" Then Horner boarded the *Sultana* for his trip home and suffered a double-barreled tragedy:

The explosion of the steamer *Sultana* and my escape from a watery grave at first seemed like a horrid dream, but in a short time I learned it was a reality. When first awakened from my slumbers it seemed as if some poor emaciated comrade had fallen upon me. The next thing I knew I was struggling in the water. I was not very well versed in the art of swimming; but fortunately for me a stick of timber came floating along. I grasped it and soon found another, and by the aid of these I thought that there would not be much danger of my drowning. While clinging to the timbers a poor fellow clutched me by the legs, and for fear that he would drown us both I pushed him off, letting one of my socks go with him. Probably well I did so, for I should not have been able to have taken him with me. . . . We [now with several other survivors on a small raft made from the hurricane deck of the *Sultana*] floated . . . along until we came to where the city guards were stationed; they fired upon us not knowing what was the matter. . . . I hallooed with all my strength and soon a party of two, with a small boat came to our rescue.[29]

For Americans on both sides, Civil War captivity was characterized by harsh, vindictive treatment up to the end of hostilities. With popular songs like "Dixie's Sunny Land" circulating in the North and South after the war, testimonies in Congress about the horrors of Andersonville and other Confederate prison camps, the reports of the Sanitary Commission, and a large number of revenge-seeking captivity narratives, there is small wonder that Reconstruction was pursued so long and so punitively. To this day, deep resentments exist concerning Civil War captivity. The Andersonville Historic Site is now federal property and is the *only* national cemetery for veterans in the state of Georgia. In the North, the proprietors of Johnson's Island in Ohio consistently refuse to allow the United Daughters of the Confederacy to decorate the graves of Confederate war dead. One can only ask if the American Civil War will ever come to an end.

The next period for major prisoner exchanges, paroles, and laments was fought against a backdrop of international rules governing the treatment of POWs. When World War I ended, approximately 75 percent of the American prisoners resided in camps close to the Rhine River near the zone occupied by Allied armies. According to Carl P. Dennett, the American Red Cross Deputy Commissioner to Switzerland in charge of American POW matters, the Americans coming out of Germany had ample food and clothing and seemed in good condition. The German government supplied Allied prisoners with the absolute minimum of food, medicine, and clothing, and if not for the steady supply of Red Cross relief packs, conditions would have been much worse, starvation would have been rampant, and many more lives would have been lost.

Exchanges between belligerents began as early as 1916, when about 17,000 Russian sick and wounded were exchanged for 8,000 Austro-Hungarians and 2,000 Germans. The British, French, and Germans concluded an exchange agreement in April 1916 that called for internment of sick and wounded in Switzerland. Britain and Germany finally agreed to their first prisoner exchange in 1917 and to a second one in 1918. In 1917, Germany exchanged sick and wounded prisoners with Japan through Holland and the United States. In that year the Russians exchanged all their German civilian internees for 4,000 Russian officers. An American exchange agreement began with the Germans in September 1918 and was signed on November 11, 1918. Although German sick and wounded were repatriated in April 1919, the general armistice superseded exchange agreements, and German prisoners in Allied hands waited until January 1920 for repatriation.[30]

For some POWs the release was simple. According to Mike Shallin, "Around the first part of November the rumors started to fly about an armistice. When it did come, the Germans actually celebrated. I don't think they gave a damn who won; it was over—that's all they cared about. Hell, you'd think we'd been allies. They'd come into the camp crowing, 'Comrade, Comrade.' A short while later, Red Cross trains started coming in from Switzerland to take us out. We were on our way home."[31] For others, release was complex—full of celebrations fused with lament, as Norman Archibald recalls:

We are leaving for Switzerland! The barracks hum; the hour has come. My right boot will not go on my left foot; it is three o'clock in the morning; where is my bread? We scurry around and chattering like magpies tie up our scanty possessions including cans of Red Cross food. Each man is aware that a longed-for hour of life is here. Each man talks, rushes, buttons his coat and arranges his little bundle. . . .

A whistle blows! blows! blows! The shrill sound, as it screeches in warning for a clear track, pierces our very souls. A clear track! A clear track . . . from Bondage to Emancipation. . . . At a glance we see Germany, Austria and Switzerland. Germany is back of us . . . BACK of us! Germany, the Germans, the prisons and hell are behind and back of us for ever. The international boundary line and, ahead, the other half of Switzerland. The impulse to run!—to dash across!

Oh Lord! I give Thee thanks. Hear me, dear Lord, and look into my grateful heart for I am thankful. Our Father in heaven, listen to my plea. Make me to remember! Make me to forget!

Oh God, I pray Thee help me to walk in peace. . . .

France! We are going to France!

We sit, mute as stone, and watch the gliding landscape. Faster now, faster . . . faster . . . and the trees are whirling past. A lone Swiss soldier, young and handsome, smiles at us. He is our friend.

The boundary line!

We cross the line and a rare emotion surges through me. Hot and cold . . . bitter and sweet . . . blind and hitherto unfelt . . . I swim in shell-pink waters but cannot see.

We are free! A solid mass of joy-crazed humanity; a passionate world let loose; a human pandemonium of cheering, yelling, screaming people stretches from the platform into a vast half-circle beyond. Thousands upon thousands of human beings crushed together in an uncontrollable tempest of savage happiness. . . .

Cheers! Cheers! Cheers! They shout, shout, shout and pictures of President Wilson are everywhere. American Flags! They wave from every conceivable spot and the Stars and Stripes—our Stars and Stripes—rise and fall, curl in and out and despite a gentle rain unfurl their welcome. . . . The train stops on the side of a steep incline, and cradled just below, in a golden mountain crevice, is the little town of Bellegarde. We get off, stretch ourselves and dig our boots into the soil of France! On the track ahead a Red Cross train waits to take us to a hospital and beneath is a bridge which spans a roaring river between us and the town. . . . The warm wave of weariness; the kind of tired that lulls one to rest without a single thought. Clean pajamas, clean bodies and I rub the whitest sheets that ever were against my face. Sheets!—imagine! The comfort and the tender care! France! France! France! Here we are, like babes.[32]

Ralph E. Ellinwood found himself free and happily on the way home. "On the morning of December 29th, at ten o'clock, a section of American ambulances rolled down the Kaiserstrauss [Kaiserstrasse] and drew up before the hotel. A loud ringing cheer greeted them as we caught the first glimpse of the small American flags mounted on the bodies of the cars. In a moment we were on our way, leaving a crowd of curious Germans gaping on the sidewalk. The last lap of our journey had begun. . . . On New Year's Day, 1919, after having been a prisoner for seven months, I set foot once more in France."[33] Clifford M. Markle observes that "no pen can fittingly describe the feelings of emotion which surged in our breasts as we pictured in our minds the repatriation. . . . That night we had some good old army chow, and all of us slept in feather beds, not awakening until noon of the following day, which was the 17th of November, 1918. On December 1st we rejoined our regiment and sailed for America four months later with a song of prayerful thanksgiving in our hearts that we had been permitted to pass through our experiences and return to our homes and families."[34]

In 1939 at the outbreak of European hostilities, the International Red Cross called on each belligerent nation to form a model draft agreement to govern the exchange of sick and wounded prisoners. Simultaneously, the IRC stated that certain protecting powers had already taken steps toward implementation. Germany, France, and Britain had agreed that repatriated sick and wounded prisoners would be transported home through the protecting power, Switzerland, but disagreed on the mode of transportation. Nothing happened until the British and Italian governments developed an exchange agreement that led to the first formal prisoner exchange in April 1942. When the United States entered World War II, the State Department informed the IRC that it would comply with all provisions of the 1929 Geneva Convention and the model agreement as well. The Germans, Italians, and Japanese responded in kind. In October 1943, the belligerents reached an agreement concerning "protected personnel," consisting of religious, sanitary, and medical people, civilian internees, and merchant seamen. Between October 1943 and January 1945, 21,000 Germans and Italians were exchanged for 13,500 Allied personnel, including 1,200 Americans. Toward the end of 1944, there were more sporadic kinds of head-for-head exchanges of seriously sick and wounded, and in May 1945, the United States repatriated 50,000 Germans it considered to be "of no use," either hard-resisting Nazis, the insane, or those whose status was such that they could not be forced to work. During the entire war, there were no prisoner exchanges between Germany and the Soviet Union.[35]

Toward the end of World War II, liberation brought the war to the Kriegies' doorsteps. Liberating Stalag VII A at Moosberg on April 28, 1945, General George S. Patton led a charge of tanks that broke through the barbed wire and barriers surrounding the camp. For the Kriegies inside, all hell broke loose when the American tanks ripped through the German defenses. At first, the Germans put up some armed resistance, but it was a weak effort. Kenneth Simmons describes the scene: "German guards were screaming, bullets were flying, tanks were shaking the ground like an earthquake, and diving planes were spitting fire."[36] The battle raged for twenty minutes. After the fighting ceased and quiet prevailed, the Kriegies came out from their hiding places and discovered that their war was finally over. The guards surrendered to the American tankers. Then they all caught a glimpse of a rather large, broad-shouldered officer lifting himself out of a tank, George S. Patton, commanding general of the Third Army. They knew it was Patton because his pearl-handled pistols were in full view. After the shock, the liberated Kriegies rushed toward General Patton, who, standing erect, looked down from the tank and said, "The war is over for you boys. You are sure going to eat tonight. I damn sure guarantee you that."[37] Patton asked how many sick men there were. "About four thousand," he was told. Angered, General Patton declared, in his gruff manner, "These German bastards are going to pay for this. The sons-of-bitches will suffer, and don't you ever forget it."[38] Then the moment arrived for Moosberg officially to change hands. General Patton ordered the German flag lowered. The camp was completely frozen as the American flag was unfurled and ascended up the pole. Time stood still. According to Kenneth Simmons,

> Tears from my eyes blurred the picture. The Stars and Stripes waved and rippled as they moved slowly toward heaven. Soldiers from General Patton's Army snapped to attention and saluted. Those of us who were able joined in with them.
>
> When the flag climbed to its full height, salutes were conducted, but eyes remained on the Stars and Stripes. Men about me were kneeling. I knelt too. While kneeling, I prayed and thanked God. I wiped my eyes, but the tears would not stop. Gene Coletti knelt beside other happy men and wept bitterly. Pirtle covered his face again. Clark stared in disbelief, Swanson blew his nose, Rinehart rubbed his eyes and coughed. Mott held his head high. His eyes were filled with tears, but he smiled.[39]

For Simmons and the other prisoners in Moosberg, the day ended finally when canteen trucks pulled up to the camp, complete with American nurses and Red Cross workers. Women! Moments later a sound truck with a loudspeaker pulled into the camp and started playing "Don't Fence Me In." After supper, the men gathered around General Patton for a short farewell. "These bastards started this war, and we finished it. It will be over in a few days, and you will be going home. You men have displayed real bravery and courage. You have survived a great ordeal. . . . I am proud that I had a part in winning this war, but most of all I am proud of liberating you men. Goodbye, and God bless you."[40]

Many American Kriegies were liberated by the Russians. Charles Miller recalls his liberation when the Red Army came to the camp. "I believe it was May 5th [1945]. . . . Eventually, the Russians came—a mob of them with women and everything—right with the Russian Army. One of the first things they did was turn the side of a truck into a stage and have a floor show! Like what the hell, it's fun time. Meanwhile, their troops were still fighting a little further east, and here we were having a floor show."[41] The Russians liberated another Kriegie, Al Johnson of Philadelphia, imprisoned in Stalag Luft 1 at Barth along the North German Baltic coast. Rather than roll into the camp in armored vehicles, the Russians stormed the camp and the nearby town on horseback. As Johnson tells it:

All of a sudden one day in comes a column of Russians! They're on horseback! They would gallop down the cobblestone streets. When they wanted to stop, they hauled the horse back on his haunches, skid and strike sparks on these cobblestones. They would slide to a halt and jump off while the horse was still sliding. . . . [When the Russians] liberated our camp, they were friendly. They asked through interpreters, "What do you guys want?" We said, "How about some fresh meat?" "Ah, good." they said and started rounding up cattle for twenty miles around. By night we had cows in our compound, buttock to buttock. You couldn't even open the barracks door without hitting a cow in the rear end. Boy, did we eat fresh meat![42]

Miller, along with thousands of other liberated Kriegies in Germany, was then taken to Camp Lucky Strike near Le Havre, France, as part of the American Recovered Allied Military Personnel Camp Program (RAMP). There they took their first hot showers, the first in years for some, and began to eat three meals a day in preparation for the return voyage to the United States. A few POWs actually hitchhiked to Paris for a few nights on the town.

Though a signatory in Geneva, Japan was not a party to the 1929 Geneva Convention because Japanese military politics prevented ratification at home. In 1942, the United States and Japan concluded a pact concerning the status of civilian internees, and several thousand civilians were exchanged for about an equal number of Japanese civilians held in the United States.[43] The IRC contacted Japan in 1944 with a reciprocal offer for the repatriation of sick and wounded prisoners. Nothing came of the proposal, probably because of the negative feelings concerning prisoners in general.

In late 1942, Camp O'Donnell on the Philippine Island of Luzon—the end point of the Bataan Death March—was evacuated, and prior to removal to prison and work camps in Japan, Formosa, Thailand, and Korea, the Japanese army sent 6,000 American POWs to Cabanatuan. By 1945, Cabanatuan contained only some civilian internees and a relatively small contingent of military POWs. The camp was not large by European standards, but was surrounded by three rows of barbed wire fence, eight feet high, four feet wide, with three guard towers twenty feet high, and machine gun pits. All the buildings in camp were constructed of wood, bamboo, and nipa palm; outside the wire, the Japanese constructed several metal sheds for a motor pool.[44] In March 1945, the camp housed American, British, and Dutch prisoners who sensed they were being mustered for the last time before their guards massacred them. On the night of January 30, 1945, the American 6th Ranger Battalion, led by Lieutenant Colonel Henry Mucci, with the help of Filipino guerrillas and Alamo Scouts, made a deep penetration behind enemy lines into the Cabanatuan prison camp. A dawn reveille formation was interrupted by the Rangers, who shot as they charged, wiping out the Japanese guards before they could kill the prisoners.[45] The results of the raid were encouraging: the American 6th Ranger Battalion inflicted considerable losses on the Japanese and liberated 516 prisoners. Casualties included one American civilian prisoner who suffered a heart attack at the prison gate during the raid; another who was left behind by accident, and two soldiers killed in action in the raid. The Cabanatuan raid was perhaps the most spectacular and successful prisoner recovery operation in American military history. General MacArthur said of it, "No other incident of the campaign has given such personal satisfaction."[46] Other Japanese POW and internment camps were liberated by invading armies, much as German camps were in Europe, overwhelmed by advancing Allied ground forces. There were no exchanges of prisoners until the war ended in August 1945, when 14,950 American prisoners were liberated.[47] The largest number, 11,400, was freed in Japan; 1,500 were liberated in the Philippines, 1,200 by the Russian army in Manchuria, 480 in Burma and Thailand, 200 in the Celebes, 150 in Korea, and only 20 in China.[48]

Laurens Van der Post, a Commonwealth POW, lamented that his prison walls served two purposes: "It was almost as if walls had come to mean not just instruments of confinement but a physical support against the vast, free, comparatively empty and unconstrained world outside."[49] His lament was easily shared by the Americans as well. At Shirakawa, Formosa, (Taiwan) in Prison Camp Number 4 late in 1944, General C. Gordon Sage of the New Mexico National Guard wrote about the hopes and fantasies of the prisoner—food, clothing, family, and vengeance—in his verse, "I Want to Go Home," a POW adaptation of "The Night Before Christmas."

> I want to go home to a place where we eat
> Oranges, grapefruit, and oat meal and wheat,
> Roast beef and baked spuds and sausages and ham,
> Turkey and chicken and hot cakes and jam;
> Pickles and sauces and onions with steak,

Biscuits and jelly and sundaes and cake,
Melons and cookies and honey on comb,
Someone come get me—I WANT TO GO HOME!

Concerning clothing and family:

I want some clothes that are decent to wear;
Something to cover the places now bare;
Give me some underwear, socks and some shoes;
Bring me a suit to replace "ersatz" blues;
Let me have matches, a hankie, a knife—
Also I'm longing for daughters and wife;
Show me arroyos, and red sandy loam;
Come get me quickly—I WANT TO GO HOME!

Concerning his vision of the justice of final victory in the war:

Bring in some planes with a star on their wings;
Bombers and fighters, attack ships and things;
Parachute soldiers and air infantry—
Landing boats, barges and tanks from the sea.
Let me be thrilled by vict'ry that flies
Dashing and diving through tropical skies;
Then take me up—and no more let me roam;
Rescue me now boys—I WANT TO GO HOME![50]

In a parody folk song, "I'm a Hungry Man from Old Bataan," an anonymous composer used the tune to "Ramblin' Wreck" to coin his political lament as a cynical jest. This song was well known in the prison camps in the Philippines and Japan.

I'm a hungry man from old Bataan,
And there's nothing in the pot,
I guess that I'm the buckeroo
The nation has forgot.

Now Franklin [Roosevelt] says, "I love you,
Now boys, you know I do—
I'll have to risk the Navy's neck,
There's nothing I can do.[51]

Sergeant Carl Nash was captured in the Philippines in 1942 and survived the Bataan Death March. In captivity, he worked in a Japanese factory

in Nagoya, Japan. His captivity ended when the Swiss arrived and told
him that the war was over.

> A Swiss legation came in about the 13th or 14th [of August] and told
> us that the war was over. When the Japanese found that out they
> all took off. All the guards were gone, and we never did see them
> anymore. Some civilians brought in a pig and some extra rice. We
> just had a ball after that for a couple of days. A couple of B-29s came
> over and dropped food on us, and we were still there for two or
> three more days before we got out. We boarded this train across the
> bay there and rode to the coast line landing of some navy personnel,
> and [there was] a big hospital ship sitting out in the bay which we
> knew we were going to get on. But in the meantime we had loaded
> up all that chow that the B-29s had dropped on our camp. We wasted
> nothing. We had corned beef, canned butter, powdered milk, beans,
> all kinds of things. We loaded it in a little bag we had called a mussette
> bag. We put it in it and lugged it to this depot, all the way to where
> the navy had landed. They put us aboard a landing craft and took
> us out to the hospital ship. As we got on the ship the corpsmen
> stripped us all off and sprayed us with DDT. We put a towel over
> our eyes. It killed the lice. In the meantime, some personnel were
> dumping all this food over the side into the bay. But I didn't care.

His lament is simple. "Getting liberated back into this country was like
being born again. I think guys like us, and some more that were in the
same situation in other wars, don't know what freedom really means until
they have lost it. Once you've lost it you might as well go on and get
yourself buried!"[52]

Carl Nash was among the fortunate American POWs released in August
1945. According to Edward Russell's *The Knights of Bushido* (1958), the
Japanese war ministry issued clear orders to prevent prisoners from falling
into Allied hands. Many American and Allied prisoners, especially pilots
and submariners, were treated as war criminals by the Japanese and suffered last-minute reprisals and executions.

In 1949, one year before the Korean War broke out, the 1929 version of
the Geneva Convention was revised in an attempt to address and correct
some of the problems experienced by soldiers in captivity during World
War II. In June 1950, both warring sides in Korea declared that they would
abide by the new provisions. Negotiations began as early as 1951 at Panmunjom and later at Kaesong. In late 1952, the executive committee of the
League of Red Cross Societies asked each belligerent to repatriate sick
and wounded. The United Nations affirmed the request; the North
Koreans ignored it. In February 1953, General Mark Clark contacted North

Korean and Chinese commanders and urged them to consider the league's request. On March 28, 1953, the communist commanders agreed to an exchange and suggested that this might be a wider window of opportunity for a general armistice.

On April 11, 1953, representatives from both sides signed an initial agreement establishing "Operation Little Switch," which began on April 20 and lasted until May 3, 1953. It exchanged 6,670 North Koreans and Chinese communists for 684 United Nations prisoners including 149 Americans. Private Carl W. Kirchenhausen of New York was the first American released. Tight faced and hobbling on frostbitten feet, he sighed, "I'm glad it came true."[53] Captain John W. Thornton, USN, in *Believed To Be Alive* (1981), recalls bitterly that the communists intentionally held some legitimately sick or wounded prisoners back during "Little Switch" because they were uncooperative, resisting "reactionaries." "As galling as this was to the rest of us, what really made us choke was the inclusion of the healthy "progressive" POWs in Operation Little Switch. There were the prisoners who had sold out long ago to our enemy and subsequently enjoyed a captivity of relative ease, comfort and good health. Their early release was in further payment of services rendered during their imprisonment—services that were at the expense of their country and their fellow POWs who resisted. We vowed, should we be lucky enough to get out, to have our day in court with these traitors."[54] As unhappy with "Little Switch" as Thornton and many other POWs were, for United Nations forces, recovery was more important than the POWs' internal camp politics. Admiral John C. Daniel, USN, one of the senior military American negotiators in Panmunjom, told *Newsweek* that "I'm not giving up hope. I am still trying to get back more."[55] After the general armistice signed on July 27, 1953, both sides established "Operation Big Switch" and exchanged a total of 88,596 prisoners.[56] In a cumbersome operation, United Nations POWs were put into cattle cars without any food for a train ride from their camps in North Korea to Keasong where they sat for days waiting for the last step of the journey, a truck ride to "Freedom Village." Under the terms of the agreement, POWs who refused repatriation were put into the custody of a Neutral National Repatriation Commission that agreed to furnish guards. After the commission took custody, the names of twenty-three United Nations' POWs were announced; in addition, 325 South Koreans had cast their lot with the communists.[57]

Many prisoners recall that they rode with their Chinese interrogators on the way to the repatriation site and relished the chance to assault them just to get even. The American military police anticipated such feelings and prevented the Chinese guards from remaining with their former charges even for a short moment. In the village John Thornton was furious as he watched healthy North Korean and Chinese prisoners heading the other way. "I fumed as I watched them and wished I could run over to plant the toe of my boot up their asses to help them move north a little quicker. But I relented and decided I had more important things to think about now."[58] After putting his deep-seated angry feelings aside in Freedom Village, Thornton and the other repatriated POWs saw the United Nations flag flying overhead. Embraces, cheering, applause, tears, food, medical attention, and friendship abounded. But for some, liberation was clothed in tragedy. Sergeant Ralph D. Moyer lamented one of the saddest moments he experienced during "Operation Big Switch."

A sergeant from Pennsylvania left his wife in a family way and headed for Korea. He spent thirty-three months as a prisoner of war. Most of us after one year's captivity did receive some mail, but he never heard from his wife. He did, however, receive two or three letters from his mother, but nothing was said in the letters about his wife and child. A few hours passed after our release, and I saw him sitting on a hospital cot with his head in his hands. He told me that he was afraid to ask for someone to send a message for fear of bad news. I took him to the chaplain's office who sent a message by short wave radio to his home town. The message came back: "Wife and child passed away at childbirth."[59]

In 1968, another prisoner release would take place on the "Bridge of No Return" at Panmunjom, Korea. After a year of negotiation and a formal apology from the United States to North Korea, the officers and crew, eighty-two men of the USS *Pueblo* were released on December 23, 1968. Present at the release was Sergeant Stan Aungst, a communications specialist, who was aghast but not surprised at what he saw.

I would say about 12:00 o'clock noon I helped bring some of the people over. . . . These people were in bad shape; I think they lost thirty to forty pounds. The Red Cross was there, basically to put them into the ambulances. One of the guys—he was thin, about six foot—said he was the Signal [Communications/Intelligence] Officer. I can see his face, but don't remember his name [Lt. Stephen Harris]. . . . I asked him how the treatment was. He said he was beaten daily. . . . I asked him if they signed. He knew what I was talking about. They wanted them to sign documents [stating] that they were spies. He said that they did, including [Commander Lloyd] Bucher. I asked him, why, what happened? Everybody has a breaking point. They took this South Korean's shirt off, got the knives out and started cutting the skin off. He told me they plucked his eye out. He said he thought the Korean had bitten his tongue off, bit clear through his tongue and never yelled, and died there on the pole. They [the *Pueblo*'s officers] were forced to watch this. He told me that the North Korean commander told Bucher if they did not sign that they were going to do that to everyone of the men, and Bucher would have to watch. . . . That's why they signed. . . . It made me more convinced that I'm not going to be a goddamn prisoner.[60]

The condition of the returning *Pueblo* prisoners foreshadowed the condition of Americans repatriated from captivity in the Vietnam War. However, the Americans were not the first to suffer an extended punitive captivity in Indochina. The French Indochina War ended officially on July 21, 1954, after more than eight years of hostilities. Upon capture, POWs handed over their clothes, shoes, and all personal possessions including their watches, jewelry, and photos. They received one pair of prison pants and a shirt and made their own sandals. In captivity, the Viet Minh forced prisoners to build their own camps. No fences held the French because escape was virtually impossible. Those who tried to escape were mostly officers, because French military regulations stipulated that it is the duty of every officer to escape. The natives received cash payments for recapturing fugitive escaped prisoners. When recaptured, prisoners were either shot or put into "reeducation" camps. Under the terms of an agreement signed by the French and the Viet Minh at Geneva, the French high command presented a list of 40,172 MIAs to the Viet Minh, but the Viet Minh announced the release of only 9,138. By August 25, 1954, one month later, the French released 20,616 Viet Minh prisoners; the Viet Minh returned only 2,714 to the French.

In the Vietnam War there were only 766 known American POWs, 629 of whom survived and returned to American control.[61] Special Forces Sergeant George Smith was captured in November 1963. After being held for two years, he was released by the Vietcong in November 1965. According to Smith, the Vietcong released him in direct response to antiwar activities in the United States.

They [the Vietcong] stated that they realized that the American people were basically peace-loving people and did not condone the actions that the United States Government was taking in South Vietnam, so they were returning two of their sons to them. . . . At Phnom Penh . . . they set up a press conference for us. International reporters were there. And someone asked a question of what I intended to do when I got back to the United States. I told him that I was going to tell the true story of Vietnam as I could see it, from my experiences. That the United States had no business in Vietnam, that it wasn't in the best interest of the American people, and that therefore we should all get out immediately.[62]

After Sergeant Smith, the Vietcong released more prisoners for purposes of political propaganda. Early in November 1967, a broadcast by the North Vietnamese government in Hanoi announced that three captured American army sergeants were being released after showing "sincere repentance over the crimes they had committed against the Vietnamese people" and "in response to the American Negro's struggle for peace in the United States." News of the pending release of the three GIs—Sergeants James E. Jackson, Jr., and Edward Johnson (both African-Americans) and Daniel Lee Pitzer—set off immediate speculation by government officials about possible or probable POW cooperation and collaboration. To forestall the effect of any antiwar statements by the released men, an eager American official in Saigon spread the word that the prisoners had been "brainwashed." He made the charge before he or any other American official had had any contact with the freed POWs to hear their side of the story or to ascertain their mental condition. Following contact, Robert J. McCloskey, the State Department's press officer, hastened to acquit the sergeants of the brainwashing stigma. "On the basis of our talks with these men, it seems clear . . . that the men withstood their long ordeal with great courage and intelligence." Meanwhile they returned to light duty at Fort Bragg, North Carolina. After a period of convalescence, one member of the trio, Sergeant James E. Jackson, narrated his eighteen-month ordeal to *Ebony* managing editor Hans J. Massaquoi:

> One thing that was constantly slapped in my face was the race situation in the United States. It was initially used to win me over without applying any of the other more drastic methods they had. They tried the nice way first. They definitely tried to make me feel that my race would put me in line for special privileges; but I could readily see that they were only making promises. All I had to do was look around me and see in what miserable shape the other Negro prisoners were in. First of all, they wanted to know why the American Negro wanted to come to Vietnam; why did he allow himself to be sent to Vietnam? They would ask me whether it is true that Negroes in America don't go to school, whether all Negroes are poor. Some wanted to know whether there were any Negro officers in the United States Army. You'd be surprised at how many people I ran into over there who told me that there were no Negro officers in the U.S. Army. These were people who were supposed to be well-informed.
>
> They even went so far as to remind me that black leaders—like Malcolm X—were being assassinated back home. They told me that Negroes were getting machine-gunned in the streets of America and that Newark and all those places had blown up. In addition to all this, they had me listen to Radio Hanoi and another clandestine

guerrilla radio station in the south. So I heard constant news about all the "black revolutions" happening in the United States. I knew that there was unrest and I knew that there was trouble, but as far as Negroes being machine-gunned in the streets and my family being in terrible trouble back home was concerned, all this I knew wasn't true. The whole thing was blown so far out of proportion as it was presented to me, I just had to write it off as being untrue.[63]

Sergeant Jackson explained his response to the release:

It was a bigger surprise to me than anybody else, I think. At first I didn't believe it. I got the first word that I would be one of three prisoners to be released from a representative of the National Liberation Front. He mentioned to me that this American peace committee had been instrumental in our release. Some of the more prominent members of that committee were Dr. Martin Luther King Jr., Dr. Spock, Floyd McKissick, Joan Baez, and Tom Hayden. Why I was chosen instead of some other prisoner, I still don't know.[64]

Seaman Douglas Hegdahl was one of the few navy enlisted men in captivity in Hanoi. He was offered early release in 1969 but refused it in accordance with the provision of the Code of Conduct and the directives against early release issued by James B. Stockdale, the senior ranking officer in the "Hilton." Hegdahl's cellmate, Commander Richard Stratton, USN, ordered him to accept the early release for one specific reason. The American government and families of the missing needed positive and irrefutable POW identification. Because the North Vietnamese refused to reveal any information to the Red Cross or anyone else, Hegdahl's information answered questions that loomed heavy in Washington concerning who was and who was not in confinement, not only in Hanoi but throughout the North Vietnamese prison system. In captivity, Hegdahl received orders to memorize the names of all the known American prisoners in Hanoi by rhyming their names to "Old MacDonald Had a Farm." When he returned home, he brought the list with him, the first documented evidence of live Americans initially believed to be missing or killed in action.

Hegdahl's startling report confirmed fears that all was not well in Hanoi. John Chafee, then secretary of the navy, discovered that American prisoners in Hanoi were systematically beaten and that their wounds were left untreated. He learned that they suffered extended periods of solitary confinement and days of sitting on a stool until unconsciousness overtook them, that the Americans subsisted on pumpkin soup, pig fat, bread, and water once a day, and that they were hanged from the ceilings in their cells (strappado) and dragged along the ground with broken legs.

Chafee concluded that despite their signatory status, the North Vietnamese intentionally ignored the provisions of the Geneva Convention relative to the treatment of POWs.[65]

In 1966 and 1967, when Colonel Francis Kelly commanded the Army 5th Special Forces Group, the rescue of prisoners became a major objective. Under the aegis of Military Assistance Command Vietnam (MACV), the Joint Prisoner Recovery Center in Saigon repeatedly attempted to recover American and allied prisoners in enemy hands. Several enemy prison camps were overrun, but the Vietcong followed a policy of moving their prisoners frequently and had standing orders to kill their prisoners if any chance existed at all for raiders to free them.[66] David Beville, a member of the Marine Force Reconnaissance Team in 1967–1968, described his experiences raiding POW camps. Preparing for the raid, the marines dropped the team a day's march from the suspected prison camp site in Laos. The tactic called for two raiding teams: one would reconnoiter the camp and if American prisoners were sighted alive, the assault group would attack. "I was weapons and demolition," writes Beville. "That time we hit the camp, we knew they were supposed to be there. Our job was supposed to be looking at it to see how many we could see, and then they were going to bring in other teams . . . SEALs and other people . . . everybody was on standby."

The marine raiders would be shocked at what they discovered.

We were about twenty miles into Laos when we hit that camp, [and] I still think they knew we were coming. They [guards and live prisoners] were gone, maybe two or three days. No fires. . . . They had been gone maybe three days. [When] we went in, there was nobody there. [except] some dead Americans they had tortured. One [American] really sticks in my mind, the black guy, [the Vietcong] castrated him. . . . We saw a guy hanged upside down, dead, by his ankles. He was nude . . . [with] blood running out of his nose, stiff for a long time. We had figured that's when they had left the camp. Evidently he was wounded and must have been shot. . . . They had taken knives [to] the black guy [before] he was shot. He had a stomach wound but wasn't dead all the way, and they just start cutting, making deep cuts on him. Long cuts on his face, all over him. Yeah, live persons when they get deep cuts turn white. He evidently was alive. I remember the lieutenant was really pissed about the guy hanging upside down, because you know the blood rushes to your head, and it just swelled the guy's head up.

Beville wanted to cut the man down, but his fellow raider yelled, "No, don't touch him." Experienced raiders knew that the Vietcong booby-trapped bodies from time to time. Beville recalls that in addition to the prisoner hanging by his feet, there were two other dead American prisoners in the camp. Each prisoner had wounds, most probably received from combat before capture. Beville concludes that they were incapacitated from the wounds and killed because their captors could not move them to another camp quickly without help. After searching the camp and carefully watching for booby traps, the marine raiders photographed the camp and the murdered American and Vietnamese prisoners without touching them. Beville's memories of the dead South Vietnamese prisoners are particularly ghastly. "There were [South] Vietnamese [POWs] there too. Evidently, the Americans and Vietnamese were kept away from one another. You could see that some of them were shot in the head; some [Vietnamese soldiers'] faces were blown off, some [shot in] the back of their heads, some [through the] side. I'd say maybe four or five [bodies]. One [South Vietnamese POW lay] without his head; the rest were all shot."[67] Finding the aftermath of murders in Vietcong prison camps was common if the raiders arrived before the evidence could be hidden. Some raids, like Beville's, went into Laos, off limits to regular combat forces and forever bound to secrecy. However, raiding and rescue missions like Beville's were commonplace in South Vietnam during the war.

When the final truce was signed in Paris in 1973, Chapter 3, Article 8, stated, "The return of captured military personnel and foreign civilians . . . shall be carried out simultaneously with and completed not later than the same day as the troop withdrawal mentioned in Article 5." However, on several occasions, the North Vietnamese sought to hold up the prisoner releases in return for action on other unrelated clauses of the agreement. In late March, during the final phase, there was a tense ten-day confrontation over the status of ten prisoners: seven American airmen, two American civilians, and a Canadian missionary who had been captured in Laos. In the end, the communists lived up to their agreement that the release of the American prisoners would be linked to troop withdrawal.[68] Finalizing the agreement, a three-day airlift removed the last American troops from South Vietnam, carefully calibrated to coincide with the release of the last group of prisoners.[69] The only uniformed Americans remaining in Vietnam after the prisoner exchange were 159 marine guards and fifty members of the Defense Attaché.

"Operation Homecoming" in 1973 gave the United States an opportunity to see and hear prisoners who returned home after one of the longest captivity experiences in American military history. In a 1989 public address, Colonel Norman A. McDaniel, USAF (Retired), remembered his release and repatriation:

On February 12, 1973 we were released. The prisoners were released in groups of about 25 over a period of three or four releases. And it was really like resurrection coming back to this great country. I had been out of it for seven years. If you will just think: if you were to close your eyes, and think back seven years and think of all the things that have gone on within that seven year period of time, you can realize what we had missed, what I had missed. Or, if you close your eyes and think ahead seven years 1996, just imagine all the things that are going to transpire between now and then. And so for me, coming back to freedom, to life so to speak, was a real challenge.[70]

Captain Giles R. Norrington, USN (Retired), also recalled his homecoming: "After 1,775 days of captivity, on the 14 day of March, 1973, I returned to . . . the United States of America. Then the fun really began. I saw it all with renewed eyes and improved vision."[71] In *Beyond Survival* (1990) Gerald Coffee laments his seven years in captivity in Hanoi. "In the first seven years of my career I had married, gone through . . . flight training . . . fathered four children . . . and trained dozens of pilots in the Vigilante. What the hell had I done in the last seven? During the prime of my life, I'd sat on my ass in some medieval dungeons, broken my teeth, screwed up my arm, contracted worms and God knows what else, and had gotten *old*. Well, I was almost thirty-nine. We sure as hell better have something to show for it."[72] Coffee then considers his relationship with his wife. "Would I be okay for her? Did she still love me? Would we make love? Did she know how much she meant to me all these years?"[73]

If there was a point-counterpoint series of statements concerning the nation's feelings about Operation Homecoming after the Vietnam War, two positions seem to stand out. Typical of the divisiveness of the Vietnam War inside the country, while America welcomed the American POWs home, celebrities of the antiwar movement damned them as war criminals. Philip Berrigan commented on February 17, 1973, that "We are over-publicizing the war-criminals that are coming home. But what else could we expect from the government but to distort the true nature of the men? The returning prisoners are just what [President] Nixon would want them to be, but they're going to have to come to terms with themselves. . . . It's not that I am against them coming home, because these men have suffered grievously over the years for their actions in this war. However, they are just what the President wants them to be, and nothing could be more demeaning."[75] Neither Norman McDaniel, Giles Norrington, nor the vast majority of the American POWs returning from Vietnam in 1973 accepted Berrigan's evaluation as anything more than a dying rhetorical gasp from the fading antiwar movement. American national television turned its attention to a small podium when Jeremiah Denton, the senior returning officer on his aircraft, walked to the waiting microphone and said: "We are honored to have had the opportunity to serve our country

. . . under difficult circumstances. We are profoundly grateful to our commander in chief and to our nation for this day. God bless America!'"[74] Unwittingly, Berrigan and Denton actually affirm one thing: Americans could excpect no less of its soldiers. Millions of people witnessed Denton and the other POWs file from the airplane on television and saw the moment captured later in magazines, news reports, and newspapers. The effect was nothing short of electric. Americans began to put away their differences over the war's controversial issues and made their first solidly positive gesture toward their returning soldiers. For the first time in American military history, POWs returned to America as heroes. The Vietnam War was over; the POWs had succeeded in becoming symbols of resistance to adversity; the country was finally proud of something and someone again.

One wonders why captivity narratives still appear regularly in the press. Terrence Des Pres observes that survivors feel obligated to the living and dead members of the prison community to tell the story. After a considerable length of time away from captivity, some prisoners lament the experience to such a degree that they come to negative conclusions and write apologies to support those conclusions. After liberation and repatriation, some former prisoners clothe themselves in years of silence. Others keep POW communities relatively intact by forming relatively exclusive organizations that provide political, medical, and psychological support for former captives. Others avoid their former comrades and simply smoulder inside until some event in life after captivity reminds them of life in the prison camp. Accepting the losses imposed by captivity and confessing to what the culture perceived as a failure has never been easy.

By writing about the experiences of captivity, former prisoners find a catharsis for personal feelings and a forum to tell the world what happened to them. Virtually every narrative of captivity from the forest wars to Vietnam contains descriptions and reflections of release, exchange, liberation, repatriation, and lament. Regardless of the individual's pathway to freedom, bringing the unnatural life behind the wire to closure is a necessity. Joe Boyle's Kriegie verse looks to the future and recounts his captivity as a mere historical interlude:

> So here's to happy days ahead
> When you and I are free,
> To look back on this interlude
> And call it history.[76]

Closure offers POWs a final opportunity to denounce a captor's excess and to damn the captors and the experience categorically and completely; in some cases, to render thanks for kindnesses; and most important, to forgive the captors, and, if possible, themselves. As POW narrators have shown, the three concluding event-scenarios—release, repatriation, and the prisoner's lament— form a continuing contest of opposites: euphoric happiness against timeless grief, personal freedom against individual lowliness, the pursuit of life against the imminent threat of death, and the perception of success against the self-accusation of failure.

PART THREE

Legacies

CHAPTER TWELVE

Missing: Unknown Soldiers
and Unresolved Mysteries

Prisoners of war shall be released and repatriated without delay after the cessation of active hostilities.

Geneva Convention (1949)

Before hostilities in Europe ended on November 11, 1918, American public consciousness accepted that in war there would be slain soldiers—officially listed as "missing in action"—who would be "known only to God." After the great conflagrations in France during World War I, sometimes only parts of bodies survived the bombardments by large-caliber artillery or mortar attacks, sometimes nothing at all remained of slain soldiers. Similar obliteration took place in World War II, Korea, and Vietnam when one side would use large-caliber weapons, including mines, to atomize the other. Responding to the mortal fear of being an unknown soldier, common soldiers began to sew their names on their uniforms, hoping that if they were mutilated in death beyond physical recognition, their comrades would know who they were, and friends and families at home would eventually know their fate. In spite of name tags stitched on uniforms, or "dog tags," the ferocious nature of the modern battlefield may still obscure fallen soldiers' identities. As the technology of war became ever more sophisticated and the killing power of weapons increased dramatically, battlefields became mass killing fields, and the dead were left to be buried under thousands of markers saying "Unknown."

One result of the inability to identify the dead after battle has been the creation of the Tomb of the Unknown Soldier in Arlington National Cemetery. Protected by a twenty-four-hour ceremonial guard, and inscribed with the words, "Known only to God," the massive tomb houses the remains of four unidentified soldiers from each of America's wars of the twentieth century: World War I, World War II, Korea, and Vietnam. The Unknown Soldier has been awarded the Medal of Honor—the highest military honor America can bestow—posthumously for action "above and beyond the call of duty." The tomb serves not only as an icon of soldierly values and sacrifice but also as a symbol of political and public consciousness of an individual's sacrifice to country.

According to Charles Stenger, 92,753 American soldiers remain MIA in

263

America's twentieth-century wars (see Appendix 4A).[1] Concerning the MIAs in the twentieth century, something has lingered in private and public consciousness since 1918: some MIAs or POWs are known to have been alive in captivity, and the search for the truth of their fates continues. Honoring and posthumously decorating the unknown war dead is one thing; addressing the issue of what happened to those who were captured alive is another. When facts, like prisoners themselves, are missing, a powerful myth acts as a circumstantial basis for action. Thus arises the myth of the missing warrior: a fervent belief held by a relatively large constituency nationwide that many live American POWs were not repatriated after the end of hostilities, but that instead, long after the wars have stopped, these soldiers remain in captivity against their will.

A major subset among images of the vanished soldier, perpetual captivity has held mythic status since Americans first began writing about the captivity experience. Myths, according to film scholar John Hellmann, have two possible effects in a culture: they can elevate a people to new achievements, or they can compel a people to defy the facts, with the disastrous result that a nation veers from reality.[2] Whether this strong popular belief can be debunked as a falsification of reality or indeed reflects a fact that has been smothered in deceit, Americans have been so moved by it that by 1991 the matter reached the United States Senate for resolution. Are all missing soldiers dead? Could they all have disappeared on the battlefield or died in captivity without the knowledge of the captors? Did thousands of American captives decide to expatriate themselves and assimilate with their respective captors? Is it unreasonable to ask why a former prisoner or a prisoner's body has not been properly buried or returned home long after the war's end? Is it not the responsibility of the former captors under international law and the customs of war to return remains after the cessation of hostilities? Did the United States government do everything in its power to accomplish this task within the scope of present diplomatic realities? Can anything be done to facilitate or effect this process?

None of these questions can be answered by the silence of the Tomb of the Unknown Soldier. American advocacy groups have rejected the concept that a war ends simply because hostilities end. Although it may seem crass and unfeeling, after World War I, three thousand missing soldiers were not enough to worry about. They could have been lost at sea, or easily vaporized by artillery, a mine, or some other modern field weapon. A similar supposition could apply to MIAs from World War II. Additionally, the celebration of the conclusion of World War II stifled many concerns about POWs, especially about those soldiers who remained missing. Such were the fortunes of war! The unpopularity of the Korean War, the issue of brainwashing, and the worries about the twenty-one

Americans who remained with the captors after "Operation Big Switch" in 1953 inspired further silence about the missing. In view of the length of the Vietnam War and its intensity from 1966 through 1972, it is amazing that the captured and missing figures were so low. Nonetheless, until the conclusion of the Vietnam War, the trend in the twentieth century seems to have been one of diminishing concern for missing soldiers.

International agreements made in Geneva in 1929 and 1949 and the United Nation's Declaration of Human Rights prohibit torture and have attempted to ameliorate the physical damage a captor can inflict on a prisoner; however, the status of "missing" falls into a hazy area not clearly defined in law. Initial status classification rests on the decision of the field commander. For example, if a wingman sees a parachute open after a pilot bails out of his burning airplane, then a possibility exists that the pilot survived the shootdown. The reverse is likewise true. Ultimately, POW status can only be confirmed by the captor, who is required by the Geneva Convention to fill out a "capture card," which is in turn sent home through the International Red Cross, or, in some cases, through the protecting power. Missing means that a person lost in a combat zone may have been taken prisoner, or may have been killed in action. Consequently, without the benefit of any substantive proof to the contrary over a reasonable amount of time, a soldier classified as MIA may subsequently be presumed dead. The fate of these soldiers remains the issue that has haunted the American conscience after every war in the twentieth century, especially when thousands of real or imaginary "live sighting" reports reach the public. To accept these reports as true is to deny the presumption of death, or at least to question it.

Concerning the Vietnam War, several opposing positions exist: those of the government, the residual antiwar movement, and the POW/MIA activists, mostly family members. One missing American soldier remains classified as a POW in a symbolic gesture of the government's public commitment to resolving the fate of all the POW/MIAs. From 1975 to 1992 the American government shifted its stand. In 1975 to 1980, the Ford and Carter administrations and the Defense Intelligence Agency responsible for POW/MIA affairs held that the 2,273 men who failed to return were either dead or had decided to stay in Southeast Asia on their own volition (see Appendix 4B). Of that number, the military services listed 1,101 as killed in action, body not recovered, and 1,172 POW/MIA, of which 133 were "discrepancy cases," that is, they were identified as alive sometime in captivity. Further reducing that number, in a cover story, *Life* magazine reported in November 1987 that there were twenty-five compelling open cases that still defied resolution.[3] During this period, officially, the government more or less accepted the probability that most, if not all, the Americans counted as MIA were dead. The aging antiwar faction agreed.

In *M.I.A.: Mythmaking in America* (1992), H. Bruce Franklin, noted antiwar activist and professor of American Studies, presents three essential points: the Geneva Convention is a utopian document that does not hold the force of law anywhere; all the MIAs are dead; and the POW/MIA controversy became an issue in American culture through Richard Nixon's prowar propaganda machine. According to Franklin, the entire POW/MIA commotion was a myth-religion that perpetuated unreasonable, neofascist, and militaristic belligerency in post-Vietnam America. Writing from a distinctly Marxist point of view, Franklin describes the POW/MIA faith as much ado about nothing, an opiate to soothe a people who refused to accept the realities of North Vietnam's victory over America, the need for social justice at home, the cry for economic egalitarianism, and the influence of radical feminism. Franklin denounces the POW/MIA movement because it serves as a medium of false hope perpetrated by the newly emerging, if not ascending, evil radical right.[4] Opposed to Franklin stand several authors who maintain that the Socialist Republic of Vietnam deliberately withheld Americans from repatriation in 1975. Larry O'Daniel's *Missing in Action: Trail of Deceit* (1979) and Rod Colvin's *First Heroes* (1987) both attempt to prove that the government ignored, deceived, and deliberately covered up its dereliction of sworn duty to bring home its live POWs. Nigel Cawthorne, a British pulp journalist who managed to collect sanitized live-sighting reports when they were made available in the late 1970s, wrote in *The Bamboo Cage* (1991) that members of the United States intelligence community knew through electronic intercepts that live POWs existed in Southeast Asia. According to Cawthorne, some officers—those who were technically interesting to the Russians—were shipped to the Soviet Union during the war. Cawthorne suggests naively that if only the United States paid the Vietnamese the 3.5 billion dollars it owed, all would be well, and the Vietnamese would probably send the remaining live POW/MIAs home.

The most important journalistic work to tackle the credibility of the POW/MIA issue has been *Kiss the Boys Goodbye: How the United States Betrayed Its Own POWs in Vietnam* (1990). Monika Jensen-Stevenson started her work on the topic as the producer of "Dead or Alive" (1986) for the television show "60 Minutes." While she conducted research, she began to encounter the kinds of informational roadblocks experienced by POW/MIA families. According to Jensen-Stevenson, the roadblocks became so severe that she left "60 Minutes" in 1986 to further investigate the POW/MIA problem. In a speech before a convention of the Forget-Me-Not Association in 1989, she accused the government of the United States, especially those people assigned to address the POW/MIA issue, as usurpers of power, power-elitist bureaucrats more interested in preserving their personal domains than in serving the interests, let alone the will, of the people.[5]

During the war, feelings of helplessness, isolation, alienation, and frustration felt by the families of POW/MIAs had been addressed by the formation of the National League of Families in 1969. Institutionally, the League of Families is connected to the Defense Intelligence Agency (DIA), whose work is to collect, catalog, and classify all data received concerning American POW/MIAs. It claims to do its work methodically, cautiously, and persistently in spite of the pressures brought to bear by families, radical activists, and entrepreneurs who say they serve the cause. In support of the DIA's efforts, the National League of Families publishes a newsletter that tells a wide readership what is going on at official levels between the American and Indochinese governments. They also warn the readership about what they believe are bogus entrepreneurial or individual efforts to recover live prisoners and MIAs, efforts the league perceives as a threat to chances to close the book on Vietnam. The league's critics complain that its primary function has been to develop positions and apply grassroots pressure to effect only the return of the *remains* of deceased prisoners from Indochina. What about live ones? Either because of the league's activities or in spite of them, the remains of America's POW/MIAs are slowly being returned to waiting families in the United States. In August 1987, 230 sets of remains returned from Vietnam, but only eighty sets were positively identified at the Central Identification Laboratory in Hawaii or CII-HI, as those of Americans.[6] In April 1989, Vietnam returned twenty-one more sets of remains to American authorities in Thailand, and in June 1989, it returned twenty-eight more sets of remains. The political impact of these activities was as significant as it was emotional.

Opposed to the League of Families is the grassroots National Forget-Me-Not Association that consists of POW/MIA family members who maintain that they have received neither sufficient nor even reasonable answers from the league or the government. Members claim to have been given false or misleading information by the government, mostly from the Defense Intelligence Agency, and virtually nothing by the league. Individual family members have searched alone and have concluded that there have been major errors, if not a major conspiracy, at all levels of government since the armistice in 1973. As a group, the National Forget-Me-Not Association believes that in its haste to end the Vietnam War, the government saved only a small percentage of the men held by the Vietnamese and none held by the Pathet Lao (communist Laotians). Thus the Forget-Me-Nots conclude that there are Americans being held against their will not only in Southeast Asia but in Korea, and, possibly, in China and Russia as well. Furthermore, they believe that the vast intelligence community inside the American government erred in its belief that the Indochinese would give up its "pearls," that is, the prisoners it held as bargaining chips in the world of international diplomacy. The association observes that as policy, the American intelligence community refuses to admit that mistakes were ever made and thus holds back information to the families, changes reports, and refuses to act on the information it has—in effect, abusing power in the name of national security. As policy, the American government refuses to cooperate with families of the missing POWs and MIAs in their search for accurate data. It refuses to acknowledge the large number of covert operations and covert units that were committed to the Vietnam War before, during, and after hostilities were formally terminated. It attempts to discredit anyone not holding its views. These attempts at disinformation and discrediting range from former generals to former enlisted intelligence operatives and occur on an institutional level, including DIA, FBI, CIA, and subsidiary intelligence-gathering organizations. Clearly, the work of journalists, scholars, and activists have created doubts, not only among POW/MIA family members, but among veterans and members of Congress as well.

Although questions surrounding soldiers missing in action have penetrated deeply into American society following all wars, the questions lingering after Vietnam were far more overwhelming than those faced by American society in 1919, 1945, or 1954. On May 30, 1990, what were believed to be the remains of five American servicemen were returned to the United States by North Korea. Vietnam is not the first war in which thousands of soldiers were lost without trace in captivity, and indeed the families and advocates of MIAs from previous wars began joining the advocates from the Vietnam War, supported in part by major veterans' organizations that have millions of active members. These representative advocacy institutions began to consider World War II and Korea in addition to the Vietnam MIAs, and with numbers of MIAs rising, demanded more substantive answers than were offered by the government to their predecessors.

The Vietnam War has been over militarily for the United States since 1973, militarily and politically for the Vietnamese since 1975. No formal diplomatic relationship between the Socialist Republic of Vietnam (SRV) and the United States existed from 1975 to 1992, for the POW/MIA issue still populates the old battlefield with skeletons. Following the end of the war in 1975, three issues stood in the way of a bilateral relationship: President Richard M. Nixon's promise of more than three billion dollars in aid, the SRV's withdrawal from Cambodia, and a lack of resolution of the POW/MIA issue. Few diplomats speak of the money issue any longer since it derived from a private communication between Nixon and the North Vietnamese. Furthermore, Congress never approved the aid because many congressmen considered it a form of tributary war reparations paid by the vanquished to the victor, or worse, an offer of ransom for prisoners.

When Nixon left the White House because of his part in the Watergate scandal, the offer left with him. With much fanfare and international publicity the SRV removed its troops from Cambodia in 1990, leaving in place an advisory team to work with the Cambodian army. Only one issue remains between the United States and the Socialist Republic of Vietnam: the fate of American POW/MIAs who were not repatriated in 1975.

Officially, the United States wants all its soldiers back from Vietnam, dead or alive. Vietnam wants to normalize relations because it needs loans and credits to clear the destruction left by the war and to compete in world markets. More important, normalization would mean the resumption of normal and peaceful diplomatic relations, including trade, international cash flow, the exchange of ambassadors, and general access to each country by the other's citizenry. One would expect to find powerful conciliatory forces at work in this arena, for everyone has much to gain and seemingly little to lose. Appearances are deceiving, however, especially when they relate to the Vietnam War. On September 29, 1990, Secretary of State James Baker met with Nguyen Co Thach, the Foreign Minister of the Socialist Republic of Vietnam, and in New York at the United Nations the American public heard the stalemate again on the evening news: the POW/MIA issue continues to stand in the way of normalization of international relations between the two countries. At the heart of the issue are basic conflicts in both sides' perceptions of their mutual responsibilities under international law. Beginning when the first Americans were captured by the North Vietnamese and the National Liberation Front (Vietcong), the old issue of status arose. The belligerents did not agree to the mutual applicability of the 1949 Geneva Convention. American military and legal historians claim that the North Koreans and communist Chinese in the 1950s, then the North Vietnamese and the National Liberation Front in the 1960s and 1970s, disregarded nearly every provision of the 1949 Geneva Convention in their treatment of American and allied POWs. Invoking their exception to Article 85, the North Vietnamese told the International Red Cross that indeed they did not recognize full applicability of the 1949 Geneva Convention to the conflict between themselves and the Americans and their allies. The International Red Cross reminded the belligerents that the articles in the 1949 Geneva Convention relative to the treatment of prisoners applied to each of the signatories regardless of whether a formal declaration of war existed or not. Both sides understood that the convention's articles applied.

Notwithstanding the convention's provisions, the North Vietnamese and the Vietcong refused to allow the IRC to inspect their respective camps. As early as 1967, President Lyndon B. Johnson asked North Vietnam and the Vietcong to allow inspections of the camps and the repatriation of all sick and wounded on both sides. The Vietnamese refused, believing that prisoner issues should be settled at the end of the conflict; however, from time to time, for political reasons, the Vietcong would release an American they thought reliable enough to spread the word of their cause at home. They maintained a position similar to the one taken by the Japanese military command against Allied airmen in World War II, that the Americans fighting against them—especially airmen—were "war criminals" and "air pirates." Thus, the Vietcong's definition of the military prisoner as criminal formed the legal and ethical dilemma that Americans faced in Indochina. Although the Americans and South Vietnamese publicly subscribed to the 1949 Geneva Convention, in practice neither side agreed on basic definitions, rights, or responsibilities of the captor toward the prisoner.[7]

Long after the cessation of hostilities in Korea and Vietnam, some Americans at home claimed that Americans remained in captivity after "Operation Big Switch" in 1953 and "Operation Homecoming" in 1973. According to Kenneth A. Steadman, Director of National Security and Foreign Affairs for the American Veterans of Foreign Wars, of the 8,177 MIAs from the Korean War, 329 were reported to be alive at one time. A delegation of veterans was invited by the North Korean government to retrieve remains in June 1989; when the time came, however, the North Koreans refused entry. When the United Nations Military Armistice Commission requested the promised remains, North Korea claimed that none existed.[8] James B. Stockdale and other former POWs report in their narratives that their captors told them that as captives (not POWs) they could be kept forever.[9]

The old antiwar constituency represented here by H. Bruce Franklin presumes that all the MIAs are actually dead or remain in Indochina willingly as assimilated captives. It claims that the American government deliberately contravened the peace agreement of 1973 and still refuses to face the reality of defeat. It glories in North Vietnam's military victory over South Vietnam, Vietnamese political reunification, and the superimposition of hardline communism on a generally unwilling South Vietnamese population as its own victory. After all, these antiwar adherents argue, the People's Army of Vietnam (PAVN) and the National Liberation Front (NLF, or Vietcong) have thousands of MIAs left unaccounted for, and the government of the United States shows no interest in that fact.

Opposed to the old antiwarriors is another, less complacent, group that believes the government conspired with its former adversaries—and sometimes with allies in the case of the Soviet Union in World War II—to keep missing persons in captivity forever. Charged by a belief in government deceit beginning in 1945, the most radical actors have been individuals with some private and limited institutional support who seek to confront the POW/MIA issue head on. As independent operators they claim to have conducted clandestine "recovery missions" inside Indo-china with financial support from sympathetic parties. The people involved in these activities consider themselves political libertarians and individuals still at war. Although relatively few, they are fully capable of using tabloid media to promote their POW/MIA activities. For several years, the *Bamboo Connection,* a government-deceit tabloid, claimed to be "a voice for American war veterans," and featured government-deceit articles such as "MIA Group Furious over Reagan Pledge," "6 Fined in Protest Over Vietnam MIAs," and "POW Activist Jailed on Father's Day." Cartoons show the federal bench resembling the three monkeys: one judge sits blindfolded, and the other two are wrapped around the mouth and ears, respectively. The caption reads, "Federal Judges Deny POWs Their Constitutional Rights!" Another cartoon shows an American eagle shackled to a Vietcong guard tower; the caption reads, "Vietnam: The war is not over till they all come home." And in what the *Bamboo Connection* called "Operation Dong the Cong," a cartoon shows a North Vietnamese Dong (money), with an inscription, "POW Reward Fund will pay 2.4 million U.S. dollars for American prisoner of war." Eventually, the *Bamboo Connection* changed its name to *U.S. Veteran News and Report,* and in 1989 John M. G. Brown's and Thomas G. Ashworth's shocking article, "A Secret that Shames Humanity," appeared. It attempts to prove with declassified government documents from the postwar period that more than 75,000 Americans were unaccounted for at the end of World War II, with sur-vivors still being held against their will today in Soviet gulags.[10]

One step beyond the tabloid press is *Bohica* (1987), a privately pub-lished book written by Scott Barnes. Barnes claims that "Bohica" is really an acronym for "bend over, here it comes again." In this work, the author claims to have been part of a private recovery operation in Southeast Asia, Operation Grand Eagle, that investigated live sighting reports in Laos. Barnes claims that as a former Green Beret, drug enforcement and CIA agent, he swam the river from Thailand into Cambodia, photographed an American POW, and returned. He also claims that in 1981 he accom-panied another American on a reconnaissance mission into Laos, located the prisoners, and received orders to kill them. Barnes should have pub-lished his book as a fictional thriller; unfortunately, the author attempted to market the book as a true account of the murky world of covert super-spook activities in the chaos of the American POW/MIA controversy.

The Skyhook II Project claims that American soldiers are still being held captive in Southeast Asia. One solicitation states: "Reliable estimates now show that as many as 253 American POWs yet remain to be rescued . . . an amazing number to survive when you consider what we've learned about their savage treatment by the North Vietnamese." Operation Home-coming is another spurious entrepreneurial exercise that fizzled. The term was used originally in 1973–1974 to signify the reintegration of former prisoners into their respective military and civilian communities. Based in California, with a few operatives located in small towns throughout the United States, Operation Homecoming, like its close relative, the Skyhook II Project, raised money from concerned citizens to bankroll its bogus overseas private operations. One such operation took place in 1987 and was reported by the Altoona *Mirror,* a small central Pennsylvania newspaper, as "Vet Returns from Asia with Bones." A staff writer reported that a Pennsylvania veteran had accompanied the president of the organization to Southeast Asia. These men claimed to have received five sets of American remains from the Laotian resistance. Actually, they brought home nothing. Most significant, the veteran (not a Vietnam veteran) stated what for him would be an absolute commitment, "I know for a fact there are Americans being held in Laos."

The Altoona story reveals a kind of negative entrepreneurism that perpetuates war psychosis—a continuing escalated hate for an enemy—that haunts many war veterans today and delays meaningful personal closures to the wartime experience in general. The overwhelming problem of individuals committed to release and raid operations outside government oversight is that letters of marque authorizing private warfare against foreign governments have been out of fashion since the American Revolution and War of 1812. The American Constitution (1787) assigns the role of diplomacy to the executive branch of government, and the Logan Act, Statute III in *Acts of the Fifth Congress of the United States* (1799), forbids private American citizens from conducting national foreign policy on their own initiative.

On the other hand, many people in the entrepreneurial or private sphere of the POW/MIA controversy recall the antiwar activists during the Vietnam War who traveled to Hanoi without government reprisals. Hanoi permitted these people to visit American prisoners for propaganda exercises. The antiwar visitors had no idea at the time that most of the American prisoners had to be tortured into speaking with them at all. Some visitors took the opportunity to broadcast propaganda messages for Hanoi on the air; others carried mail home to prisoners' families. What all the visitors had in common was that they pursued their own political agenda by conducting shadow foreign policy. None of these activists was ever prosecuted, and most (not all) of the American prisoners and nearly the entire military intelligence community sizzled with hatred for these people who flouted the sedition laws with impunity. Memories remain vivid and even impassioned among many war veterans in this respect—especially among former hard-resisting prisoners—toward Jane Fonda, Tom Hayden, Rennie Davis, Cora Weiss, David Dellinger, and many others who visited them in captivity for political and ultimately for propaganda purposes.

In the spirit of the *lex talionis*—the law of retribution that demands eyes for eyes and teeth for teeth—what was moral, ethical, or legal in principle for one side during the war could be moral, ethical, and legal for the other after it. Men and women who believe that Hanoi illegally detains Americans against their will in a gulag system see it as their higher moral duty to do something about the problem now, long after the horrors of war have ceased in Southeast Asia.

For many others, too, the shooting may have stopped but the war is not over. The missing are commemorated in local and regional popular rituals, with other icons besides the Tomb of the Unknown Soldier. On American patriotic days—Memorial Day, Flag Day, Independence Day, and Veterans Day—POW/MIA activists gather to call for the return of American POW/MIAs from the Vietnam War. On November 11, Veterans Day (formerly Armistice Day, commemorating the end of World War I), small groups gather to reenact the ritual of the missing warrior—part funeral and part initiation. Many POW/MIA memorial services take place at night. The celebrants usually stand in a circle or in a compact rectangular group; often, each person holds a candle. Many people, the organizers at least, wear metal bracelets (icons) with MIA names on them. The mood is sober, somber, thoughtful, and by and large angry. One Gloucester County, New Jersey, circular describes the spirit of the gathering.

> For some, Vietnam is still an everyday nightmare. That's because nearly 2,500 Americans are still missing in Vietnam. 2,500 people who disappeared, leaving questions in their place. Over the years since we left the conflict, hundreds of firsthand sightings by refugees and others report Americans still alive in Vietnam, Laos, and Cambodia. [They are] growing older day to day in prison camps, while Hanoi denies knowledge of them. Other reports confirm bodies being held for ransom by that same Hanoi government. Meantime, their wives and families live frozen in time, not knowing whether to remarry, to move ahead, or to hang on to hope. Now, Washington has finally admitted some of the missing could still be alive, but the wheels of government turn slowly. You can speed them up. Write your senator or congressman or write the Vietnamese Ambassador to the United Nations. . . . Americans are still in Vietnam. Let's get them out. . . . Let Hanoi know that this time Americans are together on the question of Vietnam. And we want them out. Completely.[11]

These are not isolated cults. Active, institutionalized support groups, including the Veterans of Foreign Wars, American Legion, Veterans of the Vietnam War, American Ex-Prisoners of War Association, Disabled American Veterans, American Purple Heart Association, American Gold

Star Mothers Association, Navy and Marine Corps Leagues, and the National League of Families and the Prisoners of War and Missing in Action in Southeast Asia, contain millions of veterans from World War II, Korea, and Vietnam. What distinguishes these groups from radical activists is their institutional trust in the government's commitment to account for all the MIAs of America's twentieth-century wars. To varying degrees, each group accepts the position that it is the government's business, not an individual's, to bring the missing home, dead or alive.

The government deceit theme finally worked its way into Hollywood films in the early 1980s. *First Blood* (1982) was essentially a captivity-resistance film. The central character, John Rambo, learned how to resist captors in Vietnam, and flashbacks to Rambo in enemy captivity leave no doubt that he is responding to Sheriff Teasle as he would have liked to respond to his captors in Vietnam. Overpowered, outgunned, and outnumbered at first, Rambo has no desire to make war at home and allows himself to be captured by the town sheriff and his men. Abused by his civilian captors in jail, Rambo flashes back to the bamboo cages and interrogation chamber in the jungle. In a catastrophic moment he rejects passive survivorism, snaps, resists his captors, and escapes into a war landscape he understands. There he can make war on his captors in far more violent and insidious ways than they can make war on him. With stealth, cunning, and knowledge of guerrilla tactics, Rambo invokes the undemocratic rules of guerrilla war against a community totally accustomed to the democratic rules of peace. In *First Blood,* Morrell and Stallone create more than a stereotype of a dangerous simpleton who wants to be left alone, or a man-viper who will attack if disturbed. They create in John Rambo a Jekyll-Hyde opposition of two major western heroic mythic images: Cincinnatus, the highly skilled, stoic citizen-soldier who endures harm's way when duty requires; and a vengeance-seeking, blood-lusting god of war, who, after he is captured, betrayed, and inflamed, cannot control his anger. Showing the tragedy of betrayal, Rambo as Cincinnatus returns home in peace but is shunned, mistreated, dishonored, jailed, brutalized, and betrayed by those people whose democratic values he thought he had defended. Rambo as warrior takes unqualified, catastrophically violent vengeance on his betrayers. Audiences sat stunned as Rambo, the good citizen-soldier returning from a bad war, transformed into Satan incarnate to combat government deceit and, then, tragically, into the veteran stereotype of the Vietnam War in general.

Cinematically, *Rambo: First Blood Part II* (1985) is no more than a simple melodramatic thriller, but it develops the government deceit theme from a local to a national level.[12] Rambo returns to Southeast Asia, supposedly to Laos, in order to feint a rescue, to shore up the government claim that it is actually doing something about the POW/MIA issue. The rescue mission is merely a smokescreen designed to placate the growing belief in the United States that there were Americans still in captivity against their will. When John Rambo actually finds MIAs still in captivity, an embarrassed government, represented by an outraged CIA agent, clearly has no desire to recover them at all. In D. Michael Shafer's *The Legacy* (1990), Bruce Taylor argues that Sylvester Stallone attempted to replace John Wayne as the modern "Spirit of America" with his Rambo character.[13] If the box office reveals anything about American popular culture and its relationship to consensus values, it is significant that despite being panned by critics, *Rambo: First Blood Part II* earned the third largest gross of any movie up to its time, $3.25 million in the first six days of its release. True to the government-deceit and conspiracy themes of the 1980s and 1990s, Rambo brings the men home in spite of the government, not because of it.

Missing in Action (1984), *Missing in Action II* (1985), and *P. O. W. the Escape* (1984) are all populist thrillers that tell similar stories. Each film attempts to validate one or more of the populist POW/MIA positions: a conspiracy exists between the government and the communist Vietnamese in order to resume normal diplomatic and business relationships; the government abandoned its duty to its MIAs and sold out its principles for greedy government-supported individuals (often government retirees) to establish and conduct business with the old adversary; and the true patriot achieves success only if he operates outside the corrupt system. Success in these films is defined not only by heroes recovering MIAs by force, but, more importantly, by private POW/MIA activists forcing the government to admit its errors publicly.

Uncommon Valor (1984) focuses more attention on government neglect than on government deceit. It tells the tale of a war-veteran father, Colonel Rhodes, searching for his MIA son. To make the raid, the colonel recruits his son's old unit and, in effect, reconstructs what Morris Janowitz calls the "primary unit," a brotherhood of men who were members of a military unit at a particular time functioning as a provider of social solidarity: the greater the solidarity, the greater their effectiveness.[14] Bankrolled by the very wealthy bereaved father of an MIA and manned by an intact, experienced combat force, Colonel Rhodes's primary unit raids the prison compound and successfully rescues some of the MIAs but does not retrieve his own son.[15]

Television has not exploited the government-deceit theme to the degree that the movies have. However, one segment of *Tour of Duty*, "The Raid," broadcast on August 4, 1990, finds Sarge and L-T captured. A special raiding unit went through extensive preparations and training, but when they assaulted the camp, the prisoners had been moved. Sarge and L-T have to work on their own initiative; they escape and rejoin their unit. Again, the villain is a CIA agent who constantly restrains the raiders from accomplishing their military mission; he is finally killed. In the end, the soldiers abandon trust in the army as an institution of government in favor of a more entrepreneurial reliance on self and the immediate primary unit. "The army isn't in charge; we are, us grunts." Another B thriller is a depressing hard-boiled, made-for-TV, government-deceit thriller, *The Forgotten*. Broadcast in January 1990, it stars Keith Carradine and Stacy Keach and takes the government deceit theme one step further: the government would murder American POW/MIAs if they were released or managed to escape from captivity. The plot begins when six POWs are finally released from prison in Vietnam after seventeen years of captivity. The men are taken from Vietnam to West Germany (the film was actually made in Yugoslavia) and are roughly interrogated by the resident CIA operative (Stacy Keach). After what appears to be a covert murder of one man, the rest escape the secluded American compound and attempt to seek help from the remarried German wife of one of the group. The men are pursued by American covert forces (CIA); two are killed. After extensive intrigue and gunplay, three Americans remain alive. They assault the headquarters of the American trade mission and capture the traitorous American trade negotiator—a former negotiator during the war—and hold him hostage. Keach, who was in league with the former negotiator in the first place, knows the conspiracy is in danger of being exposed, so he shoots the hostage in the chest. Keach is shot in turn by the avenging prisoners. The scope on the rifle doubles as the camera, and the audience is left believing that the whole conspiracy came from CIA headquarters or, worse, the White House.

The Vietnam postwar government-deceit thrillers send clear, prepackaged messages. American citizen-soldiers are being held against their will in Southeast Asia because the American government deceives the public and conspires with the former enemy for profit. In a clandestine paramilitary operation, the entrepreneur-hero descends into the MIA hell, retrieves the helpless victims, and returns defiantly with real evidence in hand. Corpus delicti is positively established and proves that not only did a crime exist but the former adversaries are the criminal agencies. The action formula synthesizes the familiar images of the lone rescuer (Lone Ranger) in American popular culture. Comfortable in a savage (Asian) landscape, the hero dispenses righteous and retributive (Puritan) justice to a cruel enemy (Yellow Peril); intent on defying the decadence of American governmental and business power brokers more interested in profit than honor, more concerned with diplomatic expediency than with duty, the hero assumes the government's responsibilities to its war veterans in general, represented symbolically by the POW/MIAs it left behind.

The acceptance of sets of commonly held assumptions as true constitutes a cultural belief system; series of connected belief systems create myth. In this case, the myth of the missing warrior is so pervasive that it lies beyond mere propaganda; it has replaced unavailable fact as a means of understanding the wars that shaped so much of American culture in the twentieth century.

Believing that Americans are held against their will in Southeast Asia is one thing; doing something about it is another. Some raiding activities continued past the end of formal hostilities in Vietnam. Believing that there were Americans in enemy hands in Laos, retired Colonel James "Bo" Gritz, USA, launched a short-lived raid, Operation Lazarus, on November 27, 1982, eleven years after the war was over. Gritz recruited Charles J. Patterson, a former Special Forces soldier, as his second in command. As the mission's errors unfolded, and it became evident that Operation Lazarus would become an embarrassing catastrophe, Patterson and Gritz parted company. Patterson and G. Lee Tipton wrote *The Heroes Who Fell from Grace: The True Story of Operation Lazarus, the Attempt to Free American POWs from Laos in 1982* (1985). The authors explained the rationale for the raid as Gritz saw it.

> It is assumed, due to delicate diplomatic relations between the United States, Thailand and Laos, the U.S. Government cannot commit official assets until positive proof of U.S. POW presence is provided. It is assumed, once such a determination has been made, the U.S. Government will follow the President's [Ronald Reagan's] stated policy to do whatever is required to return the POWs to U.S. control. The Thai Government can only look the other way due to their policy of providing sanctuary for Free Laos. . . . It is assumed the Free Guerrilla Forces can approach POW locations and access them by force if desired. It is also assumed that the underground auxiliary forces are adequate to support such a tactical operation and act as an evasion mechanism, should aerial support be denied in evacuating POWs to safety once liberated. It is assumed that the U.S. Government will tacitly allow the operation.[16]

This assumption was incorrect. The raiders had no legal mandate to search for American prisoners in Laos without that country's permission. Although it formed the basis for *Uncommon Valor,* Operation Lazarus turned out to be both a "mission impossible" and an embarrassment to the United States. Without any discernible permission from or connections to the American government, a team consisting of four American civilians and fifteen indigenous Laotians entered Laos illegally by crossing the Mekong River from Thailand. Being unfamiliar with the terrain, the team got lost and quickly discouraged. They were lucky to escape with their lives. When Gritz and the others returned to Thailand they were arrested and briefly jailed in Bangkok. They learned that no private citizen can attempt to free a small number of hostages or prisoners—in effect, conduct war—without the protection of a state. As Patterson and Tipton point out, an unsupported, private, independently operated raid is a crime.[17]

The belief or disbelief that POW/MIAs remain in captivity against their will defines in part the nature of the post–Vietnam War and the post–cold war America. In 1979, one MIA, Private Robert Garwood, USMC, left the Socialist Republic of Vietnam. Although Garwood claimed that the Vietnamese had held him against his will, upon his return, the United States Marine Corps tried and convicted him for collaboration with the enemy. Garwood reported that he saw live American prisoners of war in the Socialist Republic of Vietnam. The resignation in 1991 of the Director of POW/MIA affairs for the Defense Intelligence Agency, Colonel Millard Peck, USA, over the agency's policy relationships with MIA families, the government's relationship with the League of Families, the status of live sighting reports, and other evidence coming out of Southeast Asia added fuel to the fire. In July 1991, photos were released of three possible live Vietnam MIAs. Accepted by the families as pictures of their missing relatives, the photos were disputed by American government agencies, especially the Defense Intelligence Agency (DIA) in charge of POW/MIA identification, disposition, and recovery. The Vietnamese continued to deny holding Americans. In October 1991, further complicating the state of POW/MIA affairs, Oleg Kalugin, a former KGB officer, claimed that he had been involved in intelligence-gathering operations with American POWs in Vietnam in 1978. In frustration, activists and their congressional allies called for a senatorial commission to conduct investigations of DIA and the POW/MIA issue in the United States.

In November 1991, Senate hearings, known as the "Kerry hearings" after Senator John Kerry of Massachusetts, began to inquire into the nature of the POW/MIA conflict. In public and on television, the Senate interviewed DIA personnel, active and retired military officers, private activists, POW/MIA family members, authors Monika Jenson-Stevenson and Nigel Cawthorne, Ann Mills Griffiths of the League of Families, and many other citizens involved in the issue. Oleg Kalugin appeared. Although he was ostensibly refuted by former colleagues in Russia, Oleg Kalugin testified at the Senate hearings that he knew of American prisoners moved from Vietnam to Russia. Responding to the testimony, in January 1992 the DIA sent personnel to Moscow to search available KGB archives for records of Americans in Russian captivity. In June, the Senate hearings resumed after trips to Russia and Vietnam. Stirring the pot even more and supporting what Kalugin said before the Senate, President Boris Yeltsin of Russia announced in his visit to Washington, D.C., that he believed some American POWs were kept after World War II in the Soviet gulag system, some shot down during cold war intelligence gathering overflights, others transferred from Vietnam. American television journalists visited and televised a trip to a Russian labor camp in Siberia. No American prisoners were present, nor did any of the interviewed Russian guards or camp personnel have any knowledge of them.

If the Kerry hearings accomplished anything, they provided a public forum for each advocacy group to air its grievances against the government and its agencies. As expected, the major opposing positions surfaced. One group, including the DIA, the League of Families, and the major veterans' organizations, supports the notion that the government intends to find out what happened to American MIAs through diplomatic channels; the other, including families, authors, and activists, believes that government agencies are deceiving them in particular and the American public in general. The fact remains that the 1991 distribution of Vietnam MIAs per individual state is unchanged: Alabama, 42; Alaska, 2; Arizona, 23; Arkansas, 26; California, 227; Colorado, 39; Connecticut, 37; Delaware, 5; Washington, D.C., 9; Florida, 77; Georgia, 43; Hawaii, 10; Idaho, 11; Illinois, 94; Indiana, 66; Iowa, 38; Kansas, 35; Kentucky, 21; Louisiana, 29; Maine, 17; Maryland, 35; Massachusetts, 55; Michigan, 72; Minnesota, 41; Mississippi, 18; Missouri, 48; Montana, 21; Nebraska, 21; Nevada, 8; New Hampshire, 10; New Jersey, 59; New Mexico, 17; New York, 144; North Carolina, 56; North Dakota, 16; Ohio, 113; Oklahoma, 47; Oregon, 43; Pennsylvania, 113; Rhode Island, 9; South Carolina, 30; South Dakota, 8; Tennessee, 42; Texas, 146; Utah, 19; Vermont, 4; Virginia, 54; Washington, 55; West Virginia, 23; Wisconsin, 37; Wyoming, 6; Puerto Rico, 2; Virgin Islands, 1; Other, 7, for a total of 2,414 Vietnam MIAs (2,372 military and 42 civilians) listed as POWs, MIAs, or KIAs whose bodies were not recovered. According to the National League of Families, 1,190 are classified as prisoners or MIAs, Bodies-Not-Recovered.[18] The data raise several important issues. After each war in this century, thousands of soldiers could not be found, accounted for, or repatriated following an enemy's surrender or joint armistice. More important, the government has little choice other than to classify MIAs as presumed dead for family and administrative reasons after a reasonable period of time.[19]

American MIA and POW families from the forest wars to Vietnam have sought to discover what happened to missing fathers, uncles, husbands, brothers, daughters, and sons in captivity. Right or wrong, Americans have believed consistently that they have a right to that knowledge. In their view, international law and the customs of war mandate a legal responsibility, as well as a moral and ethical obligation, to bury the dead and care for the living. The Geneva Convention Relative to the Treatment of Prisoners of War, 1949, Section II, Article 118, states: "Prisoners of war shall be released and repatriated without delay after the cessation of active hostilities." Thus, the delay remains an act of unwarranted malevolence, no matter who commits it. On October 20, 1992, General John Vessey, along with Senator John McCain, a former POW and a member of the Senate Select Committee on POW/MIA, returned from Hanoi and announced that the Socialist Republic is willing to show representatives of the American government over 4,000 photos of dead Americans taken by North Vietnamese combat photographers during the war. If some American MIAs appear in these photographs, at least part of the puzzle will be solved.[20]

The POW/MIA dispute reflects tenaciously powerful traditional ideas held by many Americans who understand this issue as the last political and human vestige of the world wars, Korea, and Vietnam. With the exception of the former antiwar activists, no significant disputes exist among the contending parties about the numbers. Whether the missing are actually dead or assimilated into the former captor's culture, or whether, as popular belief suggests, they are being held in captivity against their will, this contest remains a cultural conflict, and, for the families directly affected, a deep, unhealed wound. It should be clear that when there are so many unknown soldiers, little hard evidence, and so much media attention, myth becomes not only believable, but preferable. Perhaps Mark Twain's remark that truth is so precious that it ought to be used sparingly applies here. The myth, as it appears consistently in American popular culture, is characterized by traditional storytelling techniques, a formulaic structure, and happy endings for the stoic few held against their will. The truth of the POW/MIA dispute is far less lucid and may never have an ending, happy or sad.

CHAPTER THIRTEEN

Lessons and Reflections

Only a properly historical view, a consideration of form, impact, and milieu as well as content, will enable us to see what the captivity narrative really was and came to be.

Roy Harvey Pearce (1947)

Why do captivity narratives exist? What do they do? As ethnological and ethnographic reportage, captivity literature examines the transmission, retention, and change of human values when they are challenged by captors of a different culture. This aspect of captivity is especially important when the captor's culture may have been temporary, extinct, or inaccessible at the given time. Descriptions of POW life in captivity clarify patterns of individual and group interactions as well as important elements of the material cultures of both the captors and the prisoners. They teach lessons about the personal and social psychology of captivity, about failed military operations and technologies, combat strategies, and tactics, and on occasion, they even discuss tactics of friendly (Philippines, 1942–1945) or enemy (forest wars, Philippine insurrection, South Vietnam) guerrilla operations.

Captivity reportage witnesses to the collisions of cultural values and the exigencies of daily survival. Captives are forced to identify themselves by role or function in relation to an alien culture. Writers in effect create stories by wrapping themselves in interpretive metaphors: the redeemed pilgrim, the resisting stoic or defeated hero, the rational assimilator, or the prisoner who risks escape. In each one, the writer's self is defined, the meaning of the culture is interpreted, and the significance of the captivity event comes to be understood. The common structural denominator of the captivity experience is the consistently repeated sequence of event-scenarios. What change are the combinations and recombinations of the experiential variables within them.

By approaching the captivity experience in terms of Clifford Geertz's vision of organization of social activity, institutional forms, and systems of ideas, we see that the personal narratives from the forest wars to the Vietnam War tell a special kind of war story.[1] POW narratives ask basic questions about the power of a culture's systems of traditional, commonly held ideas of right and wrong, good and bad, legal and illegal, and moral and immoral. The memoirs reveal how these conflicts work, why they exist, and how they are connected to a POW's vision of individual, collective, and cultural reality. Narrators have shown what brutality, disappointment, horror, and shame mean to them. Duty, home, family, and even human dignity are peeled from the captive. Superficial layers of culture come off easily when military, political, and personal conflicts arise; however, the inner, value-laden domains, once challenged, are much tougher to change or remove. Thus, the personal memoirs of the captivity experience counterbalance formal histories of war with metaphors that give them meaning.

Captivity narratives and related forms—poetry, paintings, photographs, sketches, novels, and movies—inevitably have their critics. Phillips D. Carleton suggests that former prisoners write their stories solely for profit. "The very truth of most of the captivities," wrote Carleton, "has counted against them, for they were not written as literature, but usually as salable tracts."[2] Carleton is quite right in this assessment, especially as it applies to civilian captives and former POWs in eighteenth- and nineteenth-century wars when the American government granted few disability pensions to POWs, leaving them often to fend for themselves. Many were destitute, with families to support. After the Civil War, some former POWs were reduced to becoming carnival freaks. Many died very young, some within a few years of repatriation. Major American veteran organizations, including the American Legion, the Veterans of Foreign Wars, the American Ex-Prisoners of War Association, the Defenders of Bataan and Corregidor, and the Veteran's Administration (VA) have shown conclusively that twentieth-century captivity disabled POWs both physically and psychologically. Consequently, each VA hospital contains one office specifically devoted to POW health and disabilities. For many, narrating the POW experience is a means to generate some needed family funds. Given that the reading public devours postcaptivity POW narratives, it is actually surprising that there have not been more in print.

Roy Harvey Pearce takes a different position in "The Significance of the Captivity Narrative" (1947). Pearce suggests that the captivity narrative yields neither historical nor ethnological data that has any significant meaning. For Pearce the importance of the personal captivity story rests on the cultural impact the narratives have on their readers. Acting as a religious confessional, overt propaganda, or simply as a popular action thriller, the captivity adventure "gives us sharp insight into various segments of popular American culture. . . . Only a properly historical view, a consideration of form, impact, and milieu as well as content, will enable us to see what the captivity narrative really was and came to be."[3] Following Pearce's suggestion and looking through a wider, more interdisciplinary lens, we can see captivity literature as part of a long-standing western oral and biblical tradition beginning in part with the books of Chronicles and Lamentations, the pre-Christian heroic lays of Northern Europe, and the secular folktales and ballads that traveled to America with the immigrants. Thus, as a synthesis of traditional oral and biblical components, the American narrative form, especially in Puritan and Catholic manifestations, evolved in part as an act of faith and redemption. It has not gone away, nor has it been replaced. The Colonies became the United States in 1783 after a long and unpopular war. Prisoners were part of that war and every war since; their experiences of survival, resistance, assimilation, and escape have become the POW narratives of today. Reliance on God has not been rejected; it became part of what Vietnam POWs call their "Four Faiths": faith in God as each POW understood God, faith in the strength of country, faith in the integrity of the POW community at hand, and only lastly, faith in one's self.

Prison camp literature is world literature. British and Commonwealth POW literature after World War I is extensive. Primo Levi's *Survival in Auschwitz,* Elie Wiesel's *Night,* Feodor Dostoevsky's *House of the Dead,* and Aleksandr I. Solzhenitsyn's epic narrative *The Gulag Archipelago* illustrate the fact that international captivity literature reflects certain universal historical and political realities. From Australia, literary critic Robin Gerster points out in *Big-Noting: The Heroic Theme in Australian War Writing* (1987) that in recent times there has been an upsurge of interest in World War II captivity narratives in Australia. Concerned with both the number of titles and the number of copies sold, Gerster suggests that the renewed popularity results in part from the fact that "customary depiction of foreign barbarity appeals readily to a xenophobic audience which enjoys its war horrors uncomplicated by moral complexity." Highly critical, Gerster notes that, "The POW narrative is the most crude kind of morality play, a story of 'good guys' who are very good, and 'bad guys' who are very nasty indeed."[4] As he understands his own postwar culture (World War II, Korea, Malaysia, and Vietnam), Gerster argues that "the old cultural commitment to the heroic ethos has become somewhat emasculated."[5] In the context of the twentieth-century, postwar, popular literary realism, Gerster is most certainly correct.[6] On the other hand, if the historical memory of war, especially of World War II, is strong, as it is in Australia, the United States, Britain, and other Allied countries, and if the permanent qualities of human suffering remain thematically powerful, Gerster's argument falters. The "old cultural commitment" will have shown itself to be much stronger, more persistent, and far more tenacious than those purveyed by contemporary literary critics schooled in trendy 1960s academic radicalism. Perhaps, when the narrator blends an understandable personal experience with an established and recognized cultural tradition, literature of the POW experience cannot avoid being popular.

Are captivity narratives true? Some are factually accurate, some are only partially accurate, and some are filled with personally interpreted fantasies. If there is one assumption that sets the tone, it is that POW narratives are perceptually true, as accurate as one person's memory can be after a long period of time. Some narratives were created from diaries; others synthesized the author's personal experience with historical facts and recollections from other POWs in the same camp. Without exception, former POWs and internees say that in captivity one's memory is heightened, for captivity is a watershed event, never to be forgotten. This is not to argue that every moment in every account was recorded with videotape accuracy; rather, the narratives consist of vivid event-scenarios that can never pass from the human memory. Are they honest personal histories of time past, or are they simply overblown statements of antipathies and vindictive diatribes against former captors? Do former POWs bother to tell the truth at all, or, as some historians suggest, might they be only dubious sources from which to unravel layers of preprocessed propaganda?

Many captivity narratives written between 1754 and 1760 were indeed anti-French, anti-Catholic propaganda. In 1756, the captive Robert Eastburn wrote, "Our enemies make a better use of a bad religion than we do of a good one." Eastburn laments that the French were united as one man while America was divided against itself.[7] Peter Williamson also chronicles what he believed were French-inspired atrocities committed against the English. Jonathan Carver, an American colonial volunteer with General Webb's expedition to strengthen Fort William Henry, was captured by General Montcalm in 1757. Survivors were permitted to leave with their muskets but without any ammunition. Montcalm promised them a protective guard, but no guard was provided and they were left unprotected. Indians attacked and easily overcame them. According to Carver, it was "a flagrant breach of every sacred law," a war crime because the French refused to control their tribal allies. There is little doubt, then, that many of the narratives written and published during and after the forest wars acted as pro-American propaganda tracts designed to ignite readers' anger against the captors as public enemies. This trend would continue into the Revolution and beyond.

During the Revolution, the English replaced the French as public enemies and perpetrators of evil, especially when they joined forces with their tribal allies, who were greatly feared for their unconventional, guerrilla warfare tactics. Thomas Jefferson makes the point very clearly in the Declaration of Independence: "He [King George III] has excited domestic insurrections amongst us, and has endeavored to bring on the inhabitants of our frontiers, the merciless Indian savages, whose known rule of warfare is an undistinguished destruction of all ages, sexes, and conditions." In addition to the Indians, British, and Hessian troops, the loyalists whom the British assigned to guard prisoners complicated captivities in the Revolution. The level of hate, or war psychosis, was high between the officers and men of the Continental army and navy and their former neighbors. The American Revolution was in a sense America's first civil war; Americans opposed Americans, and the effects were often lethal. Yet the captivity narratives of the period do not fail to insist to the reader that every word is true.

Narrative truth, therefore, often serves a purpose: not only do narrators reveal what happened to them, they remind the public in graphic terms what could happen to the readers themselves. With the introduction of the "penny dreadfuls" in the mid–nineteenth century, the reputation for veracity of the captivity narrative was severely damaged. Captivity narratives had attained so much popularity that captivity fictions were born. As a result, by the early decades of the nineteenth century the credibility of a captivity narrative was definitely in question and someone now had to attest to the narrator's accuracy. Christopher Hawkins's captivity narrative, *The Adventures of Christopher Hawkins* (1834), includes his avowal of truth. "The sufferings of my youth in my memory, and every incident or event set forth . . . I have no doubt is correct. . . . I know it is so. . . . If any one shall be so incredulous as to disbelieve this narrative, I hope that some of my early contemporaries are still alive. . . . I refer to them the truth or falsehood of this narrative and feel confident that they will sustain me in every particular claiming importance."[8]

After the Civil War, Captain Henry Wirz, CSA, Interior Commandant of Camp Sumter, Georgia (Andersonville), was indicted, tried, convicted of murder, and executed. Still Southern apologists claim that the sorrows of Andersonville, although they existed, were the fault of the system, not of the individuals. Ovid L. Futch claims that Union soldiers' captivity narratives were grossly exaggerated due to the frailties of human memory. Futch points out that narrators magnified their horrible experiences and minimized others. Self-serving reminiscences, therefore, provide little more than interesting examples of lingering mental impressions left by individual prison experiences.[9] Futch notwithstanding, narrative accounts do give powerful impressions of POW life and death in captivity. John McElroy's account of his experiences in *Andersonville* (1879) is far more than a mere "impression." McElroy insists that what he wrote was an accurate telling of what happened to him and his comrades in the Andersonville stockade.

I know what is contained herein will be bitterly denied. I am prepared for this. . . . I solemnly affirm in advance the entire and absolute truth of every material fact, statement and description. I assert that, so far from there being any exaggeration in any particular, that in no instance has the half of the truth been told, nor could it be, save by an inspired pen. I am ready to demonstrate this by any test that the deniers of this may require, and I am fortified in my position by unsolicited letters from over 3,000 surviving prisoners, warmly endorsing the account as accurate in every respect.[10]

However, McElroy qualifies his opening remarks to some degree: "The following story does not claim to be in any sense a history of southern prisons. It is simply a record of the experience of one individual—one boy—who staid all the time with his comrades inside the prison, and had no better opportunities for gaining information than any other of his 40,000 companions."[11]

Focusing on World War I, historian Richard B. Speed III points out that one ought not to believe the exaggerations of returning POWs. In his detailed study *Prisoners, Diplomats, and the Great War: A Study in the Diplomacy of Captivity* (1990), Speed argues that an international, antiwar, pacifist liberal sentiment arose in Europe and America during the nineteenth century and was responsible for the establishment of the Red Cross, the Brussels Code, the Hague Convention, and culminated in popular outrage at conditions in POW camps in Germany during World War I. Speed relies heavily on what American camp inspectors such as Senator Albert J. Beveridge and others stated in their reports and argues that conditions were not as bad as the returning prisoners reported to the Red Cross or wrote in their narratives.[12] However, any veteran of any military service knows that soldiers and sailors know about and prepare for inspections. American sailors use the term "scuttlebutt" to mean gossip. If the "scuttlebutt" has it that an inspection is coming, chances are excellent that preparations will begin. Unannounced inspections, even those made by the Red Cross or protecting powers, were fictions; according to American Kriegies, someone always knew about an inspection. Whatever daily standards may be, they are customarily exceeded during inspections. Thus inspection reports of camp conditions, although made honestly, remain at least as suspect as prisoners' narrations.

Are American captivity narratives true or not? A fact rarely considered by scholars examining POW narratives is that a great number of authors go beyond the this-is-what-happened-to-me account to ethnological and ethnographic accuracy. POWs have doubled as keen participant-observers of value systems and ethnologists of the material culture of prison camp. Certain types of POWs, especially university-trained officers and some trained journalists, found themselves in captivity in the twentieth century. This kind of observer makes many recent wartime captivity narratives more accurate than those written in the past. Evelyn Cobley states correctly that "the memoir acts as a commemoration . . . a memorial, monument, or memento to the dead and as a warning or reminder for the living."[13] Many POW and internee narratives not only serve as subjective memoirs or recollections but also possess a reasonably high degree of objective accuracy and reproduce, as honestly as possible, what was witnessed. Rarely, even in the case of sole survivors, do former POWs set out intentionally to deceive their readers. As one Kriegie writes, "No POW will ever lie to you. . . . He may not at that moment remember all there is to tell, but it will come back to him in time."[14] If narratives of captivity are written with this conviction born only by experience, then Gene Wise's comment in *American Historical Explanations* (1980) that experience is a more existentially grounded term than "reality,"[15] has found a wholly new application. With this in mind, who are we to say they are liars?

I have referred to women in captivity several times in this book. According to Frances Roe Kestler in *The Indian Captivity: A Woman's View* (1990), of the captivity narratives written from experiences in the Indian wars from the seventeenth, eighteenth, and nineteenth centuries, about 450 to 500 in approximately 1,200 editions, nearly half were composed by women.[16] The status of captured women was clear during the forest wars: in some cases, women and children were captured for the purpose of assimilating them into the tribe; in other cases, English and German women acted as commodities for trading and ransom between the Indians and the French. The French wanted to ransom the captives to convert them to Catholicism. The British attempted to ransom them back from the French, and in some cases they ransomed them directly from the Indians. As the Bouquet expedition reveals, some women gained significant social status in their captors' tribes by assimilation and marriage. Some women escaped; others died.

During the American Revolution, some American women, like Deborah Sampson Gannett, wore men's military uniforms and fought as ordinary soldiers. On May 20, 1782, Gannett put on the uniform of a Continental soldier in the 4th Massachusetts Regiment. As a soldier, she took the name Robert Shurtliff and became the first woman to become a uniformed soldier in the American army. She was wounded in action at the Battle of Tarrytown, New York, but treated herself for fears her gender would be discovered. That fear was realized, but her physician decided not to divulge her secret. Instead, Dr. Barnabus Binney decided to submit papers for Private Robert Shurtliff to be honorably discharged.[17] Other women, like Mary Patton Allan, found themselves caught in the middle of a political battlefield. John and Mary Allan were natives of Scotland who emigrated to Cumberland, Nova Scotia, in 1749. In 1776, after the battles of Bunker Hill and Lexington, John Allan declared himself for the American cause and went to Boston. Mary remained in Nova Scotia. John joined Colonel Jonathan Eddy in his disastrous raid on Fort Cumberland, Nova Scotia, on November 17, 1776, and then fought the rest of the war with the Continental army. The British responded to the Fort Cumberland raid by burning the Allan home, taking Mary prisoner, and holding her for eight months. Mary finally was released from prison and emigrated with her family from Nova Scotia to Machias, Massachusetts.[18] During the Revolution and later wars, some women took advantage of their presumed noncombatant status to act as spies; others assisted in supplying armies with food. During the Civil War, Clara Barton led an army of nurses who tended the Union wounded, and later she salvaged Andersonville as a remembrance of man's inhumanity to man. Dorothea Dix's leadership on the United States Sanitary Commission created a model for the emerging Red Cross organization forming in Europe. The Sisters of Mercy, along with uncounted legions of women in the North and South, nursed the sick and comforted the wounded. Their legacy became an American military nurse corps that found some of its members in captivity as internees in World War II.

Also during the Civil War, Belle Boyd was a Confederate spy who was captured and incarcerated in Old Capitol Prison in Washington, D.C. In Andersonville, a surprised and shocked burial detail discovered one dead Union prisoner to be a woman. Another woman refused to leave her husband and stayed in the Andersonville stockade until Confederate authorities jailed her in a nearby home. Dr. Mary Walker applied for a commission as a Union surgeon, but the Union army refused her request because of her gender. She defied the social conventions of the age and joined the army anyway as a civilian volunteer. While serving as a field surgeon with the Union army in Tennessee, Dr. Walker was captured and became a POW in the Libby Prison for Union officers in Richmond. Although she was a civilian volunteer rather than a regular uniformed surgeon, she was finally exchanged for a male Confederate officer of equal rank. Congress awarded Dr. Mary Walker the Medal of Honor, the only woman ever to receive it; however, the medal was later rescinded because she was a volunteer rather than a member of the Union armed services. Dr. Walker was too stubborn even for the United States Congress. She refused to return the medal to the government and kept wearing it until her death. Dr. Walker's medal was returned to her posthumously.

In international law, the status of women as POWs did not receive any serious attention until 1918. Article 31 of the American-German agreement accorded women the same basic legal rights in captivity as men under arms as well as special considerations relative to sanitary facilities. "All female personnel serving with the armed forces of either of the Contracting Parties, shall, if captured, be given every possible protection against harsh treatment, insult or any manifestation of disrespect in any way related to their sex. They shall be suitably and decently quartered, and provided with lavatories, bathing facilities, and other similar necessities quite separate from those provided for males."[19] No American women were POWs in World War I. However, during World War II, civilian women and military nurses were indeed captured. The 1929 convention stated that women were to be treated with all the respect due their gender.[20] Treated as internees, they were given the status of noncombatant, unarmed, nonuniformed civilians rather than POWs. One army nurse, Second Lieutenant Reba Z. Whittle, AN, was captured in Europe when her medical evacuation aircraft was disabled by enemy flak and forced to crash-land in Germany. While she was a Kriegie, Whittle served in the German Lazarett (military hospital) in Memingen treating American Kriegies. In accordance with the 1929 Geneva Convention, the Germans exchanged her quickly.[21]

In the Pacific, a number of American female nurses were captured along with their male patients at Corregidor in the Philippines early in 1942. They did not suffer anything like the Bataan Death March but were treated as internees, the legal status of which defined them as "protected persons" rather than as POWs. In camps like Santo Tomas (Saint Thomas University in Manila), Bilibid, Baguio, Batangas, Los Banõs, and many others, the Japanese victors imprisoned American civilian workers, military nurses, planters, businessmen and their families, diplomats, and journalists who found themselves in the Philippines at the outbreak of the war. Survival in the Japanese internment camps took a radical turn for the worse in 1943. As greater numbers of internees became prisoners of the Japanese army, food supplies and medical stores lessened considerably. If the internees had no outside connections among Filipinos, they would die from starvation. Mrs. Jane Fredrickson, a former internee from 1942 to 1945, summed up the condition of the American internees held in the Philippines: "By August 1945, we had one more month," meaning that because the Japanese army was starving them to death, she and her fellow prisoners had one more month to live.[22] Frederic H. Steven's *Santo Tomas Internment Camp* (1946) chronicles captivity for American civilian internees in the camp of Santo Tomas. Agnes Newton Keith published a narrative, *Three Came Home* (1947), that was subsequently made into a powerful feature film starting Claudette Colbert as Keith. Elizabeth Head Vaughn published her doctoral dissertation as *Community under Stress: An Internment Camp Culture* (1949), in which she gave the first and one of the best social scientific analyses of life, death, and survival in the Japanese army's internment camps.[23]

Reflecting a continuing interest in internment issues in World War II, especially women's views, Carol M. Petillo edited Elizabeth Vaughn's wartime notes and published *The Ordeal of Elizabeth Vaughn: A Wartime Diary of the Philippines* (1985), an internment diary which more closely approximates the uncertainties and dangers of civilian internment than those of the POW experience. This was understandable since the Japanese military code of Bushido excluded the possibility of a woman being a soldier.[24] On the other hand, as Catherine Kenny points out in *Captives: Australian Army Nurses in Japanese Prison Camps* (1986), Australian nurses' wartime experiences were considerably, if not dramatically, different from those of the Americans. In one instance, twenty-two Australian nurses in uniform with Red Cross arm bands were shot by their captors on Banka Island in 1942. Staff Nurse Vivian Bullwinkel was the sole survivor of that atrocity and testified before the Australian War Crimes Commission in 1945 and 1946. When captors were bent on destroying their prisoners, gender was no protection. To Vivian Bullwinkel, stoic heroism, luck, and the preservation of life were far more important in surviving wartime captivity than gender.[25]

There were no female POWs in Korea. In the Vietnam War there were a few women in captivity; none was an American. A British journalist, Kate Webb, narrates her story in *On the Other Side: Twenty-Three Days with the Viet Cong* (1972). Captured in Cambodia during the fighting, she discovered very quickly that her life depended on her ability to convince the Vietcong that she was not a CIA intelligence agent. After she finally convinced her interrogators that she was a sympathetic, neutral British journalist, she was set free. Monika Schwinn and her male colleague, Bernhard Diehl, wrote *We Came to Help* (1973, 1976). Their joint narrative, one of the most gripping of the Vietnam War, tells of the capture of five members of the humanitarian West German Aid Service of Malta. Stationed in South Vietnam to perform humanitarian volunteer medical duties among the civilian population, they were tricked into captivity while out for a Sunday drive in the countryside. Of the five people captured in 1968, three died in captivity from beriberi, malaria, and pneumonia. Monika Schwinn and Bernhard Diehl remained captives of the Vietcong for four years because the National Liberation Front considered the Federal Republic of Germany an ally of the United States. Diehl and Schwinn were finally transported to Hanoi and released along with the Americans in 1973.

Not until America's most recent war, the Gulf War or "Operation Desert Storm," had female American soldiers been captured as actual POWs. Two women were taken prisoner: Major Rhonda Cornum and Specialist Melissa Rathburn-Nealy. Major Cornum, a flight surgeon, suffered two broken arms, a smashed right knee, and a bullet wound in her right shoulder. She told the recently convened Presidential Commission on Women that in addition to the wounds she received in the field, she had been sexually assaulted in captivity. Specialist Nealy suffered what a *New York Times* reporter called "indecent assault." Rhonda Cornum's narrative, *She Went to War,* appeared in 1992; both women's captivity experiences wait to be revealed in full.

What are the values and virtues found in captivity? The American passion for success confronts failure at surrender and capture. Most POWs who narrate their experiences attempt to overcome the perception of failure and define what success meant to them behind the wire. Common to most narratives, especially those that focus on resistance and survival, are strong perceptions of ideals that unite incarcerated men and women into a POW community, one that according to anthropologist Robert Redfield is distinct, homogeneous, consistent, and self-sufficient. Boundaries apparent to the outside observer are expressed in the group-consciousness of the people within. The community is often small enough to function as the unit of personal observation, or, when it is somewhat larger and somewhat homogeneous, it can provide in some part of itself a unit of personal observation fully reflective of the whole; thus, activities and states of mind are much alike for all POWs in difficult circumstances past and present.[26]

The glue that binds POWs together is their ability to communicate. Even in the absolute silence of solitary confinement from the "black holes" of colonial prisons to "Alcatraz" in Hanoi, even the most rudimentary communication reinforced a sense of social relatedness among individuals to a point where they became cohesive communities during captivity and after repatriation. In captivity, with leadership exercised by senior POWs, the whole POW community often stood united against its captors. As David Westheimer dramatizes in *Von Ryan's Express,* without positive, unifying leadership, individual dissenting members often divided the community. Prisoners policed one another and relied heavily on one another for institutional support. If a prisoner collaborated or assimilated, the other members of the community took note and shunned him for what POWs considered betrayal, the worst sin of captivity. Inside the prison camp they formed institutions such as escape committees or Red Cross committees for their own welfare, protection, entertainment, or other necessities required for survival. Beginning with the Andersonville Survivors Association, after liberation, repatriation, and war's end, they formed POW veterans' associations. The American Defenders of Bataan and Corregidor, the American Ex-Prisoners of War Association, NAM-POW, and others continue to function as internal networks, political lobbies, and sometimes beneficial or protective organizations for individual members.

Prisoners' intuition dictates practicality; what works, works. Yet there is a strong reliance on a sense of what is morally and ethically correct in the face of fear. Two prized values are perseverance and courage. From the Civil War to Vietnam, thirty-four men and one woman received the Medal of Honor for valor directly related to the POW experience. Nine prisoners received it for escaping or resisting their captors, and two for heroic POW rescues. Beginning in 1944, individual efforts materialized into suggestions that POWs should be recognized with a service decoration, but the military services opposed that idea, saying there was no need. Public Law 303, a post–World War II provision of the War Claims Commission, paid compensation of $1.50 per day to any POW subjected to violations of the 1929 Geneva Convention. Public Law 97-37, the Former POW Benefits Act, expanded POW veterans' benefits from World War II and Korea to the government services for all former POWs. In 1960, President John F. Kennedy signed Executive Order 11016 authorizing the Purple Heart for POWs who were subjected to deprivation or mistreatment by captors in any future conflict. In 1971, F. Edward Herbert of Louisiana introduced a bill authorizing a lapel button for ex-prisoners. The bill was defeated. Later in 1971, Senator John G. Tower of Texas introduced the first bill to create a POW medal. As in the past, the services opposed it, and the bill withered. However, the Iran hostage crisis in 1979 changed some perceptions concerning hostile captivity.

Tensions between the United States and Iran during the 444-day Iranian crisis between November 1979 and January 1981 renewed American concern about the prisoner-hostage problem. On November 4, 1979, Iranian fundamentalist soldiers invaded the United States embassy in Teheran and captured fifty-two American embassy personnel. The Iranians caught an unsuspecting America completely off-guard. President Carter's military rescue attempt failed. After prolonged and public negotiations designed to humiliate the United States and President Carter, the American embassy hostages (technically not POWs except for uniformed personnel in the embassy staff) returned home as heroes. The Iran hostage crisis created its own popular icon: the yellow ribbon, derived not from a past tradition but from a popular song, "Tie a Yellow Ribbon Round an Old Oak Tree." More importantly, the Iran hostage crisis demonstrated that the ordeal of captivity often depends on the level of hostility that exists between captor and captive, not necessarily on the legal status based on international agreements. If nothing else, the Iran crisis heightened public awareness of the perils and dangers of captivity.

In 1985 Congress decided, against service opposition, to honor all former POWs by creating and issuing a new Prisoner of War Medal. Recipients included the 4,120 American World War I POWs, 130,201 from

World War II, 7,140 from Korea, and 766 from Vietnam. One critic pointed out that the United States is the only country in the world that has awarded a medal to individuals who surrendered to an enemy in the field of battle.[27] Dr. Robert Osbourn, in a 1985 speech to the National Former Prisoner of War Educational Conference in Dallas, Texas, commented that a POW represents a failed mission. The American ex-prisoner lives with embarrassment. The tradition of the American armed services is one of pride and success in which the POWs feel they cannot share, even when captivity is not their fault. In the end, most former POWs reject hostility against their former captors in favor of adopting quiet lives and seem very tolerant of the world around them.[28] Right or wrong, the medal now represents a mood in the United States that rewards not only the material manifestations of success but the spirit of success as well.

Between 1900 and 1967, 128 armed conflicts raged throughout the world, nearly two-thirds of which have occurred since 1945.[29] Taking prisoners, raiding prison camps, and treating prisoners in accordance with international agreements have been part of these conflicts. In January 1991, hostilities erupted between a coalition of nations, including the United States, Saudi Arabia, Great Britain, France, Italy, Canada, and others, and Iraq over the invasion and punitive occupation of Kuwait. In the first week of war, prisoners were taken on both sides. On January 19, 1991, President George Bush called the Iraqi ambassador to the White House to remind him by formal letter that his country was a signatory to the 1949 Geneva Convention. During the short one-month war, the Iraqi government refused to allow the International Red Cross to inspect the facilities it used for housing allied POWs. Conversely, the United States, Great Britain, France, and Saudi Arabia invited the International Red Cross to inspect the camps housing over 50,000 Iraqi prisoners. After the war, when allied troops entered Kuwait, they found the aftermath of atrocities not witnessed since World War II. When the field commanders met to discuss the terms of the cease fire on February 3, 1991, the first topic of conversation was the condition of the allied POWs. Latent here is not only the recognition that international law still exists to ameliorate the horrors of captivity but also the general fear that the American myth of the missing warrior might find a new landscape in a new war. During the war, a total of forty-nine American military personnel were listed as missing in action, and several journalists ventured too close to hostilities and fell into Iraqi hands.[30] (See Appendix 4C for Gulf War POW statistics.) According to the Department of Defense, the lessons learned in Vietnam, the improved communication technology, and a more friendly terrain for search and rescue acted in concert to reduce the possibilities that a former enemy could hold prisoners after the cessation of hostilities. Of the thirteen American servicemen listed as killed in action, body not recovered, twelve were lost over water, where the location of crash sites and recovery of remains presents extremely difficult problems.

In captivity, according to initial debriefing of returned prisoners by American intelligence officers, the American POWs suffered considerable mistreatment at the hands of the Iraqi army. Physical abuse ranged from electric shocks to bone breaking and routine slapping. Psychological abuse ranged from threats by the captors to cut off fingers to placing an unloaded weapon at the prisoner's head and pulling the trigger. Iraqi field commanders conducted initial interrogations to obtain military information. Later, the POWs were subjected to political interrogations akin to those used on POWs in Korea and Vietnam. After beating POWs with rubber hoses and inflicting wounds, the Iraqi interrogators forced the Americans to make recorded statements and television appearances. On February 4, 1991, the photograph of one prisoner, Lieutenant Jeffrey Zaun, USN, appeared on the cover of *Newsweek*.[31] Zaun had deliberately hit himself in the nose and face in order to make himself look terrible for the cameras. Another prisoner was connected to a car battery; the current was strong enough to cause a tooth to explode from its socket.

The Cold War ended in Europe in December 1991. In 1992, American POWs in Iraqi hands were exchanged, and Islamic hostage-takers in Lebanon freed their American hostages. In the international legal arena, beginning in 1966, the United Nations updated the 1949 Geneva Convention for participating nations and created an International Bill of Rights that included the International Covenant on Civil and Political Rights. No action was taken by the United States until President Carter submitted the covenant to Congress in 1977, and this document lay dormant until its congressional ratification in April 1992 and President George Bush's signature two months later. With this act, the United States joined 102 other countries that had ratified the document and ended a period when the United States talked about international human rights but did little.[32]

Perhaps the single most important lesson to learn from all the voices from captivity is that prisoners of war have rarely changed the course of history; wars have been won or lost, not because of them, but in spite of them. Although the technology of warfare has changed, the fearful horrors of captivity have not. For the individual soldier thrown into the uncertain life of a POW, possibly a life sentence without parole, victory becomes a day-by-day commitment to survival. Food becomes an obsession, and strong evidence suggests that a POW's will to live stems from a silent, invisible, and powerful well of religious, ethical, and moral faith.[33] Freedom becomes an ever-present dream of home and family. Some prisoners find themselves in a position to choose active self-liberation, or escape. For others, liberation, repatriation, exchange, and rescue are passive events. After repatriation, the prisoner's lament reflects the past and expresses hope for the future.

As a category of wartime literature, captivity narratives—whether first- or third-person memoirs—describe individual transformations based on pragmatic, life-saving value systems. Failure becomes success. Acts of defiance, resistance, escape, evasion, and liberation come together as the captive's defense against what on the surface may appear to be improbable odds. War is rarely, if ever, glorified or romanticized.

From coarse to elegant, their voices sing sad songs of the parts they played, large and small, in national wars that turned personal behind barbed wire. Defeat is not simply death or personal privation in a prison camp; it includes guilt generated by an individual's departure from the values of the community of prisoners for the sake of personal gain. In victory and defeat, POW narratives are dramas that expose individual human imperfections, passions, fears, and commitments when the chips are as far down as they can possibly be.

One can only hope that innocent human beings will never have their lives wasted behind barbed wire again.[34] Time is, after all, the only thing in life that is positively irreplaceable. Rather than being lost in the diffusive wake of time, the voices from captivity—loud or soft, defiant or cooperative, happy or sad, strong or weak—will continue to find a special place in the American experience.

Captivity Narrative Frameworks

A. Levels of Interpretive Distinction

1 Status	2 Polemic Intent	3 Action	4 Heroics	5 Beliefs	6 Fears	7 Faith
Captive	Jeremiad	Survive	Defeat	Success	Failure	Religion
Internee	Apology	Resist	Stoic	Abundance	Starvation	Country
Renegade	Complaint	Escape	Escape	Technology	Atrocities	Service
POW	Propaganda	Assimilate	Assimilator	Community	Solitude	Family
Hostage	Romance	Collaborate	Survivor	Duty	Weakness	Self
Evader	Entertainment	Sabotage	Raider	Law	Rejection	Community

B. Captivity Narrative Event-Scenarios

1 Precapture	2 Capture	3 Remove	4 Landscape	5 Resistance	6 Release	7 Lament
Soldier	Surrender	March	Prison	Taking Torture	Parole	Time
Airman	Shootdown	Truck	POW Camp	Military Code	Cartel	Money
Sailor	Sinking	Boat	Prison Hulk	Brainwashing	Treaty	Youth
Journalist	Overrun	Train	Dungeon	Passivity	Ransom	Family
Bystander	Invasion	Airplane	Compound	Communication	Escape	Chances
Passenger	Surrounded	Wagon	Factory/Farm	Conventions	Liberation	Rank
Statesman	Arrest	Animal	Cellar	Reeducation	Rescue	Guilt

297

Prison Ships and Prison Camps in Eighteenth- and Nineteenth-Century America

A. British Prison Ships in America 1776–1782

Wallabout Bay, New York (Brooklyn)

Prison Hulks:	John	Good Intent	Glasgow	Frederick	Chatham
	Whitby	Prince of	Good Hope	Kitty	Felicity
	Jersey	Wales			
	Preston	Grovnor	Judith	Woodlands	Myrtle
	Lord	Falmouth	Scheldt	Clyde	Scorpion
	Dunlace				
Hospital Ships:	Hunter	Persever-	Bristol		
		ance	Packet		

Prison Hulks in Charleston Harbor,
South Carolina: — Torbay — Pack-Horse
Prison Hulks in St. Lucia (West Indies): Peter

Source: Larry G. Bowman, *Captive Americans: Prisoners during the American Revolution* (Athens: Ohio University Press, 1976), 42.

B. Major Union Prison Camps

Name	Town	State	Population
Beaufort Hospital	Beaufort	South Carolina	Officer/Enlisted
Belle Plain Encampment	Fredericksburg	Virginia	Enlisted
Benton Barracks	St. Louis	Missouri	Enlisted
Camp Butler	Springfield	Illinois	Enlisted
Camp Chase	Columbus	Ohio	Enlisted
Camp Douglas	Chicago	Illinois	Enlisted
Camp Morton	Indianapolis	Indiana	Enlisted
Camp Parole	Annapolis	Maryland	Officer/Enlisted
Carroll Hall Prison	Fort Monroe	Virginia	Officers
David's Island	New York	New York	Enlisted
Elmira	Elmira	New York	Enlisted
Fort Columbus	Governor's Island	New York	Enlisted
Fort Delaware	Pea Patch Island	Delaware	Officer/Enlisted
Forest Hall Military Prison	Georgetown	District of Columbia	Officer/Enlisted
Fort Lafayette	New York	New York	Enlisted
Fort Leavenworth	Leavenworth	Kansas	Officer/Enlisted
Fort McHenry	Baltimore	Maryland	Enlisted
Fort Mifflin	Philadelphia	Pennsylvania	Enlisted
Fort Pickens	Pensacola	Florida	Enlisted
Fort Warren	Boston	Massachusetts	Officers

Appendix 2B continued

Name	Town	State	Population
Fort Wood	New York Harbor	New York	Enlisted
Gratiot Street Prison	St. Louis	Missouri	Enlisted
Hart's Island	New York Harbor	New York	Enlisted
Illinois State Prison	Alton	Illinois	Officer/Enlisted
Johnson's Island	Sandusky	Ohio	Officers
Lincoln General Hospital	Washington	District of Columbia	Officer/Enlisted
Louisville Prison	Louisville	Kentucky	Enlisted
McClean Barracks	Cincinnati	Ohio	Enlisted
Mackinac Island	Mackinac	Michigan	Enlisted
Morris Island	Charleston	South Carolina	Enlisted
Ohio State Penitentiary	Columbus	Ohio	Officers
Old Capitol Prison	Washington	District of Columbia	Political
Point Lookout	Baltimore	Maryland	Enlisted
Rock Island	Rock Island	Illinois	Enlisted
St. Helena's Church	Beaufort	South Carolina	Enlisted
St. Joseph Prison	St. Joseph	Missouri	Enlisted
Western Penn-sylvania	Allegheny City	Pennsylvania	Enlisted

C. Union Prison Camp at Elmira, New York: Morbidity and Mortality 1864

Month	POWs	Sick	Dead
September	9,480	563	385
October	9,441	640	276
November	8,258	666	207
December	8,401	758	269
January	8,602	1,015	285
February	8,996	1,398	426
			1,848

Source: James I. Robertson, "The Scourge of Elmira," in William Best Hesseltine, ed., *Civil War Prisons* (Kent, OH: Kent State University Press, 1989), 95, and *War of the Rebellion: A Compilation of the Official Records of the Union and Confederate Armies* (Washington, DC: Government Printing Office, 1880–1901), 997–1003.

D. Andersonville Deaths, 1864–1865

Year	Month	Number Held	Deaths
1864	February	1,600	
	March	7,500	283
	April	10,000	576
	May	15,000	708
	June	22,291	1,201
	July	29,030	1,817
	August	32,193	2,993
	September	17,733	2,677
	October	5,885	1,595
	November	2,024	499
	December	2,218	165
1865	January	4,931	197
	February	5,195	147
	March	4,800	108
	April		28

Source: Leon Basile, *The Civil War Diary of Amos E. Stearns, a Prisoner at Andersonville* (Rutherford, NJ: Farleigh Dickinson University Press, 1981), 117.

E. Major Confederate Prison Camps

Name	Town	State	Population
Americus	Americus	Georgia	Enlisted
Belle Island	Richmond	Virginia	Enlisted
Blackshear Prison	Blackshear	Georgia	Enlisted
Cahaba (Castle Morgan)	Cahaba	Alabama	Enlisted
Camp Asylum	Columbia	South Carolina	Enlisted
Camp Davidson	Savannah	Georgia	Enlisted
Camp Florence	Florence	South Carolina	Enlisted
Camp Ford	Tyler	Texas	Enlisted
Camp Groce	Hemstead	Texas	Enlisted
Camp Lawton	Millen	Georgia	Enlisted
Camp Oglethorpe	Macon	Georgia	Officers
Camp Sorghum	Columbia	South Carolina	Officers
Camp Sumter	Andersonville	Georgia	Enlisted
Castle Goodwin	Richmond	Virginia	Enlisted
Castle Pinckney	Charleston	South Carolina	Officers
Castle Thunder	Petersburg	Virginia	Enlisted
Charleston Jail	Charleston	South Carolina	Enlisted
City Jail	Savannah	Georgia	Enlisted
Crews Prison	Richmond	Virginia	Enlisted
Danville Prison	Danville	Virginia	Enlisted
Fort Norfolk	Norfolk	Virginia	Enlisted
Grant's Factory	Richmond	Virginia	Enlisted
Libby Prison	Richmond	Virginia	Officers
Liggons Prison	Richmond	Virginia	Enlisted
Marine Hospital	Savannah	Georgia	Officers

Appendix 2E continued

Name	Town	State	Population
Military Prison Camp	Lynchburg	Virginia	Enlisted
Old Cotton Factory	Salisbury	North Carolina	Enlisted
Old Hospital	Charleston	South Carolina	Enlisted
Paper Mill/Cotton Shed	Tuscaloosa	Alabama	Enlisted
Parrish Prison	New Orleans	Louisiana	Enlisted
Pemberton Prison	Richmond	Virginia	Enlisted
Salisbury Prison	Salisbury	North Carolina	Officers
Scott's Prison	Richmond	Virginia	Enlisted
Ship Island	Gulfport	Mississippi	Enlisted
Smith Factory	Richmond	Virginia	Enlisted
Southern Prison	Tupelo	Mississippi	Enlisted
Stockade Prison	Thomasville	Georgia	Enlisted
Tobacco Warehouses	Danville	Virginia	Enlisted

World War I and World War II Data

A. American Deaths in World War I from April 6, 1917 to November 11, 1918

Service	Troop Strength	Combat	Other	WIA
Army	2,057,675	50,510	55,868	193,663
Marines	32,385	2,461	390	9,520
Navy	80,000	431	6,856	819
Coast Guard	1,500	111	81	
Totals	2,171,560	53,513	63,195	204,002

Source: Richard K. Kolb, "Doughboys in 'No-Man's Land,'" *VFW Magazine* (November 1990): 21.

B. American Soldiers Taken Prisoner in World War I

Division	Number Captured
1	151
3	314
4	70
5	98
6	3
7	20
26	451
27	228
28	726
29	67
30	77
32	156
35	169
36	25
37	25
42	102
77	405
78	123
79	80
80	101
81	51
82	239
88	9
90	80
91	28
Total	3,798

Source: Herbert C. Fooks, *Prisoners of War* (Federalsburg, MD: J. W. Stowell, 1924), 4.

C. American Casualties and POW Losses in the European Theater: December 7, 1941–September 2, 1945

Force Strength	3,607,302
Combat Deaths	185,179
Other Deaths	17,505
Wounded	484,922
Captured	93,941
Died as POWs	1,121
Returned	92,820

Sources: "Theater Casualties," *VFW Magazine* (August 1991): 29, and "Behind Barbed Wire: POWs in the Pacific and Europe," *VFW Magazine* (November 1991): 64. The American Army air forces lost approximately 24,331 men killed and 8,175 wounded in the European and Mediterranean theaters. American POWs in Europe from 1942 to 1944 were largely airmen, except for those troops captured in North Africa and 22,554 American soldiers captured during the Battle of the Bulge in December 1944.

D. German Military Prison Camp Facilities in World War II

Designation	*Town/Map Coordinates*
Oflag IV C	Colditz, C6
Oflag VII B	Eichstätt, D5
Oflag VIII F/Oflag 74 (not on the map)	Braunschweig, B5
Oflag IX A/H	Spangenburg, C4
Oflag IX A/Z	Rotenburg, C4
Oflag X B	Nienburg, B4
Oflag XI/79	Braunschweig, B5
Oflag XIII B (not on the map)	Hammelburg, C4
Oflag XIII C	Ebelsback, C/D5
Oflag XXI B/Oflag 64	Altburgund/Schubin, Poland, B8
Stalag II A	Neubrandenburg, B6
Stalag II B	Hammerstein, B8
Stalag II E (not on the map)	Schwerin, Mecklenburg region
Stalag III A	Luckenwalde, B6
Stalag III B	Fürstenburg, B7
Stalag III C	Altdrewitz, B7
Stalag III D	Berlin/Steglitz, B6
Stalag IV A	Hohnstein, C7
Stalag IV B	Muhlberg, C6
Stalag IV C	Wistritz, Czechoslovakia, C6
Stalag IV D	Torgau, C6
Stalag IV D/Z	Annaburg, C6
Stalag IV F	Hartmannsdorf, C6
Stalag IV G	Oschatz, C6
Stalag V A	Ludwigsburg, D4
Stalag V B	Villingen, D4
Stalag V C	Offenburg, D3/4
Stalag VI G	Bonn, C3
Stalag VI J	Krefeld, C3
Stalag VII A	Moosburg, D5/6

PRISON CAMPS

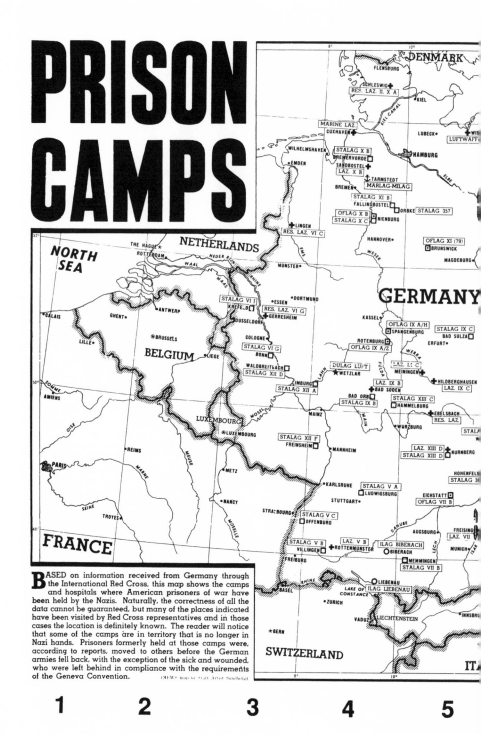

BASED on information received from Germany through the International Red Cross, this map shows the camps and hospitals where American prisoners of war have been held by the Nazis. Naturally, the correctness of all the data cannot be guaranteed, but many of the places indicated have been visited by Red Cross representatives and in those cases the location is definitely known. The reader will notice that some of the camps are in territory that is no longer in Nazi hands. Prisoners formerly held at those camps were, according to reports, moved to others before the German armies fell back, with the exception of the sick and wounded, who were left behind in compliance with the requirements of the Geneva Convention. (NEWS map by Staff Artist Sundberg)

1   **2**   **3**   **4**   **5**

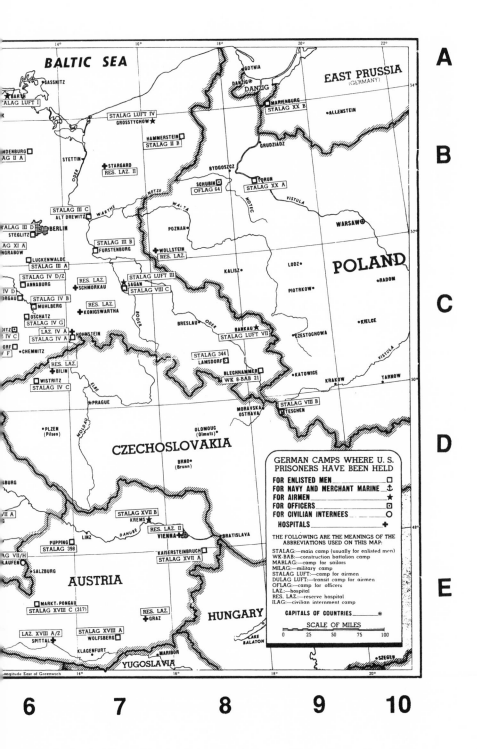

BALTIC SEA

SASSNITZ

•BARTH
STALAG LUFT I

GDYNIA

DANZIG DANZIG

EAST PRUSSIA
(GERMANY)

MARIENBURG
STALAG XX B

•ALLENSTEIN

STALAG LUFT IV
GROSSTYCHOW ★

HAMMERSTEIN
STALAG II B

GRUDZIADZ

DENBURG
AG II A

STETTIN

STARGARD
RES. LAZ. II

BYDGOSZCZ

TORUN
STALAG XX A

SCHUBIN
OFLAG 64

VISTULA

STALAG III C
ALT DREWITZ

WARTHE

NETZE

WARTA

NOTEC

WARSAW

STALAG III D
STEGLITZ BERLIN

AG XI A
NGRABOW

POZNAN•

STALAG III B
FURSTENBURG

•WOLLSTEIN
RES. LAZ.

KALISZ•

LODZ•

POLAND

•RADOM

LUCKENWALDE
STALAG III A

STALAG IV D/Z
ANNABURG

RES. LAZ.
SCHMORKAU

STALAG LUFT III
SAGAN
STALAG VIII C

PIOTRKOW•

•KIELCE

IV D
ORGAU

STALAG IV B
MUHLBERG

RES. LAZ.
KONIGSWARTHA

ODER

BRESLAU•

ODER

BANKAU ★
STALAG LUFT VII

•CZESTOCHOWA

VISTULA

OSCHATZ
STALAG IV G

ITZ
IV C

LAZ. IV A
STALAG IV A HOHNSTEIN

STALAG 344
LAMSDORF

•KATOWICE

KRAKOW•

TARNOW•

ORF
V F •CHEMNITZ

RES. LAZ.
BILIN

BLECHHAMMER
WK 8-BAB 21

WISTRITZ
STALAG IV C

ELBE

•PRAGUE

MORAVSKA
OSTRAVA

STALAG VIII B
TESCHEN

•PLZEN
(Pilsen)

MOLDAU

OLOMOUC
(Olmutz)•

CZECHOSLOVAKIA

BRNO•
(Brunn)

BURG

VII A

STALAG XVII B
KREMS ★

RES. LAZ. II

DANUBE

PUPPING
STALAG 398

LINZ

VIENNA

BRATISLAVA

AG VII/H
LAUFEN

•SALZBURG

KAISERSTEINBRUCH
STALAG XVII A

AUSTRIA

MARKT-PONGAU
STALAG XVIII C (317)

RES. LAZ.
GRAZ

HUNGARY

LAZ. XVIII A/Z
SPITTAL

STALAG XVIII A
WOLFSBERG

KLAGENFURT

•MARIBOR

LAKE
BALATON

•SZEGED

YUGOSLAVIA

Longitude East of Greenwich

GERMAN CAMPS WHERE U. S.
PRISONERS HAVE BEEN HELD

FOR ENLISTED MEN□
FOR NAVY AND MERCHANT MARINE⚓
FOR AIRMEN★
FOR OFFICERS⊡
FOR CIVILIAN INTERNEES○
HOSPITALS✚

THE FOLLOWING ARE THE MEANINGS OF THE
ABBREVIATIONS USED ON THIS MAP:

STALAG:—main camp (usually for enlisted men)
WK-BAB:—construction battalion camp
MARLAG:—camp for sailors
MILAG:—military camp
STALAG LUFT:—camp for airmen
DULAG LUFT:—transit camp for airmen
OFLAG:—camp for officers
LAZ.:—hospital
RES. LAZ.:—reserve hospital
ILAG:—civilian internment camp

CAPITALS OF COUNTRIES_____⊛

SCALE OF MILES

0   25   50   75   100

A

B

C

D

E

6   7   8   9   10

Appendix 3D continued

Designation	Town/Map Coordinates
Stalag VII B	Memmingen, D/E5
Stalag VIII A (not on the map)	Gorlitz, Silesia
Stalag VIII B	Teschen, Poland, D9
Stalag VIII C	Sagan, C7
Stalag IX B	Bad Orb, C4
Stalag IX C	Bad Sulza, C5
Stalag X B	Bremervorde, B4
Stalag X C	Nienburg, B4
Stalag XI A	Altengrabow, B6
Stalag XI B	Fallingbostel, B4
Stalag XII A	Limburg, C4
Stalag XII D	Waldbreitbach, C3
Stalag XII F	Freinsheim, D4
Stalag XIII B	Weiden, D6
Stalag XIII C	Hammelburg, C4
Stalag XIII D	Nuremberg, D5
Stalag XVII A	Kaisersteinbruch, Austria, E/D8
Stalag XVII B	Krems/Gneizendorf, Austria, D7
Stalag XVIII A	Wolfsberg, Austria, E7
Stalag XVIII C/Stalag 317	Markt/Pongau, Austria, E6
Stalag 357	Orbke, B4
Stalag XX A	Torun, Poland, B9
Stalag XX B	Marienburg, A/B9
Stalag 344	Lamsdorf, C8
Stalag 383	Hohenfels, D5
Stalag 398	Pupping, Austria, D6/7
Work Camp 21	Blechhammer, C9
Dulag Luft	Wetzlar, C4
Stalag Luft I	Barth, A6
Stalag Luft III	Sagan, C7
Stalag Luft IV	Grosstychow, B8
Stalag Luft VI (not on map)	Heydekrug, East Prussia
Stalag Luft VII	Bankau, C9
Marlag-Milag	Tarmstedt, B4
Marine (Naval) Lazarett	Cuxhaven, B4
Luftwaffe (Air Force) Lazarett 4/II	Wismar, B5
Luftwaffe Lazarett IX C	Meiningen, C5
Luftwaffe Lazarett IX C	Hildberghausen, C5
Luftwaffe Lazarett XIII D	Nuremberg, D5
Luftwaffe Lazarett VII	Freising, D5
Luftwaffe Lazarett IV G	Leipzig, C6
Luftwaffe Lazarett XVIII A/Z	Spittal, Austria, E6
Lazarett XB (Army)	Sandbostel, B4
Lazarett IX B (Army)	Bad Soden, C4
Lazarett VB (Army)	Rottenmunster, D4

Appendix 3D continued

Designation	Town/Map Coordinates
Res. Laz. II	Vienna, Austria, D8
Res. Laz. II, XA	Schleswig, A4
Res. Laz. II	Stargard, B7
Res. Laz. IV A	Hohnstein, C7
Res. Laz. VI C	Lingen, B3
Res. Laz. VI G	Gerresheim, C3
Res. Laz. (no designation)	Schmorkau, C7
Res. Laz. (no designation)	Königswartha, C7
Res. Laz. (no designation)	Graz, Austria, E7
Res. Laz. (no designation)	Berlin, C6
Res. Laz. (no designation)	Ebelsbach, C/D5
Res. Laz. (no designation)	Wollstein, B8

Source: Stan Sommers, *The European Story* (Marshfield, WI: National Ex-Prisoners of War, 1980), 22–23; map courtesy of the American Ex-POW Association.

E. U.S. Prisoners in the Pacific Theater, 1941–1945

Location	Captured	Deaths	Liberations
Philippines	22,000	5,135	1,500
Wake Island	1,555	100	
Java	890		
Japan and elsewhere	300	1,200	11,400
Celebes	255		200
Guam	400		
China	200		20
Hell Ships (Transport)		3,840	
Korean PW Camps		70	150
Burmese PW Camps		130	480
Manchurian PW Camps		175	1,200
Totals	25,600	10,650	14,950

Source: E. Bartlett Kerr, *Surrender and Survival: The Experience of American POWs in the Pacific 1941–1945* (New York: William Morrow, 1985), 335–40.

Twentieth-Century Data

A. U.S. Prisoners of War in the Twentieth Century

	WW I	WW II	Korea	Vietnam	Total
Captured and interned	4,120	130,201	7,140	766	142,227
Died while POW	147	14,072	2,701	114	17,034
Returned to U.S. control	3,973	116,129	4,418	651	125,171
Alive 1/1/91	130	67,135	3,260	600	71,125
Refused repatriation	0	0	21	0	21
MIA	3,350	78,773	8,177	2,453	92,753

Source: Charles Stegner, "Report," in Tom Williams, *Post Traumatic Stress Disorders: A Handbook for Clinicians* (Cincinnati: DAV, 1987), 131, and John S. Edwards, ed., *American Ex-Prisoners of War* (Paducah, KY: Turner, 1991), 2, 78.

B. U.S. POWs/MIAs in Southeast Asia

	POW/MIA	KIA/BNR[a]	Total
North Vietnam	348	233	581
South Vietnam	450	625	1,075
Laos	333	195	528
Cambodia	37	46	83
China	4	2	6
Totals	1,172	1,101	2,273

[a]KIA/BNR = Killed in action, body not recovered.
Source: Rod Colvin, *First Heroes: The POWs Left Behind in Vietnam* (New York: Irvington, 1987), 19.

C. Americans in Iraqi Hands during the Gulf War, 1991

	Army	Air Force	Navy	Marine Corps	Total
Captured and released	7	8	3	5	23
KIA, body recovered	0	7	3	3	13
KIA, body not recovered	0	10	3	0	13
Missing in action	0	0	0	0	0
Total	7	25	9	8	49

Source: *POW-MIA Fact Book* (Washington, DC: Department of Defense, July 1991), 34.

NOTES

INTRODUCTION

1. See Ernst Breisach, *Historiography: Ancient, Medieval, and Modern* (Chicago: University of Chicago Press, 1983), 1–4.

2. Terrence Des Pres, *The Survivor: An Anatomy of Life in the Death Camps* (New York: Oxford University Press, 1976), 30–31, 202.

3. Arthur A. Durand, *Stalag Luft III: The Secret Story* (Baton Rouge: Louisiana State University Press, 1988), 363.

4. Elizabeth Head Vaughn, *Community under Stress: An Internment Camp Culture* (Princeton, NJ: Princeton University Press, 1949).

CHAPTER ONE. SOLDIER CHRONICLES: THE BORDERS
OF MILITARY CAPTIVITY

1. For a list of all the Indian wars, as well as their causes and results, see Ray Allen Billington, *The Westward Movement in the United States* (New York: D. Van Nostrand, 1959), 16–78. For a description and list of soldier-captives taken from New England to Canada in the New England wars, see Emma Lewis Coleman, *New England Captives Carried to Canada,* 2 vols. (Portland, ME: Southworth, 1925) 2:331–85.

2. The entire narrative is contained in Alden T. Vaughan and Edward W. Clark, eds., *Puritans among the Indians: Accounts of Captivity and Redemption 1676–1724* (Cambridge, MA: Belknap, 1981), 93–131. See also Stuart Trueman, *The Ordeal of John Gyles* (Toronto: McClellend and Stewart, 1966), a third-person account of Gyles's adventures.

3. Richard M. VanDerBeets, ed., *The Indian Captivity Narrative: An American Genre* (New York: University Press of America, 1984), 15.

4. Richard M. Dorson, ed., *America Rebels: Narratives of the Patriots* (New York: Pantheon, 1953), 31.

5. Albert Greene, *Recollections of the Jersey Prison Ship from the Manuscript of Captain Thomas Dring* (1829). Introduction by Lawrence H. Leder (New York: Corinth Books, 1961), ix.

6. *Martyrs to the Revolution in British Prison-Ships in the Wallabout Bay* (New York: W. H. Arthur, 1855), 9. See also Larry G. Bowman, *Captive Americans: Prisoners during the American Revolution* (Athens: Ohio University Press, 1976), 42, for a listing of British prison hulks in New York, Charleston, and St. Lucia.

7. Ibid., 19.

8. Parker B. Brown, " 'Crawford's Defeat': A Ballad," *Western Pennsylvania Historical Magazine* 64.4 (October 1981): 311.

9. Robert A. Sherrard, *A Narrative of the Wonderful Escape and Dreadful Sufferings of Colonel James Paul* (Cincinnati, OH: J. Drake, 1869), 8.

10. U.S. House, *Report on the Spirit and Manner in Which the War Has Been Waged by the Enemy* (New York: Garland, 1978), 3–4.

11. Edward S. Wallace, "Deserters in the Mexican War," *Hispanic American Historical Review* 15:2 (August 1935): 376.

12. William Best Hesseltine, *Civil War Prisons: A Study in Prison Psychology* (Columbus: Ohio State University Press, 1930), 256. In "The Treatment of Prisoners during the War between the States" (*Southern Historical Society Papers* 1:3 [March 1876]): 123, Alexander H. Stevens argues that of the 270,000 Union prisoners in Confederate hands, only 22,576 died. The Union held approximately 220,000 Confederates, of whom 26,436 died in captivity. According to Stevens, the mortality percentages show conclusively that Union treatment of Confederates was far worse than Confederate treatment of Union prisoners.

13. Richard Garrett, *P.O.W.: The Uncivil Face of War* (Newton Abbot, Eng.: David and Charles, 1981), 90.

14. See Jefferson T. Hammer, *Frederic Augustus James's Civil War Diary* (Rutherford, NJ: Fairleigh Dickinson University Press, 1973), 9f.

15. Richmond *Dispatch*, March 12, 1863, quoted in Hesseltine, *Civil War Prisons*, 195.

16. The complete title of Corcoran's narrative is *The Captivity of General Corcoran: The Only Authentic and Reliable Narrative of the Trials and Sufferings Endured during His Twelve Months' Imprisonment in Richmond and Other Southern Cities by Brig.-General Michael Corcoran, the Hero of Bull Run*. Hesseltine believes that because of the book's overt Union propaganda, it was probably used as a recruiting device, especially for Irish immigrants in New York and perhaps in some other large cities.

17. Hesseltine, *Civil War Prisons*, 177.

18. Ibid.

19. Ibid., 192.

20. Ibid., 209. See "The Treatment of Prisoners during the War between the States," *Southern Historical Society Papers* 1:3 (March 1876): 132ff, for the complete text of the Confederate government's report presented on March 3, 1865.

21. Barziza's narrative was discovered by R. Henderson Shuffler and published in 1964 by the University of Texas Press at Austin. Shuffler writes that the Barziza narrative is "one of the rarest and least known of the published memoirs of Texans who fought in the Civil War." Further, it is "the only known published memoir of a Texan who wrote of his experiences as a prisoner during the Civil War and one of the few such accounts published on either side before the end of the conflict" (ix).

22. See Albert J. Beveridge, "As Witnessed in Germany: German System Seen in Camp, Hospital, and Prison," *American Review of Reviews* (May 1915), in Harold Elk Straubling, ed., *The Last Magnificent War: Rare Journalistic and Eyewitness Accounts of World War I* (New York: Paragon House, 1989), 266–71.

23. Ibid., 267.

24. See *Evidence and Documents Laid before the Committee on Alleged German Outrages* (London: Committee on Alleged German Outrages, 1915) and James Morgan Read, *Atrocity Propaganda 1914–1919* (New Haven, CT: Yale University Press, 1941).

25. Richard K. Kolb, "Doughboys in 'No-Man's Land,' " *Veteran of Foreign Wars Magazine* (November 1990), 21.

26. Mike Shallin, "The Guest of the Kaiser," in Henry Berry, ed., *Make the Kaiser Dance* (New York: Doubleday, 1978), 347–51.

27. Morris Janowitz, *The Professional Soldier: A Social and Political Portrait* (New York: Free Press, 1960), 219.

28. One ex-POW from Bataan wrote a letter to the author saying that his captors had asked him to go to Vichy French Indochina as a collaborative exercise. He refused and was returned to his POW community.

29. Edward Russell, *The Knights of Bushido* (London: Transworld, 1958), 73.

30. Ibid., 75.

31. For a review of the "Yellow Peril" stereotype, see Gary Hoppenstand, "Yellow Devil Doctors and Opium Dens: A Survey of the Yellow Peril Stereotypes in Mass Media Entertainment," in Christopher D. Geist and Jack Nachbar, eds., *The Popular Culture Reader* 3d ed. (Bowling Green, OH: Bowling Green State University Popular Press, 1983), 171–85. See also E. Bartlett Kerr, *Surrender and Survival: The Experience of American POWs in the Pacific 1941–1945* (New York: William Morrow, 1985), 24, for a discussion of Irvin Wallace's fictional character, Hashimura Togo, and George Feifer, *Tennozan: The Battle of Okinawa and the Atomic Bomb* (New York: Ticknor and Fields, 1992), 114–15, 120–27, for the causes of Japanese and American war psychosis—Yellow Peril vs. Yankee Peril—why Japanese killed themselves before surrender, Bushido, and Japanese feelings about an honorable soldierly death.

32. Representative government documents containing narrative testimonies include Office of the Adjutant General, *Procedures for Processing Return, and Reassignment of Exchangees in Korea* (Washington, DC: U.S. Army Center of Military History, 1951); Thomas T. Jones, "Two Hundred Miles to Freedom," *Military Engineering* 43: 295 (1951): 351–54; Bernard Cohen and Maurice Cooper, *A Follow Up Study of World War II Prisoners of War* (Washington, DC: GPO, 1954); Ray M. Dowe, "A Prisoner Can Profit," *Army Information Digest* 9:6 (1954): 41–47; U.S. Department of Defense, *POW: The Fight Continues After the Battle: The Report of the Secretary of Defense's Advisory Committee on Prisoners of War* (Washington, DC: GPO, 1955); U.S. Department of the Army, *Communist Interrogation, Indoctrination, and Exploitation of Prisoners of War* (Washington, DC: GPO, 1956); U.S. Senate, Committee on Government Operations, *Communist Interrogation, Indoctrination, and Exploitation of American Military and Civilian Prisoners,* Senate Report No. 2832, 84th Congress, 2d sess. (Washington, DC: GPO, 1957); Donald L. Manes, "Barbed Wire Command," *Military Review* 43: 9 (1963): 38–56; and Delmar Spivey, "The Soldier and the Prisoner," *Marine Corps Gazette* 49:5 (1965): 36–44.

33. See U.S. Senate, Committee on Government Operations, *Korean War Atrocities,* Senate Report No. 848, 83d Congress, 2d sess., January 11, 1954 (Washington, DC: GPO, 1954), for a variety of personal narratives.

34. See Bryan Boswell, "The Pentagon POW Scandal," *Weekend Australian,* December 9–10, 1989, 4. The author argues that the North Korean government still holds a significant number of American POWs.

35. Joe P. Dunn, "The POW Chronicles: A Bibliographic Review," *Armed Forces and Society* 9:3 (Spring 1983): 495.

36. See "The Vietnam War POW/MIAs: An Annotated Bibliography," *Bulletin of Bibliography* 45:2 (June 1988): 152–58. See also F. C. Brown's bibliographic compilations: *POW/MIA Indochina 1861–1991,* Monograph 6 (Hamilton Township, NJ: Rice Paddy, 1992); *POW/MIA Indochina 1946–1986: An Annotated Bibliography of Non-Fiction Works Dealing with Prisoners of War/Missing in Action* (Hamilton Township, NJ: Rice Paddy, 1988), and *Annotated Bibliography of Vietnam Fiction* (Mesa, AZ: Rice Paddy, 1987).

CHAPTER TWO. THE EVOLUTION OF POW STATUS:
ESTABLISHING ORDER IN CAPTIVITY

1. Telford Taylor, *Nuremberg and Vietnam: An American Tragedy* (Chicago: Quadrangle, 1970), 41.

2. Richard Garrett, *P.O.W.: The Uncivil Face of War* (Newton Abbot, Eng.: David and Charles, 1981), 17f.

3. Eoin MacNeill, *Phases of Irish History* (Dublin: M. H. Gill and Son, 1937), 228.

4. See Henry J. Webb, "Prisoners of War in the Middle Ages," *Military Affairs* 12:1 (Spring 1948): 46–49, for a brief but very good description of military captivity during this time. See also John Keegan, *The Face of Battle* (New York: Viking, 1975) for a description and discussion of the POW problem and King Henry V's solution after the battle of Agincourt.

5. Taylor, *Nuremberg and Vietnam*, 59.

6. Ibid., 60.

7. See Paul E. Sigmund, ed., *St. Thomas Aquinas on Politics and Ethics* (New York: Norton, 1988), 64f, for a discussion of St. Thomas's and St. Augustine's positions. See also Michael Walzer, *Just and Unjust Wars* (New York: Harper Collins, 1977) for discussions of "higher intention" as a rationale for both aggressive and defensive military action, morality, aggression, conventions, dilemmas, and responsibilities in war.

8. Taylor, *Nuremberg and Vietnam*, 62.

9. Ibid., 63. Donald A. Wells, *War Crimes and Laws of War* (New York: University Press of America, 1984), 63.

10. Taylor, *Nuremberg and Vietnam*, 63.

11. Ibid., 68.

12. Hamilton Vreeland, *Hugo Grotius: The Father of the Modern Science of International Law* (New York: Oxford University Press, 1917), 165f.

13. Ibid., 173.

14. Ibid., 166f.

15. Hugo Grotius, *On the Rights of War and Peace,* an abridged translation by William Whewell (Cambridge: Cambridge University Press, 1853), 387.

16. A. J. Barker, *Prisoners of War* (New York: Universe Books, 1975), 6.

17. John W. Blassingame, *The Slave Community: Plantation Life in the Antebellum South* (New York: Oxford University Press, 1979), 49–50.

18. Ibid., 50.

19. Garrett, *P.O.W.: The Uncivil Face of War,* 28.

20. Wells, *War Crimes and Laws of War,* 116. See also Taylor, *Nuremberg and Vietnam,* 65.

21. Carl von Clausewitz, *On War* (New York: Penguin, 1968), 101.

22. Barker, *Prisoners of War,* 9.

23. Herbert C. Fooks, *Prisoners of War* (Federalsburg, MD: J. W. Stowell, 1924), 272.

24. Karl J. R. Arndt, ed., *The Treaty of Amity and Commerce of 1785 between His Majesty the King of Prussia and the United States of America* (Munich: Heinz Moos, 1977), 18–19.

25. Ibid., 7.

26. Ibid.

27. Fooks, *Prisoners of War,* 13. See also Article 16 of the Treaty of Peace and Amity between the United States and Tripoli, concluded June 4, 1805. According to Ernest Dupuy and William Baumer, *Little Wars of the United States,*

American prisoners taken at sea were interned at Brasseterre on the island of St. Kitts during the 1797 Undeclared War with France (11).

28. Ernest Dupuy and William Baumer, *The Little Wars of the United States* (New York: Hawthorne, 1968), 14–15.

29. Ibid., 11.

30. Ibid., 23.

31. See Charles Andrews, *The Prisoners' Memoirs, or, Dartmoor Prison* (New York: privately printed, 1815), 11–21.

32. Ibid., 96.

33. Barker, *Prisoners of War,* 13f. Barker also explains Lieber's rationale for not taking prisoners at all.

34. Hague Conference ratified by the United States on December 3, 1909, Section 1. On Belligerents; Chapter II, Articles 4 through 20, Prisoners of War, in James Brown Scott, ed., *The Hague Conventions and Declarations of 1899 and 1907* (New York: Oxford University Press, 1918), 108–15.

35. Richard Garrett, *The Raiders: The World's Most Elite Strike Forces That Altered the Course of War and History* (New York: Van Nostrand Reinhold, 1980), 187.

36. Edward Russell, *The Knights of Bushido* (London: Transworld, 1958), 73f.

37. Garrett, *The Raiders,* 187. See also Barker, *Prisoners of War,* 212–27, for an explanation of the major points in the text of the 1949 Geneva Convention relative to the Treatment of Prisoners of War (GPW).

38. General Douglas MacArthur, quoted in Telford Talor's *Nuremberg and Vietnam* as the opening page.

39. Allen W. Cameron, ed., *Vietnam Crisis* (Ithaca, NY: Cornell University Press, 1976), 114–15, cited in Henry J. Kenny, *The American Role in Vietnam and East Asia: Between Two Revolutions* (New York: Praeger, 1984), 12–13.

40. Sydney Axinn, *A Moral Military* (Philadelphia: Temple University Press, 1989), 87f.

41. Barker, *Prisoners of War,* 15.

42. U.S. Senate. Committee on Government Operations, *Korean War Atrocities* (Washington, DC: GPO, 1954), 2.

43. Ibid., 3.

44. Axinn, *A Moral Military,* 48–49.

45. Ibid., 52.

46. U.S. Department of the Army, *Soldier's Manual of Common Tasks: Skill Level 1* (Washington, DC: GPO, 1990), 724–26.

CHAPTER THREE. CAPTIVITY LITERATURE: ANTECEDENTS AND THE CONTEXT OF AMERICAN COLONIAL NARRATIVES

1. Richard M. VanDerBeets, *The Indian Captivity Narrative: An American Genre* (New York: University Press of America, 1984), x.

2. Samuel P. Bayard, "The Materials of Folklore," *Journal of American Folklore* 66:259 (January-March 1953): 1–17.

3. Stith Thompson, *Motif-Index of Folk Literature* (Bloomington: Indiana University Press, 1957), 5:268–305. See also D. L. Ashliman, *A Guide to Folktales in the English Language* (New York: Greenwood, 1987), 60f.

4. For Ragnar Lodbrok's captivity in the heroic age, see Margaret Schlauch, trans., *The Saga of the Volsungs: The Saga of Ragnar Lodbrok Together with the*

Lay of Kraka (New York and London: George Allen and Unwin, 1949), 380f, and Oliver Elton, trans., *The First Nine Books of the Danish History of Saxo Grammaticus* (London: David Nutt, 1894), 380f.

5. Bertrand H. Bronson, *The Traditional Tunes of the Child Ballads* (Princeton: Princeton University Press, 1959), 410f. In Cecil Sharp's *English Folk Songs from the Southern Appalachians* (1932) and most other American collections, the ballad appears as "Lord Bateman" or in broadside distribution as "The Turkish Lady."

6. For a complete list and text, see Roger D. Abrahams and George Foss, *Anglo-American Folksong Style* (Englewood Cliffs, NJ: Prentice-Hall, 1968), 92–93, 101–2.

7. See George Lyman Kittredge and Helen Child Sargent, *English and Scottish Popular Ballads* (Cambridge, MA: Riverside, 1932), 95.

8. John Cotton, "The Divine Right to Occupy the Land," *Old South Leaflets, Published by the Directors of the Old South Wark, Old South Meeting House in 8 Volumes* (Documents 1–200), in Boston, *The Annals of America I* (Chicago: Britannica, 1968), 107–9. See Richard Drinnon, *Facing West: The Metaphysics of Indian-Hating and Empire-Building* (New York: New American Library, 1980), 35–61, 45, for rich details of the Pequot War and its aftermath. See also Alexis de Tocqueville, "Present and Future Condition of the Indians" (1838) in Louis Filler and Allen Guttmann, eds., *The Removal of the Cherokee Nation: Manifest Destiny or National Dishonor* (Lexington, MA: D. C. Heath, 1962), 85–93. The editors cite a letter written by M. de Senonville, the governor of Canada, to Louis XIV in 1685 explaining to the king that the French won the friendship of the Indians in America by a process of acceptance and assimilation (87).

9. Ray Allen Billington, *The Westward Movement in the United States* (New York: D. Van Nostrand, 1959), 16–78. Emma Lewis Coleman, *New England Captives Carried to Canada* (Portland, ME: Southworth, 1925) 1:1–11.

10. Alden T. Vaughan and Edward W. Clark, *Puritans among the Indians: Accounts of Captivity and Redemption, 1676–1724* (Cambridge, MA: Belknap, 1981), 139.

11. See Pauline Turner Strong, "Captive Images," *Natural History* 94:12 (December 1985): 51–56, for an extended discussion of *The Sovereignty and Goodness of God* (1682) in the context of King Philip's War on the New England battleground.

12. J. Norman Heard, *White into Red: A Study of the Assimilation of White Persons Captured by Indians* (Metuchen, NJ: Scarecrow, 1973), 2.

13. Ibid.

14. Richard Slotkin, *Regeneration through Violence: The Mythology of the American Frontier, 1600–1860* (Middletown, CT: Wesleyan University Press, 1973), 94.

15. VanDerBeets, *The Indian Captivity Narrative*, x.

16. Ibid., 3. For a large collection of 311 Indian captivity narratives in 111 volumes, see William Washburn, *The Garland Library of Narratives of North American Indian Captivities* (New York: Garland, 1978). See also Annette Kolodny's "Review," *Early American Literature* 14 (1979): 229–35; and Frances Roe Kestler's study of women in Indian captivity, *The Indian Captivity: A Woman's View* (New York: Garland, 1990).

17. VanDerBeets, *The Indian Captivity Narrative*, 7.

18. "Cry havoc!" means that no prisoners would be taken.

19. See Coleman, *New England Captives Carried to Canada* 1:52–53. Both

French and English colonies offered cash for scalps. In 1696, the Massachusetts colony declared an "Act of Reward," which declared a paid cash payment per scalp of every adult male Indian and for Indian women or children brought in as prisoners. Anyone claiming to have killed an Indian had to present the Indian scalp as proof.

20. See Kathryn Zabelle Derounian, "Puritan Orthodoxy and the 'Survivor's Syndrome' in Mary Rowlandson's Indian Captivity Narrative," *Early American Literature* 22 (Spring 1987): 82–93.

21. Slotkin, *Regeneration through Violence,* 128.

22. VanDerBeets, *The India Captivity Narrative,* 14. George Lyman Kittredge, *Witchcraft in Old and New England* (Cambridge, MA: Harvard University Press, 1929), 373. See also David L. Minter, "By Dens of Lions: Notes on Stylizations on Early Puritan Captivity Narratives," *American Literature* 45 (1975): 335–47, and William S. Simmons, "Cultural Bias in the New England Puritans' Perceptions of the Indians," *William and Mary Quarterly* 3d Series 38 (1981): 56–72. Simmons shows how the reliance of Puritan Calvinism on the printed word in the Old Testament stood diametrically opposed to anamistic native religious faith and thus helped to create the belief that the Indians were demons in service of Satan.

23. Roy Harvey Pearce, *The Savages of America: A Study of the Indian and the Idea of Civilization* (Baltimore, MD: Johns Hopkins University Press, 1953), 3.

24. Clarence W. Alvord and Lee Bidwood, *The First Explorations of the Trans-Allegheny Region by the Virginians, 1650–1764* (Cleveland, OH: Arthur H. Clark, 1912), 221–25, quoted in Billington, *Westward Movement,* 95–98.

25. Marie LeRoy and Barbara Leininger, "Narrative of Marie LeRoy and Barbara Leininger," *Pennsylvania German Society Proceedings* 15 (1906): 112–22.

26. VanDerBeets, *The Indian Captivity Narrative,* 16.

27. R. W. G. Vail, *The Voice of the Old Frontier* (Philadelphia: University of Pennsylvania Press, 1949), 26.

28. Heard, *White into Red,* 26ff.

29. Coleman, *New England Captives Carried to Canada* 2: 276–77.

30. E. G. Cattermole, *Famous Frontiersmen, Pioneers and Scouts* (Chicago: Donohue, 1888), 103. See also Molly Finney, *The Means Massacre: Molly Finney, the Canadian Captive,* ed., Charles P. Illsley (Freeport, ME: Freeport Press, 1932).

31. Cattermole, *Famous Frontiersmen,* 124.

32. Kestler, *The Indian Captivity Narrative,* xxii. Concerning the subjects of ethnological reportage one finds in Indian captivities, see Marius Barbeau, "Indian Captivities," *Proceedings of the American Philosophical Society* 94 (1950): 522–48. For a fictionalized version of the Ortiz captivity, see Andrew Lytle's 1941 short story, "Ortiz's Mass," in *At the Moon's Inn* (Tuscaloosa: University of Alabama Press, 1990), 122–50. Lytle created "Ortiz's Mass" via the report of the U.S. De Soto Commission, appointed by Franklin D. Roosevelt to research the 1539 De Soto Expedition and commemorate it in 1939.

33. Heard, *White to Red,* 1–2.

34. For a treatment of the defeated hero from Roland to Custer, see Bruce R. Rosenberg, *Custer and the Epic of Defeat* (University Park: Penn State University Press, 1974), 3. For the Sioux-Cheyenne version, called the Battle of the Greasy Grass, see William L. Byron, Jr., *Montana's Indians Yesterday and Today,* Montana Graphic Series 11 (Helena, MT: Montana Magazine, 1985), 26–29.

35. VanDerBeets, *The Indian Captivity Narrative,* 50.

CHAPTER FOUR. CONSTRUCTING THE NARRATIVE CONTOUR:
TIME, DOMAINS, SEQUENCE, AND EVENT-SCENARIOS

1. Clifford Geertz, *The Interpretation of Cultures* (New York: Basic, 1973), 362.
2. Captain Giles R. Norrington, USN (Retired), Public Address, Penn State University, 7 October 1989.
3. Pierre Boulle, *My Own River Kwai,* trans. Xan Fielding (New York: Vanguard, 1966), 170.
4. See John Cawelti, "The Question of Popular Genres," *Journal of Popular Film and Television* 13:4 (Winter 1986): 56.
5. See R. Gordon Kelly, "Literature and the Historian," *American Quarterly* 26 (May 1974): 141–59.
6. See Hayden White, *The Content of the Form: Narrative Discourse and Historical Representation* (Baltimore, MD: Johns Hopkins University Press, 1987), 1, 14. White separates the narrative from other forms of historical writing—documents, annals, and chronicles—by suggesting that narrators seize the opportunities to reflect on moral and ethical significances, thus creating a sense of wholeness or closure to their narrative discourse.

CHAPTER FIVE. BECOMING A PRISONER OF WAR:
TRANSFORMATION AND INITIATION

1. Mary Rowlandson, *The Sovereignty and Goodness of God* (1682) in Alden T. Vaughan and Edward W. Clark, eds., *Puritans among the Indians: Accounts of Captivity and Redemption, 1676–1724* (Cambridge, MA: Belknap, 1981), 64.
2. For an analog to Mary Rowlandson's approach to the captivity experience, see Peter Williamson, *Sufferings of Peter Williamson, One of the Settlers in the Back Parts of Pennsylvania Written by Himself* (1757), quoted in Richard VanDerBeets, ed., *Held Captive by Indians: Selected Narratives 1642–1836* (Knoxville: University of Tennessee Press, 1973), 216–27.
3. For the story of Barbara Leininger's cousin, Regina, see Henry Melchior Muhlenberg, "Regina, the German Captive," *Pennsylvania German Society Proceedings* 15 (1906): 87–92.
4. Marie LeRoy and Barbara Leininger, "The Narrative of Marie LeRoy and Barbara Leininger," *Pennsylvania-German Society Proceedings* 15 (1906): 111.
5. Ibid., 112.
6. John Frederick Schroeder, *Maxims of Washington* (Mount Vernon, VA: Mount Vernon Ladies Association, 1974), 154.
7. Ethan Allen, *A Narrative of Colonel Ethan Allen's Captivity Containing His Voyages and Travels Written by Himself* (New York: Georgian, 1930), 18.
8. Albert Greene, *Recollections of the Jersey Prison Ship from the Manuscript of Captain Thomas Dring* (New York: Corinth Books, 1961), v.
9. *Martyrs to the Revolution in British Prison-Ships in the Wallabout Bay* (New York: W. H. Arthur, 1855), 34.
10. "Josiah Smith to Benjamin Franklin," in William James Morgan, ed., *Naval Documents of the Revolution,* Vol. 9 (Washington, DC: Naval Historical Center, 1986), 377–78.
11. Richard M. Dorson, ed., *America Rebels: Narratives of the Patriots* (New York: Pantheon, 1953), 93.
12. H. G. Barnby, *The Prisoners of Algiers* (London: Oxford University Press,

1966), 1–10. Barnby relies heavily on John Foss's journal (1798) and James Leander Cathcart's writings, including his narrative *The Captives* (1899) and his *Diplomatic Journal and Letter Book*. See "The Diplomatic Journal and Letter Book of James Leander Cathcart, 1787–96," *Proceedings of the American Antiquarian Society* (October 1954). After his release from Algiers, Cathcart became the first American consul to Tripoli.

13. Barnby, *Prisoners of Algiers,* 111.

14. John Foss, *A Journal of the Captivity and Suffering of John Foss* (Newburyport, MA, 1798), quoted in Ernest Dupuy and William Baumer, *The Little Wars of the United States* (New York: Hawthorne, 1968), 27.

15. *Encarnacion Prisoners Written by a Prisoner* (Louisville, KY: Prentice and Weissinger, 1848), 15.

16. Ibid., 35.

17. Ibid., 40–42.

18. Stanley Weintraub, *Victoria: An Intimate Biography* (New York: Dutton, 1988), 294–95.

19. Philip Van Doren Stern, *The Confederate Navy* (New York: Bonanza Books, 1962), 57–61.

20. Charles Lanman, ed., *Journal of Alfred Ely: A Prisoner of War in Richmond* (New York: D. Appleton, 1862), 14.

21. Ibid., 15.

22. Ibid., 16–17.

23. Carl Sager, "A Boy in the Confederate Cavalry," *Confederate Veteran* 36:10 (October 1928): 374.

24. Ibid., 376.

25. John Urban, *Battle Field and Prison Pen, or, Through the War and Thrice a Prisoner in Rebel Dungeons* (Philadelphia: Hubbard Brothers, 1882), 252–53.

26. Marshall Everett, ed., *Exciting Experiences in Our Wars with Spain and the Filipinos* (Chicago: Educational Company, 1900), 233.

27. Herbert C. Fooks, *Prisoners of War* (Federalsburg, MD: J. W. Stowell, 1924), 4.

28. James W. Gerard, *Face to Face with Kaiserism* (New York: George H. Dopran, 1918), 171.

29. Ibid.

30. Ibid.

31. Mike Shallin, "The Guest of the Kaiser," in Henry Berry, ed., *Make the Kaiser Dance* (New York: Doubleday, 1978): 347–51.

32. James Norman Hall, *My Island Home: An Autobiography* (Boston: Little, Brown, 1952), 203–9.

33. In H. C. Armstrong, *Escape* (New York: Robert M. McBride, 1935), 289f.

34. Edouard Victor Isaacs, *Prisoner of the U-90* (Boston: Houghton Mifflin, 1919), 3–5.

35. Ibid., 8–10.

36. "Behind Barbed Wire: POWs in the Pacific and Europe," *Veterans of Foreign Wars Magazine* (November 1991): 54–55.

37. E. Bartlett Kerr, *Surrender and Survival: The Experience of American POWs in the Pacific, 1941–1945* (New York: William Morrow, 1985), 19–20.

38. Ibid., 339–40. For critical evaluations of the Bataan/Corregidor campaign, see Stanley L. Falk, *Bataan: The March of Death* (New York: Jove, 1984), 221–37.

39. Stanley Weintraub, *Long Day's Journey into War* (New York: Dutton, 1991), 287–88.

40. James P. S. Devereux, *The Story of Wake Island* (New York: Ace Books, 1947), 176–210. See also Weintraub, *Long Day's Journey,* 491.

41. Kenneth W. Simmons, *Kriegie* (Edinburgh: Thomas Nelson and Sons, 1960), 30. For many narrative accounts of capture in the ETO, see Joe Consolmagno, ed., *Through the Eye of the Needle: 68 First-Person Accounts of Combat, Evasion, and Capture by World War II Airmen,* published by the Stalag Luft III former prisoners of war (Baltimore, MD: Gateway, 1992).

42. Lloyd W. Pate and B. J. Cutler, *Reactionary* (New York: Harper and Brothers, 1956), 27.

43. James N. Rowe, *Five Years to Freedom* (New York: Ballantine Books, 1971), 54.

44. Van Anh, "Capturing an American Pilot," in David Charnoff and Doan Van Toai, eds., *Portrait of the Enemy* (New York: Random House, 1986), 130–34.

45. Initial remarks in a public address at Penn State University, October 7, 1989. Norman A. McDaniel in Wallace Terry, ed., *Bloods: An Oral History of the Vietnam War by Black Veterans* (New York: Ballantine, 1984), 130, 134.

46. Captain Giles R. Norrington, USN (Retired), public address, with Colonel Norman A. McDaniel, USAF (Retired), at Penn State University, October 7, 1989.

47. Harold Longacre's poem "God's Minute," appeared in American Ex–Prisoners of War *Bulletin* (July 1955): np.

CHAPTER SIX. PRISONERS UNDER GUARD:
REMOVES AND DEATH MARCHES

1. Richard VanDerBeets, *The Indian Captivity Narrative: An American Genre* (New York: University Press of America, 1984), ix.

2. J. Norman Heard, *White into Red: A Study of the Assimilation of White Persons Captured by Indians* (Metuchen, NJ: Scarecrow, 1973), 101.

3. Alden T. Vaughan and Edward W. Clark, *Puritans among the Indians: Accounts of Captivity and Redemption, 1676–1724* (Cambridge: Belknap, 1981), 64.

4. Ibid., 68.

5. Ibid.

6. Peter Williamson, *Sufferings of Peter Williamson, One of the Settlers in the Back Parts of Pennsylvania Written by Himself,* in Richard VanDerBeets, ed., *Held Captive by Indians: Selected Narratives 1642–1836* (Knoxville: University of Tennessee Press, 1973), 224f. All references to the Williamson narrative are contained in this source, 216–27.

7. Marie LeRoy and Barbara Leininger, "The Narrative of Marie LeRoy and Barbara Leininger, *Pennsylvania-German Society Proceedings* 15 (1906): 113.

8. Charles H. Metzger, *The Prisoner in the American Revolution* (Chicago: Loyola University Press, 1971), x.

9. Larry G. Bowman, *Captive Americans: Prisoners during the American Revolution* (Athens: Ohio University Press, 1976), 15.

10. Metzger, *Prisoner in the American Revolution,* 66.

11. Bowman, *Captive Americans,* 16.

12. Thomas Andros in Richard M. Dorson, ed., *America Rebels: Narratives of the Patriots* (New York: Pantheon, 1953), 93.

13. Ethan Allen in ibid., 47.

14. Ibid., 46.

15. Ibid., 47.

16. Charles Andrews, *The Prisoners' Memoirs, or, Dartmoor Prison* (New York: Privately printed, 1815), 18–19.

17. *Encarnacion Prisoners Written by a Prisoner* (Louisville, KY: Prentice and Weissinger, 1848), 44–45.

18. Ibid., 56.

19. Sir Henry Morton Stanley, *The Autobiography of Sir Henry Morton Stanley* (Boston: Houghton Mifflin, 1909), 200, 202.

20. Ibid., 201.

21. Ibid., 205.

22. Mike Shallin, "The Guest of the Kaiser," in Henry Berry, ed., *Make the Kaiser Dance* (New York: Doubleday, 1978), 349.

23. Norman Archibald, *Heaven High, Hell Deep, 1917–1918* (New York: Albert and Charles Boni, London and Toronto: William Heinemann, 1935), 235.

24. Harold Willis in H. C. Armstrong, *Escape* (New York: Robert M. McBride, 1935), 291–92.

25. Ibid., 292.

26. James Norman Hall, *My Island Home: An Autobiography* (Boston: Little, Brown, 1952), 209.

27. Carl P. Dennett, *Prisoners of the Great War: Authoritative Statement of Conditions in the Prison Camps of Germany* (Boston: Houghton Mifflin, 1919), 225.

28. Ronald H. Bailey, *Prisoners of War* (Alexandria, VA: Time-Life, 1981), 37.

29. Unpublished manuscript written by Harold R. Kipps, deceased in 1989, given to a county veterans' coordinator in Pennsylvania and sent to the author in 1990.

30. Bill F. Gurule, *Fleeting Shadows and Faint Echoes of Las Huertes* (New York: Carlton, 1987), 38–39.

31. Stanley L. Falk, *Bataan: The March of Death* (New York: Jove, 1972, reprint, 1984), 236–37.

32. Robert Considine, ed., *General Wainwright's Story* (Garden City, NY: Doubleday, 1946), 172.

33. Ibid., 174.

34. James P. S. Devereux, *The Story of Wake Island* (New York: Ace Books, 1947), 211.

35. Ibid.

36. Ibid., 212.

37. Ibid., 213. It is interesting to note that when the Japanese surrendered Wake Island back to the United States, the event took place aboard the USS *Levy,* a destroyer named after Commodore Uriah P. Levy, an American naval prisoner in Dartmoor during the War of 1812.

38. Transcription of this unpublished personal narrative given to the author in 1990.

39. Ray Marcello, "A Little Burst of Flak," *AXPOW Bulletin* 39:10 (October 1982): 20–21. It was originally copied into ex-POW Neil V. Clyman's notebook while Marcello and Clyman were imprisoned at Stalag Luft IV.

40. Kenneth W. Simmons, *Kriegie* (Edinburgh: Thomas Nelson and Sons, 1960), 208, 210–11.

41. In a letter from Mr. Thornton to the author in 1990.

42. Charles Miller, in Vladmir Pozner, *Remembering War: A U.S.-Soviet Dialogue* (New York: Oxford University Press, 1990), 58; and Studs Terkel, *An Oral History of World War II: "The Good War"* (New York: Pantheon, 1984), 407–16.

43. U.S. Senate Committee on Government Operations, *Korean War Atrocities* (Washington, DC: GPO, 1954), 4.

44. Ibid., 5.

45. Ibid., 6.

46. Letter from Ralph D. Moyer to the author, January 30, 1990.

47. Stephen R. Harris, *My Anchor Held* (Old Tappan, NJ: Fleming H. Revell, 1970), 15.

48. Lloyd M. Bucher with Mark Roscovich, *Bucher: My Story* (New York: Dell, 1970), 213.

49. Ibid.

50. Colonel Fred Cherry, USAF, in Wallace Terry, *Bloods: An Oral History of the Vietnam War by Black Veterans* (New York: Ballantine Books, 1984), 266–91.

51. Colonel Norman A. McDaniel, USAF (Retired), Public Address, Penn State University, October 5, 1989.

52. Hans J. Massaquoi, "Introductory Remarks," in Sergeant James E. Jackson, "Eighteen Months as a Prisoner of the Vietcong," *Ebony* 23 (August 1968): 114–16+.

53. Neil Sheehan, *A Bright Shining Lie: John Paul Vann and America in Vietnam* (New York: Random House, 1988), 115.

CHAPTER SEVEN. A SENSE OF PLACE:
THE PRISON LANDSCAPE

1. Mary White Rowlandson, *The Sovereignty and Goodness of God* (1682), in Alden T. Vaughan and Edward W. Clark, eds., *Puritans among the Indians: Accounts of Captivity and Redemption, 1676–1724* (Cambridge, MA: Belknap, 1981), 68.

2. Marie LeRoy and Barbara Leininger, "The Narrative of Marie LeRoy and Barbara Leininger," *Pennsylvania-German Society Proceedings* 15 (1906): 114.

3. Ibid.

4. Peter Williamson in Richard M. VanDerBeets, ed., *Held Captive by Indians: Selected Narratives, 1642–1836* (Knoxville: University of Tennessee Press, 1973), 223–24.

5. Written toward the end of 1780, this selection appears in Philip Freneau, *Poems Written and Published during the American Revolutionary War* (New York: Scholars' Facsimiles and Reprints, 1976), 36–52.

6. Ethan Allen, *A Narrative of Colonel Ethan Allen's Captivity Containing His Voyages and Travels Written by Himself,* in Richard Dorson, *America Rebels: Narrative of the Patriots* (New York: Pantheon, 1953), 55.

7. Charles Herbert, *A Relic of the Revolution* (Boston: Charles H. Pierce, 1847), 13.

8. Ibid., 45–47.

9. "Humanitas" to Lords Commissioners, Admiralty," in William James Morgan, ed., *Naval Documents of the Revolution,* vol. 9 (Washington, DC: Naval Historical Center, 1986), 612.

10. Ibid., 611–12.

11. See H. G. Barnby, "Palaces and Prisons," *The Prisoners of Algiers* (New York: Oxford University Press, 1966), 39–57, for a full description of the prisons of Algiers from 1785 to 1787.

12. Charles Andrews, *The Prisoners' Memoirs, or, Dartmoor Prison: Containing the Complete History of the Captivity of the Americans in England* (New York: Privately printed, 1815), 18–19.

13. *Encarnacion Prisoners Written by a Prisoner* (Louisville, KY: Prentice and Weissinger, 1848), 50.

14. Ibid., 58.

15. Basil W. Duke, *History of Morgan's Cavalry* (Bloomington: Indiana University Press, 1961), 470.

16. Decimus et Ultimus Barziza, *The Adventures of a Prisoner of War* (1864), ed., R. Henderson Shuffler (Austin: University of Texas Press, 1964), 75ff.

17. Buehring H. Jones, *The Sunny Land; or, Prison Prose and Poetry,* ed., J. A. Houston (Baltimore, MD: Innes, 1868), 336.

18. Ibid., 339.

19. Ibid., 455. See also *Sketches from Prison: A Confederate Artist's Record of Life at Point Lookout Prisoner-of-War Camp 1863–1865* (Baltimore: Maryland Park Foundation, n.d.), 3, and Edwin W. Beitzell, *Point Lookout Prison Camp for Confederates* (Abell, MD: Published by the author, 1972), 122, for death statistics and a general description of conditions of the camp.

20. Ibid., 453.

21. Ibid., 454.

22. Sir Henry Morton Stanley, *The Autobiography of Sir Henry Morton Stanley* (Boston: Houghton Mifflin, 1909), 205, 206.

23. Jones, *The Sunny Land,* 451.

24. The Confederate dead were not buried on Pea Patch Island; the bodies were transported from Fort Delaware to the New Jersey side of the Delaware River and buried at Finn's Point. Today, this site is a national cemetery containing 2,436 Confederate dead.

25. W. Emerson Wilson, *Fort Delaware* (Newark: University of Delaware Press, 1957), 13, 32.

26. Ibid., 14.

27. Jones, *The Sunny Land,* 456.

28. Wilson, *Fort Delaware,* 27.

29. Matthew S. Walls, "Northern Hell on Earth," *America's Civil War* (March 1991), 25.

30. Ibid., 29.

31. *War of the Rebellion: A Compilation of the Official Records of the Union and Confederate Armies* (Washington, DC: U.S. War Department, 1880–1901), 997–1003, cited by James I. Robertson, "The Scourge of Elmira," in William Best Hesseltine, *Civil War Prisons* (Columbus: Ohio State University Press, 1989), 95.

32. See ibid., 80–97, for a brief but detailed examination of the Union prison at Elmira.

33. *Report on the Treatment of Prisoners of War by the Rebel Authorities during the War of Rebellion,* U.S. House of Representatives, Report No. 45, 40th Congress, 3d sess., Serial no. 1391 (Washington, DC: GPO, 1869), 170.

34. Bernhard Domschke, *Twenty Months in Captivity* (1865), ed. and trans., Frederic Trautmann (Rutherford, NJ: Fairleigh Dickinson University Press, 1990), 38–39.

35. Edwin C. Bearss, *Andersonville Study* (Washington, DC: National Park Service, 1970), 15.

36. Ovid L. Futch, *History of Andersonville Prison* (Gainesville: University of Florida Press, 1968), 4f, 43. See also Edward D. Jervy, ed., *Prison Life among*

the Rebels (Kent, OH: Kent State University Press, 1990), xiii. Jervy's book examines the letters of Henry S. White, a Methodist chaplain from the Fifth Regiment of the Rhode Island Heavy Artillery.

37. John W. Urban, *Battle Field and Prison Pen, or, Through the War and Thrice a Prisoner in Rebel Dungeons* (Philadelphia: Hubbard Brothers, 1882), 254–65.

38. Ibid., 254f. See also Alfred Jay Bollet, M.D., "To Care for Him That Has Borne the Battle: A Medical History of the Civil War," *Resident and Staff Physician* (July 1992): 75–82. Bollet cites Dr. Joseph Jones's report given to the Confederate Surgeon General in which he reported that diet was the principal cause of disease and death in Andersonville. At his trial, Captain Henry Wirz claimed that Brigadier Joseph Winder, CSA, Andersonville's overall commandant, restrained him from allowing local aid societies from bringing vegetables to Union prisoners.

39. *Report on the Treatment of Prisoners of War by the Rebel Authorities during the War of Rebellion,* 162.

40. William O. Bryant, *Cahaba Prison and the Sultana Disaster* (Tuscaloosa: University of Alabama Press, 1990), 1.

41. Ibid., 20.

42. George L. Anderson, ed., *Colonel John Fraser, A Petition Regarding the Conditions in the C.S.M. Prison at Columbia, S.C., Addressed to the Confederate Authorities* (Lawrence: University of Kansas Libraries, 1962), 27ff.

43. Ibid., 30.

44. Carl P. Dennett, *Prisoners of the Great War* (Boston: Houghton Mifflin, 1919), 38.

45. Albert J. Beveridge in Harold E. Straubling, ed., *The Last Magnificent War: Rare Journalistic and Eyewitness Accounts of World War I* (New York: Paragon, 1989), 271.

46. Mike Shallin, "The Guest of the Kaiser," in Henry Berry, ed., *Make the Kaiser Dance* (New York: Doubleday, 1978), 349.

47. Norman Archibald, *Heaven High, Hell Deep, 1917–1918* (New York: Albert and Charles Boni, 1935), 234.

48. Edouard Victor Isaacs, *Prisoner of the U-90* (Boston: Houghton Mifflin, 1919), 23.

49. Ibid., 55ff.

50. Dennett, *Prisoners of the Great War,* 36.

51. Ibid., 230.

52. Donald Knox, *Death March: The Survivors of Bataan* (New York: Harcourt Brace Jovanovich, 1981), 153.

53. Ibid., 166.

54. Stan Sommers, ed., *The Japanese Story* (Marshfield, WI: National Ex-Prisoners of War Association, 1980), 13–14.

55. Knox, *Death March,* 198. See also John S. Coleman, Jr., *Bataan and Beyond: Memoirs of an American POW* (College Station: Texas A&M University Press, 1978), 82–104, for descriptions of Camp O'Donnell and Cabanatuan.

56. Ibid., 203.

57. Ibid., 248.

58. Douglas Valentine, *The Hotel Tacloban* (London: Angus and Robertson, 1984), 26.

59. See Edward Russell, *The Knights of Bushido* (London: Transworld, 1958), 186–88, for a more detailed description of Karenko prison camp.

60. James D. Clayton, ed., *South to Bataan, North to Mukden: The Prison Diary of Brigadier General W. E. Brougher* (Athens: University of Georgia Press, 1971), 60–67.

61. Ibid.

62. James P. S. Devereux, *The Story of Wake Island* (New York: Ace Books, 1947), 217.

63. See Stan Sommers, *The European Story* (Marshfield, WI: National Ex-Prisoner of War Association, 1980), 21, for a complete camp list.

64. See Primo Levi, *Survival in Auschwitz* (New York: Macmillan, 1959), 61. Levi tells how British POWs, who were neither criminals, political prisoners, nor Jews, were housed in the work section, or "Buna," of the camp.

65. Bill Watkins, letter to the author, December 5, 1990.

66. Warren Fencl, letter to the author, March 20, 1991.

67. Orvis C. Preston, letter to the author, November 26, 1990.

68. Charles Miller in Vladmir Pozner, *Remembering War: A U.S.-Soviet Dialogue* (New York: Oxford University Press, 1990), 56, and Studs Terkel, *An Oral History of World War II: "The Good War"* (New York: Pantheon, 1984), 407–16.

69. Captain John W. and John W. Thornton, Jr., *Believed to Be Alive* (Middlebury, VT: Paul S. Eriksson, 1981), 160.

70. Ibid., 168.

71. Ibid., 141.

72. Ralph D. Moyer in a letter to the author, January 30, 1991.

73. Ibid.

74. Stephen R. Harris, *My Anchor Held* (Old Tappan, NJ: Fleming H. Revell, 1970), 41–42.

75. George E. Smith, *P.O.W.: Two Years with the Vietcong* (Berkeley, CA: Ramparts, 1971), 155ff.

76. Rod Colvin, *First Heroes: The POWs Left Behind in Vietnam* (New York: Irvington, 1987), 161.

77. Larry Guarino, *A POW's Story: 2801 Days in Hanoi* (New York: Ivy, 1990), 16.

78. Howard Rutledge and Phyllis Rutledge, *In the Presence of Mine Enemies 1965–1973: A Prisoner of War* (Old Tappan, NJ: Fleming H. Revell, 1977), 25.

79. Ibid., 42.

80. John M. McGrath, *Prisoner of War: Six Years in Hanoi* (Annapolis, MD: Naval Institute, 1975), 111–12.

81. James N. Rowe, *Five Years to Freedom* (New York: Ballantine Books, 1971), 373–74.

CHAPTER EIGHT. THE PRISONER'S WAR:
RESISTANCE AND TORTURE

1. Edward Peters, *Torture* (New York: Basil Blackwell, 1985), 1f.

2. John H. Langbein, *Torture and the Law of Proof: Europe and England in the Ancien Regime* (Chicago: University of Chicago Press, 1977), 12.

3. Ibid., 13.

4. Ibid., 15.

5. Ibid., 16–17.

6. Peters, *Torture,* 2.

7. Richard M. VanDerBeets, ed., *The Indian Captivity Narrative: An American Genre* (New York: University Press of America, 1984), 43.

8. Peter Williamson, *Sufferings of Peter Williamson, One of the Settlers in the Back Parts of Pennsylvania Written by Himself,* in Ricahrd VanDerBeets, ed., *Held Captive by Indians: Selected Narratives 1642–1836* (Knoxville: University of Tennessee Press, 1973), 221.

9. Barbara Leininger and Marie LeRoy, "The Narrative of Marie LeRoy and Barbara Leininger," *Pennsylvania-German Proceedings* 15 (1906): 115–16.

10. Howard H. Peckham, ed., *The Toll of Independence: Engagements and Battle Casualties of the American Revolution* (Chicago: Clements Library Bicentennial Studies, 1974), 132.

11. Herbert C. Fooks, *Prisoners of War* (Federalsburg, MD: J. W. Stowell, 1924), 174.

12. *Martyrs to the Revolution in British Prison-Ships in the Wallabout Bay* (New York: W. H. Arthur, 1855), 8.

13. Fooks, *Prisoners of War,* 176–77.

14. Ibid., 177.

15. Ethan Allen, quoted in Richard M. Dorson, ed., *America Rebels: Narrative of the Patriots* (New York: Pantheon, 1953), 55.

16. William E. S. Flory, *Prisoners of War: A Study in the Development of International Law* (Washington, DC: American Council on Public Affairs, 1942), 43. For an examination of reprisal threats during the War of 1812, see George G. Lewis and John Mewha, *History of Prisoner of War Utilization by the United States Army 1776–1945* (Washington, DC: GPO, 1955), 22–23f.

17. Stanley F. Horn, *The Army of Tennessee* (New York: Bobbs-Merrill, 1941), 467.

18. Bernhard Domschke, *Twenty Months in Captivity,* ed. and trans., Frederic Trautmann (Rutherford, NJ: Fairleigh Dickinson University Press, 1990), 85.

19. John McElroy, *Andersonville: A Story of Rebel Military Prisons, Fifteen Months a Guest of the So-Called Southern Confederacy: A Private Soldier's Experience* (Toledo, OH: D. R. Locke, 1879), 360.

20. Fooks, *Prisoners of War,* 183.

21. Captain J. J. Geer, *Beyond the Lines, or, A Yankee Prisoner Loose in Dixie* (Philadelphia: J. W. Daughaday, 1864), 211.

22. Fooks, *Prisoners of War,* 182.

23. Albert J. Beveridge, "As Witnessed in Germany: German System Seen in Camp, Hospital, and Prison," *American Review of Reviews* (May 1915), quoted in Harold Elk Straubling, *The Last Magnificent War: Rare Journalistic and Eyewitness Accounts of World War I* (New York: Paragon House, 1989), 270.

24. Ibid., 270.

25. James Norman Hall, *My Island Home: An Autobiography* (Boston: Little, Brown, 1952), 207.

26. Fooks, *Prisoners of War,* 133.

27. Clifford Milton Markle, *A Yankee Prisoner in Hunland* (New Haven, CT: Yale University Press, 1920), 35.

28. One edition of the *Times* is reprinted by the Fort Delaware Society; another one was discovered in 1991.

29. Conrad Hoffman, *In the Prison Camps of Germany: A Narrative of "Y" Service among Prisoners of War* (New York: Association Press, 1920), 275. A reprint of *The Barbed Wireless* appears in Hoffman's Appendix III, "Camp Newspapers."

30. Ibid., 275.

31. See Philip M. Flammer, "Dulag Luft: The Third Reich's Prison Camp for

Airmen," *Aerospace Historian* (June 1972): 58–61; James L. Cole, Jr., "Dulag Luft Recalled and Revisited," *Aerospace Historian* (June 1972), 62–65; and Arthur A. Durand, *Stalag Luft III: The Secret Story* (Baton Rouge: Louisiana State University Press, 1988), 55–72, for details and personal narratives of life in the Dulag Luft. Kendal Burt and James Leasnor wrote von Werra's escape biography, *The One that Got Away* (New York: Ballantine Books, 1957).

32. Laurens Van der Post, *The Night of the New Moon* (London: Chatto and Windus, 1985), 35.

33. For a wide range of commentary concerning Americans in Japanese captivity, see Stan Sommers, ed., *The Japanese Story* (Marshfield, WI: National Ex-Prisoner of War Association, 1980).

34. Willie Smith, quoted in ibid., 23.

35. Ronald H. Bailey, *Prisoners of War* (Alexandria, VA: Time-Life, 1981), 25.

36. William F. Dean and William L. Warden, *General Dean's Story* (New York: Viking, 1954), 107–8.

37. Lloyd W. Pate and B. J. Cutler, *Reactionary* (New York: Harper and Brothers, 1956), 69.

38. Ibid.

39. Ibid., 92–93.

40. Stephen R. Harris, *My Anchor Held* (Old Tappan, NJ: Fleming H. Revell, 1970), 33.

41. Ibid., 34.

42. Pierre Boulle, *My Own River Kwai*, trans. Xan Fielding (New York: Vanguard, 1966), 193.

43. Robinson Risner, *The Passing of the Night: My Seven Years as a Prisoner of the North Vietnamese* (New York: Random House, 1973), 184. See also Glendon Perkins, "Hanoi Nightmare: American POW's Year of Terror," *Soldier of Fortune* 15:8 (August 1990): 25–29, 82–84.

44. James B. Stockdale and Sybil Stockdale, *In Love and War* (New York: Harper and Row, 1984), 246–47.

45. Ibid., 252.

46. Howard Rutledge and Phyllis Rutledge, *In the Presence of Mine Enemies* (Old Tappan, NJ: Fleming H. Revell, 1977), 46.

47. Larry Chesley, *Seven Years in Hanoi* (Salt Lake City: Book Craft, 1973), 53.

48. Eugene B. McDaniel, *Scars and Stripes: The Red McDaniel Story* (Dunn, NC: Published by friends of Red McDaniel, 1975), 57.

49. Stockdale, *In Love and War,* 433.

50. Ibid., 187.

51. *Newsweek,* April 16, 1973, 51. See also "Jane Fonda and Tom Hayden—Candid Conversation," *Playboy* (April 1974): 67.

52. Stockdale, *In Love and War,* 164.

53. Ralph Gaither, *With God in a P.O.W. Camp* (Nashville, TN: Broadman, 1973), 49–50.

54. Chesley, *Seven Years in Hanoi,* 65.

55. See "Fred Cherry" in Wallace Terry, ed., *Bloods: An Oral History of the Vietnam War by Black Veterans* (New York: Ballantine Books, 1984), 280–81. See also Daniel Goleman, "P.O.W.s Now Told to Resist Cooperation to 'Best of Their Ability'," *New York Times International,* January 24, 1991, A14.

56. Abraham L. Feinberg, *Hanoi Diary* (Dan Mills, Ont.: Alger, 1968), 218.

57. Ibid., 220.

58. Ibid., 221.
59. Ibid., 224.

CHAPTER NINE. THE LINE OF LEAST RESISTANCE:
ASSIMILATION AND THE RENEGADE CAPTIVE

1. John W. Blassingame, *The Slave Community: Plantation Life in the Antebellum South* (New York: Oxford University Press, 1979), 63.

2. J. Norman Heard, *White into Red: A Study of the Assimilation of White Persons Captured by Indians* (Metuchen, NJ: Scarecrow, 1973), 2, 3.

3. Ibid., 14. It is interesting to note that popular pulp fiction has again taken up this theme. Zebra Books has recent titles like *Cherokee Bride* and others that focus on the love relationships between an Indian captor and the white female captive.

4. Ibid., 26ff.

5. Girty materials can be found in U. L. Jones, *Simon Girty, the Outlaw,* ed. A. Monroe Aurand, Jr. (Harrisburg, PA: Aurand, 1931), 135–51, 152–73; and C. W. Butterfield, *History of the Girtys* (Cincinnati: Robert Clarke, 1890). For a friendly description of Girty as scout and interpreter from the British point of view, see Colin G. Calloway, "Simon Girty: Interpreter and Intermediary," in James A. Clifton, ed., *Being and Becoming Indian: Biographical Studies of North American Frontiers* (Chicago: Dorsey, 1989), 38–58.

6. W. T. R. Saffell, *Records of the Revolution* (Baltimore, MD: Charles C. Saffell, 1894), 312.

7. See R. W. G. Vail, *Voice of the Old Frontier* (Philadelphia: University of Pennsylvania Press, 1949), 314–15, 443, for a list of reprintings. The Crawford murder appears also in C. W. Butterfield, ed., *An Account of the Expedition against Sandusky under Colonel William Crawford in 1782* (Cincinnati, OH: U. P. James, 1873), and Hugh Henry Brackenridge, *Indian Atrocities: Narratives of the Perils and Sufferings of Dr. John Knight and John Slover among the Indians during the Revolutionary War* (Cincinnati, OH: U. P. James, 1867).

8. For the complete text and references to versions collected by Lyman Copeland Draper and others, see Parker B. Brown, " 'Crawford's Defeat': A Ballad," *Western Pennsylvania Historical Magazine* 64:4 (October 1981): 312, 315. Brown points out that the Crawford ballad was published along with "St. Clair's Defeat: A New Song," another broadside concerning an American loss to the British and the Indians of Ohio.

9. Ibid., 314.

10. The theme of marriage between assimilated captives was used in several feature films. In Kevin Kostner's *Dances with Wolves* (1991), two assimilated white captives marry; in Richard Harris's *Man Called Horse* (1961), an assimilated captive marries an Indian woman, and in John Ford's *The Searchers* (1957), an assimilated woman marries an Indian war chief.

11. Heard, *White into Red,* 46.

12. Ibid., 5.

13. George G. Lewis and John Mewha, *History of Prisoner of War Utilization* (Washington, DC: GPO, 1955), 14f.

14. Blassingame, *The Slave Community,* 56.

15. Ibid., 61.

16. General Santa Anna in the *New York Herald,* October 17, 1847, quoted

in Edward S. Wallace, "Deserters in the Mexican War," *Hispanic American Historical Review* 15:2 (August 1935): 379.

17. G. T. Hopkins, "The San Patricio Battalion in the Mexican War," *Cavalry Journal* (September 1913), quoted in Edward S. Wallace, "Deserters in the Mexican War," 379.

18. Ibid., 374.

19. Ibid.

20. Ibid., 382.

21. W. Emerson Wilson, *Fort Delaware* (Newark: University of Delaware Press, 1957), 13.

22. Alexander D. Brown, *The Galvanized Yankees* (Urbana: University of Illinois Press, 1963), 9, 1.

23. Sir Henry Morton Stanley, *The Autobiography of Sir Henry Morton Stanley* (Boston: Houghton Mifflin, 1909), 214.

24. Buehring H. Jones, *The Sunny Land, or, Prison Prose and Poetry* (Baltimore, MD: Innes, 1868), 338.

25. Richard E. Welch, Jr., *Response to Imperialism: The United States and the Philippine-American War, 1899–1902* (Chapel Hill: University of North Carolina Press, 1979), 42.

26. Willard B. Gatewood, Jr., *Smoked Yankees and the Struggle for Empire* (Urbana: University of Illinois Press, 1971), 15. See also Welch, *Response to Imperialism,* 113. In an ambush against his former unit, Fagan taunted them. Sergeant Washington, an old, white-haired man, "fought like a madman." Washington and Fagan were the two extremes of the race issue at this time.

27. Herbert C. Fooks, *Prisoners of War* (Federalsburg, MD: J. W. Stowell, 1924), 88.

28. A. B. Feuer, ed., *Bilibid Diary: The Secret Notebooks of Commander Thomas Hayes, POW, the Philippines, 1942–45* (Hamden, CT: Archon, 1987), 77.

29. Ronald H. Bailey, *Prisoners of War* (Alexandria, VA: Time-Life, 1981), 20.

30. Ibid., 166ff.

31. Lloyd W. Pate and B. J. Cutler, *Reactionary* (New York: Harper and Brothers, 1956), 68.

32. Andrew M. Condron, Richard G. Corden, and Lawrence V. Sullivan, eds., *Thinking Soldiers* (Peking: New World, 1955), 185.

33. John G. Hubbell, *P.O.W.: A Definitive History of the American Prisoner-of-War Experience in Vietnam, 1964–1973* (New York: Reader's Digest, 1976), 322–35.

34. Chris Doyle, "Bobby Garwood: Traitor or Victim?" *Soldier of Fortune* (September 1979): 74. See also Zalin Grant, *Survivors: American POWs in Vietnam* (New York: Berkley Books, 1985), and Winston Groom and Duncan Spencer, *Conversations with the Enemy: The Story of PFC Robert Garwood* (New York: Putnam, 1983), for critical discussions of the Garwood case.

35. Monika Schwinn and Bernhard Diehl, *We Came to Help* (New York: Harcourt Brace Jovanovich, 1973), 88.

36. Chris Doyle, "Bobby Garwood: Traitor or Victim?" 73.

37. Schwinn and Diehl, *We Came to Help,* 90.

38. Ibid., 89.

39. Groom and Spencer, *Conversations with the Enemy,* 455.

40. His story appears in a different light in Monika Jensen-Stevenson and William Stevenson's *Kiss the Boys Goodbye* (New York: Dutton, 1990).

41. David Truby, "Turncoats in Action: The Untold Story of Viet Nam's TIA,"

Military Journal 12 (June 1980): 24–25. As the Naval intelligence officer in Kien Hoa Province in 1970–1971, I received a steady stream of reports about civilian and renegade American military personnel operating with the Vietcong. Apprehending these men dead or alive became a priority for naval special operations forces (SEALS), second only to prisoner recovery itself.

42. See Chris Doyle, "Alive in Cambodia? McKinley Nolan, Turncoat," *Soldier of Fortune* (February 1980).

CHAPTER TEN. THE LINE OF MORE RESISTANCE:
COMMITTED ESCAPERS

1. Marie LeRoy and Barbara Leininger, "The Narrative of Marie LeRoy and Barbara Leininger," *Pennsylvania-German Society Proceedings* 15 (1906): 113.

2. Ibid., 115.

3. Ibid., 116.

4. For other examples of escapers in the forest wars, see Hugh Henry Brackenridge, *Indian Atrocities: Narratives of the Perils and Sufferings of Dr. John Knight and John Slover among the Indians during the Revolutionary War* (Cincinnati, OH: U. P. James, 1867), and William Smith, *Historical Account of Bouquet's Expedition against the Ohio Indians in 1764* (Cincinnati, OH: Robert Clarke, 1907).

5. Herbert C. Fooks, *Prisoners of War* (Federalsburg, MD: J. W. Stowell, 1924), 272.

6. There were other large military prisons in England at this time; however, Americans were incarcerated only in Mill, Forton, Deal (Scotland), and Kinsale (Ireland).

7. For a heavily slanted, strongly propagandistic version of life aboard the British prison ships in Wallabout Bay, see *Martyrs to the Revolution in British Prison-Ships in the Wallabout Bay* (New York: W. H. Arthur, 1855).

8. Conyngham in Robert Wilden Neeser, ed., *Letters and Papers Relating to the Cruises of Gustavus Conyngham: A Captain of the Continental Navy 1777–1779* (New York: DeVinne, 1915), 194.

9. Ibid., xlix.

10. Ibid., 194.

11. Olive Anderson, "American Escapes from British Naval Prisons during the War of Independence," *Mariner's Mirror* 41 (1955): 239.

12. Francis Abell, *Prisoners of War in Britain 1756 to 1815: A Record of their Lives, Their Romance, and Their Sufferings* (London: Oxford University Press, 1914), 215.

13. Olive Anderson, "American Escapes," 239–40.

14. Richard Garrett, *P.O.W.: The Uncivil Face of War* (Newton Abbot, Eng.: David and Charles, 1981), 35.

15. Richard M. Dorson, ed., *America Rebels: Narratives of the Patriots* (New York: Pantheon, 1953), 33. For a partial list of Continental army officer prisoners exchanged through Elias Boudinot, Thomas Franklin, and John Adams, see W. T. R. Saffell, "British Prisons and American Prisoners," in *Records of the Revolutionary War,* 3d ed. (Baltimore: Charles C. Saffell, 1894), 298–323.

16. Garrett, *P.O.W.: The Uncivil Face of War,* 42.

17. Dorson, *America Rebels,* 33ff.

18. Ibid., 96.

19. Abell, *Prisoners of War in Britain,* 237–39, 248–49.

20. *Encarnacion Prisoners Written by a Prisoner* (Louisville, KY: Prentice and Weissinger, 1848), 37.

21. Decimus et Ultimus Barziza, *The Adventures of a Prisoner of War,* ed. R. Henderson Shuffler (Austin: University of Texas Press, 1964), for the complete narrative and illuminating annotations.

22. Hundreds of first-person escape accounts, both simple and complex, appear in forty volumes of *Confederate Veteran,* in *Century Magazine,* in *Southern Historical Society Papers,* and other popular periodicals published around the turn of the twentieth century.

23. For a heroic account of John Hunt Morgan's escape from the Ohio State penitentiary, see Basil W. Duke, *History of Morgan's Captivity* (Bloomington: Indiana University Press, 1961), 486–90. Duke was Morgan's brother-in-law. See also Thomas Hines, "Morgan and His Men Escape from Prison," *Century Magazine* (January 1891), in Philip van Doren Stern, ed., *Secret Missions of the Civil War* (Chicago: Rand McNally, 1959), 155–67; James A. Ramage, "John Hunt Morgan's Escape from the Ohio State Penitentiary," *Civil War Quarterly* 10 (September 1987): 22–28; and Rod Gragg, "John Hunt Morgan," in *Illustrated Confederate Reader* (New York: Harper and Row, 1987), 211–15.

24. Thomas E. Rose, a native of Pittsburgh, was a member of the 77th Pennsylvania Volunteers, a composite unit of infantry recruited from several western Pennsylvania counties.

25. Frederick F. Cavada, *Libby Life: Experiences of a Prisoner of War in Richmond, Virginia, 1863–1864* (Philadelphia: King and Baird, 1865), 167–76.

26. See also James M. Wells, "Prisoners of War Tunnel to Freedom," *McClure's Magazine* (1904), rpt. in *Susquehanna Monthly Magazine* 16:1 (January 1991): 21–31, for a personal narrative of the Libby escape.

27. A. J. Barker, *Prisoners of War* (New York: Universe Books, 1975), 13.

28. Carl P. Dennett, *Prisoners of the Great War: Authoritative Statement of Conditions in the Prison Camps of Germany* (Boston: Houghton Mifflin, 1919), 95ff.

29. Ibid., 142–43.

30. See Ralph D. Paine, *The First Yale Unit: A Story of Naval Aviation 1916–1919* (Cambridge, MA: Riverside, 1925), 2:329–49, for the entire story of Lt. Artemus L. Gates, USNR.

31. See Edouard Victor Isaacs, *Prisoner of the U-90* (Boston: Houghton Mifflin, 1919), 148–59.

32. H. C. Armstrong, *Escape* (New York: Robert M. McBride, 1935), 289.

33. *Medal of Honor Recipients 1863–1978: "In the Name of the Congress of the United States* (Washington, DC: GPO, 1979), 446. Lieutenant Isaacs was born in Cresco, Iowa, graduated from the United States Naval Academy in 1915. Although he changed his name from Isaacs to Izac, his book, *Prisoner of the U-90,* was written under the name Isaacs. His naval records use Izac. He retired from the Navy in 1921 because of the injuries he received during his escape. He became a journalist in San Diego, California, and later served in Congress from 1937–1947. He died in 1990 at the age of 100.

34. For the story of MIS-X, see Lloyd R. Shoemaker, *The Escape Factory* (New York: St. Martin's, 1990). See also Joseph S. Frelinghuysen, *Passages to Freedom: A Story of Capture and Escape* (Manhattan, KS: Sunflower University Press, 1990), an American officer's escape narrative from an Italian prison camp, and Major Pat Reid's *Men of Colditz* (New York: J. B. Lippincott, 1954), for a narrative of his experiences as a British committed escaper in Colditz Castle. For a theatrical

treatment of escape and the American World War II military captivity experience in Germany in general, see Donald Bevan and Edmond Trzcinski, *Stalag 17: A Comedy Melodrama in Three Acts* (New York: Dramatists Play Service, 1951), and David Westheimer's novel *Von Ryan's Express* (New York: Doubleday, 1964). Westheimer's personal narrative is *Sitting It Out* (Houston, TX: Rice University Press, 1992).

35. See Eric E. Williams, *The Wooden Horse* (New York: Harper, 1958), and Edward Jerome, "The Wooden Horse," in *Tales of Escape* (Belmont, CA: Fearon-Pitman, 1959, rpt. 1970). For a comprehensive study of life in Stalag Luft III, see Arthur A. Durand, *Stalag Luft III: The Secret Story* (Baton Rouge: Louisiana State University Press, 1987); Colonel Jerry Sage, *Sage* (Wayne, PA: Miles Standish, 1985); and Delmar T. Spivey, *POW Odyssey* (Attleboro, MA: Published by the author, 1984). Paul Brickhill's *The Great Escape* (New York: Norton, 1950) describes only the British/Commonwealth side of the mass escape from the North Compound in 1944; the Americans in South and Center Compounds made some individual escape attempts from the camp but were more successful during the "Black March" in January 1945. In addition to published sources, the author interviewed Henry Burman of State College, Pennsylvania, a Kriegie who served as a "stooge" or lookout for the "X" organization in Stalag Luft III. Mr. Burman made the Black March in January 1945 and finally escaped from Stalag VIIA in Moosburg prior to liberation.

36. MI-9's August 31, 1945 report, "Statistical Summary: Return of Escapers and Evaders up to 30 June 1945," in M. R. D. Foot and J. M. Langley, *MI-9: Escape and Evasion 1939–1945* (Boston: Little, Brown, 1980), Appendix I. Foot points out that MIS-X's figures exceed 12,000 American escapes and evaders. His view is that the truth probably lies between the British and American figures.

37. Representative narratives of escape from Pacific captivity include William E. Dyess, *The Dyess Story* (New York: G. P. Putnam's Sons, 1944); Melvin H. McCoy, Steve Mellnick, and Wellborn Kelley, *Ten Escape from Togo* (New York: Hobison, 1947); and Steven M. Mellnick, *Philippine Diary* (New York: Van Nostrand, Reinhold, 1969).

38. These exploits are recorded in Edgar D. Whitcomb, *Escape from Corregidor* (Chicago: Henry Regnery, 1958); Jack Hawkins, *Never Say Die* (Philadelphia: Dorrance, 1961); and Bill Roskey, "Great Escapes: POWs Break through the Wire," *Soldier of Fortune* (May 1991): 68.

39. Donald Knox, *Death March: The Survivors of Bataan* (New York: Harcourt Brace Jovanovich, 1981), 292.

40. See Samuel C. Grashio and Bernard Norling, *Return to Freedom* (Tulsa, OK: MCN, 1972). Wohlfeld's remarks are contained in a personal letter dated October 18, 1953, to his friend and fellow prisoner, Carl Nash of Harlem, Georgia, who sent a copy to the author.

41. Edward Russell, *The Knights of Bushido* (London: Transworld, 1958), 75.

42. See Knox, *Death March,* xi–xiii. Of the Americans taken into military captivity in 1942, a little more than a third survived.

43. See. U.S. Senate Committee on Government Operations, *Korean War Atrocities* (Washington, DC: GPO, 1954).

44. Clay Blair, *Beyond Courage* (New York: David McKay, 1955), 6, 191–246.

45. Lloyd W. Pate and B. J. Cutler, *Reactionary* (New York: Harper and Brothers, 1956), 93–94.

46. Edward Marolda and Oscar P. Fitzgerald, *The United States Navy and the Vietnam Conflict* (Washington, DC: Naval Historical Center, 1986), 2:381ff.

47. See U.S. Senate, Committee on Armed Services, *Imprisonment and Escape of Lieutenant Junior Grade Dieter Dengler, USNR* (Washington, DC: GPO, 1966); Dieter Dengler, "I Escaped from a Red Prison," *Saturday Evening Post,* December 3, 1966, 27–33; and Dieter Dengler, *Escape from Laos* (Novato, CA: Presidio, 1979).

48. Quoted in Editors of the *Army Times, American Heroes of Asian Wars* (New York: Dodd and Mead, 1968), 91.

49. See James N. Rowe, *Five Years to Freedom* (New York: Ballantine Books, 1971), 432–38, for Rowe's escape from the Vietcong in December 1968.

50. Aleksandr I. Solzhenitsyn, *The Gulag Archipelago: An Experiment in Literary Investigation V-VII,* trans., Harry Willetts (New York: Harper and Row, 1979), 126.

51. George E. Day, *Return with Honor* (Mesa, AZ: Champlin Fighter Museum, 1989). Excerpt appears as "Promises to Keep," *Reader's Digest* (December 1991): 107–11.

52. See Lewis Lord, "The Medal of Honor," *U.S. News and World Report,* June 10, 1991, 65, 67, and Malcolm McConnell, *Into the Mouth of the Cat: The Story of Lance Sijan, Hero of Vietnam* (New York: Norton, 1985). For Lance Sijan's Medal of Honor citation, see *Medal of Honor Recipients 1863–1978* (Washington, DC: GPO, 1979), 922. Colonel George E. Day, USAF, also received the Medal of Honor for escape attempts and resistance; his citation appears in the same source (826), as does Admiral James B. Stockdale's (928).

53. James B. Stockdale and Sybil Stockdale, *In Love and War* (New York: Harper and Row, 1984), 467. See also George T. Coker, "PW," *United States Naval Institute Proceedings* 100:9 (October 1974): 41–46.

54. Benjamin F. Schemmer, *The Raid* (New York: Harper and Row, 1976), 171.

55. Dale Andrade, "Bring Our POWs Back Alive," *Vietnam Magazine* (February 1990): 22.

56. Schemmer, *The Raid,* 282.

57. Ibid., 236, 267.

58. Ibid., 261. See also Michael R. Conroy, "POW Rescue Game Plan," *Vietnam Magazine* (December 1992): 47–53.

59. Tom Williams, *Post Traumatic Stress Disorders: A Handbook for Clinicians* (Cincinnati, OH: Disabled American Veterans, 1987), 131.

60. Garrett, *P.O.W.: The Uncivil Face of War,* 90.

61. Barker, *Prisoners of War,* 79.

62. Ibid., 125.

63. Stanley Weintraub visited the Australian Defense Force Academy in 1988 while researching *Long Day's Journey into War* (New York: Dutton, 1991) and talked to officer instructors and students. He commented that rules and codes aside, military officer corps form an ethos of work based on success and achievement; even discussing captivity, although it is inevitable in war, seemed to be defeatist to cadets and officer candidates alike. There is a rich literature concerning health and psychological issues of POWs and escapers during World War II, Korea, and Vietnam. For World War II see Bernard Cohen and Maurice Cooper, *A Follow Up Study of World War II Prisoners of War* (Washington, DC: GPO, 1954), and U.S. War Department, Office of the Adjutant General, "Military Personnel Escaped from Enemy Territory" (Washington, DC, July 11, 1944). For postcaptivity studies after Korea, see U.S. Veterans Administration, *Study of Former Prisoners of War* (Washington, DC: GPO, 1980), and Robert J. Ursano, "The Vietnam Era Prisoner of War: Precaptivity Personality and the Development

of Psychiatric Illness," *American Journal of Psychiatry* 138:3 (March 1981): 315–18. See also the "MED-Search" section in each American Ex-Prisoner of War Association monthly *Bulletin*.

CHAPTER ELEVEN. FINAL PATHWAYS TO FREEDOM:
RELEASE, REPATRIATION, AND THE PRISONER'S LAMENT

1. Mary White Rowlandson, *The Sovereignty and Goodness of God* (1682), in Alden T. Vaughan and Edward W. Clark, eds., *Puritans among the Indians: Accounts of Captivity and Redemption, 1676–1724* (Cambridge, MA: Belknap, 1981), 75.

2. Peter Williamson, *Sufferings of Peter Williamson, One of the Settlers in the Back Parts of Pennsylvania Written by Himself* (1757), in Richard VanDerBeets, ed., *Held Captive by Indians: Selected Narratives 1642–1836* (Knoxville: University of Tennessee Press, 1973), 222.

3. Ibid., 227.

4. Herbert C. Fooks, *Prisoners of War* (Federalsburg, MD: J. W. Stowell, 1924), 277.

5. Ethan Allen, in Richard M. Dorson, ed., *America Rebels: Narrative of the Patriots* (New York: Pantheon, 1953), 58.

6. Christopher Hawkins, *The Adventures of Christopher Hawkins* (New York: *New York Times* and Arno, 1968), ix.

7. Philip Freneau, *Poems Written and Published during the American Revolutionary War,* Introduction by Lewis Leary (New York: Scholars' Facsimiles and Reprints, 1976), 51.

8. William E. S. Flory, *Prisoners of War* (Washington, DC: American Council on Public Affairs, 1942), 112f.

9. Ibid., 112.

10. Ibid., 113.

11. Ibid.

12. Jonathan Cowdery, *Captives in Tripoli, or, Dr. Cowdery's Journal* (1806), in *Naval Documents Related to the United States Wars with the Barbary Powers,* vol. 5, *1804–1805* (Washington, DC: GPO, 1944), 176–77.

13. Fooks, *Prisoners of War,* 13.

14. Richard E. Winslow III, *"Wealth and Honour": Portsmouth during the Golden Age of Privateering, 1775–1815* (Portsmouth, NH: Portsmouth Marine Society, 1988), 210.

15. From "The Log of Jeduthan Upton, Captain of the good ship *Polly,* a Privateer in the War of 1812," 8–9, entry of January 23, 1813, ibid., 209–10.

16. Francis Abell, *Prisoners of War in Britain 1756 to 1815: A Record of their Lives, Their Romance, and Their Sufferings* (London: Oxford University Press, 1914), 252.

17. Ibid., 255. See also Robin F. A. Fabel, "Self-Help in Dartmoor: Black and White Prisoners in the War of 1812," *Journal of the Early Republic* 9 (Summer 1989): 165–90.

18. *Miscellaneous Correspondence and Accounts, Prisoner of War Records,* Records of the Adjutant General's Office (Washington, DC: National Archives). See also Charles W. Elliot, *Winfield Scott: The Soldier and the Man* (New York: Macmillan, 1937), 82–83, and Pierre Berton, *The Invasion of Canada* (Boston: Little, Brown, 1980), v. 1 and 2, for a complete description of the Canadian invasion from a Canadian point of view.

19. Elliot, *Winfield Scott,* 76–77.

20. Winfield Scott, *Memoirs of Lieut.-General Scott, LL.D. Written by Himself in Two Volumes* (New York: Sheldon, 1864), 71.

21. Article III, Treaty of Ghent, quoted in George G. Lewis and John Mewha, *History of Prisoner of War Utilization by the United States Army 1776–1945* (Washington, DC: GPO, 1955), 25. See also Winslow, *Portsmouth during the Golden Age of Privateering,* 220. According to Winslow, some American privateering continued against British merchant shipping well after the treaty.

22. Anna Holstein, in Sylvia G. Dannet, ed., *Noble Women of the North* (New York: Thomas Yoseloff, 1959), 322.

23. Lydia G. Parrish in ibid., 327–28.

24. Frederick F. Cavada, *Libby Life: Experiences of a Prisoner of War in Richmond, Virginia, 1863–1864* (Philadelphia: King and Baird, 1864), 51.

25. Sir Henry Morton Stanley, *The Autobiography of Sir Henry Morton Stanley* (Boston: Houghton Mifflin, 1909), 211.

26. In Willard Glazier, *The Capture, the Prison Pen, and the Escape* (Hartford, CT: H. E. Goodwin, 1868), 350–51.

27. Ortho Becker, "A Prisoner's Lament," *Confederate Veteran* (July 1923): 79. A more complete text appears as Dr. V. Beecher, "A Prisoner's Lament," in *Confederate Veteran* (February 1923): 278.

28. C. R. Anderson, ed., *The Centennial Edition of the Works of Sidney Lanier* (Baltimore, MD: Johns Hopkins University Press, 1945), 5: 154, quoted in Daniel Aaron, *The Unwritten War: American Writers and the Civil War* (London: Oxford University Press, 1973), 266. See also Edwin Mims, "A Confederate Soldier,"in *Sidney Lanier* (Boston: Houghton Mifflin, 1905), 42–62, for a description of Lanier's experiences in Point Lookout, 1864–1865.

29. Reverend Chester D. Berry, *Loss of the Sultana and Reminiscences of Survivors* (Lansing, MI: Darius D. Thorp, 1892), 178–80.

30. Charles H. Murphy, "Prisoners of War: Repatriation or Internment in Wartime—American and Allied Experiences, 1775 to Present," in U.S. House, Committee on Foreign Affairs, *American Prisoners of War in Southeast Asia, 1971* (Washington, DC: GPO, 1971), 479–82.

31. Mike Shallin, "The Guest of the Kaiser," in Henry Berry, ed., *Make the Kaiser Dance* (New York: Doubleday, 1978), 347–51.

32. Norman Archibald, *Heaven High, Hell Deep 1917–1918* (New York: Albert and Charles Boni, 1935), 330–41.

33. Ralph E. Ellinwood, *Behind the German Lines: A Narrative of the Everyday Life of an American Prisoner of War* (New York: Knickerbocker, 1920), 162.

34. Clifford Milton Marlke, *A Yankee Prisoner in Hunland* (New Haven, CT: Yale University Press, 1920), 52.

35. Murphy, "Prisoners of War," 482–83.

36. Kenneth Simmons, *Kriegie* (New York: Thomas Nelson and Sons, 1960), 239.

37. Ibid., 240.

38. Ibid., 241.

39. Ibid., 242–43.

40. Ibid., 246.

41. Charles Miller, quoted in Vladmir Pozner, *Remembering War: A U.S.-Soviet Dialogue* (New York: Oxford University Press, 1990), 59, and Studs Terkel, *An Oral History of World War II: "The Good War"* (New York: Pantheon, 1984), 407–16.

42. Al Johnson in a letter to the author, October 13, 1990.

43. Although civilian internees were welcomed as "Civilian POWs" in ex-POW organizations, the U.S. government does not recognize them in the status of POWs nor does it presently grant them compensation or veterans' rights under existing laws. The AXPOW Association has consistently lobbied for changes in the law in this respect.

44. Forrest Bryant Johnson, *Hour of Redemption: The Ranger Raid on Cabanatuan* (New York: Manor, 1978), 21.

45. Charles M. Simpson, *Inside the Green Berets: The First 30 Years* (Novato, CA: Presidio, 1983), 128.

46. Johnson, *Hour of Redemption,* 19.

47. Murphy, "Prisoners of War," 484.

48. E. Bartlett Kerr, *Surrender and Survival: The Experience of American POWs in the Pacific, 1941–1945* (New York: William Morrow, 1985), 340.

49. Laurens Van der Post, *The Night of the New Moon* (London: Chatto and Windus, 1985), 73.

50. *AXPOW Bulletin* (July 1955).

51. Anonymous, "I'm a Hungry Man from Old Bataan," *AXPOW Bulletin* (June 1949).

52. Carl Nash's personal narrative sent to the author, November 12, 1990.

53. " 'Is Good to Be Free Again': Swap Brings III POWs Home," *Newsweek,* April 27, 1953, 42.

54. Captain John W. Thornton and John W. Thornton, Jr., *Believed to Be Alive* (Middlebury, VT: Paul S. Eriksson, 1981), 249.

55. "Eyes of World on Panmunjom as Truce Talks Start Again," *Newsweek,* May 4, 1953, 35.

56. Murphy, "Prisoners of War," 484. For a study of the conflict of forced versus free repatriation of North Korean and Chinese POWs, see Stanley Weintraub, *The War in the Wards: Korea's Unknown Battle in a Prisoner-of-War Hospital Camp* (New York: Doubleday, 1964), and Virginia Pasley, *21 Stayed: The Story of American GIs Who Chose Communist China—Who They Were and Why They Stayed* (New York: Farrar, Strauss and Cudahay, 1955).

57. Pasley, *21 Stayed,* 13.

58. Thornton, *Believed to Be Alive,* 257.

59. Ralph D. Moyer, in a letter to the author, August 10, 1991.

60. Author's personal interview with Stanley Aungst, July 1990.

61. In addition to the men released in 1973, two men were recovered from the Vietcong in 1962 before the conflict grew into an international war, two were released from China, twelve were released early by North Vietnam for various political and medical reasons, and twenty-three were released before 1973 by the Vietcong.

62. Vietnam Veterans Against the War, *The Winter Soldier Investigation: An Inquiry into American War Crimes* (Toronto: Beacon, 1972), 130.

63. "Introductory Remarks," in Sergeant James E. Jackson, "Eighteen Months as a Prisoner of the Vietcong," *Ebony* 23 (August 1968): 114.

64. Ibid., 114–16.

65. John H. Chafee, "POW Treatment Principles versus Propaganda," *Naval Institute Proceedings* (July 1971): 15–17.

66. Simpson, *Inside the Green Berets,* 129.

67. David Beville in a taped personal interview with the author in September 1989.

68. Arnold R. Isaacs, *Without Honor: Defeat in Vietnam and Cambodia* (New York: Vintage, 1984), 124.

69. Ibid., 65.

70. Colonel Norman A. McDaniel, Public Address, Penn State University, October 5, 1989.

71. Captain Giles R. Norrington, Public Address, Penn State University, October 5, 1989.

72. Gerald Coffee, *Beyond Survival: Building on the Hard Times—A POW's Inspiring Story* (New York: G. P. Putnam's Sons, 1990), 262.

73. Ibid., 263.

74. Spoken at a fund-raising dinner for the "Camden 17" in Wyndwood, Pennsylvania, February 17, 1973, and reported by *Los Angeles Times*, February 19, 1973: 7, quoted in Alan F. Pater and Jason R. Pater, eds., *What They Said in 1973: The Yearbook of Spoken Opinion* (New York: Monitor, 1974), 364.

75. Jeremiah A. Denton, *When Hell Was in Session* (Mobile, AL: Traditional, 1982), 178–79.

76. Joe Boyle, "The Fate We Share as Prisoners," in Arthur A. Durand, *Stalag Luft III: The Secret Story* (Baton Rouge: Louisiana State University Press, 1988), 363.

CHAPTER TWELVE. MISSING: UNKNOWN SOLDIERS
AND UNRESOLVED MYSTERIES

1. Charles Stenger, "American Prisoners of War in World War I, World War II, Korea, and Vietnam: Statistical Data Concerning Numbers Captured, Repatriated, and Still Alive as of January 1, 1988" (a paper prepared for the Veterans Administration Advisory Committee on Former Prisoners of War, 1988), 1. See also Tom Williams, *Post Traumatic Stress Disorders: A Handbook for Clinicians* (Cincinnati, OH: Disabled American Veterans, 1987), 131.

2. John Hellmann, *American Myth and the Legacy of Vietnam* (New York: Columbia University Press, 1986), ix.

3. "Missing," *Life* (November 1987): 111–22, 124. For numbers and resulting evaluations, see *POW-MIA Fact Book* (Washington, DC: Department of Defense, July 1991), 3; Rod Colvin, *First Heroes: The POWs Left Behind in Vietnam* (New York: Irvington, 1987), 19; and Department of Defense figures for 1986. For World War I figures and analysis, see U.S. Senate, Minority (Republican) Staff of the Committee on Foreign Relations, *An Examination of U.S. Policy toward POW/MIAs* (the *Helms Report*) (Washington, DC: GPO, 1991), 2: 1–8. There were so many errors in the *Helms Report* that some of its editors were fired.

4. As expected, Franklin's book was well received in former antiwar circles and heavily criticized by most veteran organizations.

5. For a critical review of *Kiss the Boys Goodbye: How the United States Betrayed Its Own POWs in Vietnam*, see *Indochina Chronology* 9:4 (October–December 1990): 21–22.

6. For a description of how remains are identified, see Heike Hasenhauer, "Central Identification Laboratory, Hawaii: Solving the Mystery," *Soldiers* (November 1991): 34–36.

7. For legal opinions about POWs in Vietnam, see the following articles: Bruno S. Frey and Heinz Buhofer, "Prisoners and Property Rights," *Journal of Law and Economics* 21 (April 1988): 19–47; Howard S. Levie, "Maltreatment of Prisoners of War in Vietnam," *Boston University Law Review* 48:3 (Summer 1968): 323–59; "The Geneva Convention and the Treatment of Prisoners of War in Vietnam," *Harvard Law Review* 80 (1967): 851, 856–58.

8. POW/MIA Update," *Veteran of Foreign Wars Magazine* (January 1990): 11.

9. See James B. Stockdale and Sybil Stockdale, *In Love and War* (New York: Harper and Row, 1984), and other suggested first-person captivity narratives from the Vietnam War.

10. John M. G. Brown and Thomas G. Ashworth, "A Secret that Shames Humanity," *U.S. Veteran News and Report,* May 29, 1989, 1–12. The Brown-Ashworth position appears also in the U.S. Senate, Minority (Republican) Staff of the Committee on Foreign Relations, *An Examination of U.S. Policy toward POW/MIAs* (the *Helms Report*) (Washington, DC: GPO, 1991), 3:1–27. For the Logan Act, see Title 18, "Crimes and Criminal Procedure," in *United States Code Annotated* (St. Paul, MN: West, 1987), 388.

11. Circular of the POW-MIA Awareness Committee of Gloucester County, New Jersey, 1988.

12. Capitalizing on the success of *First Blood* as a novel and later as a Sylvester Stallone action-thriller, Morrell wrote *Rambo: First Blood, Part II* (New York: Jove Books, 1985) from the screenplay.

13. Bruce Taylor, "The Vietnam War Movie," in D. Michael Shafer, ed., *The Legacy* (Boston: Beacon Press, 1990), 195.

14. Morris Janowitz, *The Professional Soldier: A Social and Political Portrait* (New York: Free Press, 1960), 219, 221.

15. This film fictionalizes Operation Lazarus, the unsuccessful, unpopular, and embarrassing Gritz raid into Laos in 1983.

16. Charles J. Patterson and G. Lee Tipton, *The Heroes Who Fell from Grace* (Canton, OH: Daring, 1985), 142.

17. Ibid., 153.

18. "America's Prisoners of War and Missing in Action: Never Forgotten," *Veteran of Foreign Wars Magazine* (September 1990), 38. Reports of the Select Committee on POW/MIA Affairs are available from the United States Senate, Washington, DC 20510-6500. See also testimonies in the *Congressional Record,* 102d Congress, 2d sess., 1991–1992.

19. See Douglas L. Clarke, *The Missing Man: Politics and the MIA* (Washington, DC: National Defense University Press Research Directorate, 1979), for a description of the complex process of establishing formal MIA status. See also U.S. House, Select Committee on Missing Persons in Southeast Asia, *Americans Missing in Southeast Asia: Summary, Conclusions, and Recommendations* (Washington, DC: GPO, 1976), and *Americans Missing in Southeast Asia* (Washington, DC, GPO, 1988).

20. According to Barbara Crossette, reporting in the *New York Times International,* November 1, 1992, A16, of the 4,800 photographs, only four resolved the fate of missing Americans.

CHAPTER THIRTEEN. LESSONS AND REFLECTIONS

1. Clifford Geertz, *The Interpretation of Cultures* (New York: Basic Books, 1973), 362.

2. Phillips D. Carleton, "The Indian Captivity," *American Literature* 15 (May 1943): 169.

3. Roy Harvey Pearce, "The Significance of the Captivity Narrative," *American Literature* 19 (1947): 20.

4. Robin Gerster, *Big-Noting: The Heroic Theme in Australian War Writing* (Melbourne, Australia: Melbourne University Press, 1987), 237f.

5. Ibid., 238. For a report on Japanese-Australian concerns about cannibalism committed against Australian and Allied POWs in World War II, see Peter Weininger, "Revenge May Have Caused War Crimes," *The Age,* August 19, 1992. Weininger reports on the contents of a half-day conference at the University of Melbourne on August 18, 1992, featuring the research of political science professor Yuki Tanaka, University of Melbourne, who claimed that the "no-prisoner policy" of Australian and American forces in the Pacific theater may well have been a form of revenge based on reports of Japanese ritual cannibalism in New Guinea from 1944 until the war's end.

6. See Peter G. Jones, *War and the Novelist: Appraising the American War Novel* (Columbia: University of Missouri Press, 1976), for a full treatment of the American war novel as genre.

7. Richard VanDerBeets, ed., *The Indian Captivity Narrative* (New York: University Press of America, 1984), 17f.

8. Christopher Hawkins, *The Adventures of Christopher Hawkins* (New York: *New York Times* and Arno, 1968), ixf.

9. His criticism appears in "Bibliographical Essay," *History of Andersonville Prison* (Gainesville: University of Florida Press, 1968), 134–42.

10. John McElroy, *Andersonville* (Toledo, OH: D. R. Locke, 1879), xiv.

11. Ibid., xvi.

12. See Richard B. Speed III, *Prisoners, Diplomats, and the Great War: A Study in the Diplomacy of Captivity* (New York: Greenwood, 1990), 9.

13. See Evelyn Cobley, "History and Ideology in Autobiographical Literature of the First World War," *Mosaic* 23:3 (Summer 1990): 35.

14. Milton Woblewski, in a letter to the author, November 26, 1990.

15. Gene Wise, *American Historical Explanations* 2d ed. rev. (Minneapolis: University of Minnesota Press, 1980), 51.

16. Frances Roe Kestler, *The Indian Captivity: A Woman's View* (New York: Garland, 1990), xii.

17. Charles E. Claghorn, *Women Patriots of the American Revolution* (Metuchen, NJ: Scarecrow, 1991), 83.

18. Ibid., 10–11.

19. William E. S. Flory, *Prisoners of War: A Study in the Development of International Law* (Washington, DC: American Council on Public Affairs, 1942), 36.

20. Ibid.

21. Second Lieutenant Reba Z. Whittle left no published narrative; however, Lieutenant Colonel Mary E. V. Frank authored "The Forgotten POW," an unpublished paper at the Carlisle Barracks, U.S. Army War College, 1990.

22. Jane Fredrickson's comments were spoken directly to the author in May 1991.

23. See Elizabeth Head Vaughn, *Community under Stress: An Internment Camp Culture* (Princeton, NJ: Princeton University Press, 1949), and "Adjustment Problems in a Concentration Camp," *Sociology and Social Research* 32 (September 1947): 513–18.

24. For studies of the internment of American women during World War II, see Lynn Z. Bloom, "Till Death Do Us Part: Men's and Women's Interpretations of Wartime Internment," *Women's Studies International Forum* 10 (1987): 75–83, and Ethel Herold, "War Memories of Ethel Herold," *Bulletin of the American Historical Collection* 10 (1982): 44–67. Women's memoirs can be found also in issues of the *AXPOW Bulletin.*

25. See Catherine Kenney, *Captives: Australian Army Nurses in Japanese Prison Camps* (Brisbane, Australia: University of Queensland Press, 1986), 33–34.

26. Robert Redfield, *The Little Community and Peasant Society and Culture* (Chicago: University of Chicago Press,1967), 4.

27. Byron Farwell, "Prisoner of War Medal," *Washington Post,* August 7, 1985, B1, 2. For veterans' positions on the POW medal, see Joel P. Smith, "Their Ordeal Rewarded," *Veteran of Foreign Wars Magazine* (February 1989): 21, and "Veterans Update," *American Legion Magazine* (December 1989), 40. In addition to the AXPOWs, both the American Legion and the Veterans of Foreign Wars were supportive.

28. Tom Williams, *Post Traumatic Stress Disorders: A Handbook for Clinicians* (Cincinnati, OH: Disabled American Veterans, 1987), 140.

29. David Wood, *Conflict in the Twentieth Century* (Washington, DC: Institute for Strategic Studies, 1968), quoted in Bruce Hoffman, *Commando Raids* (Santa Monica, CA: Rand Corporation, 1985), 3. See John G. Stoessinger, *Why Nations Go to War* 5th ed. (New York: St. Martin's, 1990), 207–14, for an analysis of twentieth-century war making. Stoessinger believes that leaders' misinterpretations of the adversary's power are perhaps the quintessential cause of war, not the actual distribution of power (213). However, the horrors of war itself introduce truth and reality to all the participants (214).

30. *POW-MIA Fact Book* (Washington, DC: Department of Defense, July 1991), 34.

31. See "Torture and Torment," *Newsweek,* February 4, 1991, 50–54.

32. Geroge Mora, "Civilian Ex-POW Committee Report," *AXPOW Bulletin* 49:9 (September 1992): 7. Mora cites President Jimmy Carter's remarks in the June 29, 1992, issue of the *Christian Science Monitor* where Carter complained that the American government failed to ratify this document and thus separated itself from the community of participating nations. For a full treatment, see Nigel S. Rodley, *The Treatment of Prisoners under International Law* (London: Oxford University Press, 1987).

33. Veterans Administration, *Study of Former Prisoners of War* (Washington, DC: GPO, 1980), 140.

34. According to an Associated Press report dated October 28,1992, the Vietnam News Agency announced that Hanoi's infamous Hao Lo Prison, the "Hanoi Hilton," would be demolished and replaced by Hanoi's first truly luxury hotel, planned to be a $29-million, 200-room facility housing banks and offices for foreign companies.

WORKS CITED

UNPUBLISHED SOURCES

Aungst, Stanley. Audiotaped interview. State College, PA, March 1990.

Beville, David. Audiotaped interview. State College, PA, September 1989.

Burman, Henry. Interviews with the author. State College, PA, 1992–1993.

Dye, Ira. "The American Prisoners of War at Dartmoor." Unpublished Paper. Charlottesville: University of Virginia, n.d.

———. "Deaths of American Prisoners of War at Dartmoor Prison during the War of 1812." Paper prepared for the HM Dartmoor Staff. Charlottesville: University of Virginia, n.d.

Fencl, Warren. Personal correspondence with the author. March 1991.

Frank, Mary E. V. "The Forgotten POW: Second Lieutenant Reba Z. Whittle." Unpublished paper. Carlisle Barracks: U.S. Army War College, 1990.

Fredrickson, Jane. Personal conversation with the author. April 1991.

Johnson, Allan E. Narrative; personal correspondence with the author. 1990–1991.

Kipps, Howard R. Unpublished personal narrative of the Bataan march and Japanese captivity donated to the author. 1988.

McDaniel, Norman A. Audiotape; public address and interviews with the author. State College, PA. October 1989, April 1993.

Moyer, Ralph D. Narrative; personal correspondence with the author. 1991–1992.

Nash, Carl. Audiotaped narrative; interviews and personal correspondence with the author. 1989–1992.

Norrington, Giles R. Audiotape; public address, personal correspondence, and interviews with the author. State College, PA, 1989–1993.

Preston, Orvis C. Narrative; personal correspondence with the author. November 1990.

Thornton, Robert J. Narrative; personal correspondence with the author. October 1990.

Watkins, William J. Narrative; personal correspondence with the author. December 1990.

Woblewski, Milton. Narrative; personal correspondence with the author. November 1990.

PUBLISHED SOURCES

Aaron, Daniel. *The Unwritten War: American Writers and the Civil War.* London: Oxford University Press, 1973.

Abell, Francis. *Prisoners of War in Britain 1756 to 1815: A Record of Their Lives, Their Romance, and Their Sufferings.* London: Oxford University Press, 1914.

Abrahams, Roger D., and George Foss. *Anglo-American Folksong Style.* Englewood Cliffs, NJ: Prentice-Hall, 1968.

Adams, Robert. *The Narrative of Robert Adams, a Sailor Who Was Shipwrecked on the Western Coast of Africa in the Year 1810, Was Detained Three Years in Slavery by the Arabs of the Great Desert, and Resided Several Months in the City of Timbuctoo.* London, 1816.

Allen, Ethan. *A Narrative of Colonel Ethan Allen's Captivity Containing His Voyages and Travels Written by Himself.* 1807. New York: Georgian, 1930.

Alvarez, Everett, Jr., and Anthony S. Pitch. *Chained Eagle.* New York: Donald I. Fine, 1990.

Alvord, Clarence W., and Lee Bidwood. *The First Explorations of the Trans-Allegheny Region by the Virginians, 1650–1764.* Cleveland, OH: Arthur H. Clark, 1912.

"American Prisoners of War and Missing in Action: Never Forgotten." *Veterans of Foreign Wars Magazine* (September 1990): 38.

Anderson, C. R., ed. *The Centennial Edition of the Works of Sidney Lanier.* Baltimore: John Hopkins Press, 1945.

Anderson, George L., ed. *Colonel John Fraser, A Petition Regarding the Conditions in the C.S.M. Prison at Columbia, S.C., Addressed to the Confederate Authorities.* Lawrence: University of Kansas Libraries, 1962.

Anderson, Olive. "American Escapes from British Naval Prisons during the War of Independence." *Mariner's Mirror* 41 (1955): 239.

Andrade, Dale. "Bring Our POWs Back Alive." *Vietnam Magazine* (February 1990): 22.

Andrews, Charles. *The Prisoners' Memoirs, or, Dartmoor Prison: Containing the Complete History of the Captivity of the Americans in England.* New York: Privately printed, 1815.

Anh, Van. "Capturing an American Pilot." In David Charnoff and Doan Van Toai, eds., *Portrait of the Enemy,* 130–34. New York: Random House, 1986.

Anonymous. "I'm a Hungry Man from Old Bataan." *AXPOW Bulletin* (June 1949): np.

Appelgate, Howard. "American Privateersmen in the Mill Prison during 1777–1782." *Essex Institute Historical Collections* 102 (October 1966): 318–40.

Archibald, Norman. *Heaven High, Hell Deep 1917–1918.* New York: Albert and Charles Boni, 1935.

Armstrong, H. C. *Escape.* New York: Robert M. McBride, 1935.

Arndt, Karl J. R., ed. *The Treaty of Amity and Commerce of 1785 between His Majesty the King of Prussia and the United States of America.* Munich: Heinz Moos, 1977.

Ashliman, D. L. *A Guide to Folktales in the English Language.* New York: Greenwood, 1987.

AXPOW Bulletin 39:10 (October 1982): 20, 21.

Axinn, Sydney. *A Moral Military.* Philadelphia: Temple University Press, 1989.

Bailey, Ronald H. *Prisoners of War.* Alexandria, VA: Time-Life, 1981.

Barbeau, Marius. "Indian Captivities." *Proceedings of the American Philosophical Society* 94 (1950): 522–48.

Barbiere, Joe. *Scraps from the Prison Table at Camp Chase and Johnson's Island.* Doylestown, PA, 1868.

Barker, A. J. *Prisoners of War.* New York: Universe Books, 1975.

Barnby, H. G. *The Prisoners of Algiers.* London: Oxford University Press, 1966.

Barnes, Scott, and Melva Libb. *Bohica.* Canton, OH: Bohica Corporation, 1987.

Barziza, Decimus et Ultimus. *The Adventures of a Prisoner of War.* 1864. Edited by R. Henderson Shuffler. Austin: University of Texas Press, 1964.

Basile, Leon. *The Civil War Diary of Amos E. Stearns, a Prisoner at Andersonville.* Rutherford, NJ: Fairleigh Dickinson University Press, 1981.

"The Battling Bastards of Bataan." *AXPOW Bulletin* (June 1949): np.

Bayard, Samuel P. "The Materials of Folklore." *Journal of American Folklore* 66:259 (January–March 1953): 1–17.

Bearss, Edwin C. *Andersonville Study.* Washington, DC: National Park Service, 1970.

Beattie, Edward W., Jr. *Diary of a Kriegie.* New York: Crowell, 1946.

Becker, Ortho. "The Prisoner's Lament." *Confederate Veteran* (July 1923): 79.

Beecher, Dr. V. "The Prisoner's Lament." *Confederate Veteran* (February 1923): 278.

"Behind Barbed Wire: POWs in the Pacific and Europe." *Veterans of Foreign Wars Magazine* (November 1991): 54–55.

Beitzell, Edwin W. *Point Lookout Prison Camp for Confederates.* Abell, MD: Published by the author, 1972.

Berry, Chester D. *Loss of the Sultana and Reminiscences of Survivors.* Lansing, MI: Darius D. Thorp, 1892.

Berry, Henry, ed. *Make the Kaiser Dance.* New York: Doubleday, 1978.

Berton, Pierre. *The Invasion of Canada.* Boston: Little, Brown, 1980.

Bevan, Donald, and Edmond Trzcinski. *Stalag 17: A Comedy Melodrama in Three Acts.* New York: Dramatists Play Service, 1951.

Beveridge, Albert J. "Report on German Camps." In Harold Elk Straubling, ed. *The Last Magnificent War: Rare Journalistic and Eyewitness Accounts of World War I,* 266–71. New York: Paragon House, 1989.

Biderman, Albert D. *March To Calumny: The Story of American POWs in the Korean War.* New York: Macmillan, 1963.

Billington, Ray Allen. *The Westward Movement in the United States.* New York: D. Van Nostrand, 1959.

Blair, Clay. *Beyond Courage.* New York: David McKay, 1955.

Blakely, Richard. *Prisoner at War: The Survival of Commander Richard A. Stratton.* Garden City, NJ: Doubleday, 1978.

Blassingame, John W. *The Slave Community: Plantation Life in the Antebellum South.* New York: Oxford University Press, 1979.

Bloom, Lynn Z. "Till Death Do Us Part: Men's and Women's Interpretations of Wartime Internment." *Women's Studies International Forum* 10 (1987): 75–83.

Bollet, Alfred Jay, M.D. "To Care for Him That Has Borne the Battle: A Medical History of the Civil War." *Resident and Staff Physician* (July 1992): 75–82.

Boswell, Bryan. "The Pentagon POW Scandal." *Weekend Australian,* December 9–10, 1989, 4.

Boulle, Pierre. *My Own River Kwai.* Trans. Xan Fielding. New York: Vanguard, 1966.

———. *The Bridge Over the River Kwai.* New York: Vanguard, 1954.

Bowman, Larry G. *Captive Americans: Prisoners during the American Revolution.* Athens: Ohio University Press, 1976.

Boyington, Gregory. *Baa Baa Black Sheep.* New York: G. P. Putnam's Sons, 1958.

Brackenridge, Hugh Henry. *Indian Atrocities: Narratives of the Perils and Sufferings of Dr. John Knight and John Slover among the Indians during the Revolutionary War.* Cincinatti, OH: U. P. James, 1867.

Bradeley, Eliza. *An Authentic Narrative of the Shipwreck and Sufferings of Mrs. Eliza Bradeley.* Boston, 1821.

Breisach, Ernst. *Historiography: Ancient, Medieval, and Modern.* Chicago: University of Chicago Press, 1983.

Brickhill, Paul. *The Great Escape.* New York: Norton, 1950.

Bronson, Bertrand H. *The Traditional Tunes of the Child Ballads.* Princeton, NJ: Princeton University Press, 1959.

Brown, Alexander D. *The Galvanized Yankees.* Urbana: University of Illinois Press, 1963.

Brown, F. C. *POW/MIA Indochina 1861–1991.* Monograph 6. Hamilton Township, NJ: Rice Paddy, 1992.

———. *POW/MIA Indochina 1946–1986: An Annotated Bibliography of Non-Fiction Works Dealing with Prisoners of War/Missing in Action.* Hamilton Township, NJ: Rice Paddy, 1988.

———. *Annotated Bibliography of Vietnam Fiction.* Mesa, AZ: Rice Paddy, 1987.

Brown, John M. G., and Thomas G. Ashworth. "A Secret That Shames Humanity." *U.S. Veteran News and Report* (May 29, 1989): 1–12.

Brown, Parker B. " 'Crawford's Defeat': A Ballad." *Western Pennsylvania Historical Magazine* 64:4 (October 1981): 311–27.

Brown, Thomas. *A Plain Narrative of the Uncommon Sufferings and Remarkable Deliverance of Thomas Brown.* Boston, 1760.

Brown, Wallace L. *The Endless Hours: My Two and a Half Years as a Prisoner of War of the Chinese Communists.* New York: Norton, 1961.

Bryant, William O. *Cahaba Prison and the Sultana Disaster.* Tuscaloosa: University of Alabama Press, 1990.

Bucher, Lloyd M., with Mark Rascovich. *Bucher: My Story.* New York: Dell, 1970.

Bundrett, Ross. "Operation Betrayal: Left to Die." *The Sun,* November 18, 1989.

Burt, Kendal, and James Leasnor. *The One That Got Away.* New York: Ballantine Books, 1957.

Butterfield, C. W. *History of the Girtys.* Cincinnati, OH: Robert Clarke, 1890.

Butterfield, C. W., ed. *An Account of the Expedition against Sandusky under Colonel William Crawford in 1782.* Cincinnati, OH: U. P. James, 1873.

Byron, William L., Jr. *Montana's Indians Yesterday and Today.* Montana Graphic Series 11. Helena: Montana Magazine, 1985.

Calloway, Colin G. "Simon Girty: Interpreter and Intermediary." In James A. Clifton, ed. *Being and Becoming Indian: Biographical Studies of North American Frontiers,* 38–58. Chicago: Dorsey, 1989.

Cameron, Allen W., ed. *Vietnam Crisis.* Ithaca, NY: Cornell University Press, 1976.

Carey, George G. *A Sailor's Songbag: An American Rebel in an English Prison, 1777–1779.* Amherst: University of Massachusetts Press, 1976.

Carleton, Phillips D. "The Indian Captivity." *American Literature* 15 (May 1943): 169–80.

Carpenter, Willis, and Roberta Carpenter. *I Was the Enemy.* Millersburg, IN: Privately printed, 1990.

Cathcart, James L. *The Captives: Eleven Years a Prisoner in Algiers.* LaPorte, IN, 1899.

Cattermole, E. G. *Famous Frontiersmen, Pioneers and Scouts.* Chicago: Donohue, 1888.

Cavada, Frederick F. *Libby Life: Experiences of a Prisoner of War in Richmond, Virginia, 1863–1864.* Philadelphia: King and Baird, 1864.

Cawelti, John. "The Question of Popular Genres." *Journal of Popular Film and Television* 13:4 (Winter 1986): 55–61.

Cawthorne, Nigel. *The Bamboo Cage: The Full Story of the American Servicemen Still Held Hostage in South-East Asia.* South Yorkshire, Eng.: Leo Cooper, 1991.

Chafee, John H. "POW Treatment Principles Versus Propaganda." *Naval Institute Proceedings* (July 1971): 15–17.

Charnoff, David, and Doan Van Toai. *Portrait of the Enemy.* New York: Random House, 1986.

Chesley, Larry. *Seven Years in Hanoi: A POW Tells His Story.* Salt Lake City: Book Craft, 1973.

Child, Francis James. *The English and Scottish Popular Ballads.* 1884. New York: Dover, 1965.

Chinese People's Committee for World Peace. *Shall Brothers Be.* Peking: Foreign Languages Press, 1952.

Circular. POW-MIA Awareness Committee of Gloucester County, New Jersey, 1987.

Claghorn, Charles E. *Women Patriots of the American Revolution.* Metuchen, NJ: Scarecrow, 1991.

Clarke, Douglas L. *The Missing Man: Politics and the MIA.* Washington, DC: National Defense U.P. Research Directorate, 1979.

Clausewitz, Carl von. *On War.* 1832. New York: Penguin, 1968.

Clayton, James, D., ed. *South to Bataan, North to Mukden: The Prison Diary of Brigadier General W. E. Brougher.* Athens: University of Georgia Press, 1971.

Clifton, James A. *Being and Becoming Indian: Biographical Studies of North American Frontiers.* Chicago: Dorsey, 1989.

Cobley, Evelyn. "History and Ideology in Autobiographical Literature of the First World War." *Mosaic* 23:3 (Summer 1990): 37–54.

Coffee, Gerald. *Beyond Survival: Building on the Hard Times—A POW's Inspiring Story.* New York: G. P. Putnam's Sons, 1990.

Cohen, Bernard, and Maurice Cooper. *A Follow Up Study of World War II Prisoners of War.* Washington, DC: GPO, 1954.

Coker, George T. "PW." *United States Naval Institute Proceedings* 100:9 (October 1974): 41–46.

Cole, James L., Jr. "Dulag Luft Recalled and Revisited." *Aerospace Historian* (June 1972): 62–65.

Coleman, Emma Lewis. *New England Captives Carried to Canada between 1677 and 1760 during the French and Indian Wars.* 2 vols. Portland, ME: Southworth, 1925.

Coleman, John S., Jr. *Bataan and Beyond: Memories of an American POW.* College Station: Texas A&M University Press, 1978.

Colvin, Rod. *First Heroes: The POWs Left Behind in Vietnam.* New York: Irvington, 1987.

Condon, Richard. *The Manchurian Candidate.* New York: Signet, 1959.

Condron, Andrew M., Richard Cordon, and Lawrence V. Sullivan, eds. *Thinking Soldiers.* Peking: New World, 1955.

Conroy, Michael R. "POW Rescue Game Plan." *Vietnam Magazine* (December 1992): 47–53.

Considine, Robert, ed. *General Wainwright's Story.* Garden City, NY: Doubleday, 1946.

Consolmagno, Joe, ed. *Through the Eye of the Needle: 68 First-Person Accounts of Combat, Evasion, and Capture by World War II Airmen.* Published by the Stalag Luft III Former Prisoners of War. Baltimore, MD: Gateway, 1992.

"Controversial Prisoner Freed." New York *Daily News,* March 5, 1973.

Copley, John M. *A Sketch of the Battle of Franklin, Tenn., with Reminiscences of Camp Douglas.* Austin, 1893.

Corcoran, Michael. *The Captivity of General Corcoran: The Only Authentic and Reliable Narrative of the Trials and Sufferings Endured during His Twelve Months' Imprisonment in Richmond and Other Southern Cities by Brig.-General Michael Corcoran, Hero of Bull Run.* Philadelphia: Barclay, 1862.

Cornum, Rhonda, and Peter Copeland. *She Went to War: The Rhonda Cornum Story.* Novato, CA: Presidio, 1992.

Cotton, John. "The Divine Right to Occupy the Land." 1630. In *The Annals of America I,* 107–9. Chicago: Britannica, 1968.

Cowdery, Jonathan. *Captives in Tripoli, or, Dr. Cowdry's Journal.* 1806. In *Naval Documents Related to the United States Wars with the Barbary Powers,* vol. 5, *1804–1805.* Washington, DC: GPO, 1944.

Crossette, Barbara. "Vietnamese Photos Resolve Fate of 4 Missing Americans. *New York Times International,* November 1, 1992, A16.

cummings, e. e. *The Enormous Room.* 1922. New York: Liveright, 1978.

Daley, James A., and Lee Bergman. *A Hero's Welcome: The Conscience of Sergeant James Daley Versus the United States Army.* Indianapolis: Bobbs-Merrill, 1975.

Dannet, Sylvia G. L., ed. *Noble Women of the North.* New York: Thomas Yoseloff, 1959.

Davis, Curtis Carrol, ed. *Belle Boyd in Camp and Prison: Written by Herself.* New York: Thomas Yoseloff, 1968.

Davis, Samuel B. *Escape of a Confederate Officer from Prison: What He Saw at Andersonville, How He was Sentenced to Death and Saved by the Interposition of President Abraham Lincoln.* Norfolk, VA, 1892.

Day, George E. "Promises to Keep." *Reader's Digest* (December 1991): 107–11.

———. *Return With Honor.* Mesa, AZ: Champlin Fighter Museum, 1989.

Dean, William F., and William L. Warden. *General Dean's Story.* New York: Viking, 1954.

Deane, Philip. *I Was a Captive in Korea.* New York: Norton, 1953.

De Brisson, M. *An Account of the Shipwreck and Captivity of M. DeBrisson.* London, 1789.

Dengler, Dieter. *Escape from Laos.* Novato, CA: Presidio, 1979.

———. "I Escaped from a Red Prison." *Saturday Evening Post,* December 3, 1966, 27–33.

Dennett, Carl P. *Prisoners of the Great War: Authoritative Statement of Conditions in the Prison Camps of Germany.* Boston: Houghton Mifflin, 1919.

Denton, Jeremiah A. *When Hell Was in Session.* Mobile, AL: Traditional, 1982.

Derounian, Kathryn Zabelle. "Puritan Orthodoxy and the 'Survivor's Syndrome' in Mary Rowlandson's Indian Captivity Narrative." *Early American Literature* 22 (Spring 1987): 82–93.

Des Pres, Terrence. *The Survivor: An Anatomy of Life in the Death Camps.* New York: Oxford University Press, 1976.

Devereux, James P. S. *The Story of Wake Island.* New York: Ace Books, 1947.

Domschke, Bernhard. *Twenty Months in Captivity.* 1865. Edited and translated by Frederic Trautmann. Rutherford, NJ: Fairleigh Dickinson University Press, 1990.

Dorson, Richard M., ed. *America Rebels: Narratives of the Patriots.* New York: Pantheon, 1953.

Dowe, Ray M. "A Prisoner Can Profit." *Army Information Digest* 9:6 (1954): 41–47.

Doyle, Chris. "Alive in Cambodia? McKinley Nolan, Turncoat." *Soldier of Fortune* (February 1980): n.p.

————. "Bobby Garwood: Traitor or Victim?" *Soldier of Fortune* (September 1979): 74.

Dramesi, John A. *Code of Honor*. New York: Norton, 1976.

Drinnon, Richard. *Facing West: The Metaphysics of Indian-Hating and Empire-Building*. New York: New American Library, 1980.

Drury, Robert. *Madagascar, or, Robert Drury's Journal during Fifteen Years Captivity on That Island*. London, 1890.

Duff, William H. *Terrors and Horrors of Prison Life, or, Six Months a Prisoner at Camp Chase, Ohio*. N.p., 1907.

Duke, Basil W. *History of Morgan's Cavalry*. Bloomington: Indiana University Press, 1961.

Dukore, Bernard F. *Dramatic Theory and Criticism: Greeks to Growtowski*. New York: Holt, Rinehart and Winston, 1974.

Dunant, Henri. *Un Souvenir de Solferino*. Geneva, 1862.

Dunkle, John J. *Prison Life during the Rebellion: Being a Brief Narrative of the Miseries and Sufferings of Six Hundred Confederate Prisoners Sent from Fort Delaware to Morris Island To Be Punished, Written by Fritz Fuzzlebug, One of Their Number*. Singers Glen, VA, 1869.

Dunn, Joe. "The Vietnam War POW/MIAs: An Annotated Biibliography." *Bulletin of Bibliography* 45:2 (June 1988): 152–58.

————The POW Chronicles: A Bibliographic Review." *Armed Forces and Society* 9:3 (Spring 1983): 495–514.

Dupuy, Ernest, and William Baumer. *The Little Wars of the United States*. New York: Hawthorne, 1968.

Durand, Arthur A. *Stalag Luft III: The Secret Story*. Baton Rouge: Louisiana State University Press, 1988.

Dye, Ira. "Physical and Social Profiles of American Seafarers, 1812–1815." In Colin Howell and Richard Twomey, eds., *Jack Tar in History*, 220–35. Fredericton, NB: Acadiencais, 1991.

————. "American Maritime Prisoners of War 1812–1815." In Timothy J. Runyan, ed., *Ships, Seafaring, and Society: Essays in Maritime History*. Detroit, MI: Wayne State University Press, 1987.

————. "Introduction." In *Records Relating to American Prisoners of War 1812–815*. East Ardsley, Wakefield, UK: EP Microform, 1980.

Dyess, William E. *The Dyess Story*. New York: G. P. Putnam's Sons, 1944.

Editors of the *Army Times*. *American Heroes of Asian Wars*. New York: Dodd and Mead, 1968.

Edwards, John S., ed. *American Ex-Prisoners of War*. 2 vols. Paducah, KY: Turner Publishing Company, 1991.

Ellinwood, Ralph E. *Behind the German Lines: A Narrative of the Everyday Life of an American Prisoner of War*. New York: Knickerbocker, 1920.

Elliot, Charles W. *Winfield Scott: The Soldier and the Man*. New York: Macmillan, 1937.

Elton, Oliver, trans. *The First Nine Books of the Danish History of Saxo Grammaticus*. London: David Nutt, 1894.

Ely, Alfred. *The Journal of Alfred Ely*. New York, 1862.

Encarnacion Prisoners Written by a Prisoner. Louisville, KY: Prentice and Weissinger, 1848.

Everett, Marshall, ed. *Exciting Experiences in Our Wars with Spain and the Filipinos*. Chicago: Educational Company, 1900.

Evidence and Documents Laid before the Committee on Alleged German Outrages. London: Committee on Alleged German Outrages, 1915.

"Eyes of World on Panmunjom as Truce Talks Start Again." *Newsweek,* May 4, 1953, 35–36.

Fabel, Robin F. A. "Self-Help in Dartmoor: Black and White Prisoners in the War of 1812." *Journal of the Early Republic* 9 (Summer 1989): 165–90.

Falk, Stanley L. *Bataan: The March of Death.* 1972. New York: Jove, 1984.

Farwell, Byron. "Prisoner of War Medal." *Washington Post,* August 7, 1985, B1, 2.

Feifer, George. *Tennozan: The Battle of Okinawa and the Atomic Bomb.* New York: Ticknor and Fields, 1992.

Feinberg, Abraham L. *Hanoi Diary.* Don Mills, Ont.: Alger, 1968.

Feuer, A. B., ed. *Bilibid Diary: The Secret Notebooks of Commander Thomas Hayes, POW, the Philippines, 1942–1945.* Hamden, CT: Archon, 1987.

Finney, Molly. *The Means Massacre: Molly Finney, the Canadian Captive.* Edited by Charles P. Illsley. Freeport, ME: Freeport Press, 1932.

Flammer, Philip M. "Dulag Luft: The Third Reich's Prison Camp for Airmen." *Aerospace Historian* (June 1972): 58–61.

Flory, William E. S. *Prisoners of War: A Study in the Development of International Law.* Washington, DC: American Council on Public Affairs, 1942.

Fooks, Herbert C. *Prisoners of War.* Federalsburg, MD: J. W. Stowell, 1924.

Foot, M. R .D., and J. M. Langley. *MI-9: Escape and Evasion 1939–1945.* Boston: Little, Brown, 1980.

Foss, John. *A Journal of Captivity in Algiers.* Newburyport, MA, 1798.

———. *A Journal of the Captivity and Sufferings of John Foss.* Newburyport, MA, 1798.

Foxe, John. *Foxe's Book of Martyrs.* Moundsville, WV: Gospel Trumpet, n.d.

Franklin, H. Bruce. *M.I.A.: Mythmaking in America.* New York: Lawrence Hill, 1992.

Frelinghuysen, Joseph S. *Passages to Freedom: A Story of Capture and Escape.* Manhattan, KS: Sunflower University Press, 1990.

Freneau, Philip. *Poems Written and Published during the American Revolutionary War.* Introduction by Lewis Leary. New York: Scholars' Facsimiles and Reprints, 1976.

Frey, Bruno S., and Heinz Buhofer. "Prisoners and Property Rights." *Journal of Law and Economics* 21 (April 1988): 19–47.

Frost, Griffin. *Camp and Prison Journal: Embracing Scenes in Camp, on the March, and in Prisons; Springfield, Gratiot Street, St. Louis, and Macon City, Mo.; Fort Delaware, Alton and Camp Douglas, Ill.; Camp Morton, Ind.; and Camp Chase, Ohio. Also Scenes and Incidents during a Trip for Exchange from St. Louis, Mo., via Philadelphia, Pa., to City Point, Va.* Quincy, Ill., 1867.

Frye, Northrop. "The Archetypes of Literature." In Bernard F. Dukore, *Dramatic Theory and Criticism: Greeks to Growtowski,* 897–901. New York: Holt, Rinehart and Winston, 1974.

Futch, Ovid J. *History of Andersonville Prison.* Gainesville: University of Florida Press, 1968.

Gaither, Ralph. *With God in a P.O.W. Camp.* Nashville, TN: Broadman, 1973.

Gallery, Daniel V. *The Pueblo Incident.* Garden City, NY: Doubleday, 1970.

Garrett, Richard. *P.O.W.: The Uncivil Face of War.* Newton Abbot, Eng.: David and Charles, 1981.

———. *The Raiders: The World's Most Elite Strike Forces That Altered the Course of War and History.* New York: Van Nostrand Reinhold, 1980.

Gatewood, Willard B., Jr. *Smoked Yankees and the Struggle for Empire: Letters* from Negro Soldiers 1898–1902. Urbana: University of Illinois Press, 1971.

Gee, Joshua. *Narrative of Joshua Gee of Boston Mass., While He Was a Captive in Algeria of the Barbary Pirates 1680–1687.* Hartford, CT, 1943.

Geer, J. J. *Beyond the Lines, or, A Yankee Prisoner Loose in Dixie.* Philadelphia: J. W. Daughaday, 1864.

Geertz, Clifford. *The Interpretation of Cultures.* New York: Basic Books, 1973.

"The Geneva Convention and the Treatment of Prisoners of War in Vietnam." *Harvard Law Review* 80 (1967): 851, 856–58.

Gerard, James W. *Face to Face with Kaiserism.* New York: George H. Dopran, 1918.

Gerster, Robin. *Big-Noting: The Heroic Theme in Australian War Writing.* Melbourne, Australia: Melbourne University Press, 1987.

Glazier, Willard. *The Capture, The Prison Pen, and the Escape.* Hartford, CT: H. E. Goodwin, 1868.

Goleman, Daniel. "P.O.W.s Now Told to Resist Cooperation to 'Best of Their Ability.'" *New York Times International,* January 24, 1991, A14.

Gragg, Rod. *The Illustrated Confederate Reader.* New York: Harper and Row, 1987.

Grant, Zalin. *Survivors: American POWs in Vietnam.* 1975. New York: Berkley Books, 1985.

Grashio, Samuel C., and Bernard Norling. *Return to Freedom.* Tulsa, OK: MCN, 1972.

Greene, Albert. *Recollections of the Jersey Prison Ship from the Manuscript of Captain Thomas Dring.* 1829. Introduction by Lawrence H. Leder. New York: Corinth Books, 1961.

Groom, Winston, and Duncan Spencer. *Conversations with the Enemy: The Story of PFC Robert Garwood.* New York: Putnam, 1983.

Grotius, Hugo. *On the Rights of War and Peace.* An abridged translation by William Whewell. Cambridge: Cambridge University Press, 1853.

Guarino, Larry. *A POW's Story: 2801 Days in Hanoi.* New York: Ivy, 1990.

Gurule, Bill F. *Fleeting Shadows and Faint Echoes of Las Huertes.* New York: Carlton, 1987.

Hall, James Norman. *My Island Home: An Autobiography.* Boston: Little, Brown, 1952.

Hammer, Jefferson T. *Frederic Augustus James's Civil War Diary.* Rutherford, NJ: Fairleigh Dickinson University Press, 1973.

Handy, Isaac W. K. *United States Bonds, or, Duress by Federal Authority: A Journal of Current Events during and Imprisonment of Fifteen Months at Fort Delaware.* Baltimore, MD, 1874.

Haney, Robert E. *Caged Dragons: An American P.O.W. in WWII Japan.* Ann Arbor, MI: Sabre, 1991.

Harris, Stephen R. *My Anchor Held.* Old Tappan, NJ: Fleming H. Revell, 1970.

Hasenhauer, Heike. "Central Identification Laboratory, Hawaii: Solving the Mystery." *Soldiers* (November 1991): 34–36.

Hawkins, Christopher. *The Adventures of Christopher Hawkins.* 1834. New York: New York Times and Arno, 1968.

Hawkins, Jack. *Never Say Die.* Philadelphia: Dorrance, 1961.

Heard, J. Norman. *White into Red: A Study of the Assimilation of White Persons Captured by Indians.* Metuchen, NJ: Scarecrow, 1973.

Hellmann, John. *American Myth and the Legacy of Vietnam.* New York: Columbia University Press, 1986.

Helsop, J. N., and D. H. Van Orden. *From the Shadows of Death.* Salt Lake City: Desert, 1973.

Herbert, Charles. *A Relic of the Revolution.* Boston: Charles H. Pierce, 1847.

Herold, Ethel. "War Memories of Ethel Herold." *Bulletin of the American Historical Collection* 10 (1982): 44–67.

Hesseltine, William Best. *Civil War Prisons: A Study in Prison Psychology.* Columbus: Ohio State University Press, 1930.

Hines, Thomas. "Morgan and His Men Escape from Prison." *Century Magazine* (January 1891). In Philip van Doren Stern, ed. *Secret Missions of the Civil War,* 155–67. Chicago: Rand McNally, 1959.

Hoffman, Bruce. *Commando Raids.* Santa Monica, CA: Rand Corporation, 1985.

Hoffman, Conrad. *In the Prison Camps of Germany: A Narrative of "Y" Service among Prisoners of War.* New York: Association Press, 1920.

Horn, Stanley F. *The Army of Tennessee.* New York: Bobbs-Merrill, 1941.

Howard, John. *The State of Prisons in England and Wales.* 3d ed. Warrington, UK: Eyers, 1784.

Howell, Colin, and Richard Twomey. *Jack Tar in History.* Fredericton, NB: Acadiencais, 1991.

Hubbell, John G. *P. O. W.: A Definitive History of the American Prisoner-of-War Experience in Vietnam, 1964–1973.* New York: Reader's Digest, 1976.

" 'Humanitas' to Lords Commissioners, Admiralty." In William James Morgan, ed., *Naval Documents of the Revolution,* 9:611–12. Washington, DC: Naval Historical Center, 1986.

Hunter, Edward. *Brainwashing: The Story of the Men Who Defied It.* 1956. New York: Pyramid Books, 1964.

Isaacs, Arnold R. *Without Honor: Defeat in Vietnam and Cambodia.* New York: Vintage, 1984.

Isaacs, Edouard Victor. *Prisoner of the U-90.* Boston: Houghton Mifflin, 1919.

" 'Is Good to Be Free Again': Swap Brings Ill POWs Home." *Newsweek,* 27 April 1953, 42–43.

Jackson, James E. "Eighteen Months as a Prisoner of the Vietcong." *Ebony* 23 (August 1968): 114–16 +.

Jacobs, Wilbur. *Dispossessing the American Indian: Indians and Whites on the Colonial Frontier.* Norman: University of Oklahoma Press, 1985.

"Jane Fonda and Tom Hayden—Candid Conversation." *Playboy* (April 1974): 67.

Jane's Dictionary of Military Terms. Compiled by P. H. C. Hayward. London: MacDonald, 1975.

Janowitz, Morris. *The Professional Soldier: A Social and Political Portrait.* New York: Free Press, 1960.

Jensen, Jay Roger. *Six Years in Hell.* Salt Lake City: Horizon, 1974.

Jensen-Stevenson, Monika, and William Stevenson. *Kiss the Boys Goodbye: How the United States Betrayed Its Own POWs in Vietnam.* New York: Dutton, 1990.

Jerrome, Edward. "The Wooden Horse." In *Tales of Escape.* 1959. Belmont, CA: Fearon-Pitman, 1970.

Jervy, Edward D., ed. *Prison Life among the Rebels.* Kent, OH: Kent State University Press, 1990.

Johnson, Forrest Bryant. *Hour of Redemption: The Ranger Raid on Cabanatuan.* New York: Manor, 1978.

Jones, Buehring H. *The Sunny Land, or, Prison Prose and Poetry.* Edited by J. A. Houston. Baltimore, MD: Innes, 1868.

Jones, Peter G. *War and the Novelist: Appraising the American War Novel.* Columbia: University of Missouri Press, 1976.

Jones, Thomas T. "Two Hundred Miles to Freedom." *Military Engineering* 43:295 (1951): 351–54.

Jones, U. L. *Simon Girty, the Outlaw.* 1846. Edited by A. Monroe Aurand, Jr. Harrisburg, PA: Aurand, 1931.

"Josiah Smith to Benjamin Franklin." In William James Morgan, ed., *Naval Documents of the Revolution,* 377–78. Washington, DC: Naval Historical Center, 1986.

Kantor, Mackinley. *Andersonville.* New York: World Publishing, 1955.

Keegan, John. *The Face of Battle.* New York: Viking, 1975.

Keiley, Anthony M. *Prisoner of War, or, Five Months among the Yankees: Being a Narrative of the Crosses, Calamities, and Consolations of a Petersburg Militiaman during an Enforced Summer Residence North.* Richmond, VA, 1865.

Keith, Agnes Newton. *Three Came Home.* Boston: Little, Brown, 1947.

Kelly, R. Gordon. "Literature and the Historian." *American Quarterly* 26 (May 1974): 141–59.

Kenney, Catherine. *Captives: Australian Army Nurses in Japanese Prison Camps.* Brisbane, Australia: University of Queensland Press, 1986.

Kenny, Henry J. *The American Role in Vietnam and East Asia: Between Two Revolutions.* New York: Praeger, 1984.

Kerr, E. Bartlett. *Surrender and Survival: The Experience of American POWs in the Pacific, 1941–1945.* New York: William Morrow, 1985.

Kestler, Frances Roe. *The Indian Captivity: A Woman's View.* New York: Garland, 1990.

King, John H. *Three Hundred Days in a Yankee Prison: Reminiscences of War, Life, Captivity, Imprisonment at Camp Chase, Ohio.* Atlanta, GA, 1904.

King, John R. *My Experience in the Confederate Army and in Northern Prisons.* Clarksburg, WV, 1917.

Kinkead, Eugene. *In Every War But One.* New York: Norton, 1959.

Kittredge, George Lyman. *Witchcraft in Old and New England.* Cambridge, MA: Harvard University Press, 1929.

Kittredge, George Lyman, and Helen Child Sargent. *English and Scottish Popular Ballads.* Cambridge, MA: Riverside, 1932.

Knox, Donald. *Death March: The Survivors of Bataan.* New York: Harcourt Brace Jovanovich, 1981.

Kolb, Richard K. "Doughboys in 'No-Man's Land.' " *Veterans of Foreign Wars Magazine* (November 1990): 21.

Kolodny, Annette. "Review." *Early American Literature* 14 (1979): 229–35.

Kunz, Josop L. "The Chaotic Status of the Laws of War and the Urgent Necessity for Their Revision." *American Journal of International Law* 35 (January 1951): 37–61.

Lane-Poole, Stanley. *The Story of the Barbary Corsairs.* New York: G. P. Putnam's Sons, 1896.

Langbein, John H. *Torture and the Law of Proof: Europe and England in the Ancien Regime.* Chicago: University of Chicago Press, 1977.

Lanman, Charles, ed. *Journal of Alfred Ely: A Prisoner of War in Richmond.* New York: D. Appleton, 1862.

Leff, Lisa. "A Long Wait Ends for Family of Maryland Native Lost in Vietnam." *Washington Post,* October 1, 1989.

Leininger, Barbara. "The Narrative of Barbara Leininger." *Pennsylvania-German Society Proceedings* 15 (1906): 107–10.

LeRoy, Marie, and Barbara Leininger. "The Narrative of Marie LeRoy and Barbara Leininger." *Pennsylvania-German Society Proceedings* 15 (1906): 111–22.

Levi, Primo. *Survival in Auschwitz*. New York: Macmillan, 1959.

Levie, Howard S. "Maltreatment of Prisoners of War in Vietnam." *Boston University Law Review* 48:3 (Summer 1968): 323–59.

Lewis, George G., and John Mewha. *History of Prisoner of War Utilization by the United States Army 1776–1945*. Washington, DC: GPO, 1955.

Longacre, Harold. "God's Minute." *AXPOW Bulletin* (July 1955): np.

Lord, Lewis. "The Medal of Honor, Profiles in Courage: Part V: Lance Sijan, 'The Mouth of the Cat.'" *US News and World Report,* June 10, 1991, 65–67.

Lytle, Andrew. *At the Moon's Inn*. 1941. Introduction by Douglas E. Jones. Tuscaloosa: University of Alabama Press, 1990.

McConnell, Malcolm. *Into the Mouth of the Cat: The Story of Lance Sijan, Hero of Vietnam*. New York: Norton, 1985.

McCoy, Melvin H., Steve Mellnick, and Wellborn Kelley. *Ten Escape from Togo*. New York: Hobison, 1947.

McDaniel, Eugene B. *Before Honor*. Philadelphia: A. J. Holman, 1975.

———. *Scars and Stripes: The Red McDaniel Story*. Dunn, NC: Published by friends of Red McDaniel, 1975.

McDaniel, Norman A. "Prisoner of War." In Wallace Terry, ed., *Bloods: An Oral History of the Vietnam War by Black Veterans,* 130–42. New York: Ballantine Books, 1984.

———. *Yet Another Voice*. New York: Leisure, 1975.

MacDonald, J. Fred. *Television and the Red Menace: The Video Road to Vietnam*. New York: Praeger, 1985.

McElroy, John. *Andersonville: A Story of Rebel Military Prisons, Fifteen Months a Guest of the So-Called Southern Confederacy: A Private Soldier's Experience*. Toledo, OH: D. R. Locke, 1879.

McGrath, John M. *Prisoner of War: Six Years in Hanoi*. Annapolis, MD: Naval Institute, 1975.

MacNeill, Eoin. *Phases of Irish History*. Dublin: M. H. Gill and Son, 1937.

Mahurin, Walker M. *Honest John*. New York: G. P. Putnam's Sons, 1962.

Manes, Donald L. "Barbed Wire Command." *Military Review* 43:9 (1963): 38–56.

Marcello, Ray. "A Little Burst of Flak." *AXPOW Bulletin* 39:10 (October 1982): 20–21.

Markle, Clifford Milton. *A Yankee Prisoner in Hunland*. New Haven, CT: Yale University Press, 1920.

Marolda, Edward, and Oscar P. Fitzgerald. *The United States Navy and the Vietnam Conflict*. Washington, DC: Naval Historical Center, 1986.

Martyrs to the Revolution in British Prison-Ships in the Wallabout Bay. New York: W. H. Arthur, 1855.

Massaquoi, Hans J. "Introductory Remarks." In James E. Jackson, "Eighteen Months as a Prisoner of the Vietcong," *Ebony* 23 (August 1968): 114–16 + .

Mealing, S. R., ed. *Jesuit Relations and Allied Documents: A Selection*. Toronto: Macmillan, 1978.

Medal of Honor Recipients 1863–1978: "In the Name of the Congress of the United States." Washington, DC: GPO, 1979.

Mellnick, Steven M. *Philippine Diary*. New York: Van Nostrand, Reinhold, 1969.

Metzger, Charles H. *The Prisoner in the American Revolution.* Chicago: Loyola University Press, 1971.

Millar, Ward M. *Valley of the Shadow.* New York: David McKay, 1955.

Mims, Edwin. *Sidney Lanier.* Boston: Houghton Mifflin, 1905.

Minnich, J. M. *Inside of Rock Island Prison from December 1863 to June 1865.* Nashville, TN, 1906.

Minter, David L. "By Dens of Lions: Notes on Stylizations on Early Puritan Captivity Narratives." *American Literature* 45 (1975): 335–47.

Miscellaneous Correspondence and Accounts, Prisoner of War Records. Records of the Adjutant General's Office. Washington, DC: National Archives.

"Missing." *Life* (November 1987): 111–22.

Moody, Samuel B., and Maury Allen. *Reprieve from Hell.* New York: Pageant, 1961.

Mora, George. "Civilian Ex-POW Committee Report." *AXPOW Bulletin* 49:9 (September 1992): 7.

Morgan, William James, ed. *Naval Documents of the Revolution.* Washington, DC: Naval Historical Center, 1986.

Morrell, David. *Rambo: First Blood, Part II.* New York: Jove Books, 1985.

Muhlenberg, Henry Melchior. "Regina, the German Captive." *Pennsylvania-German Society Proceedings* 15 (1906): 82–89.

Mulligan, James A. *The Hanoi Commitment.* Virginia Beach, VA: RIF Marketing, 1981.

Murphy, Charles H. "Prisoners of War: Repatriation or Internment in Wartime—American and Allied Experiences, 1775 to Present." In U.S. Congress, House of Representatives, Committee on Foreign Affairs, *American Prisoners of War in Southeast Asia, 1971,* 479–82. Washington, DC: GPO, 1971.

Naval Documents Related to the United States Wars with the Barbary Powers, Vol. 5, *1804–1805.* Washington, DC: GPO, 1944.

Neeser, Robert Wilden, ed. *Letters and Papers Relating to the Cruises of Gustavus Conyngham: A Captain of the Continental Navy 1777–1779.* New York: DeVinne, 1915.

Northop, Henry Davenport. *Indian Horrors or Massacres by the Red Men.* Philadelphia: National Publishing, 1891.

O'Daniel, Larry. *Missing in Action: Trail of Deceit.* New Rochelle, NY: Arlington House, 1979.

Paddock, Judah. *A Narrative of the Shipwreck of the Ship Oswego.* New York, 1818.

Paine, Ralph D. *The First Yale Unit: A Story of Naval Aviation 1916–1919.* Cambridge, MA: Riverside, 1925.

Parry, J. H. *The Establishment of the European Hegemony: 1415–1715: Trade and Exploration in the Age of the Renaissance.* New York: Harper and Row, 1966.

Pasley, Virginia. *21 Stayed: The Story of American GIs Who Chose Communist China—Who They Were and Why They Stayed.* New York: Farrer, Strauss and Cudahay, 1955.

Pate, Lloyd W., and B. J. Cutler. *Reactionary.* New York: Harper and Brothers, 1956.

Pater, Alan F., and Jason R. Pater, eds. *What They Said in 1973: The Yearbook of Spoken Opinion.* New York: Monitor, 1974.

Patterson, Charles J., and G. Lee Tipton. *The Heroes Who Fell from Grace: The True Story of Operation Lazarus, the Attempt to Free American POWs from Laos in 1982.* Canton, OH: Daring, 1985.

Pearce, Roy Harvey. *The Savages of America: A Study of the Indian and the Idea of Civilization.* Baltimore, MD: Johns Hopkins University Press, 1953.
———. "The Significance of the Captivity Narrative." *American Literature* 19 (1947): 1–20.
Peckham, Howard, ed. *The Toll of Independence: Engagements and Battle Casualties of the American Revolution.* Chicago: Clements Library Bicentennial Studies, 1974.
Perkins, Glendon. "Hanoi Nightmare: American POW's Year of Terror." *Soldier of Fortune* 15:8 (August 1990): 25–29, 82–84.
Peters, Edward. *Torture.* New York: Basil Blackwell, 1985.
Pfeiffer, G. S. F. *The Voyages and Five Years Captivity in Algiers of Doctor G.S.F. Pfeiffer.* Harrisburg, PA, 1836.
Plumb, Charles. *I'm No Hero.* Independence, MO: Independence Press, 1973.
Potter, Pitman B. "Repatriation of Korean Prisoners of War." *American Journal of International Law* 61 (1953): np.
POW-MIA Fact Book. Washington, DC: Department of Defense, July 1991.
"POW/MIA Facts Update." Washington, DC: National League of Families, 1987.
"POW/MIA Update." *Veterans of Foreign Wars Magazine* (January 1990): 11.
Pozner, Vladmir. *Remembering War: A U.S.-Soviet Dialogue.* New York: Oxford University Press, 1990.
Prelinger, Catherine M. "Benjamin Franklin and the American Prisoners of War in England during the American Revolution." *William and Mary Quarterly* 3d ser. 32 (1975): 261–94.
Prough, George S. "Prisoners at War: The POW Battleground." *Dickinson Law Review* 60:2 (January 1956): 123–38.
Ramage, James A. "John Hunt Morgan's Escape from the Ohio State Penitentiary." *Civil War Quarterly* 10 (September 1987): 22–28.
Ransom, John. *Andersonville Diary.* 1883. Introduction by Bruce Catton. New York: Berkley Publishing, 1986.
Read, James Morgan. *Atrocity Propaganda 1914–1919.* New Haven, CT: Yale University Press, 1941.
Redfield, Robert. *The Little Community and Peasant Society and Culture.* Chicago: University of Chicago Press, 1967.
Reid, Pat. *Men of Colditz.* New York: J. B. Lippincott, 1954.
Reid, Pat, and Maurice Michael. *Prisoner of War.* London: Hamlyn, 1984.
Review, "*Kiss the Boys Goodbye* . . . by Monika Jensen-Stevenson and William Stevenson." *Indochina Chronology* 9:4 (October–December 1990): 21–22.
Riley, James. *Loss of the American Brig Commerce.* London, 1817.
Risner, Robinson. *The Passing of the Night: My Seven Years as a Prisoner of the North Vietnamese.* New York: Random House, 1973.
Robbins, Christopher. *The Ravens: The Men Who Flew in America's Secret War in Laos.* New York: Crown, 1987.
Robertson, James I. "The Scourge of Elmira." In William Best Hesseltine, *Civil War Prisons.* Columbus: Ohio State University Press, 1989.
Rodley, Nigel S. *The Treatment of Prisoners under International Law.* London: Oxford University Press, 1987.
Rosenberg, Bruce R. *Custer and the Epic of Defeat.* University Park: Penn State University Press, 1974.
Roskey, Bill. "Great Escapes: POWs Break through the Wire." *Soldier of Fortune* (May 1991): 67–69, 77–79.
Rowe, James N. *Five Years to Freedom.* New York: Ballantine Books, 1971.

Rowlandson, Mary White. *The Sovereignty and Goodness of God.* 1682. In Alden T. Vaughan and Edward W. Clark, eds., *Puritans among the Indians: Accounts of Captivity and Redemption, 1676–1724,* 64–75. Cambridge, MA: Belknap Press, 1981.

Rudolf, Alice. "Vet Returns from Asia with Bones." *Altoona Mirror,* September 22, 1987.

Runyan, Timothy J. *Ships, Seafaring, and Society: Essays in Maritime History.* Detroit, MI: Wayne State University Press, 1987.

Russell, Edward. *The Knights of Bushido.* London: Transworld, 1958.

Rutledge, Howard, and Phyllis Rutledge. *In the Presence of Mine Enemies 1965–1973: A Prisoner of War.* Old Tappan, NJ: Fleming H. Revell, 1977.

Saffell, W. T. R. *Records of the Revolutionary War.* 3d ed. Baltimore, MD: Charles C. Saffell, 1894.

Sage, C. Gordon. "I Want to Go Home." *AXPOW Bulletin* (July 1955): np.

Sage, Jerry. *Sage.* Wayne, PA: Miles Standish, 1985.

Sager, Carl. "A Boy in the Confederate Cavalry." *Confederate Veteran* 36:10 (October 1928): 374–76.

Schemmer, Benjamin F. *The Raid.* New York: Harper and Row, 1976.

Schlauch, Margaret, trans. *The Saga of the Volsungs: The Saga of Ragnar Lodbrok Together with the Lay of Kraka.* New York and London: George Allen and Unwin, 1949.

Schroeder, John Frederick. *Maxims of Washington.* 1942. Mount Vernon, VA: Mount Vernon Ladies Association, 1974.

Schwinn, Monika, and Bernhard Diehl. *We Came to Help.* New York: Harcourt Brace Jovanovich, 1973.

Scott, James Brown, ed. *The Hague Conventions and Declarations of 1899 and 1907.* New York: Oxford University Press, 1918.

Scott, Winfield. *Memoirs of Lieut.-General Scott, LL.D. Written by Himself in Two Volumes.* New York: Sheldon, 1864.

Shallin, Mike. "The Guest of the Kaiser." In Henry Berry, ed., *Make the Kaiser Dance,* 347–51. New York: Doubleday, 1978.

Sharp, Cecil. *English Folk Songs from the Southern Appalachians.* London: Oxford University Press, 1932.

Sheehan, Neil. *A Bright Shining Lie: John Paul Vann and America in Vietnam.* New York: Random House, 1988.

Shepherd, Henry E. *Narrative of Prison Life at Baltimore and Johnson's Island, Ohio.* Baltimore, MD, 1917.

Sherburne, Andrew. *Memoirs of Andrew Sherburne: A Pensioner of the Navy of the Revolution Written by Himself.* Providence, RI: H. H. Brown, 1831.

Sherrard, Robert A. *A Narrative of the Wonderful Escape and Dreadful Sufferings of Colonel James Paul.* Cincinnati, OH: J. Drake, 1869.

Shoemaker, Lloyd R. *The Escape Factory.* New York: St. Martin's, 1990.

Shuffler, R. Henderson. *See* Barziza

Sigmund, Paul E., ed. *St. Thomas Aquinas on Politics and Ethics.* New York: Norton, 1988.

Simmons, Kenneth W. *Kriegie.* Edinburgh: Thomas Nelson and Sons, 1960.

Simmons, William S. "Cultural Bias in the New England Puritans' Perceptions of the Indians." *William and Mary Quarterly* 3d ser. 38 (1981): 56–72.

Simpson, Charles M. *Inside the Green Berets: The First 30 Years.* Novato, CA: Presidio, 1983.

Sketches from Prison: A Confederate Artist's Record of Life at Point Lookout

Prisoner-of-War Camp 1863–1865. Baltimore, MD: Maryland Park Foundation, n.d.

Slotkin, Richard. *Regeneration through Violence: The Mythology of the American Frontier, 1600–1860*. Middletown, CT: Wesleyan University Press, 1973.

Smith, George E. *P.O.W.: Two Years with the Vietcong*. Berkeley, CA: Ramparts, 1971.

Smith, Joel P. "Their Ordeal Rewarded." *Veterans of Foreign Wars Magazine* (February 1989): 21.

Smith, William. *Historical Account of Bouquet's Expedition against the Ohio Indians in 1764*. Cincinnati, OH: Robert Clarke, 1907.

Solzhenitsyn, Aleksandr I. *The Gulag Archipelago: An Experiment in Literary Investigation V-VII*. Translated by Harry Willets. New York: Harper and Row, 1979.

Sommers, Stan., ed. *The European Story*. Marshfield, WI: National Ex-Prisoners of War Association, 1980.

———. *The Japanese Story*. Marshfield, WI: National Ex-Prisoners of War Association, 1980.

Speed, Richard B., III. *Prisoners, Diplomats, and the Great War: A Study in the Diplomacy of Captivity*. New York: Greenwood, 1990.

Spivey, Delmar T. *POW Odyssey: Reflections of Center Compound, Stalag Luft III, and the Secret German Peace Mission in World War II*. Attleboro, MA: Published by the author, 1984.

———. "The Soldier and the Prisoner." *Marine Corps Gazette* 49:5 (1965): 36–44.

Staden, Hans. *True History of His Captivity among the Tupi Indians of Brazil*. Edited and translated by Malcolm Letts. London: Routledge, 1928.

Stanley, Sir Henry Morton. *The Autobiography of Sir Henry Morton Stanley*. Boston: Houghton Mifflin, 1909.

Stenger, Charles. "American Prisoners of War in World War I, World War II, Korea, and Vietnam: Statistical Data Concerning Numbers Captured, Repatriated, and Still Alive as of January 1, 1988." Washington, DC: United States Veterans Administration Advisory Committee on Former Prisoners of War, 1988.

Stern, Philip Van Doren. *The Confederate Navy*. New York: Bonanza Books, 1962.

———. *Secret Missions of the Civil War*. Chicago: Rand McNally, 1959.

Stevens, Alexander H. "The Treatment of Prisoners during the War between the States." *Southern Historical Society Papers* 1:3 (March 1876): 123.

Stockdale, James B. *Ten Years of Reflection: A Vietnam Experience*. Stanford, CA: Hoover Institute, 1984.

Stockdale, James B., and Sybil Stockdale. *In Love and War*. New York: Harper and Row, 1984.

Stoessinger, John G. *Why Nations Go to War*. 5th ed. New York: St. Martin's, 1990.

Straubling, Harold Elk, ed. *The Last Magnificent War: Rare Journalistic and Eyewitness Accounts of World War I*. New York: Paragon, 1989.

Strong, Pauline Turner. "Captive Images." *Natural History* 94:12 (December 1985): 51–56.

Taylor, Bruce. "The Vietnam War Movie." In D. Michael Shafer, ed., *The Legacy*, 186–206. Boston: Beacon Press, 1990.

Taylor, Telford. *Nuremberg and Vietnam: An American Tragedy*. Chicago: Quadrangle Books, 1970.

Terkel, Studs. *An Oral History of World War II: "The Good War."* New York: Pantheon, 1984.

Terry, Wallace, ed. *Bloods: An Oral History of the Vietnam War by Black Veterans.* New York: Ballantine Books, 1984.

"Thomas Andros." In Richard M. Dorson, ed., *America Rebels: Narratives of the Patriots,* 93–113. New York: Pantheon, 1953.

Thompson, Stith. *Motif-Index of Folk Literature,* vol. 5. Bloomington: Indiana University Press, 1957.

Thornton, Captain John W., and John W. Thornton, Jr. *Believed to Be Alive.* Middlebury, VT: Paul S. Eriksson, 1981.

Tocqueville, Alexis de. "Present and Future Condition of the Indians." 1838. In Louis Filler and Allen Guttmann, eds., *The Removal of the Cherokee Nation: Manifest Destiny or National Dishonor.* Lexington, MA: D. C. Heath, 1962.

"Torture and Torment." *Newsweek,* February 4, 1991, 50–54.

Towers, Edwin L. *Hope for Freedom: Operation Thunderhead.* LaJolla, CA: LaLane and Associates, 1981.

"The Treatment of Prisoners during the War between the States." *Southern Historical Society Papers* 1:3 (March 1876): 113–221; 1:4 (April 1876): 225–327.

Trueman, Stuart. *The Ordeal of John Gyles.* Toronto: McClellend and Stewart, 1966.

Turner, Eunice H. "American Prisoners of War in Great Britain." *Mariner's Mirror* 45 (1959): np.

Tyler, Moses Coit. *The History of American Literature during the Colonial Period, 1607–1765.* 1898. New York: G. P. Putnam's Sons, 1909.

Tyler, Royall. *The Algerine Captive, or, The Life and Adventures of Doctor Updike Underhill [pseudo.], Six Years a Prisoner among the Algerines.* Walpole, NH: D. Carlisle, 1797.

U. S. Congress. House of Representatives. *Report on the Spirit and Manner in Which the War Has Been Waged by the Enemy.* 1813. New York: Garland, 1978.

———. *Report on the Treatment of Prisoners of War by the Rebel Authorities during the War of Rebellion.* Report no. 45. 40th Congress, 3d sess., Serial no. 1391. Washington, DC: GPO, 1869.

United States. Congress. House of Representatives. Committee on Foreign Affairs. *The Geneva Convention Relative to the Treatment of Prisoners of War.* Washington, DC: GPO, 1970.

United States. Congress. House of Representatives. Committee on Foreign Affairs. Subcommittee on Asian and Pacific Affairs. *The Treatment of Political Prisoners in South Vietnam by the Government of the Republic of South Vietnam.* Washington, DC: GPO, 1973.

United States. Congress. House of Representatives. Select Committee on Missing Persons in Southeast Asia. *Final Report.* Washington, DC: GPO, 1977.

———. *Americans Missing in Southeast Asia: Summary, Conclusions, and Recommendations.* Washington, DC: GPO, 1976.

United States. Congress. Senate. Committee on Armed Services. *Imprisonment and Escape of Lieutenant Junior Grade Dieter Dengler, USNR.* Washington, DC: GPO, 1966.

United States. Congress. Senate. Committee on Government Operations. *Communist Interrogation, Indoctrination, and Exploitation of American Military and Civilian Prisoners.* Senate Report No. 2832. 84th Congress, 2d sess. Washington, DC: GPO, 1957.

———. *Korean War Atrocities.* Senate Report No. 848. 83d Congress, 2d sess., January 11, 1954. Washington, DC: GPO, 1954.

United States. Congress. Senate. Committee on Veterans' Affairs. *See Medal of Honor Recipients 1863–1978.*

United States. Congress. Senate. Minority (Republican) Staff of the Committee on Foreign Relations. *An Examination of U.S. Policy toward POW/MIAs [the Helms Report].* Washington, DC: GPO, 1991.

United States. Department of Defense. *POW: The Fight Continues after the Battle: The Report of the Secretary of Defense's Advisory Committee on Prisoners of War.* Washington, DC: GPO, 1955.

United States. Department of the Army. *Soldier's Manual of Common Tasks: Skill Level 1.* Washington, DC: GPO, 1990.

———. *Communist Interrogation, Indoctrination, and Exploitation of Prisoners of War.* Washington, DC: GPO, 1956.

———. *Field Manual FM 27-10: The Law of Land Warfare.* Washington, DC: GPO, 1956.

———. *Pamphlet 27-1: Treaties Governing Land Warfare.* Washington, DC: GPO, 1956.

United States. Veterans Administration. *Study of Former Prisoners of War.* Washington, DC: GPO, 1980.

United States. War Department. *War of the Rebellion: A Compilation of the Official Records of the Union and Confederate Armies.* Washington, DC: GPO, 1880–1901.

———. *General Order 100: Rules of Land Warfare.* Washington, DC, 1863.

———. *General Order 207: Instructions for the Government of Armies of the United States.* Washington, DC, July 3, 1863.

United States. War Department. Office of the Adjutant General. *Procedures for Processing Return, and Reassignment of Exchanges in Korea.* Washington, DC: U.S. Army Center of Military History, 1951.

———. "Military Personnel Escaped from Enemy Territory." Washington, DC, July 11, 1944.

United States Code Annotated. Title 18, "Crimes and Criminal Procedure." St. Paul, MN: West, 1987.

United States Sanitary Commission. *Narrative of Privations and Sufferings of United States Officers and Soldiers while Prisoners of War in the Hands of Rebel Authorities.* Philadelphia: King and Baird, 1864.

Upton, Jeduthan. "The Log of Jeduthan Upton, Captain of the good ship *Polly,* a Privateer in the War of 1812." In Richard E. Winslow III, *"Wealth and Honor": Portsmouth during the Golden Age of Privateering, 1775–1815.* Portsmouth, NH: Portsmouth Marine Society, 1988.

Urban, John. *Battle Field and Prison Pen, or, Through the War and Thrice a Prisoner in Rebel Dungeons.* Philadelphia: Hubbard Brothers, 1882.

Ursano, J. "The Vietnam Era Prisoner of War: Precaptivity Personality and the Development of Psychiatric Illness." *American Journal of Psychiatry* 138:3 (March 1981): 315–18.

Vail, R. W. G. *The Voice of the Old Frontier.* Philadelphia: University of Pennsylvania Press, 1949.

Valentine, Douglas. *The Hotel Tacloban.* London: Angus and Robertson, 1984.

VanDerBeets, Richard, ed. *The Indian Captivity Narrative: An American Genre.* New York: University Press of America, 1984.

———. *Held Captive by Indians: Selected Narratives 1642–1836.* Knoxville: University of Tennessee Press, 1973.

Van der Post, Laurens. *The Night of the New Moon.* London: Chatto and Windus, 1985.

Vaughan, Alden T., and Edward W. Clark, eds. *Puritans among the Indians: Accounts of Captivity and Redemption 1676–1724.* Cambridge, MA: Belknap, 1981.

Vaughn, Elizabeth Head. *Community under Stress: An Internment Camp Culture.* Princeton, NJ: Princeton University Press, 1949.

——. "Adjustment Problems in a Concentration Camp." *Sociology and Social Research* 32 (September 1947): 513–18.

"Veterans Update." *American Legion Magazine* (December 1989): 40.

Victor, John. *Time Out: American Airmen in Stalag Luft I.* New York: R. R. Smith, 1951.

Vietnam Veterans Against the War. *The Winter Soldier Investigation: An Inquiry into American War Crimes.* Toronto: Beacon, 1972.

Vonnegut, Kurt, Jr. *Slaughterhouse-Five or The Children's Crusade.* New York: Delacourt, 1969.

——. *Mother Night.* New York: Avon, 1967.

Vreeland, Hamilton. *Hugo Grotius: The Father of the Modern Science of International Law.* New York: Oxford University Press, 1917.

Wallace, Edward S. "The Battalion of Saint Patrick in the Mexican War." *Military Affairs* 14:2 (July 1950): 84–91.

——. "Deserters in the Mexican War." *Hispanic American Historical Review* 15:2 (August 1935): 374–83.

Walls, Matthew S. "Northern Hell on Earth." *America's Civil War* (March 1991): 25–29.

Walzer, Michael. *Just and Unjust Wars.* New York: Harper Collins, 1977.

Washburn, William. *The Garland Library of Narratives of North American Indian Captivities.* 111 vols. New York: Garland, 1978.

Waterhouse, Benjamin. *A Journey of a Young Man from Massachusetts, Late a Surgeon on Board an American Privateer.* Boston: Rowe Hooper, 1816.

Webb, Henry J. "Prisoners of War in the Middle Ages." *Military Affairs* 12:1 (Spring 1948): 46–49.

Webb, Kate. *On the Other Side: Twenty-three Days with the Viet Cong.* New York: Quadrangle Books, 1972.

Weininger, Peter. "Revenge May Have Caused War Crimes." *The Age,* August 19, 1992.

Weintraub, Stanley. *Long Day's Journey into War.* New York: Dutton, 1991.

——. *Victoria: An Intimate Biography.* New York: Dutton, 1988.

——. *The War in the Wards: Korea's Unknown Battle in a Prisoner-of-War Hospital Camp.* New York: Doubleday, 1964.

Welch, Richard E., Jr. *Response to Imperialism: The United States and the Philippine-American War, 1899–1902.* Chapel Hill: University of North Carolina Press, 1979.

Wells, Donald A. *War Crimes and Laws of War.* New York: University Press of America, 1984.

Wells, James M. "Prisoners of War Tunnel to Freedom." *McClure's Magazine* (1904). Reprinted in *Susquehanna Monthly Magazine* 16:1 (January 1991): 21–31.

Westheimer, David. *Sitting It Out.* Houston, TX: Rice University Press, 1992.

——. *Von Ryan's Express.* New York: Doubleday, 1964.

Whitcomb, Edgar D. *Escape from Corregidor.* Chicago: Henry Regnery, 1958.

White, Hayden. *The Content of the Form: Narrative Discourse and Historical Representation.* Baltimore, MD: Johns Hopkins University Press, 1987.

White, William Lindsay. *The Captives of Korea*. New York: Scribner's, 1957.

Wiesel, Elie. *Night*. 1958. Translated by Stella Rodway. New York: Avon Books, 1960.

Williams, Eric E. *The Wooden Horse*. New York: Harper, 1958.

Williams, Tom. *Post Traumatic Stress Disorders: A Handbook for Clinicians*. Cincinnati, OH: Disabled American Veterans, 1987.

Williamson, Peter. *Sufferings of Peter Williamson, One of the Settlers in the Back Parts of Pennsylvania Written by Himself*. 1757. In Richard VanDerBeets, ed., *Held Captive by Indians: Selected Narratives 1642–1836*, 216–27. Knoxville: University of Tennessee Press, 1973.

Wilson, W. Emerson. *Fort Delaware*. Newark: University of Delaware Press, 1957.

Wilson, W. Emerson, ed. *Jeff Thompson in Fort Delaware*. Wilmington: Fort Delaware Society, 1972.

Winslow, Richard E., III. *"Wealth and Honour": Portsmouth during the Golden Age of Privateering, 1775–1815*. Portsmouth, NH: Portsmouth Marine Society, 1988.

Wise, Gene. *American Historical Explanations*. 2d ed., rev. Minneapolis: University of Minnesota Press, 1980.

Wood, David. *Conflict in the Twentieth Century*. Washington, DC: Institute for Strategic Studies, 1968.

INDEX

3 1905 00047 2061

813   Doyle, Robert C.
DOYLE
        Voices from captivity

Base Library FL4471
    Bldg 749
McChord AFB WA 98438